Anti-Foreignism and Western Learning
in Early-Modern Japan

Harvard East Asian Monographs   *126*

Bob Tadashi Wakabayashi

Distributed by the HARVARD UNIVERSITY PRESS, Cambridge (Massachusetts) and London   1991

Anti-Foreignism and Western Learning in Early-Modern Japan

The *New Theses* of 1825

Published by the COUNCIL ON EAST ASIAN STUDIES, HARVARD UNIVERSITY

Printed in the United States of America
Second printing 1991

The Council on East Asian Studies at Harvard University publishes a monograph series and, through the Fairbank Center
for East Asian Research and the Reischauer Institute of Japanese Studies, administers research projects designed to
further scholarly understanding of China, Japan, Korea, Viet-
nam, Inner Asia, and adjacent areas.

Library of Congress Cataloging-in-Publication Data

Wakabayashi, Bob Tadashi, 1950–
  Anti-foreignism and western learning in early-modern
Japan.

  (Harvard East Asian monographs ; 126)
  "New theses": p. 147
  Bibliography: p. 315
  Includes index.
  1. Japan—Intellectual life—1600–1868.
2. Japan—Politics and government—1600–1868.
3. Aizawa, Yasushi, 1781–1863. Shinron. 4. Kokutai.
I. Aizawa, Yasushi, 1781–1863. Shinron. English.
1986. II. Title. III. Series.
DS822.2.W34 1986   952'.025   85-31379
ISBN 0-674-04037-6

For Yoshida Toshizumi

Contents

Contents

Foreword and Acknowledgments

Do you wish to be an author? Do you wish to make a book?
Remember that it must be new and unusual, or at least have
great charm.

—Voltaire

This book is a scholarly introduction to, and an English translation of, *New Theses (Shinron)*, a political tract that a Japanese
Confucian named Aizawa Seishisai (Yasushi) composed in
classical Chinese during the spring of 1825. My rather lengthy
introduction describes the historical background and significance
of this document—in what I hope is a new and unusual way.

New Theses was Aizawa Seishisai's most famous and important work. He wrote it as a confidential memorial, and presented
it to the daimyo of Mito domain, Tokugawa Narinobu, two
months after the Edo bakufu had issued its famous Expulsion
Edict of 1825. Narinobu not only refused to submit *New Theses*
to the bakufu as Aizawa desired, he forbade circulation of the
tract for fear of punitive measures that Edo leaders might take
against Mito. Tokugawa Nariaki, who succeeded Narinobu as
daimyo in 1829, was far less circumspect toward the bakufu,
and as a result, *New Theses* began to circulate throughout Japan
in manuscript form. Japanese language versions of the text
appeared in the 1850s,[1] and this made it possible for only mod-
erately educated members of Tokugawa society to sample its
contents. *New Theses* had a political and social impact probably
unmatched by any other single work during the final decades of
bakufu rule. It was a virtual bible to activists in the "revere the
Emperor, expel the barbarian" movement which swept through

Japan during the 1850s and 1860s, and the work gives us precious insights into the mentality of the so-called patriots of high resolve (*shishi*). Thus, *New Theses* is essential reading for anyone studying late Tokugawa or Restoration history. Prominent *shishi* such as Maki Izumi, Hirano Kuniomi, Yokoi Shōnan, and Yoshida Shōin venerated Aizawa, and made pilgrimages to visit him in Mito. Bakufu leaders such as Kawaji Toshiakira and Abe Masahiro also were among the readers of *New Theses* before its publication in 1858.[2]

One reason for the work's popularity was that it discussed many pressing issues of the day in language that allowed differing interpretations: Almost everyone active in late Tokugawa politics found support in it for policies he advocated. The text took on a life and significance of its own, apart from the author's intentions. Samurai of ability, but low rank, welcomed Aizawa's call for opening avenues of political advancement to them at the expense of their hereditarily entrenched social betters. Daimyo and their advisors trying to push through reforms were delighted to find Aizawa arguing against overly centralized bakufu control and for more domain autonomy. Yet authoritarian bakufu leaders might interpret Aizawa's section on "National Defense," for example, as supporting more, not less, centralized bakufu control. Then again, more radical bakufu reformers found support in Aizawa's proposal to overturn Ieyasu's control measures because these were outdated and unsuited to the needs of Japan as a whole. Finally, loyalist *shishi* derived inspiration from *New Theses* to move for even more radical changes: to eliminate the bakufu and restore imperial rule.

We should note in passing that *New Theses* moved men's spirits not only in the late Tokugawa era; it had long-range implications for nineteenth- and twentieth-century Japan. Meiji leaders actually carried out two of Aizawa's proposals: to establish centralized government control over Shinto shrines throughout the nation, and to create an emperor-centered state religion. Another idea Aizawa forwarded—to exploit foreign crises as a pretext to justify authoritarian controls and Draconian austerity at home—was adopted in the 1930s and 1940s. As Hashikawa Bunzō has noted, the regimentation and militarization of life depicted in *New Theses* provides all too disturbing a reminder of wartime Japanese society.[3] Finally, the idea of *kokutai,* which Aizawa formulated as a result of Western learning, would become immensely potent in modern Japanese politics. This study, however, deals with Aizawa's thought and knowledge of world affairs up to 1828, when he published the anti-Christian tract, "Some Call Me Disputatious" (*Kikōben*). In short, I discuss Aizawa and *New Theses* primarily for their historical significance in his own age. Concepts like *kokutai,* "honoring the emperor," and "the expulsion of Western barbarians" grew up and attained popularity in the second half of the Tokugawa period. Therefore the historian should examine them in that historical context, and try to remain free of the biases of his own age.

Reliable biographical information on Aizawa is sketchy.[4] During the Sengoku period his ancestors emigrated from present-day Shizuoka prefecture to a village in the northern part of what is now Ibaraki. When Tokugawa Ieyasu's youngest son, Yorifusa, obtained a fief there as a collateral house to the shogunal family, Mito domain came into being. At that time, Aizawa Sōbei moved to the castletown of Mito and served the domain in the ignoble post of bait-bird snarer; his primary duty was to capture the small birds fed to his lord's hunting falcons. It was two hundred years before the Aizawa family attained full, if lowly, samurai status. This happened during the life of Kyōkei, Seishisai's father, who must have been a man of considerable talent, for he was entrusted with the domain's rice storehouse in Ōsaka. Kyōkei stressed the importance of education for his son, and in 1791, the young Aizawa began to study under the gifted eighteen-year-old Fujita Yūkoku (1774–1826), originally the son of a merchant dealing in secondhand clothes.

Yūkoku and Aizawa knew full well that their lowly family origins imposed severe political and social restrictions. No matter how enlightened their reform proposals might be, participation in domain government was forbidden to them under the rigid Tokugawa order. As previous studies have stressed, Fujita and Aizawa espoused "attacking and expelling barbarians" (*jōi*) and played up the foreign "crisis" partly to justify their appointment to domain office and to force through unpopular reform programs. Moreover, their appointment to such positions of authority depended on support from Tokugawa Nariaki (1800–1860), who became daimyo in 1829. Aizawa remained close to Nariaki, and he was politically active and influential until his own death in 1863. In 1831, he was named head of the Mito Historiographical Institute, the Shōkōkan, and in 1841, he became head of the Mito Domain School, the Kōdōkan. By this time he was receiving a total annual stipend of 350 *koku,* and in the 1850s, this rose to 450 *koku,* which made him a man of power and high standing in Mito.

A discussion of texts is called for, since there are variant manuscripts of *New Theses,* or *Shinron.* What historians now consider the definitive *Shinron* text is the 1973 recension published by Iwanami shoten in volume 53 of its *Nihon shisō taikei* series. The editors, Imai Usaburō, Seya Yoshihiko, and Bitō Masahide, based their recension on two texts: Aizawa's original brush-written manuscript preserved in the Archives and Mausolea Department of the Imperial Household Agency, and the 1857 wood-block edition published by Gyokusandō. I have followed the 1973 Iwanami edition, but have checked it against the 1857 Gyokusandō text and an earlier Iwanami *bunko* edition of 1931. Many, if not most, of my notes to the translation rely on the headnotes to the 1973 Iwanami edition. I have also consulted the complete modern Japanese translation of *Shinron* by Hashikawa Bunzō,[5] and the short selections translated into English appearing in Ryūsaku Tsunoda, ed., *Sources of Japanese Tradition.*

In all quotations and references to *Shinron* made in my introduction, I cite page numbers to the Japanese version in the 1973 Iwanami edition. However, I have based my translation on both the classical Chinese original (also contained in the Iwanami edition) and the Japanese version. In certain contexts, I have disregarded the Japanese version and followed a reading of the classical Chinese original judged more appropriate. I have curtailed or omitted from my translation certain of Aizawa's glosses that seemed tedious or superfluous. Such deleted portions, which amount to less than 5 percent of the entire text, consist mainly of lengthy quotations from the Chinese classics.

Aizawa inserted these for pedantic as much as for documentary or explanatory reasons, and they have little meaning for modern Western readers. I have transliterated Chinese philosophical terms as Chinese, given in Wade-Giles romanization, not as Japanese.[6] In some of my notes, I was content to identify Aizawa's quotations simply as being from a certain classic, such as the *Book of Changes,* for example, without citing specific editions and page numbers.

Theories and philosophies of translation differ, and I think it proper to present mine explicitly here rather than to leave them for the reader to discover on his own. All translations, but particularly those from classical to modern languages, involve interpolation and interpretation. The translator cannot help taking certain liberties with the text if he is to capture the spirit of the original and still produce idiomatic prose. I have remained very close to Aizawa's original text, but have rejected the strict literalism that some translators prefer because it produces stilted, ponderous English prose. This, I hope, has allowed me to convey faithfully—and with no significant loss in meaning—the rancorous polemic tone that is crucial to Aizawa's tract. *New Theses* has immense significance as a historical document because it roused late Tokugawa *shishi* to violent action; they did not hurl it aside in disgust because it was boring. The historical significance of the work warrants making it accessible to Western readers. I hope the translation will stand on its own, apart from the scholarly introduction to it, and I would be happy if the general reader found it useful and enjoyable. Specialists and other critical readers are urged to compare the translation with Aizawa's original for accuracy and style. If my English version allows modern readers to understand why the original provoked such strong reactions among late Tokugawa *shishi,* my efforts will be rewarded.

In reading *New Theses* as a historical document, we must be wary of succumbing to what Herbert Butterfield has called "the transference into the past of an enthusiasm for something in the present."[7] We should not allow an enthusiasm for egalitarianism, or international good will, or the liberal tradition, to color our judgments of Aizawa and other Tokugawa thinkers. For example, they freely employed what we would consider offensive pejoratives:"stupid commoners" for Japanese townsmen and peasants; "barbarians," "foreign beasts," or "dogs and goats" for Western peoples; and "Shina" for China. But these epithets reflect biases integral to the world view shared by virtually all men of their period, class background, and education. The historian translating a document from another era does his readers a disservice if he softens its tone or substitutes less-offensive English wording in an attempt to make the author seem less prejudiced. To seek historical understanding by accepting those prejudices for what they were in Aizawa's day is not to approve of them.

This book results from several years labor in Japan and the United States. Although I take full responsibility for any errors, flaws, or shortcomings in the final product, I wish to acknowledge gratefully a few of the many persons who have expended much time and effort on my behalf.

My undergraduate mentors at UCLA from 1969 to 1972, Fred Notehelfer and Robert Epp, deserve thanks for getting my study of Japanese history off on the right foot and for their continued support and encouragement over the past decade and a half. Both read the manuscript and offered valuable advice. Robert Epp in particular should be credited for performing the arduous task of first-round editing. Few lines in the manuscript escaped his red pencil, and if, as I hope, my writing has attained some degree of clarity, I owe it to his painstaking help. No student could be blessed with a more caring, dedicated teacher.

From 1972 to 1979, Ienaga Saburō and Matsumoto Sannosuke of Tokyo Kyōiku Daigaku guided my graduate research in Japan. Both men are scholars and gentlemen for whom I have the greatest respect. Prof. Matsumoto's lectures and writings have shaped my understanding of Japanese political thought to an enormous extent. In addition to this personal instruction and guidance, Prof. Matsumoto graciously checked about half of my English translation of *Shinron* against the original and saved me from many embarassing mistakes—even when my stubbornness thoroughly tried his patience. Yamamoto Takeo of the Historiographical Institute at Tokyo University was unsparing with his time in helping me read old documents written in cursive script. Without his help, I could not have done the research for Chapter 3. Bitō Masahide's graduate seminar in early-modern Japanese history at Tokyo University was an enormously enriching experience. No one studying Tokugawa thought in general or Mito Learning in particular can remain indifferent to his scholarly achievements. Kitaoka Shin'ichi offered comments from the standpoint of his speciality—modern political history. He was the first to suggest that I add a concluding section outlining developments to 1890: Chapter 5 is the result. Igarashi Akio, Eizawa Kōji, Kurihara Takashi, Hirayama Kazuhiko, and Suzuki Masayuki—all of Tokyo Kyōiku Daigaku—provided academic advice and friendship throughout my stay in Japan.

From 1979 to 1982, Marius B. Jansen was my main advisor at Princeton; his scholarly guidance and warm personal encouragement will not be forgotten. Prof. Jansen has endured with humor, grace, and broadmindedness all criticisms and challenges posed to him by this, his most *namaiki* of students. Martin Collcutt and Ann Waswo read and reread drafts of the dissertation; because of their incisive criticisms, the present work has attained a measure of structural coherence. I would like to thank Martin also for his kind and sympathetic counsel during my Princeton years and beyond. Willard Peterson taught me Chinese philosophy for its own sake; due to his instruction, my ideas on the Middle Kingdom world view were sharpened and refined. Richard Bowring kindly read the dissertation and through his discussions, he has shown me what an intellectual historian can gain from the application of literary theory. Keith Hazelton cheerfully solved my word-processing crises at all hours of the day and night; if not for him, the manuscript would still be in the computer.

Harvard's Japan Institute, under the Acting Directorship of Albert Craig, provided me with office space and a postdoctoral fellowship from 1983 to 1984, which enabled me to revise the dissertation into publishable form. I also received generous financial support from the Japanese Ministry of Education, Tōkyū Foundation for Inbound Students, and the Nomura Foundation while in Japan.

Among those who read the manuscript while I was revising it for publication, Sally Hastings and Torii Masaru made numerous suggestions to improve style. Henry D. Smith, James Polachek, Watanabe Hiroshi, and Ronald Toby gave me pages upon pages of insightful comments, and I have incorporated much of their advice in my revisions. Prof. Watanabe, a young scholar specializing in East Asian political thought on the Faculty of Law at Tōdai, was especially generous with his time and knowledge. Ronald Toby kindly allowed me to read his *State and Diplomacy in Early Modern Japan* while it was still in manuscript. Anyone familiar with the works of Watanabe and Toby will, when they read my book, realize how much I have learned from them. Ronald Egan, my editor at the Council of East Asian Studies, Harvard University, combined Sinological expertise with saintly patience. I consider myself lucky to have profited from his thoughtful and meticulous editing.

Finally, Yoshida Toshizumi, my *sempai* at Tokyo Kyōiku Daigaku, helped me obtain many of the unpublished archival materials in Japan without which I could never have completed this study. He, more than anyone else, drilled and instructed me in the reading of Tokugawa documents; I will never forget the monthly sessions we spent at his home in Mito poring over Aizawa's writings. It is to Yoshida that I have incurred my greatest debts, both scholarly and personal; and it is to him that this book is dedicated.

Introduction

chapter one

Prologue: Looking Backward

In the second lunar month of 1825 the Edo bakufu ordered officials in coastal areas except Nagasaki to attack on sight and drive away all Western ships, whether or not clearly identified as Dutch. In the following month Aizawa Seishisai (1781–1863), a Confucian scholar of Mito Learning,[1] composed a polemical tract entitled *New Theses* (*Shinron*) justifying that policy. These events mark a great divide in early-modern Japanese history: Even though the Expulsion Edict was revoked in 1842, bakufu authority and legitimacy after 1825 hinged on maintaining national isolation (*sakoku*), conceived of as an inviolable law of the land.[2] This in turn meant being willing and able to perform *jōi*, or the expulsion of Western barbarians by force. In this study, which serves as an introduction to the English translation of *New Theses,* I show how this idea of armed expulsion evolved during the Edo period and try to explain why bakufu leaders adopted it as the guiding principle of Japanese foreign policy.

Quite rightly, we generally examine Mito Learning and the idea of armed expulsion in the context of Western impact and Japanese response leading to the Meiji Restoration during the 1850s and 1860s. Mito Learning represented a final ideological attempt to shore up the existing Tokugawa feudal order. Aizawa's thought, as articulated in *New Theses,* provided normative grounding for bakufu de facto sovereignty, its policy of national isolation, the hereditary supremacy of the samurai class, and a pre-modern economy based on agricultural self-sufficiency.[3] The Meiji Restoration could not occur, capitalism and industrialism could not advance, and a powerful centralized nation-state

3

could not emerge, until these old Tokugawa institutional arrangements were scrapped. First of all, Japan's leaders had to disown the Mito-inspired policy of armed expulsion, a policy that became unrealistic after Commodore Matthew C. Perry and Consul Townsend Harris forced Japan's ports open in the 1850s. Japan's leaders had to recognize the inevitability of "opening the country" (*kaikoku*) to trade and diplomacy, and of joining the world community of nations.

For these reasons, Japanese and Western historians have focused on the bakumatsu, or "End of the Shogunate," era from 1853 to 1868 in their attempts to understand the slogans *jōi* and *kaikoku*. Political and diplomatic historians explain that in this era the rhetoric of expelling Westerners and opening the country should not be accepted literally.[4] These slogans were not mutually exclusive. Both allowed for a wide range of usage and interpretation as changing political conditions dictated. Not only did elliptic literary forms of writing foster ambiguity, bakumatsu writers manipulated these slogans in a purposely cryptic way, for they were masters of the skillful hedge. "Expelling Western barbarians," for example, often was for domestic consumption, while "opening the country" was an expedient ploy for diplomatic maneuvering with the foreign powers. And after 1864, the rhetoric of *jōi* was little more than a pretext for overthrowing the bakufu.

Yet ambiguities and qualifications aside, this interpretation holds, *jōi* and *kaikoku* advocates shared the same basic goal: to preserve Japan's independence. They also agreed on the means to achieve that goal: national wealth and military strength. Even after 1853, *sakoku*, or national isolation, persisted as an ideal; it was transformed into the conviction that Japanese leaders should not open their country under foreign coercion, that they themselves should determine the time and the conditions under which to pursue trade and diplomacy. Advocates of armed expulsion knew full well that this policy could lead to defeats in combat with the foreigners. But a few lost battles would unify the Japanese people spiritually and inspire them to achieve equality with the West, even if this entailed importing Western arms and technology through trade and intercourse. Expulsion, then, was not an end in itself; it admitted the eventuality of opening Japan to the Western world. Nor was opening the country an ultimate goal. Instead of risking immediate military defeat, Japan prudently should accede to Western demands, at least for the time being. But Japan must use this respite to master Western science and technology, adopt Western institutions, and thus strengthen itself to recapture the ideal behind national isolation—an ability to expel Westerners should the need or desire arise. In effect, opening the country was the best way to expedite the expulsion of Western barbarians in the long run.

Some scholars reject this *jōi/kaikoku* polarity in favor of a three-stage developmental scheme to clarify the character and scope of change in bakumatsu foreign policy attitudes.[5] First, increased public engagement in the foreign policy debate through the call for expulsion meant advancing from a passive acceptance of national isolation to a positive advocacy of it. Next came acquiescence, however reluctant and resentful, in a policy of opening the ports. Finally, active support for the policy would follow. This three-step process, it is held, produced an ethical transvaluation in which Japanese leaders came to believe that national isolation was bad, and that opening the country to Western trade and diplomatic intercourse was good. This entailed repudiating the bakuhan system as unworkable and not worth supporting.

Other scholars oppose this *jōi/kaikoku* dichotomy for different reasons.[6] They see the primary issue not as a debate over whether to expel or admit foreigners to Japan, but rather, as a clash between traditional Confucian and modern Western conceptions of the world order. *Jōi* assumed a hierarchy among nations, *kaikoku*, equality between nations. Expulsionist thinkers could conceive of Japan only as the embodiment of civilization at the center of a Chinese-style "all under Heaven"; Westerners were inherently inferior beings, barbarians to be kept at bay. Opening Japan to the world in a true and meaningful sense required accepting a Europe-centered international order composed of independent and equal nation-states. Modern trade and diplomacy could take place only under these conditions: The Western powers, not Japan, determined the game's rules.

5

Intellectual historians offer a different way of analyzing *jōi* in the bakumatsu era.[7] For them, the expulsionist ideas in *New Theses* serve as a convenient departure point in tracing the breakdown of traditional modes of thought and the emergence of a modern political realism. These processes would take Japan through the Meiji Restoration and culminate in a centralized, bureaucratic nation-state. The history of nineteenth-century Japanese thought, according to this view, describes the liberation of political decision-making from Confucian moralism. Mito thinkers such as Aizawa could not perceive the foreign threat realistically—as a military problem. Instead, Aizawa construed barbarian intrusion to be a portent from Heaven signifying daimyo and samurai moral decay. Like earthquakes, volcanic eruptions, and other irregularities of nature, the appearance of Western barbarians for Aizawa was an admonition to carry out moral reform in government. According to the logic behind his premodern Confucian idea of interaction between Heaven and man, a ruler's good or bad deeds invited Heavenly reciprocation in kind. The daimyo and samurai, Aizawa believed, had brought the Western menace on themselves by governing in a lackadaisical, irresponsible manner. Mito critics such as Aizawa were convinced that *chūkō*, political reform through moral reinvigoration, of which *jōi* formed a central part, would suffice to end the foreign threat. But after 1864, when Western armed strength proved unassailable, such reformist ideas based on moral rigor lost cogency and gave way to an opportunistic realpolitik in domestic and foreign affairs.

Cultural historians argue that the empiricism of Western science and the useful knowledge gained from a study of world affairs discredited backward-looking *jōi* ideas and policies.[8] The scholars of Dutch Studies (Rangakusha) enlightened their countrymen by providing new, practical knowledge from the West. Responsible Japanese leaders came to realize the impossibility of trying to drive away Westerners by force. Pragmatic statesmen found that they must open the country to Western trade and diplomatic intercourse in order to master the secrets of Western power and wealth. Informed specialists in Dutch Studies and Western Learning challenged outmoded Mito views of state and international order; *New Theses* lost credence and currency; *kaikoku* replaced *jōi*. One distinguished scholar emphasizes the decisive role that men with Western knowledge played in refuting the xenophobic Mito policy of expulsion:

> ... the pursuit of Dutch studies had already in the eighteenth century created a body of scholars who, primarily because of their interest in science, were anxious to see the opening of the country. This tendency had been strengthened as with the lapse of time more knowledge was acquired and more was needed, until at length it became clear that the Bakufu was too weak to withstand accumulating foreign pressure.[9]

Another authority lends further support to this view:

> The kaikoku school is closely connected with the Rangakusha whose study of the West gave them a greater knowledge of world conditions than that possessed by most of their contemporaries. With greater knowledge came a more vivid realization of Japan's military weakness, and it was this that was the distinguishing feature of their thought.[10]

Mid-nineteenth-century Japanese leaders rejected direct military confrontation with the West in favor of thoroughgoing cultural borrowing. By adopting Western ideas and institutions in the name of "civilization and enlightenment," they strove to create wealth and power under a centralized nation-state.

This brief survey only begins to introduce the rich and sophisticated secondary literature on Aizawa's *New Theses*, Mito Learning, and *jōi*, but I believe it accurately reflects a pertinent range of scholarly opinion. Despite the diversity of viewpoints I have presented above, all have two themes in common: They ascribe prime importance to Western knowledge in repudiating *jōi* as an outdated idea and an unrealistic policy, and they focus on the period 1853 to 1868. By synthesizing the various scholarly theses presented above, we would arrive at something like the following consensus. First, *jōi* ideologues such as Aizawa were convinced that a "muscular Confucianism"[11] which reasserted the superiority of traditional culture and values would beat back Western encroachment. After this proved futile,

7

realists such as Sakuma Shōzan declared that, since the foreign menace was a matter of power rather than culture or ethics, Japan's leaders need but assimilate demonstrably superior military technology and science from the West. Finally, enlightened thinkers such as Fukuzawa Yukichi realized that importing such by-products and outward forms of Western civilization was not enough: Modern Western nations derived their strength from a spiritual source; so Japan must acquire this spirit of modern Western civilization as well.

In short, historians treat Aizawa's Mito Confucianism and *jōi* as representing outmoded values and a state policy that Japan had to leave behind in her quest for independence and modernity. There is much validity in this view, but it is only one way of coming to grips with the problem at hand. In this study of Aizawa's thought I will examine nineteenth-century Japanese anti-foreignism from a different perspective in the hope of gaining new insights into its historical significance. I will primarily look backward in time from 1825 to discover how the idea and policy of *jōi* emerged, rather than look forward from 1825 to discuss why this idea and policy declined.

The appearance of *New Theses* and the promulgation of *jōi* as national policy in 1825 marked the end of one epoch as well as the start of another. After more than a century of intellectual ferment, the era from 1793 to 1825 saw the perfection of an ideology to support the Japanese state in its then-existing form: a Tokugawa-led federation of regional daimyo which historians label the bakuhan system. This national ideology of "Japan as Middle-Kingdom" allowed bakufu leaders to extricate Japan from subservience to a China-dominated diplomatic world order of universal empire and culture. Equally important, it allowed them to conceive of ideas like national sovereignty and territorial integrity, ideas indispensable to the formation of Meiji nationalism. Throughout *New Theses* Aizawa calls Japan "the Divine Realm," and "the Middle Kingdom." Granted, he was not the first Tokugawa thinker to boast that Japan rather than China represented Chūgoku, "Middle Kingdom Civilization," and that therefore Japan was the superior nation. But in *New*

Theses, Aizawa achieved the ultimate synthesis of Confucian and nativist rationales for claiming Japanese superiority, and he linked the idea of Japan as Middle-Kingdom to the existing state structure more forcefully and convincingly than anyone had before. In short, his *New Theses* contained tenets of proto-nationalism: the idea and belief that all Japanese, despite their unalterable differences in social status, owe ultimate loyalty to the existing bakuhan state as the only form of political organization proper to an independent and sovereign Japan. Thanks to this ideology of Japan as Middle-Kingdom, Aizawa made the crucially important shift in world view from universal empire (*tenka*) to nation-state (*kokka*), a perceptual shift that would take decades longer in China.[12] After the appearance of *New Theses* in 1825, bakumatsu thinkers and leaders continued to conceive of a Japan-centered world order, but they realized that Japan did not dominate it. Although the Tokugawa bakuhan state claimed centrality and superiority in the international arena, a plurality of nations vied for supremacy and survival. Japan was only one of the competitors—and a small, backward one at that.

In yet another sense, 1825 marked the culmination of an important historical change. The concept of *jōi* took on a new, militant character, and found institutionalization in state policy with the promulgation of the 1825 Expulsion Edict. Earlier in the Edo period, Confucian thinkers had conceived of *jōi* in highly abstract, cultural terms; for them it had meant sweeping away, or eradicating "what is barbarian." They had seen it as eliminating alien ideas, customs, and values by edifying commoners in Confucianism. *Jōi* in this abstract, cultural sense entailed erecting barriers to prevent Japanese commoners from being "transformed" by foreign ways. In 1825, the term changed in meaning from eradicating "what is barbarian" to eradicating "the barbarians." This semantic change accompanied a shift in methods of execution—from edification to armed force—which reflected the bakufu's recognition that world conditions called for a new basic foreign policy. Before 1825, the bakufu customarily turned away foreign intruders by persuading them to leave peacefully. Edo leaders shied away from provoking encounters

9

with Westerners, sometimes even if it meant humiliating themselves. But in 1825, they publicly committed their regime to violence as a first resort, not a last resort, in upholding national isolation.

Western Learning contributed directly to the bakufu's formulation and justification of armed expulsion: We must discard any preconceptions linking knowledge of the West with an "enlightened" *kaikoku* policy. Nineteenth-century Japanese students of the West such as Takano Chōei and Watanabe Kazan argued that the bakufu should strive to exclude Westerners and uphold national isolation insofar as international developments allowed.[13] In fact, the most brilliant and informed Rangakusha of the day, a bakufu official named Takahashi Kageyasu, first proposed the 1825 Expulsion Edict.[14] Furthermore, when Aizawa composed *New Theses* that same year, he knew much more about the world outside Japan than we generally assume. Though at times mistaken, his understanding of things Western was crucial in shaping his development as a xenophobic thinker.

Some may resist this argument. Given the virulent nature of Aizawa's anti-foreign rhetoric, he and Mito Learning should be deemed irrelevant to, if not incompatible with, Western Learning and its liberalizing effects on Tokugawa thought, politics, and society. Aizawa, they would claim, steeped himself in traditional Confucian and Shinto biases. He flaunted Japanese cultural and ethnic superiority, contemptuously calling Westerners "barbarians," "dogs and goats," "wild boars and wolves," and the like. He warned of sinister Christian designs on Japan and exhorted all Japanese to hate and kill foreigners as they would hate and kill vicious, cunning predators. In stark contrast to Aizawa's xenophobia, this interpretation holds, thinkers engaged in Western Learning were forward-looking heralds of Japanese modernization. They should be viewed as liberal or progressive for wanting to transcend the narrow confines of classical Chinese or native Japanese learning. Would not the zealous pursuit of practical knowledge from Europe foster good will toward foreign peoples? Xenophobia stemming from uninformed prejudice and open-minded liberalism fostered by knowledge—these are the contrasting images that Mito Learning and Western Learning present to many.

In truth the issue is not this simple and clear-cut.[15] Seeking or possessing Western knowledge to a greater degree did not make Japanese in the nineteenth century more liberal or more kindly disposed to Westerners. As mentioned earlier, the period's most accomplished Rangakusha, Takahashi Kageyasu, proposed that the bakufu order all daimyo to drive away Western ships on sight. Nor did a lesser understanding of conditions in the West preclude some Japanese from formulating "enlightened" policies: In 1825, Aizawa perceived Japan's foreign and domestic crises much more clearly than Takahashi, and he proposed much more sensible solutions.

Few studies of the past are unimpaired by discrepancies of perception; historical hindsight often yields images of people, ideas, and events that contemporaries would have found hard to accept. Aizawa and his *New Theses* are a case in point. As we have noted, postwar historians tend to characterize his Mito Learning as feudal, traditional, backward-looking, or outmoded; in short, as a hindrance that could not be overcome quickly enough.[16] But many people in Aizawa's own lifetime saw *New Theses* in a different light. His very use of the adjective *new* in his title must have struck bakumatsu readers as deliberately provocative. To Tokugawa scholars trained in the Confucian historiographical tradition, *new* (as opposed to *ancient*) often implied something radical or unorthodox, if not downright dangerous. Wang Mang's New Dynasty in the first century A.D., and Wang An-shih's New Laws during the Sung dynasty would have been the immediate associations.[17]

Aizawa's *New Theses* of 1825 intimated much that was similarly deviant. In the 1850s, for example, Yamagata Taika, a high-ranking domain scholar in Chōshū, cast a jaundiced eye on "adherents of the Mito school in our domain" who were "misled by its heterodox teachings."[18] Regarding Aizawa's concept of *kokutai* (discussed below), Taika wrote: "The term *kokutai* appears often in Sung dynasty writings, but I have yet to come across it in Japanese works. It probably originated in Mito."[19]

11

Taika deserves no high marks for philological erudition, but his comments show that he considered Aizawa's ideas to have been "outlandish concepts not expressed by men in earlier ages."[20] He plainly did not think that Mito ideas were sanctioned by tradition, or that they could shore up the existing order. Quite the contrary, he feared that *New Theses* would lead young men down evil and aberrant paths.

Chōshū scholars were not alone in attacking Aizawa's ideas as dangerous. In 1871, the Kurume domain samurai, Kawashima Suminosuke, recalled:

Scholars both in and outside the domain school, the Meizendō, refused even to look at Mito-related writings and would not allow their students to read them either. They branded readers of Mito works "followers of Tempō Learning." They detested and spread tales about such followers, depicting them as practicers of black magic, in an attempt to imbue common folk with fear and loathing of them. Those scholars would say, "such persons possess the evil eye; if you associate with them, they will cast its spell on you."[21]

Aizawa's "new" theses seemed uncanny and extremist to many contemporaries. They labeled his Mito ideas "Tempō Learning," after the Tempō era, from 1830 to 1843. In those years his works began to circulate throughout Japan, winning the enthusiastic support of impressionable youths and earning the fearful disdain of fusty establishment scholars. In this study I argue that the idea of *kokutai* and much else that appeared new (and ominous) in *New Theses* derived from Aizawa's Western Learning.[22]

In 1825, a decade and a half before the Opium War, Aizawa perceived that the Western "barbarians" were unlike any who had confronted China or Japan in the past. He did not discern a Western military threat to Tokugawa Japan because no such threat existed. In the 1810s and 1820s, British and American whalers, not warships, were appearing frequently in Japanese waters. The Industrial Revolution had yet to tip the technological scales decisively in Europe's favor, so Westerners brandished no overwhelmingly superior weapons in the Far East. In short, expulsion by force was a safe and sound policy for

Japan to adopt at that time. Since no clear and present military danger from abroad existed in 1825, we miss the point when we fault Aizawa for failing to detect it. Instead, we should try to explain how and why he construed the foreign menace as he did.

Aizawa argued that the secret of Western strength lay in Christianity, a state cult that Western leaders propagated to cultivate voluntary allegiance both in their own peoples and in those they colonized overseas. Aizawa called the popular unity and allegiance so cultivated *kokutai,* "the essence of a nation," (and by extension, "what is essential to make a people into a nation"). This meaning of *kokutai* constituted a significant departure from customary usage. Tokugawa and Ch'ing writers used the term *kokutai* or *kuo t'i* to mean "the nation's honor" or "dynastic prestige," and in some contexts Aizawa too used the term in this sense. But in *New Theses* his use of *kokutai* also connoted "the unity of religion and government" (*saisei itchi*) used by a ruler to create spiritual unity and integration among his subjects: Only in this manner would a people be made into a nation. In antiquity, the emperor was both a spiritual and secular sovereign who conducted religious rituals as part of government. Though Aizawa claimed that this form of rule was purely Japanese and made Japan superior to foreign lands, actually he derived this idea of *kokutai* in large part from a knowledge of Christianity and the West. His studies of world geography and foreign affairs convinced him that Western leaders had attained *kokutai* better than the bakufu. In his eyes, Western power came from a spiritual source. Indeed, he equated a state's independence with its religious autonomy:

> The only nation besides our own that is not yet befouled by either Islam or Christianity is the Manchu Ch'ing empire. Countries such as Korea or Annam have also done an admirable job of maintaining their independence (*tokuritsu*) by remaining unconverted to those occult religions.[23]

In *New Theses* Aizawa covertly argued that bakufu leaders must imitate Western methods of government by using the emperor to conduct a Japanese state religion designed to win the same type of national unity and mass loyalty that Western leaders

13

had captured through Christianity. He considered national unity and mass loyalty more important than wealth and armed strength in ensuring Japan's independence as a nation. This was because he perceived that the Western threat Japan faced in 1825 was ideological, not military, in nature. Commodore Perry's steam-powered warships changed that—but not until 1853.

It is true that much of Aizawa's Western "knowledge" was based on misinformation. But his particular grasp of Western politics and society, whether accurate or not, provided a model against which to contrast and criticize Japanese institutions. Identifying what he believed to be Western sources of strength at once disclosed factors causing Japanese weakness. This prompted him to draw up radical new proposals intended to reinforce the Tokugawa bakuhan state by assimilating Western ideas and administrative practices.

Such reform programs prompted many contemporaries to look askance at *New Theses*. Discerning readers sensed that the bakuhan order could not absorb his suggested reforms and remain intact. For example, to suggest that the emperor play a crucial role in government administration in effect meant admitting that the bakufu could not rule effectively without borrowing prestige and religious authority from the imperial court. Such an admission seriously undermined the cardinal principle of bakufu political supremacy over the court, which the first three Tokugawa shoguns had been so intent on establishing. In addition, Aizawa's call for a Japanese state religion to imbue commoners with voluntary allegiance logically contradicted another categorical imperative of the bakuhan state—daimyo and warrior monopoly on military functions. This categorical imperative, usually stated as "the separation of warrior from peasant" (*heinō bunri*), justified samurai-class privilege and supremacy in Tokugawa society. But Aizawa's proposal suggested that commoners, hitherto forbidden to engage in political or military affairs, owed loyal service to the bakuhan state in wartime. And those commoners could hardly be expected to bear this large new burden without demanding large new benefits. Of course, Aizawa never intended things to go that far. But his own intentions aside, the logical implications of his *New Theses* pointed to an emperor-centered government utilizing state religious teachings to infuse nationalism, not a status-bound and domain-centered form of loyalty, in commoners. Though his original intention was to reinforce the status quo, Aizawa's ideas entailed repudiating the structural principles that upheld the Tokugawa bakuhan order.

To summarize, the era 1793 to 1825 ended an epoch and marked a turning point in Tokugawa history. In 1825, the bakufu ordered that all Western ships be fired on and driven off (*jōi, uchiharai*) and Aizawa Seishisai composed his *New Theses* in support of this unprecedented policy. Western Learning played a key role both in producing the *jōi* edict and eliciting Aizawa's approbation of it. *New Theses,* coupled with the government's policy of expulsion by force, signaled the emergence of proto-nationalism in Japan. Bakufu leaders after 1825 viewed their nation in its current form, the bakuhan state, as having surpassed China's long-held position of world-preeminence. Japan, not Ch'ing dynasty China, was Middle Kingdom Civilization. In this Japan-centered world order, Edo dictated the rules governing trade and diplomatic relations between Japan and other states. One of these rules, which bakufu leaders established in 1793, stipulated that no Westerners other than the Dutch be permitted entry into Japan. In 1825, for the first time ever, the Edo bakufu publicly committed itself to upholding this rule through the unconditional use of armed force. Thereafter, and largely because of the climate of opinion that *New Theses* helped create, politically active segments of the Japanese population made bakufu legitimacy contingent on the ability to expel Westerners from Japan by force.

Informed critics such as Aizawa were not without misgivings when they saw the bakufu put its political honor at stake in this new way, for Western Learning had disclosed serious weaknesses in Japan's defenses. Fifteen years before the Opium War, Aizawa's knowledge of world affairs convinced him that the Westerners he denigrated as "barbarians" presented a foreign menace of unprecedented scale. While Japan and China had been regressing, the Westerners had made astounding progress in important areas of government and had seized vast colonial

15

empires. Aizawa had to admit that only drastic new counter-measures would forestall territorial encroachment by the Westerners. The Edo bakufu had to reorganize Japan somewhat along Western lines in order to strengthen itself and preserve national isolation, a "hallowed law" to be enforced at any cost. Aizawa proposed how to do this in *New Theses*. He specified certain Western-inspired reforms deemed "essential to make Japan a nation" (*kokutai*). Paradoxically, his proposals would destroy the bakuhan order when pushed to their logical conclusions after 1868. But in 1825, the foreign threat facing Japan was far different from what it would be in 1853. Despite certain misgivings, Aizawa and like-minded bakufu supporters had cause for guarded optimism.

chapter two
The Civilized and
the Barbarian

Explaining the bakumatsu slogan "Expel the barbarians" (*jōi*) seems simple enough. The Japanese are civilized and are superior to Western barbarians; Western ships approaching Japan are to be driven off by force. But this simplicity is beguiling. The concepts of "civilization" and "barbarism," as applied to peoples and nations, underwent important changes during the Edo period. Roughly speaking, early in the period, Japanese thinkers saw Ming dynasty China as representing civilization in contrast to Japan which they considered a barbarian state. Since Europeans were largely out of sight and mind, they escaped ready categorization. And in any case, these categories were cultural, having little to do with military force. But by the nineteenth century, Tokugawa thinkers claimed that their nation had surpassed Ch'ing dynasty China as the center of world civilization, and they reviled Westerners as barbarians who should be expelled militarily. Only after tracing how the concepts of civilization, barbarism, and expulsion evolved during the Tokugawa period will we properly understand Aizawa's *jōi* rhetoric in *New Theses*.

Efforts to trace this evolution are complicated by problems of historical terminology. In Tokugawa times, the Sino-Japanese terms connoting civilization—Chūka and Chūgoku—were not value-free geographic names for China, as they are today. Instead, these terms were honorifics: Many Tokugawa thinkers felt that using them to designate China demeaned their own nation. Yet at the same time, a good many early Tokugawa Confucians thought of Japan, not Western countries, as barbarian.

What precisely set civilization off from barbarism as these concepts evolved over time? Just when did *jōi* take on primarily military, as opposed to cultural, overtones? How did contact with Western cultures and peoples alter these ideas? To discuss these historical issues as they would have appeared to Aizawa, I begin this chapter by borrowing two theoretical models. One, adapted from John K. Fairbank and Uete Michiari, depicts the Sinocentric Middle Kingdom world view which differentiates Confucian moral civilization from barbarism.[1] The other, which can be traced all the way back to the writings of Chu Hsi (1130–1200) defines *jōi*, or the "expulsion of what is barbarian" in cultural terms.[2] I apply these models to the thought of representative Tokugawa thinkers in order to outline the broad historical development of these key concepts central to Aizawa's *New Theses*.

CIVILIZATION: WHERE CONFUCIAN RITUAL OBTAINS

Middle Kingdom Civilization[3] was conceptualized in two dimensions: the vertical social hierarchy, on which "superior men" occupied a position midway between Heaven above and the masses of commoners below; and the horizontal-geographic plane, where inhabitants of a central realm were thought to be morally and culturally superior to aliens beyond its pale. One defining characteristic of the Middle Kingdom on both the vertical-hierarchic axis and the horizontal-geographic plane was to possess "rites, rituals, and the rules of proper behavior"— believed to be the essence of civilized existence. Another essential characteristic was to be literate in, or at least familiar with, classical Chinese. After all, people belonging to the central realm of civilization upheld the customs and conformed to the values and norms set down in classical Confucian writings. Confucians thought of commoners and aliens as similar in the sense that both required edification (*kyōkwa*) or moral transformation (*kwa*) through the mystical power of ritual and music and what Mencius called "good teachings."[4]

This identification of the Confucian literati with civilization, and of commoners and aliens with barbarism, was a highly abstract, idealized view. Theoretically, the leisure and means to pursue classical learning and thereby gain a knowledge of ritual and music were largely literati privileges. Therefore, commoners and aliens were not expected to embody civilization unless they were morally transformed or edified by their rulers from above. This ritual edification centered on making one's activities accord with one's hereditary social-status designation. In short, ritual edification was designed to produce submissive adherence to the existing social hierarchy. In like manner, edified aliens signified their proper subservience to Middle Kingdom Civilization by submitting themselves to rituals such as the kowtow.

This world view, which categorized peoples as either civilized or barbarian, was of Chinese origin and therefore was extrinsic to early Tokugawa Japan; it poorly fit the realities of Japan as a small island country. For example, "the world" as conceptualized in Sinocentric terms was "all under Heaven" (*tenka*), and it recognized no fixed national boundaries. As Arai Hakuseki (1657–1725) wrote in the context of international law, for example, "A crime is a crime anywhere on earth" (*tenka no aku wa hitotsu nari*).[5] In another usage, *tenka* designated "the realm," or the geographical extent of Middle Kingdom Civilization conceived of as China (or Japan). But according to Confucian political theory, these two conceptions of *tenka* ought to coincide: The Chinese (or Japanese) empire ideally should encompass all under Heaven, and extend to the ends of the earth. Through benevolent government and ethical example, and by extending the benefits of advanced Middle Kingdom Civilization, the emperor, the Son of Heaven, ought to incorporate aliens within it. On the other hand, if he conducted cruel government and set an evil example, not only would aliens refuse to "come to be transformed," commoners also would cease submitting to his authority.

Commoners and alien barbarians were identical in one important sense. Normally, both were ignorant of the civilized way of life defined by ritual and classical canon; both had to be morally transformed by the emperor. And both presented a threat to the existing hierarchical order characterizing Sinocentric civilization. Chinese bandit-rebels were seen as little different from barbarian invaders in that they refused to affirm and submit to this Middle Kingdom world view.[6] Whether the Middle Kingdom's borders expanded or contracted, whether barbarians remained outside it or were incorporated within it, and whether commoners acquiesced below or revolted against those above, depended on the emperor's virtue, benevolent government, ritual observances, and moral transformation.

Thus, the Middle Kingdom world view boils down to four essential characteristics: (1) *centrality* on both the horizontal-geographic and vertical-hierarchic dimensions, (2) *extensiveness* or widespread acceptance by both aliens and the lower classes in society, and (3) *superiority* based on Sinocentric moral and cultural standards. Moreover, Confucians presumed that extensiveness and superiority were inseparable: The emperor's personal virtue, the excellence of Middle Kingdom Civilization, and the "transforming power" of ritual and good teachings would win eager acceptance by commoners and foreign barbarians alike in all historical epochs. This universal acceptance found concrete form in customs or folkways that correspond to Confucian teachings and theoretically should prevail everywhere and at all times. Therefore, (4) Middle Kingdom Civilization was characterized by *timeless cultural monism.*

Jōi is another ambiguous, problematic term. It too is of Chinese origin and was alien to early Tokugawa Japan. One key example that clarifies its meaning is in Chu Hsi's commentary on the *Analects.* There he introduces the phrase, "to revere the Chou dynastic house and sweep away (or eradicate) what is barbarian."[7] This phrase glosses the following passage:

> [*Analects:*] Tzu-kung said, "I do not suppose Kuan Chung was a benevolent man. Not only did he not die for Prince Chiu, but he lived to help Duke Huan, who had the Prince killed." The Master said, "Kuan Chung helped Duke Huan to become the leader of the feudal lords (*pa*) and to rectify all under Heaven. To this day, the common people still enjoy the benefit of his acts. Had it not been for Kuan Chung, we might well be wearing our hair down and folding our robes to the left. . . ."[8]

In short, according to Chu Hsi, Confucius defended and praised Kuan Chung (7th c. B.C.), a minister who ruled by force instead of benevolence. Confucius defended him for preventing the common people's customs and manners from being transformed to alien ways. For Confucius, as construed by Chu Hsi, "wearing our hair down and folding our robes to the left" constituted a violation of ritual, or the proper rules of behavior, which set off civilized life from barbarism. In Chu Hsi's interpretation, Confucius had asserted that, by rescuing Middle Kingdom Civilization from morally and culturally backward foreign ways, Kuan Chung performed an act of *jōi*. Tokugawa thinkers before 1825 thought of *jōi* primarily as Chu Hsi's gloss indicates: the cultural sense of "sweeping away (or eradicating) what is barbarian." By tracing how this idea of "cultural *jōi*" developed in the seventeenth and eighteenth centuries, we will gain the background knowledge needed to understand why *jōi* took on military overtones in the era 1793 to 1825.

During the seventeenth and through most of the eighteenth centuries, Japan had little contact with Western cultures. As a result, Caucasians did not enter much into Japanese thinking about civilization and barbarism. Westerners were described as "red-hairs" or "Southern barbarians," but they were not objects of animosity unless they attempted to spread Christianity; Japanese in the early Edo period persecuted Christians, but not Westerners as such. The most significant disputes as to who was civilized and who barbarian centered on Japan's relationships with her Asian neighbors. As Tsukamoto Manabu[9] holds, early Tokugawa thinkers tended to admit Japan's barbarian status toward Chinese civilization; they generally did not stigmatize Westerners as barbarians. Toward the end of the eighteenth century, after the rise of Dutch Studies, Westerners did take on this stigma.[10] And after Fujita Yūkoku, Aizawa Seishisai, and their Mito Learning emerged in the early nineteenth century, many politically conscious Japanese denigrated Westerners as subhuman beasts.[11]

Japanese perceptions of China, Japan, and the West as being civilized or barbarian changed during the Edo period, and in the discussion that follows I seek to place these perceptions in dynamic historical perspective. Tokugawa thinkers, even early in the period, had not borrowed the abstract idea of Middle Kingdom Civilization from China without serious reservations. Later on, in response to attacks from Native Learning (Kokugaku) and Western Learning, scholars of Mito Learning had to create a "Japan-centered" Middle Kingdom world order substantially different from the Sinocentric view.

JAPAN: A LAND OF SPLENDID BARBARIANS

Early Tokugawa Confucians faced a difficult problem: how to Japanize the Way of the Chinese Sages without losing its universal validity and value, but also without compromising too much of Japan's cultural tradition.[12] This problem overlay more fundamental questions about the nature of civilized life itself. Could there be culture and morality apart from Confucianism? If not, how could Confucianism be detached from its Chinese moorings, from the Chinese society and way of life that produced it, and from the classical Chinese language that transmitted it? Were the categories of civilization and barbarism fixed along racial or ethnic lines? If not, how could an alien people like the Japanese leave barbarism behind and become part of Chinese civilization? Or was this really a desirable aim? Many Tokugawa Confucians found answers to these gnawing questions in this passage from the *Analects:*

夷狄之有君不如諸夏之亡也

The passage allows two radically different interpretations.[13] Following the pre-Sung commentaries, we get, "[Even though] the eastern and northern barbarians possess rulers, [they] are not as good as the Middle Kingdom which lacks one."[14] According to this older interpretation, *pu-ju* 不如 meant "do not measure up to." Chu Hsi, on the other hand, claimed that *ju* 如 meant "to be similar to," which would make the passage read, "The eastern and northern barbarians who possess a ruler are [very much] unlike the Middle Kingdom which lacks one."[15]

By adhering to the older interpretation, scholars might contend that China's superiority to the barbarians, whether based on morality, culture, language, or, in an extreme case, blood, was absolute. Other factors such as the political unity and administrative order achieved by aliens (suggested by the existence of a ruler over them) counted for nothing. Confucius emerges as confident that civilization is inseparable from the Chinese way of life.

By contrast, if scholars in later ages or foreign lands chose to follow Chu Hsi's interpretation, a whole new avenue of possibilities opened up. Confucius emerges as deferential toward aliens, as willing to acknowledge their political accomplishments and to admit that the Chinese in his day did not measure up. Because the Chinese people lacked good rulers, they suffered anarchy and civil strife. Following Chu Hsi, it might be argued that Confucius attributed equal, if not preponderate, weight to factors other than Chinese culture or race in judging the worth of men.

According to the older interpretation, narrow ethnocentric criteria determined Middle Kingdom superiority; non-Chinese were simply excluded from civilized life. But Chu Hsi's interpretation allowed Tokugawa thinkers leeway to claim quasi-Middle Kingdom status for themselves and their nation. They could acknowledge Japan to be ethnically barbarian, but still declare it superior to Ming or Ch'ing China based on other criteria within the general framework of Confucian values. Civilized life did not require Chinese lineages or inclusion in the Chinese empire; many specific aspects of Chinese culture also were dispensable.

A good number of Tokugawa Confucians adopted this cultural relativism based on Chu Hsi's portrayal of Confucius, even scholars like Itō Jinsai (1627–1705), who contentiously rejected Chu Hsi Learning on most other counts. In commenting upon the above passage from the *Analects*, Jinsai wrote,

[*Analects:*] "The eastern and northern barbarians who possess rulers are [very much] unlike the Middle Kingdom which lacks one."

[Jinsai's gloss:] Confucius was extremely attentive to the slightest change in customs of the times. . . . What a tremendous

23

change he notes here! Although the states of China are supposedly that area of the world where ritual and righteousness exist, he says that China does not measure up to the barbarians. That is why he wrote the *Spring and Autumn Annals*. . . . In it, he called "barbarian" any Chinese lord who adopted alien rituals, and he treated as part of the "Middle Kingdom" any alien who advanced to adopt the rituals of the Middle Kingdom. Confucius [impartially] praised the good as good, and hated the evil as evil. How can this distinction [of civilized and barbarian] be [arbitrarily] applied to Chinese and barbarian peoples?[16]

Here Jinsai equates "customs of the times" with the rituals men practice—whether those of the Middle Kingdom or of the barbarians. He defines "good" as practicing the rituals of Middle Kingdom Civilization, and "bad" as ignoring or rejecting them. It was wrong to attribute moral or cultural superiority to the Chinese people as such. Aliens could advance to Middle Kingdom standing by adopting the rituals and customs of the Middle Kingdom. Conversely, ethnic Chinese could revert to barbarism by rejecting Middle Kingdom rituals and customs for those of aliens. In other words, civilization and barbarism were mutually convertible categories for Jinsai.

Jinsai declared Japan to be one of the nine barbarian tribes of the east amongst whom, according to the *Analects,* Confucius wanted to settle. Jinsai, along with many early Tokugawa Confucians, acknowledged Japan's "barbarian" status relative to Chinese civilization. But this did not demean Japan, for she could boast moral excellence precisely *because* she was barbarian. Let us examine Jinsai's rationale for that assertion, based on his interpretation of this key passage from the *Analects*.

[*Analects:*] "The Master wanted to settle amongst the nine barbarian tribes of the east. Someone said, 'But could you put up with their uncouth ways?' The Master said, 'A gentleman (*chün-tzu*) once settled there, so what uncouthness can there be?'"

After identifying the Japanese as one of these nine tribes, Jinsai went on to comment that the so-called uncouthness of barbarians really stemmed from their faithfulness. From ancient times, he noted, there were reports that "a country of gentlemen" existed off to the east. Then he went on:

[Jinsai's gloss:] Confucius once said, "The barbarians with their ruler are [very much] unlike the Middle Kingdom which lacks one." From this we can see that he long held the nine barbarian tribes close to his heart. The present passage and the lament he uttered in the "put to sea on a raft" passage are identical in meaning.

No matter where under Heaven or where on earth [they may live], *all men are equally men.* Even a barbarian, if he but possesses ritual and righteousness, is a part of the Middle Kingdom. Even a Chinese, should he lack ritual and righteousness, cannot escape being barbarian. Shun was born an eastern barbarian and King Wen of Chou was born a western barbarian, but their being aliens made no difference [to their becoming sages]. Though the countries of the nine barbarian tribes are far away, none lies outside the universe (*tenchi*). Their inhabitants possess the ordinary nature of all other men. Indeed, their simplicity is always that of faithfulness, while [Middle Kingdom] Civilization is often that of falsity. No wonder Confucius "wanted to settle amongst" them.[18] (emphasis added)

When we read this gloss together with the one Jinsai added to the "put to sea on a raft" passage mentioned above, we get the point he was driving at.

[*Analects:*] "The Master said, 'The Way is not being carried out; I shall put to sea on a raft. The one who would follow me will surely be Yu.'"
[Jinsai's gloss:] This passage means the same as the "the Master wanted to settle amongst the nine barbarian tribes of the east" passage. It surely represents Confucius's long-cherished aspiration. [In China] at that time, rulers were foolish and ministers acted haughtily, so Confucius had no place to go [to implement his ideals]. Hence he wished "to put to sea on a raft" and morally transform island barbarians so that their

customs would be those of [Middle Kingdom] ritual and righteousness. Here we see the Sage's heart, which seeks to transform morally the entire world.[19]

These are amazing philological acrobatics. From the first line—"The Way is not being carried out; I shall put to sea on a raft"—Jinsai nimbly jumped to the conclusion that Confucius despaired of his homeland and desired to spread his teachings in Japan. The island barbarians there practiced faithfulness stemming from simplicity, and evinced superiority to the falsity of Chinese civilization. Confucius had a soft spot in his heart for barbarians like the Japanese; he viewed alien peoples in an egalitarian, universalistic light, since they possessed the same "ordinary nature" as the Chinese. Shun and King Wen overcame alien birth to attain moral superiority over ethnic Chinese, had they not?

Jinsai submitted one other reason for Japan's moral superiority to China, this time not only the China of Confucius's era, but the China of all eras:

Emperor Jimmu's first year of rule upon founding our nation corresponds to the seventeenth year of the Chou emperor King Hui's reign [660 B.C.]. But here in Japan the statuses of sovereign and minister have been strictly upheld down to the present day. We revere our sovereigns as though they were Heaven, and we honor them as though they were divinities. Truly, in this respect China is not our equal.[20]

Jinsai's gloss on Confucius's lament, "The Way is not being carried out," as we recall, read, "rulers were foolish and ministers acted haughtily, so Confucius had no place to go [to implement his ideals]." That is why he desired to leave China for Japan. Had he in fact done so, he would have lauded what he found there during the next two thousand years. Jinsai believed that no Chinese ruling house enjoyed the measure of faithful reverence and honor that Japan's imperial line did, hence he could boast, "China is not our equal."

We should not overemphasize Jinsai's use of the imperial institution to prove Japan's superiority to China, for this is a minor feature of his thought. Unlike the Kokugakusha, or scholars of Native Japanese Learning, he did not argue that the imperial line's longevity revealed divine will, or that it was unique to Japan, and therefore proved in itself that Japan was superior. Instead, he felt that the unbroken imperial line signified Japan's superior adherence to a set of values within the Confucian tradition—simplicity and faithfulness in strictly maintaining a hierarchic social order. Phrased differently, Japan embodied the hierarchical status order of Middle Kingdom Civilization better than China.

In asserting Japan's moral excellence, Jinsai first posited China as Middle Kingdom Civilization, examined its actual performance against certain of its own professed standards of normative culture, and noted how grievously it fell short. Then he showed how Japan, despite being a barbarian nation, actually out-performed China according to *certain other* criteria of Sinocentric moral culture. Japan was like the sage kings, Shun and King Wen: Alien birth did not hinder the attainment of moral superiority over ethnic Chinese.

Jinsai, it should be stressed, was a thoroughgoing Confucian. He once praised the *Analects* as "the greatest book ever written anywhere in the world."[21] This stands in marked contrast to Motoori Norinaga's preference for Japanese classics such as *Kojiki, Genji monogatari,* and *Shinkokinshū.* Jinsai judged Japan according to imported, Sinocentric conceptual categories and ethical standards. Most important, he conceded that Japan was a barbarian nation. He espoused elements of an egalitarian, universalistic view of man's nature found in Confucianism, but did so to allow Japan to claim superiority over China.

Jinsai emphasized the idea that customs disclosed whether a people were civilized or barbarian. If their customs corresponded to "ritual and righteousness," they were civilized, if not, barbarian. Confucius was not concerned with the Chinese people alone; he wished to transform morally all peoples on earth. A ruler performed the act of *jōi* by morally transforming alien peoples and preventing his own people from adopting alien ways; he eradicated what is culturally barbarian and ensured that customs in his land conformed to Middle Kingdom "ritual and righteousness." Jinsai explicitly defined *jōi* in exactly the same way as Chu Hsi: He employed that term in a gloss, "Revere the Chou dynastic house and sweep away (or eradicate) what is barbarian." In this gloss, Jinsai, too, praised Kuan Chung's act of *jōi,* or "eradication of what is culturally barbarian," and he went on to argue:

> The benefit received [by Confucius and his people] was that they did not become barbarian; the righteous meaning of distinctions between ruler and minister, and father and son remained intact. . . . In the Warring States period [403–221 B.C.], the common people's suffering was extreme: Only because of Kuan Chung could they nonetheless remain "people of Middle Kingdom Civilization." If not for Kuan Chung, they would have become "a barbarian people. . . ."[22]

For Jinsai, as for Chu Hsi, *jōi* meant preserving the common people's customs against barbarism and upholding Middle Kingdom Civilization construed as the Confucian hierarchical status-order in society.

Before concluding this section on early Tokugawa views of civilization and barbarism, we should note certain key ideas that thinkers in the next two centuries would carry on. Middle Kingdom Civilization was that part of the world and stratum in society where customs accorded with Confucian ritual, or ethical rules of behavior, and where people understood the classical Chinese language that conveyed that ritual. These two prerequisites to Middle Kingdom standing—ritual and classical language—did not obtain among the lower orders in Ming, Ch'ing, or Tokugawa society or among alien barbarians.[23] Commoners as well as aliens had to be edified or morally transformed. Yamaga Sokō expressed this idea when he wrote that barbarism corresponded to "where moral transformation (or suasion) does not extend."[24] The people there were ignorant of proper behavior: "Their customs are bad and they do not know good from evil."[25] Sokō noted that different lands possessed different customs due to different endowments of "vital force" (*ch'i*). But even so, he held that, because all people shared the same "moral principle" (*li*), aberrant customs could be transformed to accord with Con-

fucian norms of conduct.[26] Moreover, though he had Japan, not
Western nations, in mind, he wrote that "the sages created teachings appropriate to each land and each people's customs."[27]
Like Jinsai, he allowed room for Japan to be slightly different
from, yet superior to China. Japan, not China, was truly worthy
of the name "Middle Kingdom Civilization" (Chūgoku), he declared. However, and this is of great importance, Sokō held that
Japan was superior to China based on Sinocentric criteria of
judgment. In other words, he claimed that Japan was more Confucian than China in certain key respects—not that Japan was
superior in its own right.

Sokō stressed that barbarians and commoners had a common
nature: "The relationship between ruler and minister among
barbarians is just like that between merchants in Middle Kingdom Civilization."[28] He wrote, "When intermingling with barbarians occurs, the customs of Middle Kingdom Civilization are
transformed to profit-seeking."[29] This led to such a degenera-
tion of morals that commoners "do not differ from birds and
beasts."[30] Customs would "reach the point where commoners
despised and eliminated their rulers."[31] Thus to Sokō, Middle
Kingdom Civilization signified the extent to which moral suasion
or moral transformation prevailed. The ruler had to carry out a
form of cultural *jōi* through edification. "Since moral transformation depends on ritual and music," he remarked, "looking at
these will reveal whether the realm enjoys orderly rule or suffers
from disorder,"[32] and "Customs are improper unless there is
moral transformation."[33]

Thus, early Tokugawa Confucians (except the Kimon School,
discussed below) generally accepted the Sinocentric Middle
Kingdom world view that discriminated China-as-civilization
from barbarism. They grudgingly tended to admit that Japan
was barbarian and, hence, inferior in at least some respects to
China. They tried to find ways of asserting Japan's parity with,
if not superiority to, Ming or Ch'ing China without disavowing
Confucianism as a universalistic creed. But their strained arguments (such as Jinsai's *non sequitur* about Confucius putting to
sea) failed to convince contemporaries.[34]

In short, they tried to relativize or accommodate Sinocentric moral culture to indigenous values and socio-political realities. Thinkers like Jinsai wanted to achieve Japanese pride and independence within the Sinocentric world view: Though Japan was a barbarian country, it still could claim moral excellence based on virtues within the Chinese Confucian tradition. Later, eighteenth-century Japanese intellectuals would find such arguments far-fetched and intolerable. They relativized Sinocentric moral culture even further, and some ended up rejecting it totally.

INNATE JAPANESE SUPERIORITY: THE RISE OF KOKUGAKU

Jinsai based his view of civilization and barbarism on ancient Chinese perceptions of world geography. He conceptualized the world as "all under Heaven," or "that which Heaven covers and the earth supports," or "all within the four seas." Much as English expressions like "to the ends of the earth" or "to the four corners of the world" suggest, Jinsai's cosmology saw the world as a plane, a flat surface. The states of ancient China supposedly occupied the center of this plane and most of its surface area. This centrality and extensiveness carried assumptions of cultural and moral superiority to aliens living on the plane's fringes.[35] Jinsai himself admitted that Japan was a peripheral island: To reach it, Confucius would have had to "put to sea on a raft."

Before the advent of Western Learning, Buddhism had provided at least two alternatives to this Sinocentric view of world geography in medieval Japan. One placed Mt. Sumeru at the center of the earth and described Japan as "a peripheral cluster of lands resembling scattered millet."[36] The other was the Three Kingdoms view of Tenjiku (India), Shintan (China), and Japan. In either case, Japan assumed a marginal, insignificant position in the world.

Not every Tokugawa Confucian shared Jinsai's Sinocentric view of world geography. Asami Keisai (1652–1711) of Yamazaki Ansai's Kimon School expounded a significantly different view in "Chūgoku ben" (On defining Middle Kingdom Civilization), which he wrote in 1701.[37] Keisai declared that China's putative superiority to Japan based on geographic extensiveness had no grounding in reality:

> A map of the nations in the world shows that China (Kara) does not occupy even one one-hundredth of its surface. There are several nations (*kuni*) ten times as large as China. If we were to designate one of them "Middle Kingdom Civilization," and China, "barbarian," would the Chinese (Karahito) approve?[38]

Here Keisai calls contemporary China "Kara." He used this value-free term to claim that China is distinct from "Chūgoku," as a value-laden metaphor for civilization. Keisai denied contemporary China's claim to superiority based on geographic extensiveness, centrality, and other traditional criteria. For example, he dismissed the *Book of Rites,* which said that China's Mt. Sung-kao was the centerpoint of the world. This was claimed because measurements conducted in antiquity supposedly showed that the shadows that mountain cast in sunlight or moonlight were "perfectly equal." But, as Keisai pointed out, such would be true at all points along the sun's zenith.

> [Mt. Sung-kao] is the centerpoint of China (Kara). . . . The sun revolves in an arc over the "equatorial line." Can there be any place on the equatorial line that does not have shadows of equal length? If you measured these at various spots along it, you would find them all of equal length.[39]

Keisai himself does not propound the earth's sphericity here, though a small number of Japanese Confucians knew and accepted this theory as early as 1650.[40] Rather, his views fit into the traditional Confucian framework. What concerns us is how he used new knowledge of world geography to refute the Sino-centric association of centrality and extensiveness with superiority. China—as Kara, not Chūgoku—was not the center of a world perceived as a flat "all under Heaven." Centrality, if determined in a neutral, objective manner, no longer corresponded to some middle *point* such as Mt. Sung-kao in China, but rather, was a *line.* China was but one among many lands—and a small one at that.

New knowledge of world geography thus helped Japanese thinkers overcome Chinese Confucian standards of value by exposing these to be devoid of reality. Keisai delivered two more blows against Sinocentric civilization: a new view of international relations and a historical critique of the concept of Middle Kingdom Civilization. The first was directed against Japanese Confucians like Jinsai, who, despite claiming that Japan was superior, acknowledged that China embodied civilization while Japan was barbarian. In so doing, Keisai began to shed the traditional Confucian conception of the world as "all under Heaven" and an ideally unified empire, and to grope toward a more modern view of the world comprised of numerous independent "lands."

> Heaven envelops the earth; no matter where one travels upon it, there is no place that Heaven does not cover. Thus every land (*tochi*) is defined by the extent to which its customs prevail. Each is a full-fledged realm in itself, and none is more noble or base than any other.[41]

Here Keisai introduces a significant new conception of *tenka,* "the realm." Each land is a "full-fledged realm" in itself.[42] Each is marked off from other lands by its own distinctive customs or culture, and boasts a position equal to all others. Contemporary China (Kara) is but one of these lands, characterized by cultural distinctiveness:

> That portion of the land of China called the Nine Provinces has been cultured in manners and natural endowment (*ch'i*) ever since high antiquity. It has maintained similar customs and a common language. Hence it naturally forms a realm of its own.[43]

Keisai's second attack, related to his first blow at Japanese Confucians who mistook China for civilization itself, was his claim that such thinkers failed to place the dichotomy of civilization and barbarism in proper historical perspective. As for ancient China's relations with surrounding territories and peoples, Keisai wrote:

From the Chinese point of view, those areas where customs were unlike China's were "countries of strange shapes and ways." Areas closer to the Nine Provinces, where one could make himself understood [through written Chinese], looked like "peripheral lands." Thus they have come to call their Nine Provinces "Middle Kingdom Civilization" (Chūgoku), and surrounding areas, "barbarian."[44]

But, Keisai claimed, it was wrong to gloss over these historical facts and extend the barbarian label to other countries, least of all Japan. Moreover, Japanese Confucians ignored cultural or ethnic variations within the China of later eras. The historical boundaries of China as a designation for civilization, Keisai asserted, had never been fixed.

Areas such as Wu or Ch'u were barbarian in antiquity, and were so designated in works like *Mencius* or the *Spring and Autumn Annals*. . . . But by the end of Chou times these areas were gradually prospering and rivaled China proper (Kara). And from Ch'in and Han onward, they have clearly been part of China proper.[45]

Some of China's later capitals were located in formerly barbarian areas. Chu Hsi, who was considered the paragon of Chinese Confucian orthodoxy, hailed from a province that was part of the barbarian state of Wu in antiquity.[46] Keisai noted that China had expanded gradually during history, incorporating contiguous peoples and areas. At present, the Chinese thought of Chūgoku as "all areas under their emperor's unified rule," or "the extent to which the inhabitants' customs have been Sinified."[47] But even so, Keisai pointed out, "the land (*kuni*) of the Three Miao Tribes" and other lands inhabited by ethnic minorities "still are considered barbarian despite being included within" China proper.[48]

To clear up the confusion about which countries were civilized and which barbarian, Keisai advocated eliminating these Sinocentric categories entirely. Instead, he suggested substituting the terms "our land" (*waga kuni*) for one's own land and "foreign lands" (*ikoku*) for all other countries.[49] Every nation then could use these value-free designations toward all other nations. What is more, the inhabitants of each *waga kuni* should consider it primary, though of course peoples in all other lands would consider it secondary.[50] This would skirt the problem of cultural superiority or inferiority built into the Sinocentric terms, Middle Kingdom and barbarian, and it would make each country equal to all others.

For Keisai, as for Jinsai, Shun, the ancient Chinese ruler, was the ideal sage for Japanese Confucians to emulate, though for different reasons. In Jinsai's mind, Shun was an ethnic barbarian who overcame his alien birth and achieved sagehood. For Keisai, Shun's single-hearted devotion to his perverse father, an unalterable blood relationship, constituted sageliness and indicated the Way for Japanese Confucians to follow. Shun's fate was to have been born the son of an evil man, but his "self-evident duty" lay in assiduous filial devotion to such a father.[51] By the same token, Japanese Confucians could not help having been born in a land "of eastern barbarians" which had never produced a sage (as Sorai lamented),[52] or whose cultural refinement did not match China's. But this should cause them no despair. Through wholehearted devotion to the land of their birth, they too could attain moral excellence.

Despite this attempt to shed the Sinocentric categories of civilization and barbarism, Keisai was still committed to Confucian moral culture. His model was, after all, the Confucian sage Shun, and the exemplars in his writings were Chinese loyalists. The Kimon School, in which he was a leading figure, espoused Confucian-Shinto syncretism in which Chu Hsi's teachings supposedly corresponded "by coincidence" to those of Shinto. This insistence on "coincidental correspondence" (*myōkei*) may seem like quibbling, but to Keisei, it was immensely significant. Members of the Kimon School prided themselves on being independent from the syncretism of Hayashi Razan, who identified Japan's Way of the *kami* with the Confucian Way in more Procrustean fashion. Keisai asserted that a universal corpus of normative culture known as the Way, revealed in concepts like moral principle (*li*) and the Five Elements, had grown up coincidentally in both Japan and China; so neither country was superior. Both Ways, though in essence identical, found separate expression in the Chinese and Japanese classics. "The *Book of Changes* is a 'Chronicle of the Gods' [in *Kojiki* and *Nihon shoki*] for China just as 'The Chronicle of the Gods' is a *Book of Changes* for Japan."[53]

There was a logical inconsistency in Kimon-School pluralism. Keisai would have each particular "land" possess its own customs, culture, and moral values to which its inhabitants must remain true. Yet at the same time, he professed a universal Way valid in all times and places. Kokugakusha, or scholars of Native Learning such as Motoori Norinaga (1730-1801), strove to eliminate this logical inconsistency by basing all value judgments on purely indigenous criteria.

Norinaga vehemently rebuked Japanese Confucians who used Sinocentric ideals of moral, civilized behavior to disparage Japan. One such Confucian, Dazai Shundai (1680-1747), chastised the ancient Japanese for their custom of half-brother–half-sister marriages: this violated the Confucian taboo on incest between persons of the same surname. Shundai therefore condemned the ancient Japanese as living like the "birds and beasts."[54] Not until the Confucian classics reached Japan, he charged, did his countrymen learn proper moral behavior. At the same time, Norinaga was no less critical of Japanese apologists like Toba Gi (Yoshiaki), who justified this ancient custom in light of extenuating circumstances.[55] Norinaga's view was:

> Japanese intellectuals consider this ancient practice a disagreeable defect of our Divine Land, so they appeal to this or that cleverly contrived theory hoping to cover it up or explain it away. Yet none has come up with a convincing argument because they are all set on servile fawning toward China. If not, it would not matter that we differ from China.[56]

Norinaga vigorously opposed this type of Confucian monism and advocated pluralism in cultural and moral standards:

35

> China (Morokoshi) is China; our Imperial Land (Mikuni) is
> our Imperial Land. Today is today; the past is the past. Con-
> fucians who judge affairs based solely on the standard of Chi-
> nese customs, and contemporaries who denigrate [ancient]
> practices based solely on present-day customs, are not being
> fair.[57]

This was not just an attempt to relativize normative Sinocentric culture. Norinaga examined Japanese customs and morals
with the empathy of what we now call "historical understanding." Past periods of history, like different nations, were distinct
cultural units that must be judged according to their own particular standards. In *Man'yōshū* days, half-brothers and half-
sisters married, and in the Heian times of *Genji monogatari,*
men visited and married into the households of women. But
such seemingly immoral customs were right and proper in those
periods. It was improper for contemporaries to condemn those
practices based on alien or present-day standards of right and
wrong.

In Norinaga's Kokugaku, discovering and clarifying the original meaning of Japan's classics was the only proper form of
scholarship and correct method of understanding Japan's own
unique Way. In one of his most vituperative attacks on Japanese Confucians (like Jinsai and Sokō) and Confucian-Shinto
syncretists (like Ansai and Keisai), Norinaga wrote:

> They envy China (Karakuni) for its supposed possession of
> the Way, and bend over backwards arguing that precisely the
> the same Way exists in Japan as well. This is just like the man
> who, after being teased by a bunch of monkeys for his lack of
> body hair, feels ashamed. He searches frantically for any of
> the thinnest hairs he can find on his body, proudly points to
> these, and says, "See, I've got hair too." Are they not dimwits
> who fail to see that the lack of body hair is more to be
> esteemed?[58]

Japanese Confucians, Norinaga held, based all value-judgments
on putatively timeless and universal normative concepts (such as
yin-yang, li, the Five Elements, or the Five Constant Virtues).

They assumed that these norms had to find expression in Japan's ancient classics as well as in China's, so they "bent over backwards" to read those alien norms into the Japanese texts. (The *Kojiki* story of Izanagi and Izanami, for example, became a "parable" or "allegory" said to symbolize the distinction between male and female that Confucians valued.)[59]

But the above quotation discloses far more. Norinaga repudiated all Japanese claims to cultural and moral superiority over China that were based on imported Sinocentric criteria. He insisted that the Chinese sages—especially the Duke of Chou—were not paragons of morality. After overthrowing the Shang dynasty and usurping the throne, they deceitfully invented moral norms like the Heavenly Mandate, virtue, and the Way to justify their perfidy and to protect themselves against similar uprisings by their subjects in the future.[60] Using an argument similar to one employed by Chinese Taoists,[61] Norinaga argued that Chinese Confucians felt a special need to enunciate repeatedly or espouse emphatically moral norms like the Way, righteousness, or the rules of ethical behavior, because they did not truly practice those virtues.[62] In ancient Japan, by contrast, people felt no special need to enunciate moral norms or rules of ethical behavior because their conduct was naturally good.[63]

In short, the Chinese invented and espoused normative concepts like the Way or the loyalty of subject for ruler. But in point of historical fact, they overthrew their ruling dynasties more than twenty times. The ancient Japanese had lacked such moral concepts, but thanks to their innate goodness, they revered one ruling house throughout all time. That is why lacking a normative Way, like the absence of body hair, was "more to be esteemed."

Norinaga's arguments to claim Japan's superiority over China were just as far-fetched as Itō Jinsai's, but the crucial difference between their rationales is quite clear. Jinsai attributed the imperial line's longevity, and Japan's superiority, to the presence of Confucian virtues; Norinaga, to their absence. Norinaga held that "men know all they need to know about the rules of ethical behavior naturally, through the spirit of the deities. They have no need of moral teachings."[64] Confucian moral precepts were not the "good teachings" Mencius said they were: In truth they despoiled men of goodness. Edification or the transformation of a people's customs signified nothing beneficial. Neither the geographic extensiveness of Sinocentric moral culture nor its widespread acceptance by people within China proved its excellence. Norinaga wrote:

> The fact that the Chinese masses revere the sages as they revere Heaven is because they have been deceived by those sages, not because the sages were truly honorable. If we assume that being revered by many people is tantamount to true moral excellence, what do we make of Shinran? Present-day followers of the Ikkō Sect, who revere him as its founder, are far more numerous than the [Chinese] Confucians who revere their sages. But does this prove that Shinran's virtue is greater than that of the sages?[65]

Shinran, the Chinese sages, and Christians[66] were deceivers, pure and simple. Norinaga denounced them for the falseness of their views but he did not fear them. Unlike Confucians such as Aizawa, he did not equate the widespread acceptance of a particular teaching with its moral and cultural superiority. One final example, dealing with world geography, should demonstrate this point.

From 1786 to 1787, Norinaga and another prominent scholar of Native Learning, Ueda Akinari (1734–1809), debated fiercely about (among other things) the world as depicted on Dutch maps. Akinari turned to the Dutch "map of the globe"[67] and said:

> Only a few countries use and understand ideographs; the rest have strange names we have never heard of, and many of them are vast in size. When we try to pick out our Divine Land, we see that it is but a tiny island, a single leaf floating on the surface of a wide pond.[68]

To which Norinaga replied:

> How funny it is that you view this world map with such curiosity. In this day and age, has anyone *not* seen such maps?

Does anyone *not* know that our Divine Realm is not very extensive? The nobility or baseness, beauty or ugliness, of a thing does not hinge only on whether it is large or small. . . . An inferior nation, even if large, is still inferior; our superior land, even though small, is still superior.[69]

Norinaga listed these reasons for Japan's superiority despite being small: (1) Being the land where the Sun Goddess was born, Japan was the fountainhead of all other nations. (2) Japan's imperial line was unbroken since the beginning of time. (3) Japan possessed the only classics containing the gods' true revelations. (4) Japan produced the world's best rice. (5) Japan had never been conquered by foreign powers.[70]

Western Learning did not directly challenge any of these Kokugaku "reasons" for Japanese superiority. But all of them hinged on unquestioning belief in the literal truth of Japan's oldest classical text, the *Kojiki,* where they supposedly were revealed. And Western knowledge did challenge this credulity. Norinaga recognized value in Dutch Studies because it awakened Japanese thinkers to the error of "slavish adherence to Chinese ways and values."[71] He also echoed the views of many Japanese about Chinese Confucianism and Dutch Studies in the late eighteenth century:

By learning about world affairs one ought to realize the excellence of our Divine Realm. But they [the Rangakusha] refuse to revere our Divine Realm because they believe slavish adherence to Chinese ways and values is bad. This makes them think that slavish adherence to anything is wrong. So they place ultimate value in slavishly adhering to this attitude of rejecting slavish adherence.[72]

Norinaga affirmed the Rangakusha's stubborn skepticism and refusal to commit themselves wholeheartedly to China. But he would not tolerate such attitudes toward Japan.

Kokugaku was by far the most influential movement in eighteenth-century Japanese thought. After Norinaga, Tokugawa thinkers might profess respect for Chinese or Western civilization, but not to the extent of national self-effacement in the manner of "Sorai, the eastern barbarian."[73] From the late eighteenth century onward, for better or worse, "the Japanese spirit" (*wakon*) would be supreme, would have to be lauded for its own sake. Only then might thinkers supplement it with Chinese or Western "learning" (*kansai, yōsai*). In 1807, for example, the Dutch Studies expert Ōtsuki Gentaku wrote:

Japan is a small land compared with others, but she is an empire whose ruling imperial house has remained intact throughout the myriad ages. This is why Japan is superior to other countries, and why they revere and stand in awe of her. . . .[74]

An understanding of eighteenth-century intellectual developments just presented is needed to place Dutch Studies and Western Learning in balanced historical context. Students of Western and world affairs played a decisive role in formulating a modern conception of Japan in the international order. But their achievement was possible only because the Sinocentric Middle Kingdom world view already had been largely relativized and repudiated. We shall now see how two Dutch Studies experts, Sugita Gempaku and Maeno Ryōtaku, rejected Chinese claims to cultural and moral excellence, and how one of them, Ryōtaku, took the label of superiority off of China and applied it to the West.

THE EXCELLENCE OF WESTERN BARBARIANS

Sugita Gempaku (1733–1817) and Maeno Ryōtaku (1723–1803) were domain doctors of Dutch medicine, but their basic values and world view were unmistakably Confucian. Ryōtaku began studying Dutch in 1770 at the age of 47, Sugita, one year later, at the age of 39. Sugita seems mainly to have read Dutch books on his specialty, medicine. Ryōtaku, as his writings show, informed himself about far more Western subjects. But as we shall see, certain tenets central to their Confucian philosophy made their reaction to Western Learning decisively different from that of Kokugakusha such as Norinaga.

In 1775, one year after he helped complete the translation of the Dutch anatomical text *Ontleedkundige Tafelen*, Sugita wrote *Words of a Fanatic Doctor* (*Kyōi no gen*). The title is of no small significance. Sugita portrayed himself as "fanatic" in his desire to sally forth to do battle with the forces of Tokugawa medical obscurantism. He compared his zeal to that of Po-i and Shu-ch'i of the fallen Shang dynasty, who refused to serve the victorious Chou dynasty, vowing to die rather than submit.[75] Sugita had two objectives in composing this work. First, he sought to assimilate advanced Western medical techniques, demonstrably superior to those of China, through the time-honored Confucian method of canonical sanction. Second, he relativized (but did not totally repudiate) Sinocentric civilization through arguments similar to those advanced by Jinsai, Keisai, and Norinaga.

Words of a Fanatic Doctor is a dialogue between Sugita, the fanatic doctor, and a sympathetic friend who urges him to abandon his infatuation with Western surgery and return to the Way of Chinese medicine. The tract begins with a vitriolic denunciation of Sugita by a third character, a doctor of Chinese medicine steeped in Confucian prejudices. The author, Sugita, carefully differentiates the term "Chūka," Middle Kingdom Civilization, from "Shina," a neutral designation for China, without connotations of moral and cultural superiority. The bigoted doctor of Chinese medicine and Sugita's friend use "Chūka," but Sugita himself uses "Shina" to show his less approving view of China.[76]

The doctor of Chinese medicine bases his arguments on Sinocentric criteria long discredited by Keisai and Norinaga: "Countries like Korea or the Ryūkyūs (and by logical extension, Japan) are not far removed from Middle Kingdom Civilization,"[77] since they had adopted the classical Chinese language and Confucian culture. The doctor's grounds for asserting Japan's excellence are identical to Jinsai's: faithfully embodying aspects of a superior Sinocentric civilization. Japan is culturally and geographically closer to China's Middle Kingdom Civilization; thus it is far less barbarian than Holland. Unlike the Japanese, the Dutch do not read classical Chinese and have not heard the sages' teachings. Holland "is located in the remotest area of any dwelt in by the barbarians; its customs are utterly different [from those of the Middle Kingdom]."[78]

Having thus vented his spleen, the prejudiced doctor of Chinese medicine left. We should note that his arguments were anachronistic even by Confucian standards in the eighteenth century. It is easy to imagine why Sugita endowed him with so combative an attitude: Men of the doctor's stripe were beleaguered not only by students of Dutch Learning, but also by Kokugakusha and Confucian-Shinto syncretists.

In contrast to Jinsai, who viewed Japan as barbarian, and Keisai or Norinaga, who scarcely mentioned Westerners, Sugita's doctor of Chinese medicine in 1775 vehemently denigrated the Dutch as barbarian. As Satō Shōsuke argues, only with the rise of Rangaku did intense animosity against Western knowledge, as distinct from Christianity, appear.[79] People most threatened by the new learning were among the first to lash out at it. Sugita's detractor was a doctor of Chinese medicine, not a scholar of Confucianism itself. His value to society lay in an ability to dispense Chinese technical skills, but Western science discredited them. With his personal worth thus impugned, he could only fall back on Chinese moral culture, but Kokugakusha like Norinaga denied its validity. At that point, the merits of Sinocentric culture could be rescued only by infusing it with native Japanese elements, the goal of Confucians like Keisai and Aizawa. We should keep these points in mind when reading the following passage:

> In China (Shina), they have already realized that traditional methods of astronomy, calendar-making, and the various arts and crafts are in error. Since late Ming times they have been studying many Western (seiyō) methods. . . . For example, the globes they now rely on are far different from those of antiquity. This shows that they adopt what is good from the West and abide by these [superior methods]. *It is only our own Japanese doctors of Chinese medicine who cling to outdated practices.* How sad indeed![80] (emphasis added)

Sugita did not belittle Shina, or contemporary China, in all respects. Here he praises the Ming and Ch'ing Chinese for appreciating and adopting advanced Western technical skills in contrast to unregenerate Japanese doctors of Chinese medicine.

Even in China, homeland of Middle Kingdom Civilization, Confucians had sense enough to import the best from the West; Tokugawa Confucians ought to follow suit. Sugita did not disparage Confucianism itself. He only attacked Confucians who "cling to outdated practices," and he provided the following rationale for assimilating demonstrably superior Western techniques.

The sage kings of ancient China (Shina) did, it is true, "edify the people by 'differentiating' Middle Kingdom Civilization from barbarism." But to Sugita, this did not mean esteeming the former and despising the latter unconditionally. Some peoples had strong customs, in the sense of being impervious to acculturation; other peoples' customs were weak and easily altered. The sage kings, in their sagacity, knew that Chinese customs were of the weak sort. Hence:

> It was to prevent Chinese customs from becoming indistinguishable from those of the barbarians that they established proper rules of ritual behavior, esteemed Middle Kingdom Civilization, and despised barbarism.[81]

The sages' bias against barbarians was functional, not absolute. They differentiated their own Middle Kingdom Civilization from barbarism only "to protect their people with a barrier." In this connection, Sugita, like Jinsai nearly a century earlier, cited Kuan Chung's act of cultural *jōi:* "Confucius said, 'If not for Kuan Chung, we would be wearing our hair down and folding our robes to the left.' Thus he praised Kuan Chung's great achievement."[82]

But such efforts to "build barriers" and prevent the transformation of Chinese customs to those of the barbarians proved futile:

> From Ch'in times onward, after the Way of Hsia, Shang, and Chou had declined, China's borders were violated by the northern barbarians. The First Ch'in Emperor [like the ancient sages] realized the weakness of his people's customs and built the Great Wall. After Han times, the Chinese could not prevail against the northern barbarians. . . . In the Yuan and Ch'ing periods, the entire country became Tungusland. . . .

Now, a little over one hundred years after K'ang-hsi made the country strong and prosperous, the Thirteen Provinces of China and all its myriad people wear barbarian dress and are fettered by barbarians. But not one of them feels any shame. The weakness of their customs makes them thus. [83]

The Chinese sages sought to eradicate what is barbarian in order to prevent their people's customs from being transformed. But this did not preclude assimilating advanced barbarian techniques. There is a seeming contradiction here, at least from a traditional Confucian standpoint. Would not customs be transformed and the people made barbaric by adopting these barbarian techniques? No, says Sugita, because Chinese moral culture is not the only form of civilized life:

Hidebound Confucians and run-of-the-mill doctors of Chinese medicine don't know how large the world is. Having heard about two or three countries in the East (Tōyō), they think that China (Shina) is the greatest of all nations. . . . They charge that the barbarians' customs lack rules of ethical behavior. [84]

Thus far Sugita seems merely to be repeating hackneyed arguments to claim Japan's superiority over China by relativizing the Sinocentric Middle Kingdom world view. But his method of relativization differs from Keisai's or Norinaga's:

Ritual, music, and the other accoutrements of civilization exist to maintain the statuses of noble and base. Does *any* country lack statuses of noble and base? Does *any* country lack ritual and music? Confucius said, "[Even] the barbarians have a ruler." To have a ruler and honor him is [the essence of] ritual. [85]

Sugita, like Jinsai, followed Chu Hsi's intepretation of this *Analects* passage. But for Sugita, the barbarians were the Dutch, not the Japanese. He universalized the concept of ritual, or the rules of ethical behavior, by making it, like the differentiation of civilization from barbarism, functional rather than absolute. The function of ritual, music, and the other accoutrements of civilization was to distinguish noble from base, and this distinction obtained in every nation of the world. Therefore the ritual, music, and accoutrements of civilization in all nations possessed equal value. Ch'ing China had no monopoly on this value; Chinese civilization was not world civilization.

Sugita went on to relativize the Way itself, which he defined as "leaving evil behind and progressing to goodness."[86] This Way found embodiment in "customs" that differ according to the area in which one lived; Dutch customs were fully compatible with it:

> The Way is not something established by the sages of China (Shina). It is the [universal] Way of Heaven and Earth. Wherever sun and moon shine, wherever dew and frost form, there are nations, there are people, and there is the Way.[87]

Chinese customs represented but one form of this universal Way; any attempt to force those customs on the inhabitants of different climates would seriously harm their health.[88]

Sugita's most devastating attack on the Sinocentric Middle Kingdom world view, however, resembled Norinaga's: accusing China's ancient medical sages of moral duplicity. Sugita defined sageliness as "wisdom, caring for people's lives, and refusing to deceive them."[89] Yet, argued Sugita, Chinese medical texts attributed to the sages were based on speculation and forced metaphysical analogies to yin-yang, the Five Elements, and similar vacuous theories. They were proved false when compared with accurate Western anatomical drawings. To treat patients according to such faulty Chinese texts and medical practices was to fail "to care for people's lives"; it was, in fact, "to deceive them." Only Dutch medical texts and techniques, confirmed to be true and accurate, allowed one to fulfill the requirements of sagehood.

There was a clear limit to Sugita's championing of the Dutch cause, however. In *Keiei yawa* (1802), he asserted, "I discovered the true principles of medicine to exist in far-off Holland."[90] However, in his Preface to *Kaitai shinsho,* the translation of *Ontleedkundige Tafelen,* he noted that the word "dissection" (*kaibō*) had appeared in an ancient Chinese medical text, and from this he concluded:

45

The Chinese (Karahito) must have possessed this method [dissection] in antiquity, but men in later ages did not receive it. They now futilely place their faith in worthless practitioners of medicine and spew forth groundless theories. Thus, for thousands of years since antiquity we have remained ignorant of this method's true nature. Ah, how sad indeed![91]

Here Sugita emphasizes that dissection was known in ancient China but subsequently disappeared. This idea of a Way lost in China and Japan since antiquity but discovered thereafter in the West was an important concept for Aizawa, as we shall see. The above passage underscores Sugita's antiquarian leanings,[92] and shows the limits of his antipathy to Confucianism.

Sugita proclaimed Dutch moral superiority over the Chinese sages in *Kyōi no gen,* but a perusal of his other works, particularly *Yasō dokugo* (1807) and *Nochimigusa* (1787), shows that he did not repudiate Confucianism in general. For example, he began *Yasō dokugo* by citing twenty-two irregularities in natural phenomena and other recent inauspicious omens. Then he stated, "These are all warnings from Heaven that men should reform morally."[93] This way of thinking is reminiscent of Chinese Han dynasty Confucianism and suggests intellectual debts to it.[94] We should also note that he composed *Kyōi no gen* in classical Chinese, and that it was exceptional among his writings in criticizing the sages. Sugita, then, retained considerable respect for Sinocentric civilization.[95] How should we interpret these seeming inconsistencies in his thought?

Sugita repudiated Confucian moral culture in order to assimilate superior Western medical techniques—and for that purpose only. In his mind, these techniques could be appropriated and utilized without disrupting traditional ways of thought or existing socio-political institutions. Maeno Ryōtaku's study of things Western, by contrast, would show that such assimilation might entail repudiating the established political order.

Maeno Ryōtaku (1723–1803) took up Dutch Studies for different reasons and out of different interests. In *The Beginnings of Dutch Studies (Rangaku kotohajime)*, Sugita noted: "Ryōtaku, due to his outstanding talents, wanted to make Rangaku his life's work, to attain a full mastery over Dutch, and thereby learn about conditions in the West. His great ambition was to acquire the ability to read all their books."[96] Maeno read much more widely about Western subjects than Sugita; he avidly learned about "conditions in the West" and compared Tokugawa institutions unfavorably with what he discovered. Maeno probably did more than anyone else to establish systematic instruction in the Dutch language during the mid-Edo period.[97] His numerous works consisted mainly of Dutch primers and translations on a wide variety of subjects, including medicine, natural science, and geography. But only one of these works, *Kanrei higen* (1777), informs us of his thought.[98]

In *Kanrei higen* (Comments on narrow-mindedness to be kept secret), Maeno rejected the Chinese Five Elements theory, traditional cosmology, and the Confucian view of nature. In their place he advanced the Aristotelian idea of four elements and other theories of Western science. What concerns us, however, is his idealistic portrayal of Western conditions and the unfavorable implications this had for Sinocentric moral culture. Maeno equated superior Western achievements in *Naturkunde* or natural science,[99] with a superior morality.[100] The essence of *Naturkunde,* Maeno assumed, was *kyūri,* or "investigating Principle exhaustively."[101] But at the same time:

> Through *Naturkunde* they revere Heaven, honor the deities, conduct government, seek out the truth, become conversant with affairs and proficient in techniques, correct [defective] goods, and make effective use of tools. Thus, their emperors (*teiō*) disseminate virtuous teachings, their princes maintain the state, their people are secure in their livelihoods, and their arts and crafts attain perfection. *Their sphere of moral suasion must truly be vast!*[102] (emphasis added)

As a Confucian, Maeno linked learning and government to geographical extensiveness: Virtuous European rulers implemented superior Western knowledge in political administration, and this necessarily extended their sphere of moral suasion. From an important non-Dutch author, Matteo Ricci, Maeno learned of the constant strife characterizing Ming China before

47

the Manchu takeover. Echoing Norinaga he wrote, "From the Shang and Chou down to the Ming, they have overthrown more than twenty dynasties."[103] But in contrast, he noted:

In European states, no one has ever succeeded in becoming the ruler of a nation (*tenka kokka*) through violent usurpation. Since they have never had a haughty and unprincipled Chieh or Chou on the throne, they never had a treacherous overthrower like T'ang or Wu.[104]

Because Ming leaders failed to heed Matteo Ricci's remonstrances to reform, Maeno believed, their dynasty fell to the Manchus.[105]

By introducing and contrasting European methods of succession and of selecting state officials with Chinese or Japanese methods, Maeno implied Western superiority:

In Europe, Italy [i.e., the Vatican] is sovereign in matters of moral transformation. . . . Responsibility for government is delegated to priest-officials, of whom there are seventy-two. When the king dies, each noble and commoner writes on a secret ballot the name of that priest-official who he believes has enough virtue to be a worthy successor. The minister who gets the most recommendations accedes to the throne. This method is used to select the priest-officials as well.[106]

This was not only true in "Italy": "European countries in general use this method to select successors to the throne when heirs are lacking or to fill vacancies among priest-officials. They show no favoritism in choosing an heir or granting office."[107] In addition to the election system, Maeno discovered an important form of Western rule: the unity of government and religion, conducted by state officials invested with religious authority. This authority derived from a head of state whose sovereign powers were spiritual rather than political. As we shall see, this idea of the unity of government and religion assumed great significance in Mito Learning.

We must also understand Maeno's knowledge of world geography and the Western moral superiority he extrapolated from it. He stated that Europeans formerly believed that the three continents of Europe, Asia, and Africa made up the entire world.[108] However, "in the second year of Meiō [1493], an Italian named Columbus set off to prove that there was yet another continent in the Western sea." Maeno believed that Columbus was a "savior of other lands," a missionary of impeccable moral standing. After discovering the New World, he and other Europeans, such as Magellan and Amerigo Vespucci, founded many colonies there. For Maeno, the known world had expanded to include two new continents, North and South America. ("Centrality" by this time had long ceased to be an issue.)[109]

Unlike Kokugaku scholars, the Confucian Maeno logically attributed European geographic extensiveness to the efficacy of European kyōhō, or religion.[110] First he noted the basic similarity between Confucianism and other "teachings" (oshie or kyō):

> Christianity (tenshukyō), the state religion (kokkyō) of Holland, and the teaching (oshie) of Africa . . . all have the same aim: to save and nurture widowers, widows, orphans, single persons, the sick and disabled, and the destitute and suffering, and *to base edification and government on this policy.*[111] (emphasis added)

This passage is pregnant with meaning: In it Maeno anticipated Aizawa on several points. First, Maeno propounded the basic universality of all religious "teachings." Second, he stated that their essence is to care for the needy and helpless in society. Third, he held that implementing such teachings is, or should be, the responsibility of the ruler; religion is inseparable from government. Fourth, Holland had established its own state religion:

> Holland is the only nation [in Europe] that excludes the religion (hō) of other lands and has established [its own] separate religion. Many of its colonies such as New Holland in North America, Jakarta and Australia in Asia, and Magellanica,[112] also believe in this religion. North and South America were originally frontier areas developed by Europeans, who rule over the various lands located there. The natives revere the Europeans as sage-rulers (shinsei). How much more so do most of them adhere to European religions.[113]

We should note one more point about Maeno's universalistic view of religions:

> When ancient sage kings (sennō) established teachings and brought men under moral transformation, there were bound to be variations according to time and place. But even so, when we examine the consequences of those teachings—order or rebellion, prosperity or decline—and when we appraise the geographic extent to which these teachings and moral suasion spread—near or far, narrowly or broadly—it seems that these two outcomes depend on whether the teachings had been established well or poorly.[114]

Maeno did not express himself as lucidly as we might wish, but he sought to convey the following ideas. Whether a nation enjoys peace and orderly rule or suffers anarchy and demise depends on the quality of the religious teachings that its ancient sage kings had established. The "good teachings" Mencius talked about would gain widespread reverence, but poor teachings would win acceptance only in a limited area if at all. As we noted, Maeno disparaged China for its frequent dynastic changes, and on this point he did not differ from Keisai or Norinaga. Unlike them, however, he praised European nations, not Japan, for never having overthrown a ruling dynasty.[115] To Maeno, every country—not China alone—had had "ancient sage kings." And China's frequent dynastic turnovers reflected a lack of domestic order stemming from the poor teachings that the Chinese sages had established.

To Maeno, the religious teaching of the Western sages was best; that Christianity had spread over far more of the globe than any other teaching proved this.[116] Better knowledge of world geography and demography broke down the Sinocentric Middle Kingdom world view held by Japanese Confucians: "Buddhism has spread over one-fifth of Asia, Confucianism, one-tenth of Asia. Christianity dominates the rest of the world."[117] People inhabiting but one-tenth of one of the world's five continents believed in Confucianism; Christianity had transformed all other nations. Confucian norms of excellence were unlike the particularistic criteria Norinaga set up to claim Japanese superiority. Middle Kingdom Civilization, whether represented by China or Japan, held universal pretensions. Widespread non-acceptance over the globe had to discredit the Confucian Way and Sinocentric culture in Maeno's eyes.

Maeno refrained from publishing *Kanrei higen* for fear of incurring bakufu displeasure, explaining, "To extol the customs of foreign lands surely violates bakufu law."[118] Nevertheless, this manuscript circulated privately among doctors, translators, and technical experts serving bakufu and daimyo domains.[119] Although it is difficult to gauge the direct impact of his ideas on Tokugawa thinkers, we know for certain that men like Fujita Yūkoku and Aizawa Seishisai were familiar with Maeno's work.[120] They took over his sympathetic views of the West and used these for their own purposes—creating an ideology of hatred to shore up the bakuhan order.

THE MITO SYNTHESIS: JAPAN AS MIDDLE KINGDOM

By the late eighteenth century, the Sinocentric Middle Kingdom world view had been so relativized, or compromised to Japanese values and socio-political realities, that it was untenable. Radical refashioning through massive injections of Native Learning was needed to make it acceptable once more. Tokugawa thinkers had attacked this imported world view largely to retain a sense of pride in their own land. They welcomed Western Learning, particularly its superior techniques and knowledge of world geography, in part because it discredited Confucianism and Sinocentric civilization even further. The world no longer was a flat "all under Heaven"; it was a sphere, where Ming or Ch'ing China could not claim centrality and superiority. Customs and social mores in Japan and elsewhere, though different from those prescribed by Confucianism, possessed equal validity and worth. Some Tokugawa thinkers discovered that Christian teachings were more effective than, and therefore superior to, Confucianism in morally transforming barbarian peoples all over the globe. In general, Japanese Confucians—but not Kokugaku thinkers—

had to admit this when they looked at the world map, for Christendom encompassed a territory far more vast than their putatively superior Middle Kingdom Civilization.

Western Learning brought to light hard facts that could not be wished away; Mito Confucians like Fujita Yūkoku and Aizawa Seishisai had to make radical adjustments in the Sinocentric Middle Kingdom world view in order to retain its cogency and their own sense of worth in society. Forced to admit the unrealness of Middle Kingdom Civilization on the horizontal-geographic plane, Yūkoku and Aizawa reasserted all the more tenaciously its moral rightness for the vertical, socio-political hierarchy within Japan. In 1791, Yūkoku wrote:

> How vital indeed it is to rectify names and adhere strictly to prescribed statuses within the realm, *for names and statuses can no more be altered than can Heaven and Earth.* [It is written,] "Heaven and Earth exist; hence ruler and subject exist. Ruler and subject exist; hence the high and low exist . . ." Unless the names of "ruler" and "subject" are rectified, the statuses of high and low will not be strictly adhered to. The noble will become the base and the base will become the noble, the exhalted and despised will lose their respective places in society, the strong will overpower the weak, the many will oppress the few, and the day of doom will be near at hand.[121] (emphasis added)

Yūkoku and Aizawa asserted that the Tokugawa hereditary status system and bakuhan state structure were part of nature, beyond men's power to alter.[122] This fit the needs of the Tokugawa ruling class quite well, because it meant that its position was immutable. Whether Yūkoku and Aizawa actually believed this claim is doubtful. But they proclaimed that the statuses of high and low, rulers and subjects, must be "rectified," by which they meant unconditionally upheld.

In the late eighteenth century, Yūkoku's awareness that Europeans were spreading Christian teachings in the territories they colonized effected him profoundly. From Honda Toshiaki, Mamiya Rinzō, Mogami Tokunai, Kondō Jūzō, Ōhara Sakingo, and others, Yūkoku learned of Russian proselytizing and colonizing north of Japan. I discuss the information these men gave to Yūkoku and Aizawa more fully in the next chapter. Here I note only that Maeno's vision of a Christian-dominated world inspired fears that Yūkoku held for Japan. Yūkoku made Middle Kingdom Civilization on the perpendicular socio-political order absolute because he was acutely aware of the danger stemming from contacts between Japanese commoners and Christian barbarians. In a letter dated the second month of 1797, he offered the following advice on defense measures to ward off Russian encroachments. Purely military countermeasures were "not practicable."

> First of all, since popular unity and integration (*jinwa*) have been lost, the four classes will scatter before the enemy. Should the Russian barbarians entice our stupid commoners (*gumin*) with their wicked [Christian] teachings and sugar-sweet words, should they beguile them with lucrative benefits, [we will suffer the same fate as Chou, the wicked last ruler of the Shang dynasty:] "those in the front lines will turn their halberds on troops to the rear." It goes without saying that we will suffer this at the hands of stupid commoners, who are afflicted with hunger and cold, but perhaps also at the hands of those officials among us who seek personal gain in disregard of righteousness. All of this may be exaggerated, but still, the barbarians will advance like lightning by sea and land. If we remain oblivious to this threat, we can expect help from no quarter.[123]

Yūkoku keenly perceived Japan's susceptibility to Russian incursion through religious conversion and economic inveigling. To understand his message fully, we must search out the *locus classicus* of his quoted phrase, "those in the front lines will turn their halberds on troops to the rear." This comes from the (spurious) "Successful Completion of the War" chapter of the *Book of Documents,* where King Wu's campaign to punish Chou, the wicked last ruler of the Shang dynasty, is decided:

> [The Shang] troops were as numerous as the trees in a forest, but none opposed us. Their troops in the front lines turned

their halberds on troops to the rear, attacked, and fled. The
blood flow was enough to carry away their shields. Thus did
we topple the Shang. . . .[124]

Yūkoku feared that if barbarian armed forces appeared on Japanese soil, "stupid commoners" would not only fail to support
domain leaders, they would join forces with the enemy. By
implication, he put himself and the entire daimyo-samurai ruling
establishment in the position of wicked King Chou, whose neglect of kingly duties created alienation among the commoners
and led to the demise of the dynasty.[125] Japan's bakufu and domain rulers must take heed. They must eliminate the hunger
and deprivation afflicting "stupid commoners" so that collabora-
tion with the enemy would not take place. Given social and
economic conditions in eighteenth-century Mito domain, Yūkoku's allusion to mass defection causing the Shang demise was
not far-fetched. As he himself reported, between 1726 and
1798 Mito's population dropped from 318,475 to 229,239 because of starvation and flight.[126]

Yūkoku argued that Japan's rulers had to win "popular unity
and integration" (jinwa), which Mencius perceived as the true
key to national strength. In waging war, Mencius held, favorable
weather was not as important as topographical advantage, and
topographical advantage was not as important as popular unity
and integration. According to accounts by Maeno Ryōtaku and
other informed students of Western affairs, European rulers
somehow had managed to implement the Way in their domestic
politics and thereby win voluntary support from their peoples.
Yūkoku realized that rulers in Japan had to do likewise. If not,
barbarian takeover was inevitable.

Jōi, conceived of as sweeping away or eradicating what is culturally barbarian, was an attempt to build barriers between
Japanese commoners and foreigners. Mito thinkers stressed the
need to carry out internal reforms and conduct edification to
make those commoners less susceptible to barbarian transformation. But even more important in the minds of nineteenth-
century Mito Confucians such as Aizawa was the use of brute
force; military action assumed a new and important place

alongside moral transformation in notions of how to eradicate what was barbarian. Aizawa glossed *jōi* as follows:

> [Ieyasu] constantly exhorted men living in an age of orderly rule to remain prepared for [warfare and] upheaval. Should Japan be lax about military training in peacetime, she will invite foreign encroachment. . . .
>
> [Ieyasu] warned that civil wars result in victory or defeat, prosperity or decline, only for daimyo houses. *Defeat by a foreign nation, however, would disgrace the entire country of Japan* (Nihonkoku). For this reason, he strictly banned the evil Westerners from coming to Japan after he had discerned their wicked designs on our Divine Realm. Hidetada and Iemitsu carried on his policies. By the Kan'ei era [1624–44], they had annihilated the [Westerners], eliminated the source of their evil forever, and made foreign lands stand in awe of our nation's might.[127] (emphasis added)

Aizawa here incorrectly asserts that the first three Tokugawa shoguns had instituted the policies of national isolation (discussed in the next chapter) and indiscriminate armed expulsion of Westerners. Mito scholars portrayed Westerners as rapacious barbarians intent on capturing the hearts and minds of "stupid" Japanese commoners—so called because the scholars were convinced that commoners could be easily converted to Christianity and induced to forsake their rulers. Here the Confucian emphasis on virtue and edification has disappeared. According to Aizawa, Ieyasu advocated that foreigners seeking to transform Middle Kingdom Civilization be eradicated by violent means. Aizawa applied the Middle Kingdom world view and the concept of *jōi* directly to the nineteenth-century Tokugawa polity and its relations with foreign countries. He anachronistically attributed to Ieyasu a consciousness of Japan as a nation-state on the brink of war with Western nations.

To Aizawa, the Tokugawa state was more than the sum of its constituent parts. The bakufu-led federation of daimyo domains that constituted Japan as a national unit represented civilization; Western countries were contemptible barbarian lands. Aizawa, unlike Jinsai, did not consider the civilized/barbarian dichotomy mutually convertible: Japan might regress to barbarism if her commoners were transformed to Christianity, but Westerners could never advance to civilized status on a par with the Divine Realm. Japan must maintain her superiority over foreigners through military force; to suffer defeat would be an unbearable humiliation for all Japanese daimyo and samurai.

But despite fears of transformation by Christianity, Aizawa, like Sugita, recognized the value of adopting advanced Western techniques to supplement Confucian moral culture.[128] In *New Theses,* he wrote:

> Small arms were first cast by the Western barbarians, but we in the Middle Kingdom (Chūgoku) imported and refined these weapons so much that the Ming Chinese (Minhito) named them "Japanese guns," not "Barbarian guns." This shows their deep respect for our ingenuity. Let us repeat this *tour de force* in the field of shipbuilding.[129]

He went on to say:

> The Russian khan, Peter, once traveled to Holland disguised as a carpenter to learn the art of building ships. This took place in the Genroku era [1688–1703], and there is little doubt that Russia began to possess huge warships and sophisticated navigating skills at that time. Even the barbarians heed this vital matter. How can we in the Middle Kingdom ignore it?[130]

Throughout *New Theses* Aizawa would call Japan the "Middle Kingdom" or the "Divine Realm," but not out of cultural or intellectual complacence. In the above passages, not only does he insist on Japan's need to assimilate advanced Western technology; he advocates emulating the leader of a less-advanced barbarian state who had done so. He points with pride to the praise Ming Chinese gave to Japan regarding its adoption of, and improvement on, Western technical expertise. Aizawa would affirm Chinese moral culture, infuse it with elements of Kokugaku myth, and seek to reinforce it with superior Western techniques.

Aizawa's greatest fear was that the bakufu might not be able to adopt and utilize the benefits of Western Learning without succumbing to the danger it posed—Christian subversion. Despite this fear, he argued that Edo leaders should assimilate from the West as much useful information as possible, particularly on "international affairs, firearms, and ship construction."[131] There was nothing wrong with studying Western subjects as long as the bakufu monopolized the fruits of those labors:

> Some take pleasure in reading strange books written in far-off, foreign lands. Their activities do not need to be a crime against the Tokugawa ruling house (*kokka*). Quite the contrary, if they placed the knowledge thus gained at bakufu disposal, their services would be of great value.[132]

With the rise of Mito Learning in the late eighteenth and early nineteenth centuries, politically conscious Japanese came to regard bakufu and domain governments as constituting an ideally federated nation-state. They cast off the barbarian status they formerly had acknowledged toward China, and now claimed centrality and superiority throughout the world for Japan in her own right. Together with these radical changes in world view came a momentous revision of bakufu foreign policy. National isolation, upheld by the indiscriminate armed expulsion of Western ships, emerged in the era 1793 to 1825. The following chapter describes how Western Learning helped create this crucial political development.

chapter three

Knowledge and
Hatred of the West

THE ROAD TO NATIONAL ISOLATION: MISCONCEPTIONS OF "SAKOKU"

In 1838, Takano Chōei and his colleagues in Western Learning were apprehensive about how the bakufu would treat a Western ship they mistakenly assumed was approaching Japan. In fact, the bakufu had already driven away the vessel in question (named the *Morrison*) one year before. Chōei, however, believed that the eminent English Sinologist, Robert Morrison, was commanding the ship and was repatriating Japanese castaways. And he distrusted Morrison's motives:

> The bakufu has always stipulated that other nations return our castaways by placing them in custody of the Dutch, that only the Dutch repatriate them. England is a neighbor of Holland; the English should be well aware of this law. Indeed, a few years ago [in 1830], a Japanese ship from Bizen was cast ashore in the English territory of India, and on that occasion, the English repatriated our nationals through the Dutch. Why are they using one of their own ships to return our castaways this time? Moreover, if they simply wanted to return castaways, they could place anyone in charge of the mission. Why do they assign so high-ranking an officer as Morrison? None of this sets right.[1]

Chōei reasoned as follows: The Dutch and English were competing for commerce and empire in the Far East, and the Dutch had been slandering the English as pirates to be kept out of Japan; this was to protect their monopoly on Japanese trade. Morrison realized that bakufu officials, misled by these Dutch slanders, would enforce the 1825 Expulsion Edict. By the overtly humanitarian act of returning Japanese castaways, however, he would allay suspicions of English rapacity and set about achieving his ulterior motive—to prevail on the bakufu to grant England trading privileges. But Chōei argued:

> From the beginning of the present [Tokugawa] dynasty, the hallowed law (*goseidō*) of national isolation (*sakoku*) has limited our trade with barbarian nations to Holland; it allows trade with no others. Therefore granting permission to trade is unthinkable. And at any rate, the law (*osadame*) holds that because visits by Western ships are bothersome, we must fire on and drive them off. . . .[2]

By the 1830s and 1840s, Takano Chōei, Aizawa Seishisai, Watanabe Kazan, and many other Japanese were under the impression that *sakoku,* or national isolation, was a policy dating from the beginning of Tokugawa rule, if not earlier.[3] They believed that it restricted Japan's "barbarian" trading partners to Holland, and that it demanded the armed expulsion of all other Western nationals. Thus, only the Dutch might return Japanese castaways. Most important, they believed that this hallowed law was an integral part of the Tokugawa ruling system and that bakufu leaders would enforce it any any cost—even to the point of sinking foreign vessels that were returning shipwrecked Japanese nationals. By the 1830s and 1840s, altering or rescinding *sakoku* was unthinkable to many, if not most, Japanese.

Such nineteenth-century notions were anachronistic.[4] The Edo bakufu's 1825 Expulsion Edict was not a reaffirmation of its so-called "Seclusion Edicts of the Kan'ei Era" issued from 1633 to 1639. National isolation and the expulsion of foreigners, as consciously-conceived state policies, came into being between 1793 and 1825. They owed their existence not only to bakufu design, but also to waning Dutch power, compared with that of Britain and Russia, in Far Eastern waters.

On the one hand, Matsudaira Sadanobu formulated and instituted national isolation (*sakoku*) as bakumatsu thinkers would understand it, when he rejected Russian overtures for trade and diplomatic relations in 1793. (The term *sakoku* itself, however, was coined in 1801.) In 1793, Sadanobu referred to venerable conventions forbidding Japan from trading with countries other than Ch'ing China and Holland, and from exchanging diplomatic messages with countries other than Korea and the Ryukyus.[5] In 1804, the bakufu explicitly declared to the Russian ambassador, Nicolai Petrovich Rezanov, that those conventions were inviolable national laws,[6] and it repeated this declaration to Russia in 1813.[7]

On the other hand, the bakufu's policy of driving away foreigners by force emerged in final form with the Expulsion Edict of 1825. The text reads:

We have issued instructions on how to deal with foreign ships on numerous occasions up to the present. In the Bunka era [1804–17], we issued new edicts to deal with Russian ships. But a few years ago, a British ship wreaked havoc in Nagasaki [the *Phaeton* Incident of 1808], and more recently their rowboats have been landing to procure firewood, water, and provisions. Two years ago they forced their way ashore [in Satsuma domain], stole livestock and extorted rice. Thus they have become steadily more unruly, and moreover, seem to be propagating their wicked religion among our people. This situation plainly cannot be left to itself.

All Southern Barbarians and Westerners, not only the English, worship Christianity, that wicked cult prohibited in our land. Henceforth, whenever a foreign ship is sighted approaching any point on our coast, all persons on hand should fire on and drive it off. If the vessel heads for the open sea, you need not pursue it; allow it to escape. If the foreigners force their way ashore, you may capture and incarcerate them, and if their mother ship approaches, you may destroy it as circumstances dictate.

Note that Chinese, Koreans, and Ryukyuans can be differentiated [from Westerners] by physiognomy and ship design, but Dutch ships are indistinguishable [from those of other Westerners]. Even so, have no compunctions about firing on [the Dutch] by mistake; when in doubt, drive the ship away without hesitation. Never be caught offguard.[8]

The stipulations of this edict plainly reveal why it was epoch-making. Two new types of Westerners, the Russians and British, had appeared in Japanese waters in the late eighteenth and early nineteenth centuries. The Japanese could not tell the various Western ships and peoples apart, and as we shall see, this confusion created unprecedented difficulties which forced the bakufu to revise current foreign policies. Moreover, these new Western nationals, unlike the Dutch, refused to obey bakufu-dictated rules governing Japan's foreign relations. They had become "steadily more unruly"; brute force now was called for. The Dutch would continue to be permitted entry at Nagasaki—but only there. Should they or other Westerners approach Japanese shores anywhere else, they faced immediate armed expulsion. The indiscriminate and unconditional character of the 1825 Expulsion Edict made it decisively different from earlier bakufu decrees ordering that Westerners be excluded or expelled from Japan. Let us briefly trace how bakufu methods of dealing with foreign ships evolved from the Kan'ei era (1624–43) down to the late eighteenth century. This will provide the historical background needed to clarify why Western Learning prompted early nineteenth century thinkers and leaders to institute policies of national isolation and armed expulsion of Westerners. In short, why did increased knowledge of, and contact with, Western peoples and cultures lead to xenophobia in men like Aizawa Seishisai and Takano Chōei?

It is important to keep in mind that during the 1500s and 1600s Japan and the Western world were still very far apart geographically. In those centuries, the only Europeans to visit Japan were the Spanish, Portuguese, English, and Dutch. The so-called "Seclusion Edicts of the Kan'ei Era" issued from 1633 to 1639 were motivated primarily by the desires to eradicate Christianity and to establish bakufu controls over trade.[9] These edicts prohibited Iberian missionaries from coming to Japan and Japanese nationals from leaving the country. They did not apply to the Dutch, who were permitted to trade in Japan. And they were not binding on the English, who had left Japan voluntarily in 1623 due to economic distress at home and to a number of military setbacks incurred against Dutch forces in the Far East.[10] The Kan'ei edicts ordered only the Portuguese and Spanish out of Japan; only these two peoples were subject to armed expulsion should they return, and the Spanish never did.

In effect, then, the Edo bakufu excluded no foreign peoples other than the Portuguese from Japan. After the decline of China as a maritime power in the sixteenth century and the issuance of the Kan'ei edicts which halted Japanese naval development, Portugal and Holland were left as the main competitors for mastery of the seas in East Asia. It is a little-known fact that during the seventeenth century, Dutch, not Japanese, forces "expelled" most foreigners from the oceans surrounding Japan. From 1629 to 1635, for example, the Dutch navy destroyed over one hundred fifty Portuguese ships in Far Eastern waters. In 1641, Dutch forces seized the key Portuguese colony of Malacca, and in 1642, captured Taiwan from Spain, thereby overpowering these two European rivals and establishing colonial supremacy in the region.[11] As long as Dutch naval power went unchallenged in the Far East, Tokugawa Japan largely was spared troublesome visits by other foreign peoples. But in the late eighteenth and early nineteenth centuries, Russia and England arrived to challenge the Dutch, and the resulting confusion forced bakufu leaders to institute a policy of indiscriminate armed expulsion in 1825.

In contrasting the Kan'ei edicts of the 1630s with the 1825 Expulsion Edict, we should note that the earlier edicts did *not* authorize local daimyo to attack and destroy foreign ships on sight. Instead, the bakufu ordered daimyo to escort intruding vessels to Nagasaki under armed guard.[12] Presumably, bakufu officials there were responsible for sending them away. Not until the 1640s and 1650s did the bakufu authorize daimyo in coastal areas to destroy Iberian ships. But it stipulated that the daimyo should do so only if those ships tried to call at a port or put men ashore; if the ships merely passed by or anchored offshore, the daimyo should take no hostile action.[13] Second, the sole instance of the bakufu actually destroying a Western vessel under the Kan'ei edicts took place in 1640. Besides sinking the Portuguese ship in question, bakufu forces killed sixty-one of those on board and deported thirteen others to Macao.[14] The bakufu itself would not exercise force against an intruding Western vessel again until 1837, when it drove away the *Morrison*. During the two centuries between 1640 and 1837, the bakufu's basic policy toward foreign vessels was to avoid armed confrontation. Edo leaders repeatedly commanded daimyo in coastal areas to try to persuade foreign ships to leave peaceably, and to seek bakufu intercession if necessary, but to use force only as a last resort.

Thus the Kan'ei edicts of the 1630s, which excluded only the Spanish and Portuguese from Japan, did not constitute a policy of *jōi* in the key nineteenth-century sense of indiscriminate and unconditional armed expulsion. In 1647, a mere eight years after the last Kan'ei exclusion edict was issued, two Portuguese men-of-war appeared in Nagasaki Bay. The bakufu magistrates there ordered the captains to surrender munitions before coming ashore, but this order was ignored. In haste, the magistrates put troops from nearby domains on alert, informed Edo of the intruders' presence, and awaited orders. The bakufu replied that there was no need to expel these ships because they bore a royal ambassador informing Japan of Portugal's independence from Spain and the accession of a new Portuguese king.[15] If either the Nagasaki magistrates or bakufu officials in Edo had construed the Kan'ei exclusion edicts in the nineteenth-century sense of *jōi*, they would have ordered those vessels destroyed immediately. But quite to the contrary, the magistrates supplied food, water, and firewood to the Portuguese ships—even though their captains contemptuously had defied orders to surrender their arms.[16] In one case, local daimyo destroyed a foreign ship under the Kan'ei exclusion edicts: Fukuoka, Hirado, and Karatsu clansmen attacked and sank a Western vessel in 1644. But their act plainly violated the 1640 bakufu decree enjoining daimyo to escort such vessels to Nagasaki peaceably.[17]

During the seventeenth century, then, the only Westerners that the Japanese knew from direct contact were the Spanish, Portuguese, English, and Dutch. The Edo bakufu subjected the Portuguese alone to armed expulsion, and only if they tried to land, not if they merely appeared in Japanese waters. Prior to the nineteenth century, the bakufu used force against foreigners only in the Kan'ei era, from 1624 to 1644. From the second half of the seventeenth century, the bakufu became increasingly lenient. For example, it customarily rewarded with thirty bales of rice Dutch, Chinese, or Korean ships that returned ship-wrecked Japanese nationals. In 1685, it even extended this kind-ness to the Portuguese.[18]

The policy of *sakoku,* or national isolation—in the sense of limiting trade and diplomacy to specific countries—also came into being in the period 1793 to 1825. The Kan'ei edicts did not prohibit trade with foreign countries other than Holland and Ch'ing China. When the English ship, the *Return,* arrived in Nagasaki requesting permission to reopen trade with Japan in 1763, the Nagasaki magistrates received its captain hospitably, and bakufu officials in Edo also showed a desire to grant his request. The Dutch factory captain on Dejima in Nagasaki Bay, however, pointed out that the English and Portuguese ruling houses were related through marriage, intimating that England too, was a Christian country that should be banned from coming to Japan. (Of course, the Dutch offered this in-formation out of a desire to preserve their monopoly on Euro-pean trade with Japan.) It was solely for this reason—fear of Christianity—that the bakufu refused the English request to reopen trade.[19]

In their communiqué, bakufu officials said nothing about Japan's trade being restricted by law to Ch'ing China and Holland, because no such law existed. Non-Western foreign peoples, from Siam, Annam, and Cambodia, who had traded with Japan earlier in the century were *not* prohibited from re-turning. These peoples stopped coming after the 1640s largely because the Dutch navy forcibly prevented them from reach-ing Japan. This was to protect the Dutch East India Company's trading interests in the Far East.[20] Officials in the Company also used a variety of obstructionist tactics against Chinese, French, and Danish merchants to maintain their monopoly on Japanese trade.[21] Thus, Japan's lessened trade and diplo-matic contacts with the outside world in the sixteenth century did not result solely from the bakufu's Kan'ei edicts. The Dutch did their best to cut foreigners off from Japan, and this helped create the illusion of a closed country from the 1640s onward.

In 1739, Captain Martin Spanberg visited Japan commanding a fleet of Russian vessels. His party landed and bartered goods at Ojika in Sendai domain, Awa (Chiba), and Shimoda.[22] The party also reportedly left behind pieces of silver and written messages containing sketches of crosses. The bakufu promptly confiscated these notes and turned them over to the Dutch for deciphering, but showed little further interest in the Russians' activities.[23] After the fleet departed, the bakufu instructed daimyo that in the future, foreigners should be apprehended if they attempted to land, but otherwise they should be left to go away. It issued no statements about the need to shore up defenses or drive away foreigners by force.

In 1771, Baron Moritz Aladar von Benyowsky landed in Awa (Chiba), Tosa in Shikoku, and on Amamiōshima in Satsuma domain.[24] He delivered messages through Satsuma officials addressed to the Dutch on Nagasaki, and in one of these, warned that Russia had fortified the Kuriles and was planning to attack Matsumae. Implicit in his statement, however, was that Russia's southward advance endangered the Dutch position in Japan. His message leaked to the Japanese in garbled form, and caused in the last quarter of the century great consternation over a possible Russian threat from the north. Here we need only note that officials in Awa, Tosa, and Satsuma supplied provisions to Benyowsky without incurring bakufu punishment. A British ship landed at Kumano in the Tokugawa collateral domain of Kii in 1791, and it also received supplies and hospitable treatment. The bakufu's lack of punitive measures following these and similar incidents indicates indifference to, or even tacit approval of, local daimyo who provided food, water, and firewood to foreign ships.

In 1777, a Russian ship appeared in Ezo requesting permission to trade. The following year, Matsumae domain officials answered that all Japanese trade with foreign nations was handled at Nagasaki, so the Russians must go there to make their petition. The Russians refused, saying that the Dutch were in Nagasaki.[25] Even at this late date, however, Matsumae officials said nothing about Japan's trade being legally restricted to China and Holland because the idea was not yet widely held or firmly established.

The Russian ambassador, Adam Laxman, made the first serious challenge to the Dutch monopoly on Western trade with Japan when he arrived in Ezo (present-day Hokkaidō) in 1792.[26] Matsudaira Sadanobu, then head of the bakufu, was willing to open a port to Russian trade in Ezo temporarily, as a way of keeping the Russians from coming to Edo Bay and discovering the lack of Japanese defenses. He clearly did not advocate opening the country to trade as a matter of principle, only as an expedient. At any rate, in 1792 he led Laxman to believe that going to Nagasaki to make his petition was merely a formality, that the bakufu would permit trade. However, in the following year, 1793, Sadanobu replied, making the following points:

1. From ancient times, Japan has been bound by the following proscriptions: (a) when a ship from a country not maintaining diplomatic relations with the bakufu approaches shore, we must seize or destroy it at sea. (b) Every foreign ship, even those returning Japanese castaways, may call at no port other than Nagasaki. (c) Should a foreign ship from a country without diplomatic ties be "cast upon our shores,"[27] we must turn it over to the Dutch in Nagasaki; they will repatriate it. (d) We must destroy any ship from a country not maintaining diplomatic ties that is cast upon our shores, and we must permanently incarcerate its crew.

2. But in consideration of the trouble you took to return our nationals and your ignorance of our laws, we shall allow you to return home on the condition that you never return to this port (Nemuro).

3. We do not understand the languages of countries with whom we have no diplomatic ties. Hence, we do not know the proper appellations used to address your sovereign, and we are unsure of what constitutes correct protocol.[28] This precludes an exchange of messages, though we do not disapprove of your returning our shipwrecked nationals.

4. We may not permit you to call at Edo even though your sovereign has so instructed you. Our reasons are: (a) We exercise

strict controls in our dealings even with those countries who maintain trade or diplomatic relations with us. (b) No foreign ship may call anywhere besides Nagasaki. Our authorities at all other ports are instructed to destroy any foreign vessel that approaches shore.

Sadanobu accepted the Japanese castaways that Laxman returned at Nemuro, and presented him with a permit (*shimpai*) to enter Nagasaki. However, let us examine the points in his replies against the historical record: There was only one instance of the bakufu destroying a foreign ship, this in 1640. The bakufu consistently held that force be used only when the intruders themselves were belligerent. There was no basis for the statement that foreign vessels returning Japanese castaways may do so only at Nagasaki: Laxman was the first to try elsewhere. That the bakufu could have no dealings with countries other than those already maintaining trade or diplomatic ties was true only for diplomatic relations, not trade. The bakufu never banned *all* countries other than Ch'ing China and Holland from coming to Japan; the Dutch had obstructed the others from coming, or else those countries abandoned their interests in Japan voluntarily. It was untrue that ships blown ashore from countries without diplomatic ties were sent to Nagasaki and their crews repatriated on Dutch ships. It was also untrue that the bakufu confiscated all ships, and permanently imprisoned all persons, from countries not maintaining diplomatic ties. Only Dutchmen were returned on Dutch ships. Ryukyuans and Koreans were repatriated on their own ships at Nagasaki or through Satsuma for the Ryukyuans and Tsushima for the Koreans. Moreover, the bakufu imprisoned and executed only Western missionaries such as Sidotti; not *all* Westerners cast upon Japanese shores. Benyowsky's visits, which had caused such a stir, were still within living memory—and he had been sent away safe and sound.

Historical inaccuracies aside, Sadanobu's replies in 1793 established national isolation and the armed expulsion of Westerners as time-honored bakufu laws. In 1825, a scant thirty-two years later, when the bakufu issued its Expulsion Edict and Aizawa Seishisai composed *New Theses,* these not-so-hallowed laws became part of the established political order. Their revocation, as Takano Chōei lamented in 1838, was now unthinkable. National isolation and armed expulsion received support from politically conscious Japanese in all schools of thought; their popularity was by no means limited to followers of Mito Learning or Native Learning. Why did these policies, which had come into being so recently, win such widespread belief and acceptance? To answer this question, we must examine what information Japanese thinkers were receiving on Western and world affairs during the late eighteenth and early nineteenth centuries. Such information quickly fostered support for anti-Western foreign policies.

AIZAWA'S VIEW OF CHRISTIANITY: CONQUEST WITHOUT WARFARE

Maeno Ryōtaku and other informed students of world affairs discovered that Western barbarians had developed superior religious teachings used as an integral part of government. The Europeans had perfected techniques of edification, which along with their benevolent and just political institutions, won appreciative support not only from their own peoples, but also from less-advanced barbarians in areas they annexed, such as the Americas, Africa, Australia, Siberia, and the Pacific islands off to Japan's south. Consequently, Western religious "teachings" and forms of government dominated a far greater portion of the earth than did any abstract Middle Kingdom Civilization. In 1795, Ōhara Sakingo (1760?–1810), one-time advisor to Matsumae domain, summed up the crisis facing late eighteenth-century Japan:

Their [the Russians'] customs allow popular unity and integration (jinwa) to be well established. High and low act as one. Even the lowly and base are recruited if they be talented, so all government officials are men of worth. Moreover, since they have but one religion (hō) as a state teaching (oshie), once their people revere that religion, they do so for the rest of their lives. They consider its essence to lie in serving their sovereign while they live. In death as well, they believe themselves to be repaying the benefits of that religion, so they do not feel the slightest remorse. All of them—the sagacious and stupid according to their callings and the high and low according to their statuses—are united in striving to expand their territory.[29]

Ōhara Sakingo, Fujita Yūkoku, and Aizawa Seishisai saw Christianity as the means that Western rulers used to achieve *jinwa*, or popular unity and integration, which was the key to national strength, wealth, and expansion. Aizawa conceived of *kokutai* and other ideas and policies outlined in *New Theses* largely out of a desire to achieve the same kind of popular unity in Japan that he believed Christianity and Christian-inspired government had created in Western nations. He construed *kokutai*, or what is essential to a nation, as the spiritual unity and integration that make a territory and its inhabitants a nation. He did not formulate this idea based *solely* on a perception of what Christianity was and how it spread. But I believe that Christianity was of prime importance and thus requires careful examination.

Aizawa was no less impressed than Maeno Ryōtaku or Ōhara Sakingo with the fact that Christianity, rather than Confucian culture and values, had won the allegiance of most of the earth's inhabitants. It seems likely that his shock and chagrin at this discovery prompted him to conceive of the concept of *kokutai*, as outlined in *New Theses*. Despite the hostility Aizawa displayed toward Christianity in word and deed, it profoundly impressed him. His particular understanding of Western affairs made him hate and fear Christianity for the threat it posed. But at the same time, he sought to obtain for the bakufu the benefits in Christianity that made it threatening. The following two episodes are revealing in this respect.

In the fifth month of 1792 the bakufu suppressed Hayashi Shihei's works and sentenced him to house arrest in Sendai. But by coincidence, Adam Laxman arrived in Nemuro later that year seeking permission to trade. This ominous event seemed to bear out Hayashi's warnings that Muscovite ships were fully capable of making their way to Japanese shores. A letter composed by Aizawa sometime during the 1850s describes his reactions to this event which he remembered from his childhood:

> In 1792 when I was at the tender age of eleven, the Russian barbarians arrived in northern Ezo. When Master Yūkoku told me about their fearsome, cunning nature, my blood began to boil and I resolved then and there to drive them away. I built an earthen statue of Laxman and derived great pleasure by lashing it with my riding whip. From then on I vowed to devote myself to learning. [30]

Like all historical documents composed decades after the events they purport to describe, this letter of Aizawa's requires cautious examination; the historian must be wary of any image that Aizawa might have wanted to project of his youth. Even so, we can cull important insights. In addition to the fact that Aizawa nurtured an intense dislike of Russians, we learn that his resolution to devote himself to a lifelong pursuit of learning was first sparked by what he considered a foreign threat. He perceived a great danger in Laxman's arrival in Ezo, which remained for the most part unexplored, uncharted, and beyond the pale of Japanese civilization. The letter continues:

> The only thing that allows the barbarians to achieve their sinister designs is their wicked doctrine, which they use to incite stupid commoners to rebel. The only way we can counteract that wicked doctrine is to elucidate the Great Way of Justice. When our Great Way is clear to all, the barbarians' wicked religion will be foiled, and with it, their sole tactic of subversion. This is what the ancients meant by "counteracting the enemy's stratagems in advance" and "capturing the hearts and minds of the foe." [31]

The "wicked doctrine" is Christianity, which Yūkoku and Aizawa believed was the prime weapon that Europeans used to subdue and colonize foreign nations.

This same letter informs us of Aizawa's personal conviction that Heaven had conferred upon him a mission to extirpate heresy from the face of the earth. This mission would find fulfillment only through the combined efforts of a "sagacious thinker" (Aizawa himself) and a "Great Hero."[32] The original model for this Great Hero was probably Peter the Great. But the phrase Great Hero and Man of Talent and Virtue as mentioned in *New Theses* undoubtedly refer to Tokugawa Nariaki, whom Aizawa had personally tutored.

In stark contrast to this irrepressible hostility toward Laxman, Aizawa expressed unconstrained admiration for another foreign visitor to Japan's shores—Giovanni Battista Sidotti, the Jesuit missionary interrogated by Arai Hakuseki in 1709. In an undated essay entitled "A Tract to Enlighten the Roman [Sidotti] (As Might Have Been Written by Arai Hakuseki)," Aizawa praised the Italian:

> You, sir, enjoy the blessings of and derive inner strength from your religion and system of government. Upon the order of your Pope you have traversed thousands of miles of desolate ocean, seeking only to disseminate the religion you hold so dear to your heart. I am deeply touched and impressed by your sense of patriotism, which fully accords with our own values of loyalty and truth.[33]

For Aizawa, Christianity was Russia's means of encroachment in Ezo; as such, he feared and hated it. At the same time, he considered Christianity the source of Sidotti's courage, fortitude, and spiritual strength; it was the inspiration for Sidotti's "patriotism" (*hōkoku no kokoro*). It prompted Sidotti to forsake home and family and to devote himself wholeheartedly to overseas expansion and aggrandizement (or so Aizawa thought) in dutiful compliance with the will of his spiritual lord. Aizawa, then, attributed courage, fortitude, and patriotism to Sidotti's faith in Christianity. These were the very qualities that he and Yūkoku sought to instill in the samurai class, a class whose physical prowess and spiritual vitality, they along with Hayashi Shihei, Ōhara Sakingo, and Sugita Gempaku judged, had been sapped by two hundred years of peace and soft living.

Aizawa at first understood Christianity as Confucian ritual and music, but like Maeno Ryōtaku, he came to think of it as similar to the modern-day idea of state religion.[34] This institutionalized state or civil religion, Ōhara and Aizawa concluded, was the secret behind Western military might and expansion because it enabled European rulers to unite and mobilize their own as well as foreign peoples. In *Chihoku gūdan* (1795), Ōhara had written:

> Though the Russians scheme to annex other lands, they do not necessarily send troops directly. At times they use trade to conclude treaties of amity; or they first spread their state religion (*sono kuni no oshie*), and after winning the allegiance of the people [in question], convince them that it is not wrong to revolt against their sovereign. Thus they stir up trouble between that sovereign and his people and then send troops to take over the country.[35]

In Aizawa's mind as well, Christianity was an effective vehicle of sedition that allowed European rulers to practice the precepts of the Chinese military strategist Sun Tzu—to "vanquish enemies without resorting to battle" and achieve "the best of all victories," namely, "taking over enemy homelands intact."[36] This image of the Cross as a power capable of subverting Japan and her civilized Confucian way of life explains both Aizawa's revulsion for Christianity and foreign peoples and his envious admiration of them. It was this ideological weapon, not Western armed might, that men such as Ōhara and Aizawa feared most in the late eighteenth and early nineteenth centuries. But how did Aizawa arrive at such an image of Christianity? What were the specific sources of his Western knowledge?

Aizawa was not, as is commonly believed, a blind and ignorant xenophobe. In fact, he was fairly well-informed on world affairs. He was one of only a handful of Japanese, excluding bakufu interpreters or officials, who had interrogated a Westerner directly. If we are to evaluate accurately his anti-foreignism and *jōi* thought, we must know the sources and the extent of his information on the outside world before he wrote *New Theses* in 1825. Furthermore, we should attempt to compare his knowledge of world developments with that held by other students of Western affairs during the late eighteenth and early nineteenth centuries. Fortunately I have had access to two of his unpublished, early manuscripts, *Chishima ibun* (1801) and *An'i mondō* (1824).[37] Careful analysis of these two documents gives us a clear understanding of Aizawa's Western Learning.

In the Tokugawa period, the only authorized points of contact with the outside world were Nagasaki and Matsumae in Ezo.[38] It is vital to bear in mind that even in the late eighteenth and early nineteenth centuries, "Ezo" was uncharted territory: It stood for all land(s) north of Matsumae domain, at the southern tip of present-day Hokkaidō. Aizawa, for example, thought Ezo included Siberia, Manchuria, Kamchatka, Sakhalin, and the Kuriles. But more important, Japanese thinkers also thought of "Ezo" as a cultural entity; it was that area where Japanese customs and folkways did not obtain, where the inhabitants were believed to be culturally, if not racially, different from Japanese in Japan proper. Hayashi Shihei, for example, argued that the frontier boundary between Japan and Ezo had been pushed further and further north during history as more and more territory came under "the dynasty's sphere of moral suasion." He placed the current borderline at "Kumazeki,"[39] (now pronounced "Kumaishi"), and defined this as "the limit to which Japanese customs extend."[40]

Thus Ezo was Japan's only point of direct contact with peoples and cultures less advanced than her own. It was the only area that Japanese Confucians could, with some semblance of validity, designate barbarian (*i*) in contrast to their own Middle Kingdom Civilization (*ka*). Particularly during the "northern crisis" of the late eighteenth century, many Japanese thinkers began to think of Ezo as a possible avenue of foreign incursion by military or non-military means. It is clear from the writings of concerned thinkers such as Kudō Heisuke, Sugita Gempaku, Honda Toshiaki, Ōtsuki Gentaku, Hayashi Shihei, Mamiya Rinzō, Ōhara Sakingo, and Habuto Seiyō, that in the eyes of a small group of well-informed "Europe-watchers," Russia presented a grave threat to Japan's northern frontier.

Opinion was divided on the exact nature of this threat and how to meet it. The most aggressive advocated forestalling Russia by occupying and developing Ezo. Modern historians discuss their proposals in terms of "colonizing" or "annexing" Ezo. But actually, these thinkers spoke of "edifying" and "transforming" the barbarian customs of the natives living there as the means of gaining control over that territory. For example, Hayashi Shihei, who considered the Japan-Ezo cultural border to be at Kumaishi, argued: "We should make Sōya and Shiranushi in the northernmost part of Ezo the limit to which Japanese customs extend, and thereby incorporate the territory of Ezo into Japan."[41] Such a move constituted overseas expansion, since even to irredentists like Hayashi, Honda, and Mogami, Ezo was a foreign land.[42] Shiranushi, in fact, was on the island of Sakhalin.

Opposed to the expansionists was a peace faction consisting of men like Nakai Chikuzan, Nakai Riken, Yamagata Bantō, and (early in his career) Matsudaira Sadanobu. These men were "grateful that Heaven had made Ezo a desolate frontierland,"[43] a barren buffer-zone against Russia to the north. This peace party believed that the best way to deal with the Russians was "to have nothing to do with them,"[44] to keep away from them "as one would from a mad dog."[45] To occupy and develop Ezo, they reasoned, would only expose Japan to danger. "To settle the area and spend money and grain attempting to develop it would not produce a return on our outlays in the foreseeable future." When prosperity finally did come to Ezo, "the Russians would only further be tempted to invade it."[46]

The crux of the debate lay in whether Japan's leaders should respond aggressively or passively to the Russian threat. Should the bakufu take over and develop Ezo, thereby risking a greater frequency of encounters? Or should the bakufu leave the area as a "natural firebreak,"[47] thus avoiding direct contact with the Russians as much as possible? Of course, at the bottom of this latter viewpoint lay the fear that encounters might lead to embarrassing military defeats. On the other hand, the expansionists worried about Russian encroachment through the "transformation" of native Ezo customs.[48] The following ideas expressed by Hayashi Shihei in 1786 convey this fear, and at the same time introduce new conceptions of civilization and barbarism:

The Ezo are the same kind of people [as the Siberians who are now part of Russia], but their country has never undergone civilization. In antiquity there were no precious goods, no grains and silk, no writing, no ceremonial dress, and no methods of measuring time. Food-gathering and sexual intercourse were the only activities known. The Ezo remain just as they were in antiquity because no sagacious man has appeared to edify them. . . .

Japan, China (Kara), Korea, and Holland now are civilized nations but at the time of their foundings, their peoples were just like the Ezo of today. However, sagacious men appeared and took pains to edify them during the following millenia. That is why they have become civilized nations. If a sagacious man appeared and edified the Ezo, they too would become a civilized nation. . . . The custom of their land is to exalt Japan. If we but edified them a little, their customs immediately would be transformed [in submission to us].[49]

The relativization of the Middle Kingdom world view described in the last chapter has led to an interesting conclusion in this passage. Hayashi placed Japan, China, Korea, and Holland on an equal level as civilized nations (*ka*) that had evolved from a similar state of primitiveness that the Edo people then lived in. According to Hayashi's view of history, civilization (*bunka* or *bumbutsu*) developed in a cumulative, progressive fashion everywhere. A given country's level of civilization could rise due to the edification of its people through advanced teachings. Indeed, a people such as the primitive Ezo would eagerly aspire to be "transformed" and to obtain the benefits of civilized life. Japan's vulnerability to incursion from the north lay precisely in such aspirations. Ōhara Sakingo wrote:

The natives [of Ezo] are still like people in high antiquity: they have never heard any religious teachings (*oshie*) and suffer from a spiritual void (*kūshin*, literally, "empty hearts"), which makes it easy for the Russians to disseminate their teaching.[50]

If the Russians took advantage of this spiritual void and seized Ezo, sooner or later they would be able to spread their own culture among those whom Yūkoku and Aizawa called the "stupid commoners" in Japan proper.

THE THREAT FROM THE NORTH: RUSSIA

The urgency of this northern crisis and the debate over how to meet it were not lost upon thinkers and officials in Mito. Tachihara Suiken (1774–1823), head of Mito's Historiographical Institute (Shōkōkan) in Edo, was a close personal friend of Honda Toshiaki's and secured copies of Honda's private manuscripts (which were never published) for Mito domain archives.[51] Tachihara also obtained manuscripts and valuable information verbally from Ōhara Sakingo,[52] probably the most belligerent member of Japan's expansionist party in the late eighteenth and early nineteenth centuries. Tachihara was so impressed with Ōhara's *Chihoku gūdan* that he presented it to bakufu senior councilors, Matsudaira Nobuakira and Honda Tadakazu, for official inspection in 1795.[53] Copies of Honda's and Ōhara's manuscripts did exist in Mito and presumably were available to Aizawa through Yūkoku.[54]

In 1785–86, when Tanuma Okitsugu dispatched a bakufu exploring expedition to Ezo and other territories north of Japan, Tachihara managed to get a Mito clansman, Kimura Ken, included. (Kimura's report on the mission, *Suiko hikki,*[55] was consulted and cited by Aizawa in *Chishima ibun.*) Tachihara passed on this concern over the northern threat to Yūkoku, then his prized pupil. Aizawa began his studies under Yūkoku in 1791, at the age of nine. He clearly was impressed by his teacher's anxiety over Russia's presence in the north and by the ramifications it had for Japan's political and social order:

> Master Yūkoku had always been troubled deeply by the barbarians' prying along our coasts. In 1794 [sic], the Russians came to eastern Ezo seeking permission to trade. The master knew their ulterior motives all along. . . . He believed that if we allowed these Western barbarians to achieve their aims, darkness would shroud the entire universe.[56]

At the time of Laxman's first visit to Ezo in 1792, Aizawa was ten. The statue-whipping episode related earlier indicates his emotional and violent reaction to foreign activities near Japan. Had Aizawa been content to go on lashing his statue, we might properly label him a blind and ignorant xenophobe. Instead, he went on to survey world conditions and Western (mainly Russian) history. His studies bore fruit in *Chishima ibun,* which he completed in 1801, at the age of nineteen. In this work he drew upon over twenty-five major Chinese and Japanese sources,[57] some of which were translations of Jesuit works, and many of which bakufu censorship had made inaccessible to the general Tokugawa readership. That Aizawa examined proscribed reading material suggests that he entertained real concern over Russian incursions and that he felt compelled to study conditions in Europe.

Chishima ibun begins with a brief historical outline of Ezo and of Japanese contacts with neighboring territories in ancient times. Aizawa explained the geographic features of the area and gave an account of Japanese military triumphs and glories there. In antiquity, Imperial Prince Yamato Takeru and other heroes such as Abe no Hirafu and Regent Jingū had extended Japan's frontiers through brilliant campaigns. The Kuriles as well as the Three Kingdoms of Korea, Siberia, and Manchuria on the Asian mainland, had all sent tribute-bearing ambassadors to the imperial court, thereby showing their submission to imperial virtue.[58] In short, Japan then stood in a position comparable to China's at the apex of the world order as Middle Kingdom Civilization. But for reasons unexplained by Aizawa, Japanese dynastic prestige in later ages plummeted so much that foreign barbarians withheld their tribute-bearing ambassadors and ceased coming to Japan in search of moral transformation. What was worse, those same barbarians grew strong and impudent enough to assault Japan. First, the Jurchen attacked during the reign of Emperor Goichijō (r. 1016–35), and the Mongols invaded two centuries later. On the latter occasion, Emperor Kameyama's prayers and Hōjō Tokimune's measures for *jōi* produced the divine wind that saved Japan from destruction. Aizawa noted that shortly after Hideyoshi's brief period of glory on the

mainland, Manchu barbarians overran Middle Kingdom Civilization in China, and Russian barbarians took over all parts of Ezo
except the domain of Matsumae.[59]

After presenting this brief historical background, Aizawa
asserted that people living in northeastern Japan and on the
Japan Sea coast should not be ignorant of events on the continent because "we are separated by but a strip of water."[60] This
need to know about affairs on the Asian mainland was now
more urgent than ever due to the rise of Russia—a great power
expanding eastward with frightful speed, and believed to be harboring designs on the Japanese portion of Ezo. On this note,
Aizawa began his description of Russian strength and analyzed
its sources.

Russia began its eastward advance in the seventeenth century.
It had not chosen that direction voluntarily, for a number of
strong powers in Europe and in the south thwarted Russia's
ambitions on these fronts. Consequently, Russia opted to acquire
the less lucrative, but easy-to-conquer, sparsely-populated territories in Asia as a first step to self-strengthening and enrichment.
This eastward expansion inevitably brought Russia into conflict
with Ch'ing dynasty China. It also forced Russia to construct
border fortresses and to dig canals and build roads in order to
improve Russia's military transport system. As a result, Russia
had come to lie much closer to China. Aizawa displayed his
cognizance of a shrinking world by observing, "Whereas it used
to take six years to reach China from Moscow, it now requires
but four months."[61]

Later conquests brought Russia, which had grown to be a
European colossus, even closer to Japan. This aroused in Aizawa
a gripping sense of imminent danger. Russia's subjugation of the
greater part of Kamchatka in 1698 clearly evoked irredentist
sentiments in him: "According to Honda Toshiaki, Kamchatka
was formerly part of Ezo, and as such, should be under Matsumae control. But we have been ignorant of this for more than a
hundred years since that territory was stolen from us."[62] Aizawa
noted with alarm that the Russians were building forts and
trading-posts in their newly acquired areas, and that from these
bases, they were converting the natives to Russian manners

and customs. He had this to say about their settlement of Siberia:

> When the Russian barbarians took over Siberia, it was a vast wasteland with few inhabitants. That is why they settled many people there and turned the area into a prosperous territory. One of the keys to their success in this undertaking was the large numbers of prisoners they dispatched to Siberia as settlers.[63]

We should note that thirty years later Tokugawa Nariaki would propose the same tactic as part of a bold scheme for Mito to acquire and develop Ezo.[64] (After the Restoration, the Meiji government actually implemented this plan in Hokkaidō.)[65]

Aizawa stated that "in 1624, a 'Captain X' was the first Russian explorer to make his way to the islands near Kamchatka and give them Russian names," and that "in 1729, Captain Bering arrived in St. Lawrence."[66] It piqued Aizawa to learn that "according to Kondō Jūzō, the Russians called themselves 'men from the Land of the Rising Sun'" in an effort to awe the simple-minded natives into submission.[67] Aizawa described how Russian conquests continued under "Captains Chirikov and Spanberg," until "North America and Sakhalin came under Russian control." He declared that "all their undertakings are turning out exactly as they wish." Guided by the "detailed map of Siberia that they recently drew up," they were digging canals in all parts of the region to facilitate transportation and communications.

Aizawa had discovered that Russia's trading activities were bringing prosperity to Siberia. With the wealth thus gained, the Russians were "building military academies and institutions of higher education for the sons of nobles" and "primary schools" ostensibly to instruct the children of commoners. Aizawa complained that Russian leaders were building forts and trading-posts in Japan's former territory of Kamchatka as well. The Russians were "transforming the natives culturally so that they would follow Russian manners and customs." He cited Kudō Heisuke to the effect that "by 1730, the natives in Kamchatka were paying tribute to Russia."[68]

"As early as 1735–38, Russia's Queen Anna," Aizawa asserted, "had had her eye on the Ch'ing empire and Japan." At that time, however, she was directing her main efforts to the south and west. Therefore, Russia's policy was to use trade as a means of reconnaissance, "to see if these two Asian nations were strong or weak." In 1739, for example,

> Foreign ships came to Mutsu and Awa, and after giving pieces of silver to people on shore, went on their way. When questioned about this affair, the Dutch in Nagasaki replied that this ship was a Russian vessel that had departed from Muscovy the previous year.[69]

Having read a translated Western work entitled *Barbarian Gazetteer* (*Teki shi*), Aizawa related with great alarm:

> Russia does not seem to have annexed the Ezo Islands until that time [1741]. But now [in 1801], the only islands left to us are Kunashiri, Etorofu, and Karafuto [Sakhalin]. All the rest were snatched away before we knew what was happening. *Teki shi* lists the Ezo Islands (which the Russians claim), and ends the account saying, "the large southern-most island in the Ezo Archipelago is called 'Matsumae'." This means they think they already own the island containing Matsumae![70]

Aizawa thought that Russia considered itself the owner of what today is Hokkaidō.

According to the reports of Kondō Jūzō and Kimura Ken, Japanese castaways landing on Siberian and Kamchatkan shores received cordial treatment. Aizawa believed that the Russian government welcomed them by awarding them lucrative teaching positions in the state-sponsored language school.[71] Furthermore, he discovered that those castaways assumed Russian names, married Russian women, and adopted Russian customs in general. In short, they were transformed to follow Russian ways. With the aid of these teachers, the Russians "learned to read Japanese *kana.*" They "found out all they wanted to know about Japan's geography and climate, and about our people and customs." From Kondō, Aizawa learned to his horror that "because of such castaways, Kaempfer's book[72] could be written," a book "containing a large detailed map of Japan showing the locations of castles and the deployment of all daimyo throughout the country."[73]

From the Chinese work, *Hsi-yü wen-chien lu* (Records of things seen and heard in the West),[74] Aizawa learned that in 1735 Russia had stopped paying tribute to its overlord, a country called "K'ung-ge erh,"[75] which Aizawa incorrectly supposed to be the Holy Roman Empire. Aizawa believed that this "K'ung-ge erh" was a small, weak power. But because it was the spiritual head of Europe's ruling houses, he presumed, all of them pledged fealty to it and were united to smite any enemy who might dare oppose it. Aizawa reasoned that this position was somewhat like that of the Chou House in China's feudal period.[76] Due to that breach of loyalty, full-scale war broke out between Russia and an allied army of federated European states under K'ung-ge erh hegemony.

In 1770, Russia took a sound drubbing during this conflict. It lost "two hundred thousand men and suffered invasion by hundreds of thousands of foreign troops."[77] Under such circumstances, its plans for expansion received a serious setback. Russia had to seek peace and reaffirm fealty to K'ung-ge erh by again pledging to pay the yearly tribute it had discontinued in 1755. What is crucial to note is Aizawa's assumption that Russia's drive westward was stopped abruptly and with staggering losses by 1770, and that in addition, the country was burdened with huge war indemnities. For these reasons, Aizawa concluded, Russia would expand toward eastern Asia in the future, as it had done earlier in history.[78] It would seek territory and booty in the east to pay off war reparations.

Aizawa described the Beyowsky affair[79] of 1771 as Russia's first step toward conquering Asia. He quoted Mogami Tokunai to the effect that Benyowsky surveyed Japan's coast in command of three ships, and that he carried a map of the Orient showing Japan in detail.[80] From another of Honda's works, however, Aizawa was heartened to learn that although the Russians claimed Ezo for themselves, the natives there still considered the Matsumae clan their *kamoidono,* a corruption of the Japanese word for "divine lord."[81] Nevertheless, Russian fishermen and trappers came to the Ezo Island of Uruppu in 1772 to fish and obtain otter skins, and Honda reported that by this time all islands as far south as Shimoshiri were really under Russian control. This prompted Aizawa to resolve, "We must take Karafuto [Sakhalin] before they do!"[82]

Regarding otter skins, Aizawa first quoted from Mogami Tokunai's *Ezo sōshi:* "Otter skins are a special product of our Divine Realm and are trade-items shipped to China through Nagasaki. Recently the Russian barbarians have been marketing these skins directly to Peking. . . ." Then he commented: "If this is true, the whole world probably thinks that Russia has snatched away our vassal state of Ezo, where we obtain this item."[83] This passage reveals that in 1801 Aizawa did not oppose trade as being contrary to hallowed bakufu laws; he implicitly supported it assuming that it be conducted under strict bakufu control.

Aizawa then noted that a Russian named Ishiyuyo first appeared on Uruppu Island in 1780, and he observed:

Kondō Jūzō writes, "The Russians subjugated Shimoshiri a mere thirty years ago but the inhabitants' manners and customs were thoroughly transformed to those of Russia within ten years. The natives, both men and women, adopted Russian hairstyles, began to wear hats and shoes, started to carry rifles and gunpowder, learned to speak Russian, and took up the practice of dangling Russian Buddhas from their necks."

The Russians periodically dispatch officials and priests to the various Ezo Islands to collect taxes and to instill affection and submissiveness in the natives. This Ishiyuyo later would employ Christianity to seduce the inhabitants of Etorofu into submission. From this fact we can assume that he was the scoundrel who transformed Shimoshiri to Russian customs as well.[84]

Next, Aizawa presented an account of Ishiyuyo's method of operation as reported by Kondō:

In 1785, three Russians including Ishiyuyo landed on Etorofu. They erected a Cross and taught the natives their cult's magic sign. A certain native named Haushise became especially close to the [Russian] barbarians, grew his hair long, and took on other Russian customs. Later, Kondō Jūzō questioned him, and he said, "When the Russians gave us images of their Buddha and taught us their magic sign, they told us, 'If you believe in this image, your catches of fish will always be bountiful, your boats will never be shipwrecked, and your prayers will all be answered.'"[85]

In addition, the Russians handed out *sake* and *mochi* (which Kondō mistook for wine and bread[86]) to the primitive natives. By bartering such luxury items, and more importantly, by dispensing a religion promising happiness and well-being in this world, the Russians captured Ezo. They "transformed" the folkways and won the allegiance of the simple-minded inhabitants at little cost to themselves.

Aizawa was not alone in his opinions. The Rangakusha, Ōtsuki Gentaku, also cited the account by Kondō Jūzō and commented:

> They erect Crosses, teach their religion, and give Buddhas to the barbarian-natives. Thus they have come close to transforming fully the natives' folkways. . . . I am overwhelmed by the astuteness of Hayashi [Shihei]'s foresight: Over twenty years ago he predicted this would happen.[87]

After some prodding, Aizawa noted, Kondō got the "deceitful Ishiyuyo" to reveal his true motives for coming to Ezo. Aizawa paraphrased Kondō's remarks:

> Ever since the time of their King Peter, [the Russians] have been annexing territories and appointing military governors to rule these. In order to acquire all of Ezo, they first wanted to employ trade as a pretext for surveying conditions there and determining whether an immediate takeover was possible. That was their motive for wanting to establish trade relations with the bakufu, and this is why they minutely survey the geography of our Divine Realm.[88]

In *Chishima ibun,* Aizawa implied that one main source of Russian strength lay in the ability, resourcefulness, and energy of Peter the Great. It was Peter who first "unified the formerly independent Red, White, and Black states of Russia into a single nation,"[89] Aizawa observed. Russia's rise to become a great power stemmed from Peter's assiduously executed reforms:

> He devoted all his energies to stabilizing the people's livelihoods and enriching the nation. He achieved great things indeed. He planted vineyards and orchards to secure a sufficient supply of food for his people. He established schools to propagate the official religion. He drilled Russia's army, and with it, struck terror in the hearts of Russia's foes.[90]

This view of Peter as a heroic reformer, and of Russia's methods for territorial aggrandizement, certainly distressed Aizawa. Peter emerges as a benevolent and dedicated "ruler-edifer," who, after ensuring his people's livelihood, elevated their morals, spiritually unified them, and imbued them with a sense of reverence toward himself.

Russia did not absorb foreign nations and peoples through military conquest and harsh subjugation; it did so peacefully, by transforming manners and customs to Russian ways. Through such voluntary "transformation," the natives in annexed lands received the material benefits of civilized life: food, clothing, advanced technology, and firearms. Equally important, they obtained spiritual strength through Christianity, which guaranteed the fulfillment of their desires for gain in this world. As a result, they could not help feeling spontaneous affection for, and allegiance toward, their new Russian masters.

Peter had recognized Russia's backwardness and its need to learn from the West. For that reason, Aizawa noted, he dispatched students abroad to learn skills and to investigate conditions in Europe. "With the wealth he obtained through trade with Britain, Holland, and the Ch'ing empire," Aizawa observed, Peter "bought books on law, science, religion, mathematics, and astronomy" from advanced European countries, and he founded "great centers of learning in Moscow and St. Petersburg." Aizawa praised the capital's splendor and strength as a fortress, and he outlined Peter's educational achievements. He even noted the number of rubles that Russia expended annually for education and the number of volumes stocked in Russian university libraries.[91]

Peter updated, strengthened, and enlarged Russia's armed forces. By studying European techniques of navigation and by building scores of warships, he created a Russian navy that grew to become the world's most powerful, or so Aizawa believed. What probably impressed Aizawa most was Peter's personal involvement and total commitment to the goal of national wealth and strength. Peter was not satisfied with importing books and hiring foreign teachers; "he personally went to the West disguised as a workman to master the techniques of building large ships."[92]

Thus, the nineteen-year-old Aizawa's survey of Russian affairs told him that with proper leadership, even a divided, weak, subvassal state, a state by no means blessed with good climate and geography, could develop into a leading world power. Let us further analyze the reasons for Russia's phenomenal growth as Aizawa perceived them.

To begin with, Russia's leaders from the early seventeenth century possessed certain fixed, long-range objectives: the attainment of national unity, the securing of popular allegiance, the creation of wealth and strength for the state, and territorial expansion. In pursuing these objectives, Russian leaders were beset by sudden reversals and unexpected obstacles. But they, and especially Peter, pursued their long-range goals with flexibility. Though adhering to fixed objectives, they adjusted themselves to world conditions, a dexterity that they demonstrated, for example, by expanding to the east when frustrated in the west. Second, though barbarians, the Russians recognized the need to learn advanced techniques from Europe in order to realize their long-range objectives. Finally, though barbarians, their leaders had achieved a level of cultural development that allowed them to invent an efficacious Way for achieving unity at home and expediting expansion abroad. The above conclusions, the fruit of Aizawa's Western Learning, can be culled from *Chishima ibun* and would be woven into his opus, *New Theses*, twenty-four years later.

We cannot justifiably accuse Aizawa of ignoring Japan's need to obtain and assimilate knowledge about the outside world. His prime concern in 1801 was Japan's insufficient knowledge of world affairs, or as Ōhara Sakingo put it, "They know more about us than we do about them."[93] Aizawa sought to learn about conditions in the West and to place this knowledge at bakufu disposal. This is why he composed *New Theses* and sought to submit it to bakufu senior councilors in 1825.

THE THREAT FROM THE SOUTH: SPAIN AND (NEW) ENGLAND

The bakufu's successful settlement of the Takadaya-Golovnin Incident in 1813[94] lent credence to the hard-line approach to foreign affairs conceptualized as *jōi*. After exchanging prisoners, the bakufu delivered a memorandum to the Russian negotiators. It read in part:

> Our nation's laws prohibit the establishment of any new trade or diplomatic relations with foreign countries. . . . Our officials are instructed to fire on and drive off (*uchiharau*) any foreign ship approaching Japan proper and the Ezo Islands. There will be no change in this [policy].[95]

On top of that, the Russians were informed:

> It is a national law that any foreign ship not calling at Nagasaki will be driven off (*uchiharau*). Christianity is strictly prohibited. Anyone disseminating it among Japanese people is subject to the ultimate punishment.[96]

The Russians accepted these stipulations without qualms; 1813 marked the end of Russian requests for trade until mid-century. Aizawa, then, had cause to believe that a proclamation banning trade and Christianity, coupled with the threat of force, persuaded unwanted intruders to stay away. So he adopted this militant stance against British and American merchant ships and whalers, which appeared from the south in great numbers during the 1810s, and 1820s.

At some time during these years Aizawa read Arai Hakuseki's *Seiyō kibun,* which together with his earlier study of conditions in Russia, was instrumental in reshaping his world view.[97] Then in the summer of 1824, his interest in the world outside Japan received a jolting new stimulus when a fleet of foreign whalers approached the Mito coast at Ōtsuhama and twelve crewmen came ashore.[98] These foreigners were promptly apprehended, and the domain government dispatched Aizawa and Tobita Shiken, another of Yūkoku's students, to question the intruders about their motives for landing. Aizawa had five days alone with the prisoners before the arrival of the bakufu official, Koyama Zenkichi, and his two interpreters, Takahashi Kageyasu and Yoshio Chūjirō.

Aizawa's *An'i mondō* is an account of his encounters with the captain of the captured foreign crewmen. He later submitted this document to domain authorities.[99] Its main portion records the questions and answers he exchanged with the prisoners. The appendix, "Bemmō" (Exposing foolish fancies), is as the title indicates, Aizawa's exposé of the wishful thinking indulged in by domain and bakufu officials about the foreigners' true motives. Although he wrote that his sessions with the prisoners "did not allow me to obtain detailed information on foreign affairs," Aizawa was sure that he "did discover the general outlines of recent world events."[100] In a separate memorial to the daimyo, Fujita Yūkoku was even more enthusiastic about Aizawa's performance, calling it "an achievement unmatched since Arai [Hakuseki]'s interrogation of the Roman [Sidotti]."[101] That was more than slightly exaggerated praise.

Let us examine *An'i mondō* closely, since it tells us what additional knowledge of world affairs Aizawa acquired between 1801 and 1824. The first problem he faced in interrogating the prisoners was communication, a problem compounded by his ignorance of their true nationality. Aizawa arrived at the scene believing that the intruders were from Russia, and came prepared to question them in Russian.[102] He brought along a notebook in which he had jotted down a few Russian words mastered from earlier reading about the West. He also brought reference works, including a map of the world and Katsuragawa Hoshū's *Bankoku kōkai hyōkizu* (Navigation-flags of the world).[103]

Upon discovering that their leader, "Captain Gibson," could read neither Chinese ideographs nor Japanese *kana,* Aizawa wrote the word "Russia" in Russian script. Gibson, however, responded by writing Arabic numerals and the word "England" in the English alphabet. Aizawa, who believed that all Western languages were phonetically related, pronounced these numerals and letters "according to Dutch pronunciation."[104] It is highly unlikely that Aizawa's knowledge of any European language was more than paltry. Even so, his language ability, meager as is must have been, coupled with his earlier reading in Western Learning, helps explain why the domain selected him to conduct these interrogations.

Through written notes, facial expressions, gestures, the drawing of pictures, and the services of a local jailer who had acquired a smattering of conversational English (and would later be punished for it), Aizawa obtained bits and pieces of not wholly inaccurate information on contemporary world affairs and new national boundaries. His main objectives, however, were to find out why this party of foreigners had come to Japan and to investigate what they had been doing on shore before they were apprehended. Gibson claimed that the original fleet to which he belonged numbered thirty-five ships and that they had set sail from their home port thirty-two months earlier. When Aizawa inquired why they had come to Japan, Gibson replied that his particular detachment of ships came in search of whales. But on the following day, when Aizawa spread a map of the world in front of Gibson and repeated this query, a crewman named Middleton engaged Captain Gibson in heated debate. According to Aizawa,

> The second man [Middleton] walked over to the map, placed his hand on our Divine Realm, and repeatedly drew it in a sweeping motion straight toward England as if to say, "We will make the Divine Land, too, into an English colony."[105]

Then Aizawa was quick to add,

> I was not the only one who interpreted his action in this way; everyone present thought so. Then, on the next day when I repeated my question, Gibson drew a picture of a whale and said they had come for whales. This plainly was an attempt to cover up the truth that came to light the day before.[106]

In their memorials to the domain, Yūkoku and Aizawa sought to convince doubting officials that foreigners were by nature deceptive and cunning, that they posed a dire threat to Japan's existence. Yet behind this outlandish interpretation of the Englishman's hand-sweeping, there was more than an irrational hatred of foreigners. To Aizawa, foreigners *did* pose a threat to Japan, as the following two pieces of misinformation gained from Gibson show. The first was about an island called "Naideshikoetsu," which Aizawa imagined to lie north of the Ogasawaras, due east of the Mito coast. Aizawa lamented that "Gibson, a foreigner, considers this island part of Japan, but our own people do not even know it exists!"[107] Second, Aizawa learned from Gibson that the Spanish were exploiting a "Marabariko Island" (also unidentifiable), which Hakuseki's *Seiyō kibun* reported to lie due south of the Ogasawaras and to be rich in gold and silver.[108] These two bits of misinformation obtained through interrogations heightened his anxiety over European colonization near Japan. He concluded that Japan was caught in a pincer movement between Russia from the north and England and Spain from the south:

England, Russia's ally, has annexed both ends of the African continent and has settled and developed India. Even nearer to Japan, Russia's comrade, Spain, has already devoured most of the Ogasawara Islands to the south; so this territory is in effect an English colony. From these advanced bases, the British ply between points throughout the Far East: We must think of them as being right on our border. Their ships anchor in Far Eastern waters, and on one pretext or another, they seize every opportunity to become friendly with our people, to draw maps, to measure the ocean's depths off our coasts, to land on our shores, in short, to probe our defenses.[109]

The fear that European powers other than Russia also were closing in on Japan by colonizing territories and assimilating peoples nearby was very real to Aizawa. It was all the more gripping because of the particular tactics he believed they were using:

They now endeavor to annex all nations in the world. The wicked doctrine of Jesus is an aid in this endeavor. Under the pretext of trade or whatever, they approach and become friendly with peoples in all areas, secretly probing to see which countries are strong and which weak. If a nation's defenses are weak, they will seize it by force, but if there are no weaknesses to pounce on, they take it over by leading the people's minds astray with their wicked doctrine [of Christianity]. In this manner the Westerners have acquired many, many colonies located thousands of miles across the sea from their homelands.[110]

In *An'i mondō*, Aizawa asserted that neither Gibson's statements nor the fanciful thinking of bakufu officials should be taken seriously. He refused to view the Ōtsuhama Incident as an isolated act; he saw it as the last in a series of illegal English intrusions into Japanese territorial waters that included the *Phaeton* Incident of 1808 (described below), and also the *Brothers* Incident of 1818 at Uraga, in which "Christian books" translated into classical Chinese were distributed to Japanese looking on from shore.[111] As Shinobu Seizaburō has noted, Aizawa did not perceive Gibson to be an individual, a lone whaler who happened to be English.[112] Instead, he saw Gibson as part of an English *nation*. Gibson's lies must not be believed:

> Even if we were to give him the benefit of the doubt [as an individual], they [the English as a whole] have been probing our coasts for decades now. At one time they bribed the Hollanders to allow their ships to call and dock at Nagasaki under false pretenses [of being Dutch vessels]. They forced their way into Nagasaki Bay, wreaked havoc and caused the death of a bakufu magistrate there.[113]

Here we see Aizawa's grounds for regarding English requests for water, provisions, and firewood to be a form of reconnaissance, the prelude to attack or subversion.

Such suspicions were not peculiar to Aizawa. Seventeen years earlier the Dutch Studies expert, Ōtsuki Gentaku, had expressed bitter resentment over the activities of the Westerners in Japanese waters. Ōtsuki cast a jaundiced eye upon what he considered deceitful trading practices perpetrated by New England merchant-ship captains in violation of bakufu law from 1797 to 1807.[114] Gentaku also linked these violations to the *Phaeton* Incident of 1808. By placing these events in historical context, we can understand the suspicions raised by both Japanese thinkers.

Holland suffered revolution and an invasion by the French in 1794–95, and this gave birth to a Batavian Republic forced into a wartime coalition with France against England. Therefore, Dutch shipping and colonial outposts, including Dejima, became fair game for British men-of-war. By the late eighteenth century, the naval supremacy that Holland had enjoyed in the Far East was over, and this Dutch weakness exposed Japan to visits by other Western nations who sought trade or territorial concessions. Holland's maritime power atrophied so much that Dutch East India Company officials had to charter foreign vessels to maintain their trade with Japan. Of the twenty-two merchant ships flying the Dutch flag that called at Nagasaki between 1797 and 1817, eight were Dutch and nine were American.[115] Of the remaining five privately owned vessels hired by the Dutch, three were British, one was Danish, and one was from Bremen. In addition, American ships not chartered by the Dutch made four visits to Nagasaki, which brings to thirteen the number of American visits to Japan during this twenty-one year period between 1797 and 1817. In 1803, one American skipper, Captain William Robert Stewart, requested permission to trade with Japan, not as a hired agent of the Dutch, but as a private American citizen half a century before Perry.

Dutch officials on Dejima were unwilling to disclose information about conditions in Europe or wartime developments that might lead to an abrogation of their trading privileges or endanger their very existence in Japan. Holland itself was incorporated into the French Empire in 1810. Its last colonial holding, Java (under whose jurisdiction Dejima lay), fell to British armed forces in September of 1811. From then until August of 1816, when the British returned most of their captured former Dutch possessions to the newly reinstated Dutch monarch, Dejima was the only spot on earth where the tri-color royal Dutch flag flew.[116] It is no wonder that news of America's War of Independence, the French Revolution, the Napoleonic Wars, and other information harmful to Dutch interests went unreported or was misrepresented in the official reports submitted to the bakufu.[117]

Ōtsuki Gentaku, however, had access to more accurate information through his contacts with bakufu interpreters in Nagasaki and through his interrogations of Tsudayū, a Japanese castaway whom Rezanov returned to Sendai domain (where Ōtsuki was serving) in 1804.[118] In 1807, one year before the *Phaeton* Incident, Ōtsuki wrote Book One of *Hoei mondō*. In it, he discussed the problem of American ships calling at Nagasaki in Dutch employ. Ōtsuki knew that "New England" was a British colony in North America, but he did not know that the Americans had formed an independent nation in 1783. Because the ships calling at Nagasaki were registered in places like "Providence" or "Boston new [sic] England," he concluded that the so-called "American" ships regularly putting into Nagasaki Harbor were really English.[119] Moreover, Ōtsuki had learned about the French Revolution and Napoleonic Wars from Tsudayū. He had discovered that the King of Holland had fled to England in the wake of "great civil disorder"—revolution and invasion from 1794 to 1795—in his own land.[120] Ōtsuki reasoned that the British were forcing the vanquished Dutchmen in Nagasaki to falsify the identity of those ships calling there under the Dutch flag. In other words, he believed that these vessels really were (New) English, but that under duress, the Hollanders had to report them as their own.[121]

Ōtsuki knew that English forces were capturing Dutch colonial outposts in other parts of the world, and assumed that they would try to take over Dejima also.[122] He suspected that these (New) English ships were on spy missions to prepare for such an assault.[123] Since Britain and Russia had allied against Holland in campaigns on the European continent before, he judged that these two powers might well ally again to seize the Dutch-monopolized markets in Japan by forcing trade agreements on Japan or even invading her.[124]

In the *Phaeton* Incident of 1808, British sailors had forcibly abducted Dutch officials in the custody of the Nagasaki Magistrates. This violent act heightened Ōtsuki's suspicions, expressed in Book Two of *Hoei mondō* (1808). He was unconvinced by the Dutch explanation that a British warship, flying the Dutch flag, had forced its way into Nagasaki Harbor in search of Dutch ships to seize. Ōtsuki, the Dutch Studies expert, firmly believed that the *Phaeton* was in Japanese waters to spy for Britain's ally, Russia,[125] and urged that the incident be subjected to more rigorous scrutiny.[126] Clearly, then, a distrust of foreigners as deceitful and threatening was not limited to Mito xenophobes like Aizawa. Moreover, Japanese thinkers, whatever their scholarly affiliation, did have certain grounds for distrust.

Throughout his life Aizawa believed that trade and Christianity were stratagems intended to facilitate a Western takeover. To understand fully the logic behind this belief, we must examine the Western knowledge Aizawa gained from Arai Hakuseki.[127] Aizawa was critical of Hakuseki's historiography and attitude toward Japan's imperial house.[128] But he lavished praise on Hakuseki for discerning Christianity's potential threat to Japan's social and political order.[129] Aizawa read Hakuseki's *Seiyō kibun* sometime between 1801 and 1824, and Sidotti's recorded statements in the work easily confirmed the fears about European expansion that Aizawa had gained from earlier readings on Russia. What follows is not a thoroughgoing exposition of *Seiyō kibun*. Instead, my aim is to present certain viewpoints or statements expressed by Sidotti and Hakuseki that exacerbated Aizawa's xenophobia.

Many historians hold that Hakuseki's dissociation of Western arts and science from the "dangerous heresy" of Christianity greatly stimulated Japan's importation and assimilation of advanced technical knowledge from Europe.[130] Be that as it may, Hakuseki did not deny that Christianity was dangerous; he insisted that the bakufu should continue to proscribe it.[131] He held that Christianity was a doctrine unsuited to and incompatible with Tokugawa Japan's bakuhan state and social order. The fall of the Ming dynasty, he asserted, was due in no small part to its religious tolerance.[132] In opposition to Hakuseki, Sidotti argued that the Vatican was different from secular states such as Holland, Spain, or France; "Rome [the Vatican] has never conspired to annex an inch of foreign territory throughout its 1380 year history."[133] Furthermore, Sidotti reported, "nations meet their ruin because of their rulers' mistakes, not because of any particular religion."[134] The rise and fall of regimes, and the social stability or instability of nations, stemmed from purely political factors—their rulers' ability or incompetence. The religion and spiritual beliefs that their peoples embraced were of no consequence. Since state security and individual belief were separate things, religion posed no political danger. Japanese secular authorities, Sidotti said, should not outlaw his missionary activities. Sidotti went on to argue that when secular powers such as Spain and France did annex foreign nations, the conquered native peoples either lacked proper rulers due to their primitiveness, or else were so embroiled in political turmoil and warfare that existing rulers had lost popular support.[135] Since neither situation was true in Japan's case, Sidotti concluded, there was no reason to ban his proselytizing.

Despite genuine sympathy for Sidotti's plight, Hakuseki replied that tolerating Christianity would "naturally and inevitably lead to subversion from within,"[136] even though Sidotti himself did not desire such results. The existing polity rested on the moral absolutes of "loyalty of retainer for ruler and filial devotion of child for parent." Any belief in a transcendent Creator necessarily would lead retainers and sons to "slight ruler and parent."[137] That would constitute "heresy" in the Mencian sense,[138] and would undermine the value system supporting the Tokugawa bakuhan state. Hakuseki's attitude can be conceptualized abstractly as a form of cultural *jōi:* eradicating what is barbarian to prevent the transformation of civilized customs within Japan.

But more important to this discussion is the rightness of a state-instituted orthodoxy that Hakuseki hinted at. This was a potent legacy not only to Aizawa, but also to most later Japanese thinkers, for it denied the principle of the individual's religious or spiritual autonomy. If state authority is to uphold political stability at home and territorial integrity against foreign nations, Hakuseki implied, it must have the authority to control the people's spiritual and religious lives. It also must be free to propagate any set of beliefs or values best-suited to its socio-political structure and to exclude any doctrines that might prove harmful.

A second point in *Seiyō kibun* that undoubtedly caught Aizawa's attention was that Western missionaries had been thoroughly trained in languages and familiarized with local cultures before arriving in the Far East. Sidotti had already studied Japanese for three years in Rome; then he received further schooling in Japanese language, manners, and customs from Japanese nationals on Luzon.[139] Moreover, Sidotti carried with him a book on Japan written in a foreign language.[140] This indicated to Aizawa that Europeans were compiling and disseminating information on Japan among themselves.

Third, Hakuseki related that Western missionaries recruited native Asians to assist in proselytizing. When Hakuseki questioned Sidotti about Li Ma-tou, Matteo Ricci's Chinese name, Sidotti replied that he knew nothing about the man. This answer raised suspicions in Hakuseki's mind.[141] Hakuseki mistakenly believed that Li Ma-tou was born in Kwangtung Province, that he was a Chinese national educated in Christendom and sent back to China to win converts for the Church among his countrymen. "According to a certain Dutchman," Hakuseki wrote:

> The foreign missionaries look for bright little children in the lands where they proselytize, round them up, and send them to Europe for education in Christianity. When this education is completed and the children are grown up, they are returned to their homelands to preach the Gospel. In this way, the undiscriminating and less intelligent among the native populations are converted.[142]

The fourth and most upsetting piece of information that Aizawa gained from *Seiyō kibun* concerned the non-aggressive manner in which European rulers annexed foreign lands, a manner all too similar to the Way of the ancient sage kings. European rulers bestowed the fruits of their advanced civilization on primitive peoples and thereby induced them to submit voluntarily.

In describing how Spain and France "annexed and colonized foreign countries," Sidotti related through Hakuseki that in the territory called "New Spain," "the inhabitants had no ruler to maintain order," "the weak fell prey to the strong," and "people ate the flesh of corpses."[143] On Luzon as well, "the inhabitants were living in nakedness . . . not far from beasthood" until the Spanish came.

> The Spanish taught the natives how to grow food and sew clothes, saw to it that goods and commodities circulated throughout the territory; then they led the natives along the proper Way through Christianity. Thus, for the first time ever, the natives could enjoy security of livelihood. That is why they gladly submitted to the Spaniards. Before long, they even asked to have their land incorporated into the Spanish Empire so that they might enjoy the blessings of direct rule by the King of Spain.[144]

Despite its historical inaccuracy, this portrayal of Spanish missionary activities presented by Hakuseki, based on what he learned from Sidotti, matches to a tee the requirements that Yūkoku and Aizawa used to define sagehood. Their definition (discussed in the next chapter) was to dispense the "Way of nourishing the people, eliminating hardship from their lives, and providing them with ethical instruction and spiritual fulfillment."[145] This meant that Spanish activities in the Philippines resembled the Confucian Way as Yūkoku and Aizawa understood it.[146]

Finally, European rulers as described by Sidotti were farsighted and energetic, quite unlike faint-hearted Japanese such as Nakai Chikuzan, Nakai Riken, Yamagata Bantō, and (initially) Matsudaira Sadanobu, who refused to take over Ezo. European leaders vigorously pushed through programs of overseas colonization despite protests lodged by petty, economy-minded advisors who doubted the profitability of such ventures. Most important, this far-sightedness and drive stemmed from the European rulers' faith in Christianity. Hakuseki quoted Sidotti:

One minister remonstrated with the Spanish king, "Isn't it better to ignore the requests of such natives [to be incorporated into the Spanish Empire]? We should forget about annexing their lands, which, after all, are thousands of miles away. To administer such lands would only strain our resources."

But the king replied, "No. By making it possible for foreign peoples to enjoy economic security in life and to escape the sufferings of death, we can repay a large measure of God's blessings to us."[147]

WESTERN LEARNING AND CONFUCIAN WORLD VIEW

Aizawa learned about world geography, about how much of the globe Christianity and Islam controlled compared with Confucianism, and about the methods European rulers supposedly used to colonize foreign lands. This new Western knowledge destroyed the Sinocentric Middle Kingdom world view for him just as it had for Maeno Ryōtaku and Ōhara Sakingo. Aizawa could not remain sanguine about who represented civilization, and who, barbarism.

At a basic, general level, Confucian political theory holds that a sage, or a True King, is one who conducts benevolent government in accordance with the Way, nurtures his people as a loving parent cares for his children, sees to it that their material needs in life are met, reassures them spiritually, and "transforms" them morally.[148] Such an ideal ruler theoretically did not need armed force to bring alien peoples under control: Barbarians submitted voluntarily. They eagerly "came to be transformed." T'ang, virtuous founder of the Shang Dynasty, was such a True King. In describing T'ang's campaigns to "bring government to all under Heaven," Mencius wrote:

In eleven expeditions he became matchless in the Empire. When he marched on the east, the Western Barbarians complained, and when he marched on the south, the Northern Barbarians complained. They all said, "Why does he not come to us first?" The people all longed for his coming as they longed for rain in time of severe drought.[149]

Aizawa's Western Learning turned this scheme of affairs topsy-turvey: Could it be that lowly Western barbarians had appropriated the Confucian Way and were using it to their own advantage? In antiquity, China under the former sage kings and Japan under its own former sage emperors had dominated the world spatially and demographically. This was because Chinese and Japanese sage rulers had implemented the Way for their peoples and extended it to barbarians. This idealized Sinocentric world view now was untenable. First, in terms of simple geographic extensiveness, the surface area of the Middle Kingdom (whether China or Japan) proportionate to the world as a whole shrank drastically. "All under Heaven" was not dominated by a Middle Kingdom in the center with barbarian peoples existing precariously along the fringes of the known world. Instead, Aizawa now realized, barbarian lands such as North and South America, Australia, Siberia, Africa, and the Middle East constituted a far greater portion of the earth's land mass and supported populations far larger than China and Japan. Second, these barbarian lands and peoples had come under the moral suasion of the Christian God or the Islamic Allah, not the Confucian sages, and much less Amaterasu. Worse still, as *Chishima ibun* reveals, Aizawa believed that large areas once under Japanese moral and cultural hegemony—Siberia, Manchuria, Kamchatka, Sakhalin, and the Kuriles, all of which he labeled "Ezo"—had succumbed to Russia through Christian "transformation."

These upsetting realizations led to a bigoted reassertion of Japanese Confucian cultural superiority in the more vituperatively anti-foreign passages of *New Theses*. I believe that these discoveries impelled Aizawa to formulate his idea of *kokutai*— the spiritual unity and cohesion needed to make a territory and its inhabitants into a nation (discussed in the next chapter). Aizawa had to admit, even in spite of himself, that European leaders deserved respect. They had created a civilization and religion whose sphere of moral influence was much vaster than that of either the Ch'ing empire or Tokugawa Japan.

Furthermore, he could not deny that Amaterasu's sagely Way, Middle Kingdom Civilization, Japan's divine imperial house, and its *kokutai*—all of which had created spiritual solidarity and helped assimilate barbarian peoples during antiquity—had degenerated grievously by 1824. Aizawa addressed these gripping issues in *New Theses,* which he composed the following year.

chapter four
Aizawa and
His *New Theses*

Today, students of Western political history consider the separation of church and state to have been an important step in the formation of modern European nations. The textbooks tell us that Machiavelli's views on government were modern, as opposed to medieval, in that he distinguished the ruler's personal morality as a private individual from his public responsibilities as a head of state: For the prince, reprehensible personal conduct was often praiseworthy statecraft. After Machiavelli, Western rulers for the most part would exclude ethics and religion from the affairs of government; and as a result, the nation-state in modern Europe became a purely secular institution.

Most Japanese students of Western affairs in the second half of the Tokugawa period, however, did not think of contemporary European states in this way: They perceived Christianity to be an integral part of Western government. Their studies told them that "religion and government" as well as "administration and edification" were one in the West.[1] And most importantly, they believed that this non-separation of church and state was the secret of Western greatness and strength. Such an understanding of the contemporary West produced two noteworthy reactions among the Japanese: genuine admiration and genuine fear. A few thinkers, such as Maeno Ryōtaku and Shiba Kōkan, praised Western nations as benevolently-ruled utopias in which Christian teachings had a humanizing, salubrious effect on government. But by and large, Japanese thinkers—including the Rangakusha—stressed the dangers, not the virtues, presented by Christian-inspired Western governments.

In the late eighteenth and early nineteenth centuries, better knowledge of world affairs alerted many Japanese thinkers to a foreign crisis in the form of Christian non-military conquest. This in turn heightened their sensitivity to domestic unrest and to the need for relieving distress among the masses by implementing benevolent government and Mencius' "good teachings," which would produce popular unity, integration, and allegiance. Only then could bakufu leaders meet the foreign threat successfully.

Western Learning also forced many Japanese leaders to feel a keen need for *jōi*. Before the nineteenth century, as we have seen, *jōi* had been mainly cultural in nature: It meant sweeping away or eradicating what is barbarian through Confucian edification, so that the common people would not be attracted to evil foreign ways. This would keep the foreign menace from exacerbating domestic instability. Cultural *jōi* was a logical Confucian response to the threat of foreign encroachment disclosed by Western Learning.[2] Students of both Western Learning and Mito Learning supported *jōi*. But by the nineteenth century, *jōi* took on predominantly military overtones: the indiscriminate expulsion of Westerners by force. In this chapter I briefly discuss the proposal for armed expulsion that Takahashi Kageyasu, a Rangakusha, made to the bakufu in 1824. Then I introduce Aizawa's thinking on the same subject as outlined in *New Theses* and in his 1828 anti-Christian tract, *Kikōben* (Some call me disputatious).

RANGAKU AND EXPULSION BY FORCE: TAKAHASHI KAGEYASU

Expulsion by force became bakufu policy in 1825, when it promulgated the so-called No Two Thoughts Expulsion Edict. This nullified earlier edicts issued in 1806 and 1807, which had stipulated that intruding vessels, particularly if disabled, be supplied with fuel and provisions and persuaded to leave peacefully.[3] By contrast, the 1825 edict ordered that foreign ships be fired on and driven off summarily. Yet in a separate edict issued at the same time, the bakufu ordered:

It has always been a violation of bakufu law for persons on Japanese rice transports and fishing vessels to become friendly with crews on foreign ships at sea. At this time it has been newly decreed that foreign ships approaching any inlet be fired on and driven off. Hence, boatmen and fishermen must observe the above prohibition all the more strictly. They should take pains to steer their boats away from and to avoid encountering foreign ships at sea as much as possible. Should [commoners] cover up contacts with foreigners and such facts be brought to light later on, persons involved will be subject to the ultimate punishment. . . .[4]

Clearly, the bakufu sought not only to keep foreigners from approaching Japan, but also to keep commoners in Japan from approaching foreigners. It had to erect a barrier between Japanese commoners and alien barbarians so that the former would not be "transformed" by the latter.

The Rangakusha Takahashi Kageyasu[5] had originally proposed the 1825 Expulsion Edict one year earlier. Takahashi, who read Russian and English in addition to Dutch, argued in a memorial that recent British incursions were perpetrated by whalers whose crews entered Japanese territorial waters on purely private business.[6] He claimed that these foreigners were not representatives of any government and harbored no evil designs on Japan.[7] Because their crews were at sea for months at a time, they constantly suffered from malnutrition and occasionally had to obtain fruits and vegetables. Thus they meant no harm. But although they were told repeatedly not to return, they inevitably kept coming back to acquire foods essential to their health. To fire on them and drive them off without warning might seem to "lack benevolence," Takahashi admitted, but the foreigners had repeatedly taken advantage of the bakufu's good will; their brashness was becoming intolerable. Unless the bakufu adopted a tougher line, he declared, there would be no end to the foreigners' intrusions. Trying to get rid of these foreigners was like "brushing flies away from a bowl of rice."[8] The "stupid barbarians," he wrote, would seek provisions not only from duly constituted bakufu officials, but also through illicit bartering

at sea with "mean and lowly" Japanese commoners, who by nature were atracted to novel and exotic Western goods. During
such clandestine meetings, Japanese commoners and British seamen would become friendly, and the British would begin to
spread Christianity. Takahashi cited at least three instances of
Englishmen distributing Christian books to commoners on
Japanese craft at sea, and asserted, "this proves they intend to
increase such activities."[9] We should note in passing that Takahashi, like Chinese Confucians, used the mouth radical to write
the characters for "England" and "English"—this to express
contempt for their barbaric nature.[10]

From a purely military standpoint as well, Takahashi proposed
that the bakufu should revise its procedures to deal with foreign
vessels which were appearing off Japan's coasts. To mobilize a
great number of troops and set up a grand encampment as was
done at Uraga when the *Brothers* arrived in 1818, he claimed,
was "like using a four-foot cleaver to chop off a chicken's
head." Bakufu officials might think this an imposing show of
strength, but actually such overreactions earned the foreigners'
ridicule and contempt. Not only that, to display this much
force every time a foreign ship appeared offshore placed oner-
ous burdens on both daimyo and commoners.[11]

Takahashi's idea of expulsion by force was, in a sense, an attempt to use his knowledge of the rules governing Western
diplomacy to uphold the Japanese policy of isolation (*sakoku*):

According to the laws of European nations, cannon are
mounted along the coast, and when ships of a nation with
whom trade relations are maintained enter the harbor, signals
are exchanged by flag. When ships from a nation with whom
diplomatic relations are not maintained try to enter, blank
rounds are fired from the nearest cannon on shore. It is customary for those ships to leave the harbor after thus being
informed that entry is not permitted.[12]

Takahashi fully expected the foreigners to leave peaceably. Although the bakufu always had recourse to the use of live ammuni-
tion, he assumed that the need would not arise. He advocated

erecting batteries along northeastern Japan's Pacific coastline
and in Edo Bay, and gave special instructions for doing so:

> Yoshio Chūjirō [a Rangakusha] possesses a barbarian book
> describing the principles of gunnery in detail. I recently com-
> pleted the translation of it that I had planned, and if it would
> be of service to the bakufu, I will quote some passages from it.
>
> Although cannon are most effective when fired from a low
> elevation, the stone ramparts they are mounted on should be
> built high, so that the cannon are visible far out at sea. Then
> the foreign ships may go away without our having to fire at
> all.[13]

If the foreigners approached shore despite these deterrents, they
should be issued a stern warning written in Dutch, English, and
Russian: "The law of our country is that all foreign ships appearing in our waters shall be fired on and driven off (*uchiharau*).
Any ship that has approached in ignorance of this law should
withdraw immediately."[14] For good measure, Takahashi proposed that more detailed pronouncements be delivered through
the Dutch to English officials at their trading station in Bengal.
These pronouncements would inform British authorities about
sakoku and order them to keep their ships from fishing within
ten *ri* (approximately twenty-four miles) of the Japanese
coast.[15]

Takahashi used his translating skills, his knowledge of European protocol, and what he thought to be advanced Western
military technology to formulate a more effective, up-to-date
method of *jōi,* his policy of expulsion by force. In Takahashi's
case, Numata Jirō's thesis that the Rangakusha reinforced bakufu rule by supplying advanced Western technical knowledge
seems borne out by the evidence. Takahashi's main intent was
to use *jōi* to simplify and standardize the bakufu's case-by-case
methods of turning away foreign ships, whose visits were becoming increasingly numerous and irksome.

Takahashi's thinking was unmistakably Confucian. Regarding
disabled foreign vessels, for example, he wrote that out of benevolence, "we must rescue even enemy ships." He continued:

If we [repair and] send it home after giving its crew the usual admonishment about our laws prohibiting visits by their ships to Japanese waters, they truly will admire our benevolence and will tell their countrymen to comply.[16]

Takahashi's attitude toward Japanese commoners was similar to Yūkoku's: They "by nature" are easily alienated from their rulers and readily feel affection for foreigners. They are attracted to "novel and exotic" gadgets that foreigners barter, and are susceptible to the Christian teachings that foreigners spread. The situation had reached the point where foreigners "do not have to entice [our commoners] at all; they naturally feel affection for them." Takahashi noted: "This is an unavoidable part of human sentiment, but we may not permit them to feel this way toward the foreigners [whose presence in Japan] is prohibited."[17] For Takahashi, bakufu law was bakufu law. Only by building barriers, by physically separating aliens and commoners, could bakufu leaders prevent their subjects' "transformation" to barbarian ways. This would end the trouble from abroad and keep Japan's socio-political order intact. Like Arai Hakuseki, Takahashi believed that foreigners came to Japan with no intention of subverting it. And like Hakuseki, he reasoned that their activities inevitably led to subversion nonetheless. Therefore foreigners and their religion had to be shut out.

But the situation in Takahashi's day differed from that of Hakuseki's in one key respect: Foreigners, in Takahashi's own words, kept coming back to Japan like flies to a bowl of rice. Despite his vast knowledge of the West, Takahashi could not comprehend this changed world situation: Unilateral bakufu fiat simply would not keep Westerners away any longer. As Aizawa charged, people like Takahashi "relied on the barbarians' staying away . . . upon something not within our power to control."[18]

Takahashi's views may seem naively foolish, but we must not forget that his was one of the finest minds of the age and that he knew more about the West than any other Japanese then. The basic flaw in his proposal for firing on and driving off Westerners was that he assumed *all* foreigners would obey bakufu commands as docilely as did the Chinese and Dutch.[19] Like Takano Chōei fourteen years later, Takahashi believed that the bakufu needed only to explain the inviolability of *sakoku* as Japanese law and the British would obey it.[20] He viewed English whalers simply as private individuals. He did not think about the state authority to which they would appeal in protest against the arbitrary treatment that Edo meted out.[21] Takahashi could not conceive of an English government redressing its subjects' grievances by demanding not only that the bakufu permit foreign ships to call at Japanese ports, but also that Japan accept the entire system of laws governing relations between Western states. Unlike Holland, Ch'ing China, Korea, and the Ryūkyūs, England and other Western nations would not maintain relations with Japan on the unequal terms that Edo dictated. Quite the contrary, three decades later they forced their own unequal terms on the bakufu.

Fujita Yūkoku was justified in faulting many Rangakusha for their inability to perceive the nature of state authority and national integration in Western countries: "Though bakufu interpreters [like Takahashi] may understand the barbarians' speech and be able to read their writings, they cannot understand the true 'barbarians' nature' (*ryojō*)."[22] Takahashi, for all of his Western expertise, was blind to the spiritual cohesion that turned peoples into nations. That is why he did not take the Western threat from Christianity as seriously as did Yūkoku and Aizawa. Nor did Takahashi understand that the world situation had fundamentally changed by the nineteenth century. To him, the rightness of *sakoku* as well as Edo's ability to uphold it seemed self-evident. The barter-goods that English seamen brought were trifling items they "happened to have on hand,"[23] not a potentially valuable source of national revenue. Christianity posed a possible danger to the existing order, but the bakufu could easily avert that danger by strictly enforcing *sakoku*. Japan's problems would disappear if the bakufu built barriers between "stupid barbarians" and "mean and lowly" Japanese commoners. It could accomplish this by ordering the expulsion of Western ships and constructing coastal batteries visible far out at sea.

Takahashi proposed *jōi* out of exasperation over frequent foreign annoyances, not from a compelling sense of crisis. This basic complacency is underscored by his lack of specific reform plans to alleviate distress at home. Ironically, Aizawa, with far less Western Learning than Takahashi and scant ability to communicate with foreigners, nevertheless discerned the "barbarians' nature" (*ryojō*) more acutely. It was Aizawa who perceived the popular unity and support that lay behind Western strength. Equally important, Aizawa contrasted these sources of foreign strength with domestic factors creating Japanese weakness. He saw clearly that trouble from abroad endangered Japan precisely because distress at home made Japan vulnerable to it. To eliminate this internal vulnerability, Aizawa concluded, the bakufu must emulate Western leaders, who used Christianity as a state religion (*hōkyō*) to secure popular unity and allegiance. Let us examine Aizawa's ideas on these subjects as expounded in *New Theses* and "Some Call Me Disputatious" (*Kikōben*).

THE WORLD SITUATION IN 1825 AS SEEN IN "NEW THESES"

New Theses contains five treatises: "What is Essential to a Nation" ("Kokutai"), "World Affairs" ("Keisei"), "The Barbarians' Nature" ("Ryojō"), "National Defense" ("Shugyo"), and "A Long-Range Policy" ("Chōkei"). To facilitate analysis we can divide these treatises in two groups: (1) "World Affairs" and "The Barbarians' Nature" contain the fruits of Aizawa's Western Learning, in these he describes the unprecedented crisis facing Japan in 1825. "National Defense" outlines Aizawa's concrete measures to meet that crisis. (2) "Kokutai" and "A Long-Range Policy" explain what a people need to be a nation, stipulating which factors had created spiritual unity in Japan's antiquity, why that unity later disappeared, and how the bakufu could and must recover it.

Historians, based on the certainty that comes from hindsight, usually deprecate "World Affairs" and "The Barbarians' Nature" as inaccurate, outdated sources of knowledge about the West.[24] Viewed from the 1850s and 1860s, it is undeniable that Aizawa's information on world affairs was long out of date: No informed

Japanese in that era believed the Mogul empire to be a world power. Likewise, many specific proposals that Aizawa made in "National Defense" to strengthen Japan, such as returning warriors to the land or reestablishing a rice economy, were reactionary and would have weakened her against the foreign powers. But we must remember that Aizawa drew up *New Theses* in 1825, a decade and a half before the Opium War. Though some of his specific defense proposals and information on world affairs were outdated, his fundamental messages possessed lasting value. They were (1) the world situation facing Japan is dissimilar in crucial ways to anything in her history, (2) the Western barbarians are unlike those dealt with up to now, and (3) the bakufu must devise new policies to overcome the unprecedented danger it faces. It was these fundamental messages, not Aizawa's misinformation, that late Tokugawa leaders and *shishi* took to heart. In 1849, for example, Kawaji Toshiakira, though generally critical of *New Theses*, wrote, "The author . . . knows not only of Japan, but of foreign countries as well. . . . Of his seven sections, 'Ryojō' (The Barbarians' Nature) is by far the best."[25]

In "World Affairs," Aizawa wrote that because of recent Russian and British encroachments, "those seeking to defend our territory cannot afford to be ignorant of changed world conditions or unconcerned with policies to deal with them."[26] He did not think that Westerners posed a danger of mass invasion; Japan faced primarily a non-military threat. A knowledge of Western affairs and world geography had given him a healthy respect for Russian or Turkish armed forces, but only when they fought against other Eurasian continental powers. In the final analysis, he still believed that the sea effectively guarded Japan against any direct, full-scale, military takeover. Russia, Turkey, Britain, and Spain could not assemble assault fleets large enough to conquer Japan by storm;[27] there was little danger of all-out invasion and occupation similar to that posed by Mongol forces in the thirteenth century. To be sure, Western military power was a factor to be reckoned with, but not the most menacing factor. During the 1810s and 1820s, when unarmed whalers were the main intruders into Japanese waters, this appraisal—shared by Takahashi Kageyasu—was not rash or unrealistic.

Takahashi had dealt with the Christian threat almost in an offhand manner; Aizawa not only took it seriously, he analyzed its nature and causes with sophistication and thoroughness. Aizawa mainly feared an indirect Western takeover of Japan through Christian "transformation." The Westerners would employ Christianity, cultural assimilation, and economic inveiglement to fill their ranks; first they would capture the Ezo tribes in the north and other primitive peoples on Pacific islands to Japan's south, and then seduce the "stupid commoners" in Japan proper. In *New Theses* he carried this reasoning one step further: After capturing Japan through Christianity, Russia would recruit Japanese forces to help conquer the Ch'ing empire.[28]

Aizawa displayed no small respect for the Western barbarians when he attributed to them an ability to employ the strategy used by Chao Ch'ung-kuo and Chu-ko Liang. Like these legendary Chinese geniuses of military tactics, Western generals procured provisions in the enemy's homeland and enlarged their own armies by first taking over small states and conscripting captured enemy troops.[29] The Westerners also practiced *Sun Tzu*'s dictums: They "defeated enemy armies without resorting to battle, and they conquered territories intact, which is the best of all possible victories."[30] Thus, Aizawa was fundamentally at odds with Takahashi (who belittled foreigners as *merely* "stupid barbarians") in assessing the Westerners' capacity to wreak havoc. Aizawa, too, denigrated Westerners, calling them "stupid barbarians," "dogs and goats," and other like names. But such blustering and vilification should not obscure the fact that he took their threat in dead earnest. To counter the enemy's astute strategy directed against Japan (and, ultimately, the Ch'ing empire), Aizawa asserted the need for a consistent, sustained program of religious and cultural "counter-transformation" supplemented by armed might. Such a long-range policy, he claimed, originally had been devised and carried out in antiquity by Amaterasu, Jimmu, Sujin, and other sage emperors (*shinsei*). Aizawa's knowledge of the West led him to believe that European leaders recently had appropriated this long-range policy for themselves and had turned it against Japan; whereas in Japan, it had fallen into disuse. Herein lay the West's non-military threat and Japan's vulnerability to it.

World affairs, like other political matters, are subject to continual change, Aizawa claimed. They must be understood by carefully observing and analyzing both historical and contemporary conditions. Japan's leaders had to revise old, rigid conceptions of the world order and of the barbarians. They had to make these views conform to new situations; only thus could the bakufu formulate appropriate new policies. In "World Affairs," "The Barbarians' Nature," and "National Defense," Aizawa displayed his understanding of a changed world. Not only were the Westerners of contemporary times materially stronger and technologically more advanced than barbarians in ages past, they had made great strides in the realm of spirit:

> As civilization (*jimbun*) steadily progresses, even barbarians partake of its blessings and learn [the technique of] creating religious injunctions and precepts to guide their peoples. Their towering fortresses surrounded by deep moats are a far cry from their crude huts and tents of yesteryear; their huge warships and cannon are a vast advance over their mounted bowmen of bygone days.[31]

For Westerners as well as for Japanese, "civilization" had progressed in a linear and cumulative fashion.[32] The biggest difference between earlier barbarians and those of today, Aizawa argued, was the unity and strength that contemporary Westerners derived from Christianity and Islam:

> In eras past, their only means of winning and maintaining obedience among their vast hordes was to lure with promises of booty and to intimidate with displays of force. As a result, those hordes lacked integration and permanence. But now the religions (*kyōhō*) of Islam and Christianity have provided Western leaders with these two elements and more. Today, each barbarian tribe, while maintaining its own territory, allies

itself with all others to convert the entire world to their religion. This is indeed a far cry from the past.[33]

We have seen that new knowledge of the West forced Aizawa to question, at least to himself, the notion of Japan as Middle Kingdom Civilization and to look at her geographical position in global perspective. Politically and militarily, he now had to size up Japan against six foreign powers. In stark contrast to Taka-hashi Kageyasu's complacence, Aizawa's appraisal of Japan's place in the world was a grim one. The bakufu's policy of uni-lateral national isolation was becoming difficult to uphold. Japan's fate was less of Japan's own making than contingent on developments in far-off lands and on decisions made by foreign rulers over which the bakufu had little or no control.

Aizawa compared the seven great empires that dominated the contemporary world to the seven great kingdoms of China's ancient Warring States period (403–221 B.C.).[34] In so doing, he disclosed his true assessment of Japan's international standing. Japan was in a position even more hazardous than that of the weak state of Yen; more precisely, it was analogous to Chou,[35] a tiny kingdom whose precarious existence hinged on the toler-ance of other, greater powers though its cultural tradition was the richest and most venerable. He compared Russia to Ch'in, ancient China's eventual unifier. For Aizawa, Russia, Turkey (the Ottoman Empire), and the Ch'ing empire were the world's greatest powers in 1825; they would be the decisive participants in the upcoming struggle for global supremacy. Aizawa's knowl-edge of things Western forced him to recognize that even lesser powers such as Britain and Spain enjoyed a clear edge over Japan in precious metals and raw materials due to their posses-sion of overseas colonies.[36]

Russia, though suffering serious military setbacks on its west-ern front, remained the world's most powerful empire, and was building up strength for a final drive to unify the world by sub-duing its long-standing nemesis, Turkey.[37] But before that, Aizawa believed, Russia would try to dispose of the Ch'ing em-pire on its eastern front. To accomplish this, it first would use Christianity to win over the Ezo territories north of Japan in

111

concert with its British and Spanish allies, who were striving to capture Pacific islands to Japan's south. Russia and Britain then would subvert Japan proper by Christianizing its "stupid commoners," and would beguile a new generation of "Japanese raiders" (*wakō*) into attacking and weakening China. With the Ch'ing thus crippled, Russia could deliver the coup de grace from the north.[38] Aizawa's analysis reduces Japan to little more than a pawn in Russia's chess game of world conquest; Japan was a third-rate power, more affected by, than actively shaping, world events. Indeed, Japan's national security seems to hinge on the Ch'ing and Turkish empires' ability to contain Russian expansion on the Eurasian continent.[39] Aizawa notes with more than a little alarm: "The great empires are dividing up the earth. Today we find ourselves alone in a hostile world, like the defenders of a solitary fortress under siege by enemy forces."[40]

"NEW THESES" ON DOMESTIC REFORM

Aizawa's knowledge of the West informed him about conditions in European nations that contributed to their strength. After comparing conditions abroad with those at home, he formulated administrative reforms—some of which were quite radical—to reinforce bakufu rule and Japan's socio-political order against foreign encroachment. His vituperation against the West, far from showing contempt, expressed admiration and envy:

> Barbarian leaders possess the nature of dogs and goats. . . . But their customs are savage and they constantly wage war; they could not establish and maintain their states through a policy of keeping their subjects ignorant and weak [as we do]. Hence they register and conscript their subjects into armed service and further augment their ranks with other barbarian peoples [whom they convert] on overseas campaigns.[41]

Related to the Western leaders' capacity to cultivate unity and allegiance in their peoples through Christianity, Aizawa here perceives that their national strength stemmed from an ability to conscript large segments of their populations into military service. In short, Western leaders indoctrinated their peoples with a state religion and thus inspired them to enlist and fight valiantly in mass national armies. This situation contrasted starkly with the perception that Fujita Yūkoku had of Japanese commoners: not merely refusing to support bakufu and domain leaders, but eagerly joining the enemy's ranks. Aizawa realized that Japan's present "feudal" (hōken) state system, laid down by ancient sage emperors and reinstituted by Tokugawa Ieyasu, made it impossible "to conscript commoners again [as was done in antiquity]."[42] He fully shared Yūkoku's fears about Japanese commoners, writing, "commoners today are totally lacking in pluck and can hardly be expected to achieve great exploits in a battlefield situation."[43] But when "transformed" by Christianity,

> Our people would consider it an honor and a privilege to die for this foreign god; and this willingness to die, this fearless-ness, would make them fit for battle. Our people would gladly cast their riches into the sacrificial coffers of this foreign god, and those riches would finance barbarian campaigns.[44]

Western leaders did not keep their subjects ignorant and weak. But the Edo bakufu, following policies laid down by Ieyasu in another era, was doing just that. In Ieyasu's day, the realm suf-fered from too much military might: That made it difficult to uphold order. Therefore, after carefully weighing conditions in the realm, Ieyasu adopted a policy "to weaken the empire and make commoners ignorant; and he succeeded on both counts."[45] Aizawa concluded that what had once been an astute policy, now helped make Japan vulnerable to foreign encroachment. But we should note that Western Learning helped him reach that conclusion by informing him about the West's strengths; this invited contrasts with factors in Japanese politics and so-ciety that created weakness.

The same can be said for his analysis of problems stemming from the bakufu-imposed system of daimyo alternate attendance in Edo (sankin kōtai) and the concentration of samurai in castle-towns. These measures, too, Ieyasu had adopted in a different era—when powerful daimyo on the periphery presented the greatest threat to bakufu security.[46] At that time it was wise to

113

concentrate daimyo in Edo and in castletowns, make them ex-
pend their wealth in corvée labor and extravagant consumption,
and thereby prevent them from cultivating strength in outlying
areas far from bakufu control.[47] But in 1825, that threat to
bakufu authority no longer existed; old policies calculated to
produce daimyo weakness and deprivation only exacerbated
contemporary problems.[48] Thus, Aizawa wrote, "Can we
blithely ignore the need to adjust state policies to meet the demands of changing times?"[49] His knowledge of conditions in
Western nations and of changed global realities awakened him
to the anachronisms in bakufu policies, and made him realize
that responsible leaders in Edo could not remain complacent
about the situation. This was why he proposed that the bakufu
itself seize the initiative to revise outdated policies and push
through drastic reforms:

> Even if the bakufu insists on maintaining the realm by means
> of obsolete traditional measures, our coastal areas, for in-
> stance, are weakly defended. Should a particular daimyo's do-
> main be attacked and suffer defeat [by foreigners], the bakufu
> would be forced to send him back to his domain to strengthen
> his forces anyway. It is far wiser to take the initiative and
> send him back to begin with, rather than wait until conditions
> deteriorate to the humiliating point where there is no other
> choice.[50]

In addition to reforming the *sankin kōtai* system and relaxing
other traditional policies that weakened and impoverished the
daimyo domains, Aizawa advocated stationing warriors in
coastal garrisons. He also urged creating coast guard forces to
engage enemy vessels at sea rather than rely solely on cannon
to repulse them as Hayashi Shihei and Takahashi Kageyasu had
proposed earlier.[51]

But more important, he suggested creating a form of peasant
militia to supplement the warrior-class garrison forces.[52] This
is one crucial issue on which Aizawa's Western Learning clashed
with his prior political allegiances. Since he knew that the
strength of Western nations stemmed in large part from their
leaders' ability to indoctrinate and recruit commoners into

armed service, Aizawa could not help concluding that the Tokugawa system of hereditary social statuses hindered self-strengthening in Japan. He no doubt envied Western leaders and wished that the bakufu could institute similar systems to indoctrinate and enlist Japanese commoners. But such a reform would entail repudiating the hereditary distinction between warrior and commoner (*heinō bunri*), a structural principle that the Tokugawa bakuhan order based itself on. This, of course, Aizawa would never do.

A close examination of his proposed militia reveals that he would allow peasants to become sentinels in the garrisons, not regular troops.[53] He had little hope that commoners would render distinguished service, writing, "Our only enlistees would be feeble old men or indolent delinquents, and neither would do us much good."[54] Commoners would simply warn of the enemy's approach, and refrain from collaborating. This clearly was a halfway measure: to have peasants serve in Japan's armed forces, but not as full-fledged soldiers. It stemmed from Aizawa's half-hearted attitude toward Japanese commoners. He wished to entrust them with a share of the nation's defense, but did not trust them enough to make it a crucial share.[55] At the bottom of this dilemma lay the fundamental contradiction between what a knowledge of the West told Aizawa must be done to strengthen Japan, and what his commitment to the existing Tokugawa socio-political order stopped him from doing. In 1825, when the West posed no great military threat, such halfway measures and half-hearted attitudes sufficed; after Perry's intrusion in 1853, they would not.

Aizawa thus owed much to Western Learning for his understanding of contemporary international affairs and conditions in foreign countries, as outlined in "World Affairs" and "The Barbarians' Nature." This changed view of world conditions led him to examine traditional bakufu policies and existing institutions in a critical light, and to devise bold new plans for creating military strength. Aizawa's proposals would prove insufficient to meet Japan's needs after 1853, but given the social and political conditions of 1825, his ideas seemed extreme, not too mild. Aizawa called on the bakufu to abandon Ieyasu's policies of weakening and impoverishing the daimyo—measures instituted solely to uphold Tokugawa supremacy—because they made Japan as a whole vulnerable to foreign encroachment.

Western Learning had five significant ramifications in Aizawa's thought. First, he began to recognize in a blurry and imperfect way the emerging nation-state (or empire) system in a global context. Second, he acknowledged the cultural advances achieved by barbarian rulers, advances that enabled them to mobilize their peoples spiritually in pursuit of national goals. Third, he learned that no nation could hope to be a great power without winning the voluntary support and allegiance of its people. Fourth, he tacitly admitted that Japan had failed in this task: Japan was a small, weak nation needing drastic reform. Finally, he realized—but could not openly admit—that pushing these reforms through to their logical conclusions might entail dismantling the existing Tokugawa bakuhan order.

THE SAGES AND THEIR "EXPEDIENT DEVICE"

The Western barbarians had achieved national strength; Japan had not. Aizawa comprehended this failure in historical perspective and in terms of human emotional needs. As he put it, Western leaders had "stolen the sages' *ch'üan*" while Japanese leaders had let it slip away. But what was this "expedient device," the *ch'üan*, that the ancient sages had possessed? Just how had Western leaders stolen it? Did this theft make them equivalent to the sages, at least in some crucial respects? To answer these questions and fully understand the implications of Aizawa's new proposals, we must look closely into the meaning of this key Chinese term, *ch'üan*. Aizawa's anti-Christian tract, *Kikōben* (1828) provides important clues.

The tract's title, "Some Call Me Disputatious," is taken from the "T'eng Wen Kung" chapter of *Mencius*. In that chapter, Mencius places himself in a tradition of sagely personages, Yao, Shun, Yü, and Confucius, who did battle with floods, wild beasts, barbarians, and heretical teachings that repeatedly arose to victimize men in Middle Kingdom Civilization during history. In Mencius' own time (372-289 B.C.?), the new heresies of Yang

Chu and Mo Tzu called for extirpation. Hence, he railed, "Some call me disputatious, but do I have any choice?" Aizawa adopted this line from Mencius's harangue to project the image of himself as a staunch moral teacher seeking to subdue this latest and most dangerous heresy, Christianity. The essay, composed in classical Chinese, is a dialogue between a Chinese master of the Confucian classics and one of his disciples. In response to the disciple's query, "Why is the 'True Way' upheld so feebly while evil heresies flourish in the world?", the Chinese master (Aizawa) replies: "The barbarians have only one technique, but are able to expound their ideas and beguile stupid commoners because they have stolen the sages' *ch'üan* and use it to take advantage of what is easy to do. . . ." How should we interpret the meaning of "the sages' *ch'üan*"? And how do Western leaders use it to "take advantage of what is easy to do"?

Although it would be a mistake to suppose that Aizawa adhered to Ogyū Sorai's views in all matters, recent scholarship attests that Sorai influenced him considerably.[56] The "Way of the former sage kings" according to Sorai consisted of ritual, music, laws, and institutions.[57] The ritual and music were of cardinal importance, since for Sorai, the sovereign should be a "ruler-edifier" who induced acceptance of his teachings by utilizing *ch'üan* rather than by relying on words:

> The former sage kings realized that words alone were insufficient to edify people, and therefore created ritual and music. They realized that political institutions and laws alone were insufficient to bring peace and stability to the people, and therefore created ritual and music to exercise *kwa*, "an inducing influence" over them. . . . When one follows ritual, one comes under this "inducing influence" and unconsciously obeys the laws of the sovereign. How can any evil result? Could political institutions and laws ever be as good [i.e., efficacious] as this?[58]

According to Sorai, *kwa*, or what I have thus far translated as "moral suasion" or "transformation," should not take place through wordy explanations or ethical injunctions; instead, the ruler should achieve it through the "reality of ritual

117

performance." Hence, I translate Sorai's *kwa* as "an inducing influence." Through it, the performer of ritual induced those viewing it to enter a psychological state of oneness with him and to carry out the deeds that he willed. Each sage king in antiquity, Sorai held, brought the people under his inducing influence through ritual, and thereby made sure that they "unconsciously obeyed" his laws. Aizawa termed this potency "the mystical, efficacious function of ritual and music."[59] For Sorai and Aizawa, the purposeful utilization of ritual to produce an inducing influence was one important element of *ch'üan*. Sorai had written:

> The harm stemming from Tzu-ssu and Mencius is that they desired to explain their views thoroughly and make understanding easy for the listeners. This is the way of the litigant, one who seeks to get his views accepted quickly. In this case, *ch'üan* lies with the listeners. Such is not the Way to edify people. *Ch'üan* lies with the edifier since he follows the Way of the Ruler-Edifier. The skilled edifier always ensnares his learners with technique (*jutsu*), makes them feel long at ease, alters their perceptions, and induces them to change their ideas. Hence, the edifier does not rely on words, yet manages to make his learners understand as a matter of course. . . .
>
> This is what the former sage kings and Confucius did. The former sage kings did not explain ritual and music in words, but rather demonstrated these in reality. When we reach Mencius, we find that he debates in an annoying, domineering fashion, trying to argue his listeners into submission. He who seeks to make his listeners submit through wordy explanations has already failed to make them submit voluntarily. A teaching is something dispensed to those who believe in the edifier. People [in antiquity] believed in the former sage kings, and the disciples of Confucius believed in him. . . . Through wordy arguments, Mencius sought to make people—who did not originally believe in him—believe in him.[60]

Sorai here asserts that in the era before Tzu-ssu (492–431 B.C.) and Mencius, the sage kings and Confucius had rejected polemics as a means of getting their ideas accepted. For a teacher or ruler-edifier to rely on polemics meant that *ch'üan*—the ability to weigh pros and cons, to deliberate on the propriety or impropriety of a matter, and to decide which course of action was expedient to pursue—lay with the listeners. Since these listeners were skeptical of the ruler-edifier to begin with, they presumed to judge whether or not his teachings were valid and warranted compliance. By contrast, Confucius and the ancient sages recognized the need to win the people's unquestioning trust before edification could take place. They would "ensnare" the people with the "technique" of ritual and music, and thus place the people under their inducing influence. This caused the people to obey without realizing that their obedience was being manipulated. In this sense, *ch'üan* lay with the sages: It was they who weighed conditions in a given situation and decided what was proper for the learners to do. Since they already had made the people believe in them, they produced compliance without opposition. This *ch'üan,* Sorai argued, rightly belonged *only* to the sages: "For [mere] men to seek to seize the *ch'üan* of the former sage kings is stark impudence, a grand delusion, or else a gross overestimation of their own [human] capacities."[61]

Aizawa's ideas on the sages' *ch'üan,* as expressed in *Kikōhen,* were basically the same as Sorai's:

In general, human sentiment is such that man cannot but feel reverent awe for the power of Heaven. The sages' idea of Reverence for Heaven meant serving Heaven as one would serve one's parents, placing forebears in the position of Heaven, and then serving them as one would serve it. Ritual and music exist for this purpose, and these devices for "making the people follow the Way" are found in it [the sages' "Reverence for Heaven"]. Therefore when the people respectfully serve their sovereign with the same reverent awe that they feel toward the power of Heaven, sovereign and Heaven become one, and the ruler mercifully nurtures the people. This is the sages' Great *Ch'üan* for ordering the realm and ruling the people.

But the barbarians have set up a false god and beguile their peoples with it. Therefore, they are able to make their peoples

119

revere rulers [i.e., themselves] with the same reverent awe that those peoples feel for Heaven. Though their teachings are not the true teachings found in nature, these are sufficiently cogent to let them steal the sages' *ch'üan*. . . . They make [their peoples] look upon them as one with Heaven.[62]

The above discussion of *ch'üan* by both Sorai and Aizawa should allow us to grasp what they meant by it. *Ch'üan* consisted of three elements: (1) "weighing" (*hakaru*), or giving careful consideration to the relative merits of all possible courses of action before determining which is proper to follow,[63] (2) the "provisional" or "expedient" (*kari no, gon*) implementation[64] or adoption of a measure deemed proper to attain calculated ends, and (3) in Japanese Confucianism, the idea that *ch'üan* should be a "prerogative" (*kengen*) that the ancient sages alone might exercise.[65]

Aizawa argued that the sages had utilized ritual and music as a "device" that accorded with the requirements of human sentiments. In their wisdom, they knew that all human beings had, among other needs, an irrepressible longing to revere Heaven—another point Sorai stressed. A survey of Aizawa's works shows that he considered the following attributes to be part of the common people's nature:

To fear Heaven and revere the spirits is inherent in man's nature.[66]

The natural sentiments of the people are that they cannot help coveting personal gain and standing in awe of the spirits.[67]

At this time of the year [spring, the planting season], it is a natural human sentiment for the people to pray for an abundant harvest. For this reason, invocations to the Buddhas and to the Christian Heaven take place.[68]

The masses by nature cannot avoid an unconscious and irrepressible abhorrence of the world to come. Unless they put their minds at ease and attain a measure of self-composure, they will inevitably believe in doctrines of [paradise and hell in] the world to come.[69]

In short, the people had certain emotional needs: to overcome their anxiety toward death and the afterworld; to cope with their fear of Heaven, spirits, and other supernatural forces; and to seek assurances of personal gain and prosperity in the present life. As he phrased it in *New Theses,* the people were in need of a spiritual source of reliance within. The ruler-edifier was supposed to fulfill such emotional needs by using the sages' ritual and music: "The responsibility for performing these rituals; that is, for recompensing Heaven, worshipping ancestors, praying for good fortune, and eliminating calamities and evils rests with rulers."[70] Through this "device" of ritual and music, a ruler followed Confucius' maxim to "make the people follow the Way," and induced them to "serve their sovereign with the same reverent awe that they feel toward the power of Heaven."[71] In other words, the ruler performed ritual in a calculated manner to meet his people's emotional needs: "[Man] is conscious of his own life and death, particularly when faced with the prospect of dying. That is why the sages elucidated the proper religious rituals."[72]

It had been the sages' prerogative to establish ritual and music as a device to facilitate government. Rulers in later ages or alien lands might—indeed, ought to—utilize that device. But they should not presume to invent and use new, heretical forms of the device as the Europeans had done in Christianity. In Aizawa's mind, Christianity's false doctrines of Heaven and hell were no different from the concepts of heavenly paradise and hell in Buddhism. Although Aizawa did not share the admiration for Indian pseudo-sages that the author of *Honsaroku* felt,[73] both thinkers held the same conception of *ch'üan,* as here stated in that work:

Shaka, knowing that India was difficult to govern because its people were not of a docile nature . . . carefully considered how best to deal with Indian customs. He made up the fictions of heavenly paradise (*gokuraku*) and hell (*jigoku*) as an expedient method of government. He taught the people that if they did good in this world, they would be born in heavenly paradise, but if they did evil, they would fall into hell. In

121

truth, heavenly paradise and hell do not exist; these were [invented] for the purpose of governing the realm. The mind of the Buddha was indeed great: This idea corresponds to the principle of government. It is *ch'üan tao:* the "Way of Expedient Method." [74]

In Aizawa's eyes, Western barbarian leaders had done the same thing. But they were more clever because they instituted and used their religious *ch'üan* as an integral part of government. In *Kikōben,* as we recall, Aizawa stated, "They have stolen the sages' *ch'üan* and [use it to] take advantage of what is easy to do." [75] In *New Theses* he expressed the same sentiments:

> [Japanese commoners] are attracted to pernicious doctrines from abroad because they need a basis of spiritual reliance within. It is no surprise that the followers of evil [the Christian barbarians] *take advantage of this spiritual void* and this fear of the hereafter to deceive our commoners into embracing their notions of paradise and hell. [76] (emphasis added)

Like the Indian Buddha, Western pseudo-sages had set up a "false god"; they had created a type of ritual and music that resembled those of the true sages closely enough to deceive "stupid commoners." [77] The efficacy of this Christian ritual and music in fact equaled that of the true sages: Barbarian leaders "made their peoples revere rulers with the same reverent awe that those peoples [naturally] feel for Heaven." [78] This stolen *ch'üan* allowed them to gain popular unity and support at home; this was the true source of their strength. And moreover, Christian ritual and music permitted Western leaders to win over local populations on overseas campaigns:

> In recent years, the wily barbarians have established ethical precepts of their own that sound very much like the genuine ones prescribed [by the sages] in antiquity. Armed with their Way of wickedness, they eat into the people's hearts and minds. The barbarians' teachings are not [Mencius'] "good teachings," but they pass these off as "teachings" just the same, and this allows them "to capture the people's hearts." [79]

Through this notion of the sages' *ch'üan* and its supposed theft and utilization by barbarian leaders, Aizawa grasped what was essential to a nation's sovereignty and territorial integrity—political concepts beginning to take shape in the minds of nineteenth-century Japanese thinkers.

"KOKUTAI" AND "A LONG-RANGE POLICY"

Aizawa's *New Theses* explained how the bakufu might create national strength and wealth in 1825 to meet the Western threat posed mainly by Christianity. This threat, though unique in its magnitude, was not unprecedented in Japanese history. Earlier, Buddhism had entered Japan.

> The practitioners of this doctrine sought to transform our Divine Land into another India, to convert innocent subjects of our Middle Kingdom into followers of the Indian barbarians. When transformed by barbarism within, how can "what is essential to a nation" (*hokutai*) remain intact? ... Due to their adoration of India, those members [of the True Pure Land Sect] forsook our Middle Kingdom; due to their devotion to Buddhist clerics, they forsook ruler and parent.[80]

Partly because of this earlier Buddhist "transformation" of Japanese customs, beliefs, and values, Japan's *kokutai,* or "what was essential for it to be a nation,"[81] had been gravely endangered. Heresy and dissension within created national weakness which foreign enemies could exploit. In 1825, Aizawa feared that subversion by alien heresies, not invasion by Western military forces, chiefly threatened the independence and integrity of Japan's bakuhan state. Aizawa's knowledge of the West had shown him that a nation must possess something of more basic importance than wealth and armed strength:

> Just what is essential (*tai/t'i*) for a land and people to be a nation (*kuni*)? Without four limbs, a man is not a man. Similarly, a nation also possesses some essence [or requisite and defining entity that makes it a nation] (*kokutai*).

Certain people stress the need to enrich our country and strengthen our arms in order to defend our borders. But the foreign beasts now seek *to take advantage of the fact that people in outlying areas crave a source of spiritual reliance,* and furtively seduce our commoners into betraying us. Should the barbarians win over *our people's hearts and minds,* they will have captured the realm without a skirmish. Then the wealth and strength that these people stress will no longer be ours to employ. In effect, we would provide arms for the brigand and provisions for the bandit. What a pity if, after all our meticulous planning and painstaking effort, we merely ended up joining the enemy's ranks![81] (emphasis added)

Wealth and strength were worthless unless Japan's people willingly placed these resources at the bakufu's disposal. Conversely, if foreigners won the people's allegiance, Japan's autonomy and territorial integrity would cease. Securing "our people's hearts and minds" was essential to the bakufu as a national government. Sage emperors had accomplished this in antiquity: "All people in the realm were of one heart and mind; they were so endeared of their rulers that separation was unbearable."[82] This national spiritual unity—the voluntary affection and trust that commoners felt for their rulers—was what Aizawa basically meant by *kokutai* in *New Theses.* As Bitō Masahide argues in his seminal articles on Mito Learning, rulers produced this affection, trust, allegiance, and unity from above through manipulation.[83] The threat from Christianity and the West would be overcome only when bakufu rulers achieved this original *kokutai.* Only then would wealth and strength take on meaning for the nation.

Western rulers recently had "stolen the sages' *ch'üan*" and learned the technique of creating religious doctrines to instill unity and loyalty in their peoples. In stark contrast, Japanese rulers had neglected and lost this *ch'üan.* Aizawa, the historian, delved into Japan's past to discover what had gone wrong and how to set it right again. His conclusion was: "The Way that Amaterasu used in antiquity to administer the realm, to achieve spiritual unity among the people, and to endear them inseparably to their rulers can be used today."[84] In "Kokutai" and "A

Long-Range Policy," he clarified how this Way had produced popular allegiance in antiquity and proposed how to recover it.

Yūkoku and Aizawa held that the sages' original intent (whether they be Chinese or Japanese) was to nourish the people, eliminate hardship from their lives, and provide ethical instruction and spiritual fulfillment.[85] Basing himself on myths found in *Kojiki* and *Nihon shoki,* Aizawa asserted that Amaterasu bestowed the gift of rice upon her people because of her great concern for their welfare.[86] Thus, rice was her sacred gift to the Japanese people alone. As her descendents, they were obliged to treasure and revere this cereal, to display unceasing gratitude to her, and to extend this feeling of gratitude to her lineal descendents on the imperial throne.[87] Amaterasu also had provided the Japanese people with silk to make clothing[88] and with other items that made daily life less toilsome. As a result of this original gift of rice bestowed by Amaterasu, and in part because Japan was climatically suited to the cultivation of grains, Japanese customs and folkways had been cast along certain distinctive lines: "Our people do not eat flesh and drink blood as the barbarians do; hence, our country has been known as 'The Land of Ripening Rice Crests' since ancient times."[89] Such particularities of diet and dress, Aizawa held, were an important part of Japan's *kokutai* and had to be preserved.

Amaterasu's imperial descendents also had established *Kuni no miyatsuko, Agata nushi,* and other administrative organs in antiquity. These organs governed the people and enabled them to enjoy personal security within a stable social framework. In this manner, sage emperors had laid down a political and social order that Aizawa labeled "feudal" (*hōken*). First created in antiquity, it was reestablished by Tokugawa Ieyasu. This *hōken* system corresponded to the bakuhan state, was an integral part of Japan's *kokutai,* and as such, might not be altered fundamentally.

Finally, Amaterasu provided her people with ethical instruction. This was not expressed in words; it was embodied in the Three Imperial Regalia and conveyed through religious rituals. The jewel, mirror, and sword, embodied virtue, wisdom, and courage respectively.[90] The Daijō, Niiname, and other rituals were means to teach loyalty and filial devotion.[91] This was the Way that, according to Aizawa, Amaterasu had established in antiquity—nourishing the people, eliminating hardship from their lives, and providing them with ethical instruction and spiritual fulfillment.[92] The last aspect of this Way—Amaterasu's methods of edifying her people and meeting their emotional needs—is the most important to consider here.

Aizawa conceived of Amaterasu and early Japanese sage emperors such as Jimmu, Tenji, and Sujin, as identical to Yao, Shun, the Duke of Chou, and other former sage kings of the Confucian pantheon because they all had created rites and music as the Way to facilitate government.[93] Aizawa's ideas on the Way and sageliness did not derive solely from Sorai. With regard to Amaterasu and her Way, Aizawa wrote:

> In antiquity, *Amaterasu (Tenso) established teachings (oshie) in accordance with the "spirit-like processes of nature" (shen tao)*, thus elucidating loyalty and filial devotion and prescribing the rules of conduct by which men live. It is by means of these teachings that the realm can be maintained for all eternity.[94] (emphasis added)
>
> In antiquity, *Amaterasu (Shinsei) established teachings (oshie) in accordance with the "spirit-like processes of nature" (shen tao)*, and thereby captured the hearts of the people. Her teachings were the only doctrine by which popular allegiances could be secured.[95] (emphasis added)

The Way that Amaterasu established was *shen tao*. Aizawa took the above phrases verbatim from the *Book of Changes:*

> When they [the sages] gaze upon the spirit-like processes of nature *(shen tao)*, the seasons unfold in proper order. *The sages established teachings in accordance with these spirit-like processes of nature (shen tao)*, and the realm submits [in proper order].[96] (emphasis added)

Aizawa here reveals his intellectual debts to Yamazaki Ansai and Asami Keisai for the idea of "coincidental correspondences": He substitutes the Sun Goddess, Amaterasu, (*Tenso, Shinsei*) for "the sages," and inserts "loyalty and filial devotion" as the specific teachings that she established "in accordance with *shen tao*." For Aizawa, as for Asami Keisai, the Way revealed itself coincidentally in both Chinese and Japanese classics: China's *shen tao* and Japan's *shintō* were separate but essentially similar Ways.

By means of such sagely teachings, Aizawa believed, the realm could be induced to submit voluntarily. And so it was in antiquity. But how? Following Sorai, Aizawa writes, "This ultimate ethic of loyalty and filial devotion existed without overt expression and was unconsciously adhered to by all in antiquity."[97] In that era, Japan's sage emperors gained the people's willing compliance to the teachings of Amaterasu, founder of their imperial line. They did this not by resorting to arguments or explanations, but by employing the mystical, suggestive power of ritual:

> In antiquity, religious ritual corresponded to government, administration was ultimately identical with edification, and the people looked to their leaders for the fulfillment of their desires. . . . There was a ritual for every meaning His Majesty sought to convey, and through these rituals, the people became aware that the Emperor's [heartfelt wishes were] intended to benefit them. They rejoiced in this realization and their loyal and filial devotion were made pure and directed to but one object.[98]

In this manner, the sage emperors of antiquity achieved spiritual unity; "each person was loyal to his own ruler and all revered the imperial court." Through state-prescribed rituals, each sage emperor conveyed the meaning of "service to Heaven," "reverence for ancestors," "love of the people," and gratitude to Amaterasu for her original gifts of rice and silk which nurtured and clothed his people.[99] The imperial descendants of Amaterasu communicated this gratitude not through explanations or lectures, but through the Niiname and Daijō rituals, during which each emperor personally consumed newly harvested grain every fall and at the beginning of his reign. By viewing the emperor himself cherishing this precious commodity bestowed by Amaterasu, all persons who witnessed the ritual could not but come under his inducing influence (*kwa*). The

127

people became one with him in reverent appreciation for blessings received, and they submitted to the Way without question. This was the sages' *ch'üan* for securing the people's trust and allegiance.

Another important characteristic of *kokutai,* or the spiritual unity and popular allegiance which had made Japan strong and wealthy in antiquity, was that all spiritual authority stemmed from the imperial court: It outlawed other teachings and ritual practices as heresies. "The performance of all religious rituals was subject to Court control, and the myriad deities of the land were integrated within a [centralized] system."[100] Former sage emperors had worshipped local deities and heroes by distributing cloth offerings (*heihaku*) to shrines in the provinces, and thereby inspired reverent loyalty in people living there.[101] They had secured popular support in outlying areas through other methods as well. In antiquity, sacrificial rice fields and ritual sites for the Daijō and Niiname rituals were selected anew through divination on each occasion. Every year the rituals took place in different provinces, so people in all parts of the realm could witness the proceedings.[102] Moreover, people not residing in the province where one or the other ritual took place could still view the imperial processions passing along the nation's highways.[103] Residents of the province where the ritual took place bore its expenses; they felt honored and privileged to play a part in its successful completion.[104]

Sujin was the sage emperor who perceived most astutely the need to carry out ritual performances in view of as many of the realm's people as possible:

In those days, the Court still followed the ancient custom of worshipping the Sacred Mirror, the embodiment of Amaterasu [privately] within the imperial palace. The emperor [Sujin], however, was awe-struck and ill at ease. Therefore he transferred this imperial treasure to Kasanui, where he worshipped it publicly. He hoped to turn it into an object that everyone in the realm might revere with him. His Majesty's action was intended to make reverence for Amaterasu something common to the court and people, and to show the people that their worship of Amaterasu at once constituted reverence for the imperial court.[105]

Aizawa presents an enlightening explanation for Sujin's actions:

By worshipping Amaterasu [privately] within court enclosures, earlier emperors had offered the full measure of their sincere devotion to Her, it is true. But the significance of [earlier] emperors' ritual acts was lost on the people below. By worshipping Amaterasu publicly, Emperor Sujin displayed his sincere devotion to the whole realm. Thus, the people grasped the significance of His Majesty's act [directly and sensually], not through explanations or lectures.[106]

Aizawa then attributed to Sujin sageliness and political acumen equal to that of the Duke of Chou:

The ancients [i.e., Mencius] said, "Filial devotion by the realm *en masse* is the ultimate in filial devotion." When the Duke of Chou was praised in antiquity for having attained the "ultimate in filial devotion," it was because everyone in the realm [joined him] in worshipping his ancestors, each person according to his proper status. The Duke of Chou did not worship his parents within ritual-hall confines, but in public, together with his people. No doubt he had the same idea as Emperor Sujin.[107]

Here we see another important element of "sageliness" for Aizawa—political calculation behind the conduct of ritual.[108] Aizawa argued that through religious rituals, Japanese sage emperors of antiquity had produced spiritual unity and allegiance, and thereby achieved *kokutai*. In later eras this *kokutai* disintegrated for two reasons. First, "wicked heresies" (*jasetsu*) from abroad, such as Buddhism and Christianity, created spiritual divisiveness. Second, "changed historical forces" (*jisei no hen*), such as those leading to warrior supremacy and the establishment of bakufu rule, required the altering of political institutions.

129

But the original blame for Japan's loss of *kokutai*, Aizawa tacitly admitted, lay with the imperial court:

> In later ages, rulers conducted these affairs [rituals and politics] in an abbreviated and simplified manner. The sacrificial rice fields and ritual sites employed in the Daijō ritual [which formerly had been located in different provinces from year to year], became permanently established [in Ōmi, Tamba, and Bitchū Provinces]. The ritual itself then became limited to the area in and around the capital. The emperor's will and the significance behind his religious rituals were lost upon the people in the realm as a whole. . . .
>
> Thus [in later ages], rulers might explain and lecture to every household and domicile in the land; yet not a soul could be made to understand. These same rituals, though extant today, have lost their [mystical, transforming] function. How lamentable indeed![109]

Astute sage emperors such as Sujin had taken pains to perform state rituals in full public view in order to achieve the desired effects. But from the mid-Heian period onward,[110] emperors (and shoguns) neglected and ignored the political ends that religious rituals and their mystical, suggestive power should be employed to achieve. Latter-day rulers "simply conducted rituals in a perfunctory fashion, ignoring the significance contained therein." As a result, "the myriad deities and countless rituals lacked systematic organization and coherence; the people no longer directed their devotion to a single object."[111]

Aizawa did not reprove latter-day emperors explicitly, but alert readers will readily discern his critical attitude. Those emperors failed to utilize religious rituals to evoke voluntary affection and trust from the people—this was the fundamental reason why Amaterasu's Way declined in Japan. Unlike Confucian historians in the early and mid-Tokugawa eras, who criticized emperors for turpitude, Aizawa placed the imperial court above moral judgment. Yūkoku and Aizawa skirted the question of the emperors' moral and political culpability through the concept of *sei*, "historical forces or conditions."[112] According to their view, the seizure of imperial prerogatives at court by Fuji-wara regents (*sesshō*) and civil dictators (*kampaku*), the eclipse of this *sekkan* government due to rising warrior clans in the provinces, Yoritomo's establishment of bakufu rule, the period of disorder, civil war, and Ieyasu's reestablishment of bakufu rule that followed—were all beyond human power to alter. These developments resulted from "historical forces or condi-tions" or from a "constant tendency" for "orderly rule and anarchy" to follow each other in recurring fashion.[113] This con-cept of *sei*, the impersonal forces, conditions, or laws that moved history, in Aizawa's view, required no further explanation and absolved emperors of all personal responsibility. Even so, Aizawa had to admit that the spiritual unity created by sage emperors in antiquity diminished and disappeared when later emperors stopped performing religious rituals properly. And Japan's peo-ple became susceptible to foreign heresies such as Buddhism and Christianity because of that spiritual disunity and unrest:

> In subsequent ages rulers lacked vision and planning, and they made but a pretense of serving Heaven and revering ancestors. As a result, the people lost their object of reverential awe in life and their place of repose in death. Doubts and fears arose among them, and they began to yearn for a source of spiritual reliance. Then the Western barbarians succeeded in striking further anxiety in the commoners' hearts by spreading doc-trines of paradise and hell.[114]

At present, commoners "embrace the foreigners' words of reli-gion as they long for a mother's compassion; they are attracted to any pernicious doctrine from abroad because they need a basis of spiritual reliance within. . . ."[115] It was this "spiritual void," which Ōhara Sakingo also had detected, that was so easy for the barbarians to take advantage of. This was Japan's great-est vulnerability to foreign incursion in the late eighteenth and early nineteenth centuries.

In antiquity, Aizawa argued, Japan's sage emperors had "trans-formed" barbarians such as the Ezo, Emishi, Hayato, Kumaso, and the inhabitants of Korea, Siberia, and other lands on the con-tinent to the ways of civilization. Now the tables were reversed:

> The Western barbarians have grown tremendously powerful in recent times; what is more, they too have learned how to discern prevailing conditions confronting them and to ply stratagems of their own. . . . They have appropriated the very stratagem that our sage emperors in antiquity once used to subjugate barbarians, and at this moment, seek to turn it against our Middle Kingdom.[116]

Although their teachings were wickedly false, barbarian leaders seemed to display certain characteristics of sageliness. The threat posed by them necessitated a reapplication of "the sages' *ch'üan*" by bakufu leaders responsible for Japan's defense: "We must transform them [the Western barbarians] by appropriating the very Way they now seek to use to transform us."[117] The Tokugawa bakufu could achieve *kokutai* as it once existed in antiquity by utilizing the emperor to conduct religious state rituals.[118] At present, the emperor was "conducting these rituals in an abbreviated and simplified manner," he "made but a pretense of 'serving Heaven' and 'revering ancestors'"; and he did so within court enclosures as emperors before Sujin (who lacked sagely acumen) had done. The bakufu now had to place the emperor on public display, so that it could exploit the mystical, transforming power latent in his officially prescribed rituals and thus create popular unity and allegiance. In short, Aizawa argued that the bakufu should and must avail itself of the emperor's religious authority to shore up its own political authority.

Western Learning played a key role in shaping Aizawa's concept of Japan's *kokutai*. Knowledge acquired from abroad convinced him that the strength of Western nations stemmed from their rulers' use of religion as an integral part of government. Through Christian "ritual and music," rulers in the West produced spiritual unity and allegiance at home. And away from home, "they defeated enemy armies without resorting to battle and conquered territories intact" which was the best of all possible victories[119] according to *Sun Tzu*. The bakufu, Aizawa urged, should emulate these shrewd foreign leaders by reviving Amaterasu's Way, her form of ritual and music, which in Japan had fallen into neglect after the coming of Buddhism, the rise of

132

Fujiwara regencies, and the emergence of warrior rule. Aizawa's knowledge of contemporary Western political institutions, though not abundant and often inaccurate, provided an alternative model with which to contrast the existing Tokugawa sociopolitical order. This contrast led him to restudy his own nation's history to determine why and how the separation of "religion and government" and of "edification and administration" had taken place. Through this reexamination of history—including the so-called Age of the Gods, which earlier Confucian historians had dismissed as mythology—Aizawa concluded that a long process of secularization had occurred in Japanese society. This secularization, which increased with each change in historical conditions or "Great Transformation" in Japan's past, had weakened and impoverished the nation both spiritually and materially.[120]

In sum, Western Learning convinced Aizawa that the main foreign threat to Japan's bakuhan state in 1825 was not a military threat; it stemmed from the popular spiritual unity that he believed Western rulers had achieved through their state cult of Christianity. This discovery led him to compose *New Theses,* in which he argued that the bakufu must establish a similar state cult to create a similar form of popular spiritual unity, or *kokutai.* Only then could Japan overcome its present foreign crisis. He urged bakufu leaders to include religious elements in their administration, not through proscription or family-temple registration systems, which served merely to suppress deviance, but by evoking voluntary, active allegiance among Japan's masses. Aizawa proposed that the bakufu could compensate for inadequacies in its traditional methods of social control—so unsuccessful in winning popular support—by reviving and utilizing the Emperor's religio-political role as the performer of prescribed state rituals.[121] Then religion and government, as well as administration and edification, would be one in Japan too.

Like his knowledge of conscription in the West, Aizawa's understanding of the supposed unity of Western religion and government led him to submit a reform proposal that ultimately proved incompatible with the structural principles of the Tokugawa bakuhan state. Ever since issuing the "Regulations for

Court and Nobility" (*Kinchū narabi ni kuge shohatto*) in 1615, the bakufu had striven to dissociate itself from court-related sources of authority or legitimacy in various ways. For example, scholar-advisors to the bakufu such as Arai Hakuseki and Ogyū Sorai had urged that Edo institute its own separate court ranks and rituals. By acknowledging, even tacitly, bakufu dependence on the spiritual authority of emperor and court for functional administrative purposes, Aizawa unknowingly introduced the possibility of an alternative locus of sovereignty in the bakuhan state. His proposals went beyond current legitimizing theories of the investiture (*miyosashi, go-inin*) of authority from court to bakufu. Aizawa would make the emperor the principal performer of religious rituals which formed a key part of shogunal state administration. Of course he believed that the popular unity and allegiance instilled by the emperor's performance of state rituals necessarily would shore up bakufu rule. To him it was a foregone conclusion that emperor and court remain under bakufu control. Aizawa was writing, we should recall, in an era of possible but not imminent military danger from abroad. Moreover, bakufu leaders had yet to discredit themselves toward the court in any way. Thus his argument for using the emperor's religious authority to bolster bakufu political supremacy was sensible and compelling. In 1825, this seemed an ideal way to reinforce secular bakufu rule. But after 1853, historical conditions changed so drastically that neither Japanese nor foreigners would tolerate a form of state authority divided between secular and sacred sovereigns.

chapter five
Epilogue: Looking Ahead

In 1855, Ikebe Tōzaemon, a samurai from Yanagawa domain, shrewdly appraised the political position held by Tokugawa Nariaki, former daimyo of Mito and the then advisor to the bakufu on coastal defenses. Nariaki had been an avid exponent of *jōi* since 1825.

> He advanced such views before anyone else in the realm; [now] he cannot bring himself to act on them. You might say he has climbed to the peak of a steep mountain. He cannot go up any further, but he cannot back down either.[1]

Ikebe detected a disparity between rhetoric and reality. With the coming of Commodore Matthew C. Perry's steam-powered warships in 1853, the Mito slogan of *jōi*, or armed expulsion, lost much of its former appeal. The measure that Nariaki had clamored about for thirty years was now plainly unworkable.

Awkwardly perched atop his mountain peak, Nariaki conceded that much. In a reply to Abe Masahiro's call for advice on how to deal with Perry's demands and armed threats, he wrote, "Driving away the barbarians might not be such a good idea now."[2] In explaining this tactical about-face to his trusted retainers, Fujita Tōko and Toda Tadaakira, Nariaki meekly confided:

> When Westerners came in the past, they never intended to start a war. When we fired on them [as ordered in 1825], they would in fact go away. But now they come spoiling for a fight; they are waiting for us to attack. If we do, we will just be playing into their hands.[3]

135

By 1853, Nariaki had come to realize that attacking Westerners gave them an excuse to invade Japan or extort concessions—and that "might not be such a good idea." Unlike earlier Western solicitors knocking on Japan's door, Perry was ready to exploit such an excuse. In 1853 he came fully determined and fully able to make the bakufu do what he wanted: revoke its policy of national isolation. Thereafter, Nariaki clung to *sakoku* and *jōi* more from obstinate pride than conviction.

The rhetoric of national isolation and armed expulsion emerged in the era 1793 to 1825. It remained cogent until 1853 because, as Nariaki pointed out, Westerners did in fact go away when fired on. In 1844, for example, Fujita Tōko quoted Nariaki's statement that "the barbarian presence in our seas is hateful, but not a grave menace."[4] Perry's arrival in 1853, however, presented Japan with a real military crisis. For the first time in Tokugawa history, a foreign power defied bakufu-dictated rules governing Japan's relations with the rest of the world; and armed expulsion gave way to realpolitik. Mito ideologues and Japanese leaders had to stop fancying their nation as Middle Kingdom Civilization. They had to repudiate a state policy of expelling Western "barbarians" by force, and open Japan to trade and diplomacy under rules imposed by the West. The alternative was to suffer colonization.

The class-bound form of *sonnō,* or "revering the emperor," peculiar to Aizawa and Mito Learning also lost cogency after the 1850s.[5] Aizawa's intention was that bakufu leaders utilize the emperor in Kyoto to perform religious rituals as an integral part of government. He believed that these ritual acts would inspire the people's reverent submission in peacetime and their active loyalty in wartime. When he wrote *New Theses* in 1825, Aizawa assumed that Japan would remain at peace, that foreigners could never mobilize enough military strength to threaten or humiliate the bakufu, whose legitimacy had come to rest on an ability to expel Westerners by force. But in the 1850s and 1860s, the bakufu was indeed so threatened and humiliated. Western powers coerced Edo leaders into signing treaties that opened the Divine Realm to trade and permanent foreign residence; this violated a "hallowed" national law that the emperor himself sanctioned. In the course of diplomatic wranglings over treaty ratification, both Japanese and Western negotiators realized the need for an ultimate source of political authority in Japan whose commands would be obeyed. This brought to a head the issue of where actual sovereign power lay: with the court or the bakufu. Politically active Japanese had to choose whether to obey the emperor, who ordered Westerners expelled from Japan, or the shogun, who had let them in under duress. In either case, Western military pressures—unforeseeable in 1825—now foiled Aizawa's original plan for the emperor's spiritual authority to reinforce bakufu secular authority.

After the late 1850s, knowledgeable men such as Tokugawa Nariaki and Aizawa Seishisai discarded the rhetoric of expulsion, but rank-and-file *shishi* continued to accept it at face value. Aizawa wrote *New Theses* in 1825 to shore up bakufu prestige and authority, but after 1853, the tract roused *shishi* to flout that authority. By 1860, Aizawa discovered to his horror that slogans he had endorsed in *New Theses* now were being used to justify insurgency: "I understand [the rebels at] Nagaoka proclaim that their actions are to 'revere the emperor' and 'expel the barbarians.' But in truth they twist the meaning of those words to suit their own purposes."[6] And in 1862, a year before his death, Aizawa was obliged to advocate opening Japan to Western trade and diplomatic intercourse.[7] His ideas of armed expulsion and reverence for the emperor—in their particular forms expounded in *New Theses*—suffered repudiation after 1853. But in other forms, they contributed to the formation of a Japanese nation-state later in the nineteenth century. Let us look ahead, beyond 1853, to examine how.

By the late eighteenth and early nineteenth centuries, Japanese thinkers had relativized and repudiated the Sinocentric Confucian view of world order. They no longer considered Japan a barbarian nation which was civilized only to the extent that its people assimilated Confucian moral culture. Early Tokugawa Confucians such as Itō Jinsai and Ogyū Sorai had recognized Japan as barbarian, and China as Middle Kingdom Civilization. For them, the Way of China's ancient sages embodied civilized life for all peoples. But they insisted that because contemporary Japan practiced that Way more faithfully than contemporary China, Japan could boast moral excellence despite being barbarian. Such rationalizations of Japanese superiority based on Sinocentric moral and cultural norms, however, were too far-fetched to be persuasive and too nationally demeaning to be acceptable.

Later in the Edo period, Confucian-Shinto syncretists such as Yamazaki Ansai and Asami Keisai declared that the imported Chinese categories of civilization and barbarism were irrelevant. They argued that China's Way of the sages corresponded "coincidentally" to Japan's Way of the *kami*. Since these Ways, though separately expressed, were in essence one, both Japanese and Chinese customs and morals possessed equal worth. Still later, Motoori Norinaga and other Kokugaku thinkers retorted that Japan was a superb nation in its own right: Its culture and morality were superior because they were different from, not the same as, China's. Meanwhile, the applied technology and the improved knowledge of world geography supplied by Western Learning debunked all Sinocentric conceits, whether invoked by China or Japan. Thinkers in all schools welcomed this advanced Western knowledge, largely because it was useful, but also because it discredited Chinese claims of cultural superiority.

By the early nineteenth century, Mito thinkers such as Aizawa were struggling to work out an acceptable synthesis. They revived Confucian moral culture by infusing elements of Kokugaku myth, but proclaimed that Japan's native Way was primary and esteemed Chinese moral norms as a supplement.[8] Equally important, they felt constrained to respect and assimilate useful Western skills and knowledge to make up for deficiencies in traditional Japanese or Chinese learning.[9] In 1834, Tokugawa Nariaki, for example, grudgingly conceded the superior size, speed, strength, and navigability of "barbarian" ships. He admitted that Japan must acquire and use advanced Western techniques for shipbuilding in order to create a powerful navy and merchant marine. But he insisted on designing the outside of all new vessels in a conspicuously Japanese style, so that the borrowed barbarian techniques would not show through.[10]

These currents of thought signaled the beginnings of national consciousness—over and above simple ethnic pride—in nineteenth century Japan. Throughout the Edo period, Japanese thinkers and leaders had been proud of their land and asserted that pride against Chinese claims of moral or cultural excellence. But the criteria on which they based their assertions changed significantly over time; these became increasingly irrational and centered on the putative uniqueness of Japan's imperial line. By the late eighteenth century, Motoori Norinaga made it respectable, if not imperative, for Japanese thinkers to profess a belief in the literal truth of *Kojiki* myths which described Japan's divine national origins. After him, the Tokugawa climate of opinion was decidedly different: One asserted Japan's superiority to foreign lands most convincingly by citing the descent of its unbroken imperial line from the Sun Goddess. Bakumatsu leaders might borrow advanced Western skills and knowledge in order to strengthen their nation—but they were loath to admit their indebtedness openly.

Japanese thinkers in the mid-nineteenth century clearly recognized how drastically their world outlook and cultural values had changed compared with the Ch'ing dynasty Chinese. For example, in 1842, Saitō Chikudō, a poet of classical Chinese and scholar in the bakufu's Shōheikō Academy, wrote an essay called "The Origins and Outcome of the Opium War" ("Ahen shimatsu"). In it, he stated that right and wrong, justice and injustice, were self-evident: The wicked British had sold China a hateful narcotic that they banned at home. They were "ugly barbarians," who were ignorant of the rules of proper behavior and righteousness. But what had allowed them to defeat the Ch'ing empire, a "grand, huge nation of humanity and righteousness?" he asked.[11]

After pondering this question repeatedly, I concluded that English victory and Ch'ing defeat, English cleverness and Ch'ing ineptness, had nothing to do with [the moral issue of] opium. Instead, the crux of the matter lay in a more commonplace, everyday attitude of long-standing. Namely, there are many countries in the universe, and each differs from the others. Who can say that one of them is civilized, and the rest,

139

barbarian? But China (Kando), presumes itself Middle Kingdom Civilization (Chūka) and considers other peoples despicable animals, mysterious beings devoid of spirit.

They know nothing of the Westerners' shrewdness or of highly sophisticated machines because they have never considered these valuable as such. . . . When the Chinese (Kan) devise strategies to ward off Western incursion, they simply rant, "barbarian, barbarian."[12]

Unlike Ch'ing leaders, who clung to fixed notions of Sino-centric civilization and of barbarism, bakumatsu Japanese—even those steeped in Chinese literary traditions—quickly recognized and actively assimilated superior Western knowledge and skills. They did so while sneering at China for cultural complacence, exhalting the innate excellence of their Divine Realm, and disparaging Western peoples as barbarian. After 1825, Japanese intellectuals pretentiously claimed Middle Kingdom standing for their nation, but they knew full well that their claim lacked any basis in reality.

This gnawing awareness of the discrepancy between rhetoric and reality disposed Japanese leaders to adjust to changing world conditions by transforming the Tokugawa bakuhan polity into a Western-style nation-state. Although Aizawa flaunted Japan's superiority to the so-called Western barbarians, a careful reading of *New Theses* shows that his blustering lacked self-assurance. Western Learning forced him to abandon the traditional Sinocentric conception of the world as "all under Heaven"—an ideally universal empire where a uniform Confucian moral culture ought to prevail. Instead, he perceived the world as an arena where seven large territorial units, analogous to the seven great kingdoms of China's Warring States period (403–221 B.C.), vied for spiritual and military hegemony. Aizawa saw Japan as but one of these seven "territories."[13] He compared her to Chou in ancient China—an insignificant state which existed precariously in a world dominated by far larger and stronger powers. In sum, Western knowledge made him admit Japan's inferiority to the West in certain crucial respects.

Aizawa feared an indirect Western takeover through Christian transformation, or what we today would call ideological subversion and cultural assimilation. Therefore a Western military threat was not the uppermost worry in his mind. But he nonetheless recognized Japan's armed weakness. Western countries, for example, enjoyed a decisive edge in raw materials over the Divine Realm:

> The barbarians appropriate lead, copper, iron, sulfur, and other precious metals from their far-flung overseas possessions (*kaigai shokoku*), so they never suffer from a shortage of these metals. We, however, must rely solely on deposits of these metals found in our homeland (*uchi*), so we are at a clear [material] disadvantage when defending ourselves against foreigners.[14]

Bringing to light this source of Western strength had to make him question the status quo he sought to reinforce. Since Westerners had benefited greatly by expanding overseas, Aizawa could not help wondering if Japan should follow suit.

Beneath his puffed up claim that Japan was the Middle Kingdom lay a realistic perception of Japan as merely *naichi,* or "Japan proper."[15] Aizawa so designated Honshū, Shikoku, and Kyūshū, in contrast to "overseas lands"[16] (such as the Ezo or Ogasawara Islands), which he feared would succumb to Christian subversion. His use of *naichi* foreshadowed modern Japanese thinking on foreign policy. Until Japan's defeat in 1945, the term denoted its four main islands (including Hokkaidō), as opposed to *gaichi,* or areas such as Korea, Taiwan, and Sakhalin, which Japan colonized or annexed. Unlike Meiji leaders, Aizawa did not advocate overseas expansion beyond Ezo.[17] But his terminology indicates how mindful he was of Japan's being a small country, whose weakness compared with Western nations stemmed partly from a bakufu-dictated "hallowed law" that kept Japanese bottled up at home.

Japan, Aizawa realized, was not really the Middle Kingdom, and Westerners were not simple barbarians. Aizawa's pejorative, "Western barbarians," should not obscure his genuine respect for their achievements and his rational understanding of their capabilities.[18] They had stolen the sagely device of religious

141

teachings implemented in government to instill active allegiance in commoners. Their use of Christianity created the spiritual unity essential to turn Western peoples into nations (*kokutai*); it allowed them to mobilize popular energies in pursuit of state goals. Equally important, Aizawa believed that Christianity enabled Westerners to subvert the lands they sought to colonize:

> The barbarians employ occult religions and other mysterious doctrines to seduce foreign peoples into their fold. Should the barbarians win our commoners over to their cause, their paucity of numbers would become a great multitude. . . . "Whenever they arrive in a country it is doomed because they conquer it from within by recruiting the local inhabitants into their ranks. . . ."[19]

This permitted them to conquer foreign nations intact—to practice the precepts of Sun Tzu and other legendary tactical geniuses. Here was the secret of Western strength and what made Aizawa hate the West so fiercely.

Aizawa was not the only late Tokugawa thinker convinced that Westerners used Christianity as a state religion to create popular unity and national strength. Nakajima Hirotari (1792–1864), a Kokugaku scholar from Kumamoto domain and contemporary of Aizawa's, considered Christianity a "trick" that European rulers used to "make their peoples docile and easy to lead." Nakajima also suggested that bakufu leaders master the Westerners' "technique"—their calculated use of religion to facilitate political control. In Japan, "the Way of the imperial land," by which he meant Shinto, should be made to serve this purpose.[20]

Nineteenth-century Japanese thinkers and leaders expressed fascination for the idea of "national essence," perceived as the spiritual cohesion supposedly achieved in European nations due to a unity of state and church. In 1856, Yokoi Shōnan wrote:

> Although our land possesses the Three Teachings [Confucianism, Shinto, and Buddhism], it is a national polity (*kokutai*) lacking a [national] faith. The Way of the sages is an amusement for scholars; the Way of the *kami* is irrational and

absurd; Buddhism deceives foolish commoners, but is not a Great Way that both high and low will accept. How, then, can we unify the people's hearts and minds? How are we to govern and edify? These are the most grievous ills afflicting us now.

When we examine conditions in Western countries, however, we find [a stark contrast]. Although I have no detailed understanding of [present-day] Christianity, I know that *it differs from the Christianity brought [to Japan] in the Tembun era [1532-54] as night differs from day.* It is based on the Will of Heaven; its main doctrines follow the rules of ethical behavior; and its religious teachings dictate commandments [for the people to obey]. *It is a religion that combines government and edification.* From sovereign on down to commoners—all are true to its commandments.[21] (emphasis added)

Shōnan feared Christian-inspired Western government as much as Aizawa, but was more candid about praising it. He too believed that Japan's leaders had to imitate European rulers, who skillfully used Christianity to cultivate popular unity. Knowledgeable Japanese in this era did not think of Christianity as the same faith that sixteenth-century Spanish and Portuguese missionaries had propagated.[22] Quite the contrary, they elevated it to the level of Confucian ritual and music—an efficacious "device" that sagacious Western rulers exploited to make their peoples love and fight for their countries.

Itō Hirobumi also perceived the value of, and need for, state religion. On 18 June 1888, he explained what prompted the Meiji oligarchs to draft Japan's imperial constitution:

In Europe, constitutional government has had over a thousand years since its inception. Not only are the people thoroughly familiar with it, *religion serves as a "linchpin" for them.* [Religion] has seeped deeply into the people's hearts; their hearts and minds are united in this faith.

But in our country religions are very weak; none of them can serve as a linchpin in the state. At one time Buddhism was strong and bound the hearts of high and low together, but it is now on the wane. In sectarian Shinto, followers carry on the teachings of sect founders, but it has little of the power of a religion to unify and direct the people's wills. . . . In our country, the only thing that can serve as a linchpin is the imperial house. [23] (emphasis added)

In other words, only by making the Japanese people revere the imperial line, could Meiji leaders attain the spiritual unity that Western nations enjoyed because of Christianity.

These nineteenth-century thinkers and leaders realized that to maintain Japan's sovereignty and territorial integrity in the face of Western encroachment, it was essential for its government to win popular support and loyalty, and that to achieve this task, some form of state religion was imperative. The *Imperial Rescript on Education* issued in 1890 lucidly reveals this concern, and we should note that its drafters borrowed a line from the section entitled, "What is Essential to a Nation" ("Kokutai") in Aizawa's *New Theses:* "All the people of the realm be of one heart and mind." [24] This need guided the Meiji government's policy of nationalistic ethical instruction in compulsory education and its use of state Shinto to inculcate popular reverence for the emperor.

This persisting fascination with the Western-inspired idea of *kokutai* discloses an important qualitative change in how politically-conscious nineteenth-century Japanese conceived of their nation. In earlier Tokugawa political parlance, the term "nation" or "state" (*kokka*), had denoted the daimyo "lands and house" to which samurai were in hereditary liege. Thus, it stood for a daimyo's domain and the samurai belonging to it. Following that class-bound usage, Aizawa expanded the concept to include the entire realm (*tenka*): He conceived of the current Japanese state as a bakufu-led federation of all daimyo domains and warrior bands. [25] This "nation" or "state" still did not include all persons living in Tokugawa Japan, only the military aristocracy; it excluded "stupid commoners" whose loyalty Aizawa distrusted.

However, Aizawa's knowledge of world affairs showed that Japan's bakuhan state was only one of several states struggling to preserve independence in the world. This realization compelled him to grope toward the idea of a nation construed as "the land and people," or *kokumin* in modern-Japanese usage. Western Learning suggested that Japan was gravely imperiled unless Edo leaders exploited the emperor in Kyoto as a unifying symbol to inculcate active political allegiance in *all* Japanese people, irrespective of their hereditary status. Aizawa's concept of *kokutai* thus broadened the idea of what properly constituted the Japanese nation in two crucial dimensions. He proposed that the imperial court and the common people—hitherto strictly excluded from the state's political life—must begin to assume limited but key roles in it.

When pushed to its logical conclusions, this proposal meant dismantling the existing order. As long as no true military crisis forced the issue, Aizawa and other bakufu supporters were free to ignore those logical conclusions. But when faced with a real Western threat after 1853, people began to see that the shogun could not rule Japan without borrowing spiritual authority from the imperial court, and the daimyo could not defend Japan without demanding some form of military service from the non-samurai classes. Thus the bakuhan system was structurally incompatible with the drastic institutional changes that Aizawa's proposed reforms ultimately entailed: an emperor-centered state and a mass conscript army. Regardless of Aizawa's original intentions, after 1853 his concept of *kokutai* turned into an ironic contradiction. What he deemed "essential" to sustain the Tokugawa polity proved decisive in undoing it.

New Theses
Aizawa Seishisai

New Theses: one

Prefatory Remarks

(Note: In the translation that follows, the glosses were written by Aizawa himself.)

Our Divine Realm is where the sun emerges.[1] It is the source of the primordial vital force (*yuan ch'i*) sustaining all life and order.[2] Our Emperors, descendents of the Sun Goddess, Amaterasu, have acceded to the Imperial Throne in each and every generation, a unique fact that will never change. Our Divine Realm rightly constitutes the head and shoulders of the world and controls all nations. It is only proper that our Divine Realm illuminates the entire universe and that our dynasty's sphere of moral suasion (*kōkwa*) knows no bounds. But recently the loathsome Western barbarians, unmindful of their base position as the lower extremities of the world,[3] have been scurrying impudently across the Four Seas, trampling other nations underfoot. Now they are audacious enough to challenge our exalted position in the world. What manner of insolence is this?

(Gloss: The earth lies amid the heavenly firmament, is round in shape, and has no edges. All things exist as nature dictates. Thus, our Divine Realm is at the top of the world. Though not a very large country, it reigns over the Four Quarters because its Imperial Line has never known dynastic change. The Western barbarians represent the thighs, legs, and feet of the universe. This is why they sail hither and yon, indifferent to the distances involved. Moreover, the country they call America is located at the rear end of the world, so its inhabitants are stupid and incompetent. All of this is as nature dictates.)

These barbarians court ultimate ruin by ignoring the moral laws of nature and refusing to accept the lowliness of their status.

But alas, the normative forces of Heaven and Earth must wane as well as wax: "When the power of men is immense, they overcome Heaven."[4] Unless a Great Hero bestirs himself to assist Heaven's normative processes, all creation will fall prey to the wily, meat-eating barbarians.

Yet today, when I propose great plans to benefit the realm people look at one another in astonishment; they are all taken aback. This is because they cling to conventional ideas and to outmoded, inaccurate sources of information [about foreign countries]. *Sun Tzu* says, "Do not rely on the enemy's staying away; be ever prepared to keep him away. Do not rely on his not attacking; make yourself immune to any attack."[5] If we govern and edify well, if we make the people's morals pure and their customs beautiful, if we induce high and low alike to embody righteousness, if we enrich the people and strengthen our arms, if we make ourselves immune to attack from even the strongest of enemies, all will be well. But if we neglect these tasks, if we are complacent and lax, what is there for us to rely on?

But skeptics argue, "They are only barbarians in merchant ships and fishing boats. They pose no serious problem; there is no grave danger." Such skeptics rely on the barbarians' staying away, on their not attacking; they rely on something not within our power to control. Should I question them about our military preparedness or immunity to attack, they would be dumbfounded. Ah, how can we prevent the world from falling prey to the barbarians?

Unable to suppress my anger and grief, I respectfully present my views to the bakufu (*kokka*). This memorial contains five essays: (1) "What is Essential to a Nation" ("Kokutai") wherein I relate that Amaterasu founded our nation on the twin precepts of loyalty and filial devotion, that She esteemed martial virtues, and that She attached supreme importance to nurturing Her people. (2) "World Affairs," wherein I describe important developments in the international situation. (3) "The Barbarian's Nature," wherein I discuss the barbarians and their designs on us. (4) "National Defense," wherein I assert the need to enrich the nation and strengthen its arms. (5) "A Long-Range Policy," wherein I propose how to edify the people and purify their folkways.

These five essays were inspired by the prayer that "Heaven will return to normal and again control men's destinies."[6] In this memorial I outline the theses on which I pledge my life in service to Heaven and Earth.

New Theses: two

What is Essential to a Nation
[*Kokutai*] (I)

The ancient sage kings (*teiō*) did not maintain the realm, prevent unrest, and uphold everlasting domestic tranquillity by forcing their people into submission. Such methods may work for a single reign [but not forever]. Instead, the ancient sages relied on something else: "all people in the realm were of one heart and mind"; they were so endeared of their rulers that separation was unbearable.[7] This is what we can really rely on.

Ever since earth became distinct from the firmament and men came into being, a Divine Line of Emperors descended from the Sun Goddess, Amaterasu, has ruled the realm. Can it be mere coincidence that no one has ever had evil designs on the Throne? Loyalty of subject for ruler is the greatest moral precept of the cosmos. Affection between parent and child is the ultimate form of blessing within the realm. This greatest of moral precepts and this ultimate form of blessing exist together between Heaven and Earth; they slowly and steadily seep into men's hearts in all places and eras. By understanding and utilizing these sentiments of loyalty and filial devotion, the ancient sage kings regulated the realm and forever upheld nature's moral order among their people.

In antiquity, the Heavenly Progenitress, Amaterasu, set down the precepts on which to base this nation. Her Imperial Throne was divinely ordained, Her virtue was divinely bestowed, and through these, She carried out the Processes of Heaven. All of Her achievements were the work of Heaven itself. She incorporated Her virtue in the Jewel, Her wisdom in the Mirror, and Her Majesty in the Sword. Being the embodiment of Heavenly Beneficence and possessed of Heavenly Majesty, She ruled over all nations according to the dictates of Heavenly Wisdom.

When Amaterasu bequeathed the realm to Her Divine Grandson, Ninigi, She also bequeathed to Him these Three Regalia as symbols of the Imperial Throne and as manifestations of Her Heavenly Virtue. She decreed that Ninigi step in to carry out the divine tasks hitherto accomplished naturally through the Heavenly Processes, and that thereafter the Three Imperial Regalia be handed down faithfully from generation to generation for ages eternal. The majesty of our Imperial House descended from Amaterasu is inviolable. The distinction between ruler and subject was established, and the greatest virtue of all, loyalty of subject for ruler, was made manifest. In bequeathing the Mirror to Ninigi, the Sun Goddess said, "When you look at this Mirror, think of it as myself." Throughout the myriad generations, Emperors have worshipped this Mirror as the embodiment of Amaterasu Herself. When they gazed into it, they caught a glimpse of what they perceived to be Her sacred image, though what they really saw was their own reflection as Her offspring. When making sacrificial offerings at ritual time, a communion between men and gods inevitably occur. One cannot help revering ancestors, expressing filial devotion, being circumspect in behavior, and cultivating personal virtue. The affection between parent and child also is thus warmly displayed, and this affection, which is Amaterasu's ultimate blessing, bursts forth in all its splendor.

[In antiquity,] Amaterasu established the norms of human conduct—the twin precepts of loyalty of subject for ruler and affection between parent and child—and She bequeathed these to the myriad generations. These precepts constitute the ultimate Way of Heaven: affection between parent and child radiates inwardly, and the loyalty of subject for ruler manifests itself outwardly. Through loyalty, the honorable were honored; through filial devotion, parents were shown affection. Thus, for good reason, the people "were of one heart and mind" and were inseparably endeared to their rulers. Thus, for good reason, the ultimate ethic of loyalty and filial devotion existed without being expounded and was adhered to unknowingly by all.

The Sun Goddess exists amid the firmaments and beams down radiantly on earth. Her Divine Descendants occupy the Imperial

Throne and serve Her by devoting Themselves wholeheartedly
to Their people in Her stead. Religious rituals and government
are one and the same. The Emperor's Heavenly duties of administration and the Heavenly Processes realized through him constitute His devotion to Amaterasu. Because His Majesty reveres
His Heavenly Forbears and cares for His people, He is one with,
and His Throne is as everlasting as, Heaven itself. Can this be
otherwise? Each succeeding Emperor strives to recompense
Amaterasu's blessings by personifying filial devotion, honoring
the tombs of Imperial Forbears, and revering Her prescribed set
of religious rituals. Hence, religious rituals and political institutions are well-established in the land.

Nothing better exemplifies the principle of recompensing
ancestral blessings and remaining true to ancestral will than the
Emperor's role in the Daijō Ritual,[8] the first thanksgiving ceremony following his coronation. During this [religious ritual],
His Majesty partakes of newly harvested grain and offers it to
the Heavenly Deities.

> (Gloss: In antiquity the term "Divine Progenitress" referred
> only to Amaterasu, and "Heavenly Deities" was a general
> designation for the gods collectively.)

Amaterasu obtained the best rice seeds [from the god Uke-
mochi], and desired to nurture Her people with them, so she
planted them in Her august rice field. She also placed silk co-
coons in Her mouth and began to spin thread, thus introducing
sericulture to mankind. Hence Amaterasu graciously secured the
basis of Her people's livelihood—their food and clothing. When
She bequeathed the realm to Her grandson, Ninigi, She also bequeathed the seeds from Her august rice field. This shows that
Amaterasu was greatly concerned about ensuring Her people's
food supply and that She attached special meaning to rice. This
is why we cook the newly harvested rice and offer a generous
portion of it to the Gods of Heaven during the Daijō Ritual.

> (Gloss: [In antiquity,] prior to each Daijō Ritual the province
> where it was to take place was selected by divination. Once
> the location of the sacrificial rice field and ritual site were

thus chosen, the Iname and Negi branches of the Urabe *uji* were dispatched as reapers. They harvested the crop and presented part of it to His Majesty. The remainder of it was brewed into dark and light varieties of *sake.* The rice presented to His Majesty was threshed and cooked at ritual time. He then personally placed it in sacrificial bowls and offered it to the gods in the Enthronement Hall. In this ritual He displayed filial devotion to His ancestral gods and personified the meaning of recompensing Amaterasu's blessings.)

The Emperor distributed Imperial Cloth Offerings to shrines throughout the land at the time of His Daijō Ritual. These Cloth Offerings had been spun from smooth and rough material.

(Gloss: When the god Ame no Futotama served Amaterasu, he had his retainer Ame no Hiwashi weave coarse *yū* garments made from the bark of the *kōzo* tree. Later on, Emperor Jimmu dispatched a descendant of Hiwashi's to Awa Province with *kōzo* and flax seeds, and ordered that these be planted there. Thereafter, the Imibe *uji* of Awa, descendants of Hiwashi, presented rough cloth to be woven into Imperial Cloth Offerings distributed at every Daijō Ritual. This is a good example of descendants honoring and carrying on the hereditary calling established by their forbears.)

Thus, all participants in the Daijō Ritual display the principle of recompensing ancestral blessings.

His Majesty performs ritual cleansing to purify himself before the Daijō Ritual. His emergence into the Ritual Hall goes unheralded, and He enters barefoot in order to personify the highest Reverence. The simplicity of His garments symbolizes Reverence and a desire to avoid stylistic refinement.

When She bestowed the realm to Ninigi, Amaterasu decreed that Ame no Koyane divine the will of the deities and that Ame no Futotama assist Ninigi in any way possible. Bearing this in mind, we can grasp the import behind the roles played in the Daijō Ritual by the Nakatomi *uji,* who are descendants of Koyane, and the Imibe, who are descendants of Futotama. The Nakatomi deliver auspicious prayers to His Majesty and the

Imibe present Him with the Imperial Jewel, Mirror, and Sword. [In antiquity] these functions were faithfully carried out at each successive Daijō Ritual. It was as if the Nakatomi and Imibe received their original decrees from Amaterasu anew on every occasion.

(Gloss: Amaterasu decreed that Koyane, Futotama, and three other gods escort Ninigi to earth. She also decreed that they set up sacred bush-barriers around him to afford him divine protection in the same manner that they would do in Heaven. When Emperor Jimmu pacified the realm, he also set up these sacred bush-barriers. He ordered Taneko, Koyane's descendant, and Ame no Tomi, Futotama's descendant, to present a mirror and sword at the Daijō Ritual and to distribute Imperial Cloth Offerings to shrines throughout the land. All aspects of this ritual were meticulously observed for countless reigns. When Emperor Sujin worshipped Amaterasu at Kasanui Village, he ordered the Imibe *uji* to instruct the descendants of the gods Ishikoritome and Ame no Mahitotsu to cast replicas of ancient-style mirrors and swords and to place these in the Imperial Palace. Emperor Sujin did this because these two deities once had served Amaterasu; Ishikoritome, by forging the Jeweled Mirror, and Ame no Mahitotsu, as a goldsmith. The Imibe offer these articles to the Emperor during each Daijō Ritual. This action symbolizes the care shown to objects handed down from ancestors and the concern that these not be lost or damaged.)

In addition, the Imibe procured and presented all other articles used during the ceremony. Each participant in this Daijō Ritual carries out the same hereditary ceremonial function in accordance with ancestral will, and each performs his role carefully down to the last detail, just as his particular forbear did on the day that Ninigi descended to earth. Thus, ruler and retainer alike cannot but remain true to Amaterasu's original decrees.

(Gloss: Futotama led the gods Hiwashi, Taoki Hooi, Hikosachi, Kushiakarutama, and Mahitotsu in serving Amaterasu. Ame no Tomi, Futotama's offspring, instructed the descendants of the above gods to produce mirrors, halberds, shields, and other necessary objects to be offered to His Majesty during the Daijō Ritual. This was performed in obedience to ancestral custom. To give additional examples, [the *Engi shiki* says that] the Tomo no Miyatsuko light fires, the Azumi fan these fires, and the Kuramochi remove reed pot lids. These and other similar ceremonial roles were observed throughout the ages in each family line.)

When the Emperor, Amaterasu's own flesh and blood, solemnly performs this Daijō Ritual in Her honor, Her own countenance presents itself to all who gaze on His Majesty. The Court nobles looking on, both high and low, imagine themselves to be in Amaterasu's presence. This feeling [of communion] arises naturally among them and cannot be suppressed, for they too are descendants of the gods. Their own ancestors once served Amaterasu and Her Imperial Descendants by performing deeds of merit on the people's behalf. Their names are found in our set of officially prescribed classics, and the eldest son in each noble house leads its members in worshipping its forbears.

(Gloss: In antiquity, old families and clans who became *Kuni no miyatsuko* or *Agata nushi* gave their members a sense of unity by worshipping clan ancestors.[9] For example, the Miwa no Kimi, descended from Ōnamuchi, worshipped him generation after generation. The same was true for the Chichibu no Miyatsuko, descended from Omoikane, and for all other prominent clans. By Emperor Tenji's time, *uji* heads known as *konokami* were referred to as *ujinosō* in the *Taihō Code*. This is an example of embellishing an old, established custom with a new name. In later ages, gods particular to certain localities were called *ujigami,* and their worshippers were known as *ujiko.* This is another vestige of an ancient practice.)

Each noble house displays filial devotion to its own divine founder at home, and by participating in the Daijō Ritual as a public function, it worships Amaterasu, the progenitress of all the gods.

(Gloss: In antiquity, the Omi, Muraji, and Tomo no Miyatsuko made certain that the various *uji* under their command upheld hereditary callings. The aforementioned Imibe organized the various Imibe *uji* scattered throughout the country in this way also. The Imibe located in Awa descended from Hiwashi are a good example. [In that era,] every *uji* performed its hereditary ceremonial role in each successive Daijō Ritual.)

When we recall how ancestors reverently served the progenitress of our Imperial Line and other Heavenly Deities, how can we ignore ancestral will? How can we turn against our ruler? Through such rituals, filial devotion is transmitted from father to son, and from son to grandson. Each carries on the wishes of his parent and bids his offspring to do likewise. The passing of a thousand generations produces not the slightest change in their filial sentiment. Loyalty and filial devotion have always been one and the same: Filial devotion is transformed into loyalty to ruler, and loyalty is demonstrated by respecting the wishes of forbears. Edification of the people and the reform of their folkways is accomplished: The ruler places the people under his "inducing influence" (*kwa*) without recourse to injunctions or exhortations. Religious rituals are a means of political rule, and political rule is identical to ethical inculcation. Throughout history, edification and administration have been inseparable: When the people are taught simply to revere Amaterasu and Her Divine Imperial Line, their allegiances are undivided and they are blind to all heresies. Thus we achieve both spiritual unity among the people and the union of Heaven and man. This was the ancient sage kings' one true reliance for maintaining the realm, and was the basis on which Amaterasu founded our nation.

Just as the myriad things stem from Heaven, man stems from his ancestors. He acquires his body from his forbears and his vital life force (*ch'i*) from the cosmos. For this reason, not even the basest of commoners remain unawed when told about the spirits of Heaven and Earth. When government, edification, laws, and decrees all stipulate reverence for Heaven and recompensing ancestral blessings, spiritual unity among the people is a foregone conclusion. The hearts and minds of men stem from the mind of the cosmos. When their hearts and minds are unified, their spiritual powers (*ch'i*) are heightened. When their hearts and minds are unified so that these accord with the mind of the cosmos, men obtain the primordial vital force that sustains all life and order (*yuan ch'i*) in the cosmos. Since the people of our realm possess this consumate *yuan ch'i* at birth, their manners and temperament are cordial and warm. This phenomenon is known as the unity of Heaven and man. When the people are induced to think of antiquity, their customs are purified, they recompense the blessings originally bestowed by Amaterasu, and remain forever true to the wishes of their ancestors. . . .[10]

In antiquity [the feudal lords] known as *Kuni no miyatsuko* and *Tomo no miyatsuko* inherited their family posts from, and performed sacrificial ceremonies to, their ancestors generation after generation.[11] Near the midpoint of our nation's history[12] [Nara and Heian times], Court nobles and Imperial collaterals monopolized hereditary posts within their own clans. More recently [Kamakura and Muromachi times], warrior families arose, each of which bound its members with ties of filial reverence. Yet even in this period, members of the prominent clans continued to worship their own ancestral progenitors [who in turn originally had worshipped Amaterasu]. Because these prominent families remained true to their ancestors, no one dared blaspheme the Imperial Institution, and all recognized its inviolable majesty. Since the difference between loyalty and treachery was as plain as night and day, no one would aid and abet evildoers. The perfidious were hard put to exist in the world, much less could they achieve their villainous designs.

Although we have had troubled eras in our past, the majesty of our Imperial Throne remained undisturbed. It is quite true that certain Imperial Highnesses suffered exile,[13] but no one dared lay hands on the Three Sacred Treasures. It is also true that certain subvassals [such as the Hōjō] exercised power for generations on their own behalf, but no one dared depose his overlord. Amaterasu founded our nation on the precepts of loyalty and filial devotion, and these virtues exist among the people even today; it is quite natural that our Divine Line of

Emperors has remained unbroken and coeval with Heaven and Earth. This shows the firmness of our nation's Divine foundations under Amaterasu and the longevity of Imperial virtue.

May we then conclude that the Imperial Dynasty's benevolent government and illustrious virtue have been impeccable? No, normally, nothing under Heaven is entirely free of evils. Many evils now exist, but they stem from two distinct sources—changing historical forces and wicked doctrines. Before we can rectify what is deformed or revive what has declined, we must examine these evils in detail.

Changing Historical Forces. In antiquity, Amaterasu laid the foundations for Her Heavenly Tasks and lovingly cared for Her people. She appointed Heavenly Village Chiefs to look after the tillers of the soil and dispatched warrior gods to bring peace and order to the land. Thus She prompted the people to revere the Imperial Court. But the creation of earth by Heaven was just completed; the world remained nebulous and confused. The Four Quarters awaited pacification. Local tribes and territorial chieftains divided up the land among themselves and defied Imperial attempts at unification for generations.

When Emperor Jimmu, founder of our Imperial Line, pacified the realm, He enfeoffed rulers known as *Kuni no miyatsuko* and commanded them to minister to the needs of gods and men. Emperor Jimmu bound all of these feudal houses by means of noble titles and pledges of fealty. He brought all people under Imperial sway so that the entire realm enjoyed orderly government. . . .[14]

With the passing of time, administration grew lax and insurrections occasionally broke out. But Emperor Sujin suppressed these rebellions, administered the land, edified the people, levied taxes and corveys, and increased the number of *Kuni no miyatsuko* feudatories. In this way, he pacified even the remotest corners of the realm. The next several Emperors spared no efforts to administer the land and people; as a result, the Imperial Dynasty's sphere of moral suasion (*kōkwa*) became ever more vast and the nation's territory expanded correspondingly. All land was the Emperor's land, all people were the Emperor's people. We achieved spiritual unity and all under Heaven enjoyed orderly government.

But later, the ways of ease and comfort set in. The Court lacked vision in its decision-making, and high officials abused their powers by establishing private estates. The land and people soon became divided into two distinct groups: First there remained Dynastic lands and subjects, the Miyake and Minashiro; second, aristocratic families, such as the Omi, Muraji, and *Tomo no miyaytsuko,* acquired private landholdings and populations. When the land became divided, the people lost their former spiritual unity. [At this dark hour,] Emperor Tenji revived the Dynasty's fortunes. After valiantly squashing an attempted coup at court,[15] His Majesty (then Heir Apparent) served Emperor Kōtoku and Empress Saimei. He carried out long-needed reforms and instituted a totally new form of government by converting the old feudatories into administrative units called "provinces and districts" and appointing governors to rule over these. By creating a centralized form of administration, Emperor Tenji abolished the private ownership of land [and people]. Every inch of territory, every single person submitted to the Imperial Dynasty, and all under Heaven enjoyed orderly government.

Yet after a number of generations, the Fujiwara seized power. The ways of insolence and presumption again set in among Court officials, causing them to vie with one another in founding private estates (*shōen*) and bringing the people under their own control. In the provinces, warrior families who had ingratiated themselves with these aristocrats worked to subdivide and annex the land, making slaves of Imperial subjects. The realm became divided; its map had as many crisscross lines as a turtle's shell. In short, regionalism was the order of the day.

When Minamoto no Yorimoto was appointed Overlord-General, all land and people became subject to Kamakura. Under the Kamakura and Muromachi shoguns there were eras both of prosperity and anarchy, but in general, these shoguns countermanded decrees from the Throne because they were in actual control of the land and people. Wars broke out because the old aristocratic families and local magnates sought to retain their hold on the land and people. The strong devoured the weak; insurgents appeared one after another. The realm was in constant turmoil and the people suffered incredibly. Amid such confusion, they were confused about whom they should submit to. The courageous fought valiantly, each dying for his own lord. But because name did not conform to status, their loyalty was not true loyalty, and their filial devotion was not true filial devotion. True loyalty and filial devotion steadily wasted away—and with the appearance of that scoundrel, Ashikaga Yoshimitsu, the virtue of name and status reached its lowest ebb. Although a subject of the Emperor, he kowtowed before the Ming dynasty and demeaned himself as its vassal. But no one in the realm found this odd in the least. His action amounted to treason, since it induced the Ming to look on the Imperial Court as a sub-tributory.[16] So grievously did he disgrace our nation (*kokutai o kaku*) [before the world]. But no one in the realm found this odd in the least!

Thus, the principle of name and status, and above all, that of sovereign and subject, were debased. Folkways became increasingly depraved, and the virtues of recompensing Amaterasu's original blessings and of remaining true to ancestral will were all but forgotten. In succession to family headship, political or economic advantage took precedence over legitimacy of bloodline. This gave rise to the evil custom of adopting heirs from outside one's extended family.[17] If persons without blood ties may be grafted together as parent and offspring, then conversely, the blood line connecting true parents and offspring, and by extension, ancestors and descendants, may be severed. If so, everyone would be ignorant of the immutability of Heaven's ethical principles. The most extreme example of this can be discerned in the practice of allowing Imperial Princes to take the tonsure. Because of this evil practice, we almost brought the Dynastic Line to extinction. . . .[18] Unless the ruler unifies land and people, he cannot govern and edify. Ultimately, loyalty and filial devotion will cease to exist altogether, and the Way of Heaven and Man also will fall to ruin.

But "history's cycle of orderly rule and anarchy"[19] is the normal course of events on earth: When Heaven tires of disorder, Great Heroes arise. For example, Toyotomi Hideyoshi, though a mere commoner, rose up and created order out of chaos. He served the Throne as *kampaku,* issued commands throughout the realm, and unified the land and people. Next, Tokugawa Ieyasu came to the fore. Loyalty and filial devotion were the sole means by which he laid the foundations of a two-hundred year peace. He issued injunctions for his descendants to follow, and this they did to the letter. At the appropriate time, Ieyasu led the lords of the land to Kyōto to honor the Imperial Court, and the Emperor bestowed awards, offices, and Court ranks on them. Government over all land and people in the realm became unified. All revered Imperial benevolence and submitted in awe before bakufu virtue. Orderly rule, then, was the order of the day.

But because peace has prevailed for so long, lassitude has set in. The typical daimyo today enjoys a life of ease and softness from birth. His lack of measures to deal with natural disasters causes him no concern. Renegades roam freely throughout his domain, but he takes no steps to outlaw them. Foreign barbarians reconnoiter our perimeter, but he pays them no heed. This amounts to forsaking the land and people placed in his charge. The typical retainer today thinks only of his own well-being, not of loyalty to domain (*kokka*) or of solving problems on its behalf. He is lax and irresponsible, is a disgrace to his ancestors, and is unmindful of blessings received from his lord. When daimyo and retainer alike are this derelict in their duty, how can we unite the land and people? How can we maintain the spiritual solidarity that makes land and people a nation (*kokutai*)?

When a Great Hero seeks to rouse the realm to action, his only fear is that the people will not respond. But when leaders of mediocre talent temporize and gloss over problems, their only fear is that the people may indeed respond. Hence they patch up affairs to create an aura of normality and calm. They even allow foreigners to land on our shores, and afterward, in high and low places, cover up the truth by declaring that those barbarians were fishermen in search of provisions. Such [handling of this recent affair] [20] betrays an attitude of minimizing the potential threat posed by the barbarians, an attitude which can only spell trouble.

Leaders today do not heed this danger. They sit back smugly, and when such an incident occurs, take stop-gap, temporizing measures that lead us unwittingly to the brink of disaster. They are truly a deplorable lot. Can anyone with foresight help grieving in silent protest? But the bakufu has just ordered that barbarian ships be destroyed on sight. [21] It has publicly declared that it, along with the whole realm, regards foreigners as the enemy. Everyone in the realm took heart after learning of this decree and now eagerly await the chance to execute it. Such is the indomitable strength of the people's spirit!

Our current state structure cannot be other than feudal (*hōken*) because that is the system of government Emperor Jimmu first instituted [and Tokugawa Ieyasu restored]. [22] Tokugawa Ieyasu founded national peace exclusively on the principles of loyalty and filial devotion because these are the moral precepts that Amaterasu first prescribed. If we make use of and regulate the strength of the people's indomitable spirit, if we base ourselves on those moral precepts first utilized by Amaterasu to administer the realm, if we rectify the name and status of ruler and subject and make warmer still the affection between parent and child, and if we induce spiritual unity throughout the Divine Realm, how can armed expulsion be beyond our power? A chance like this will not come again in a thousand years—we must exploit it! Seeking to clarify the evils to be rectified, I cannot help bearing in mind "changing historical forces."

Wicked Doctrines. In antiquity Amaterasu [23] established precepts in accordance with *shen tao,* "the spirit-like processes of nature," [24] and thereby captured the hearts of Her people. Her teachings were the one and only doctrine to secure popular allegiance. She transmitted Her august message of "serving Heaven and worshipping forbears" to later ages so that all might know the meaning of "recompensing Her original blessings" and "remaining true to ancestral will."

When the first Emperor, Emperor Jimmu, worshipped the

gods of Heaven and subdued the rebellious, He set up a ritual site [at Tomiyama]. He worshipped Amaterasu and displayed filial devotion to the fullest. Emperor Sujin worshipped the deities, reverently served His Heavenly Progenitress, and distributed Her set of religious rituals throughout the realm. Consequently, all people recompensed Amaterasu's original blessings, remained true to their ancestors, and revered the Imperial Court as they would revere the deities of Heaven. Each served his respective overlord with filial devotion, and the people united themselves in spirit to perform deeds of loyalty, so that folkways were purified and uplifted.

Emperor Ōjin obtained the Confucian classics and circulated them throughout the realm. These classics contain the precepts of Yao, Shun, the Duke of Chou, and Confucius. Their land is close to our own, and its folkways and natural *ch'i* are similar to ours. The sages' teachings are based on the concepts of "Heaven's Will" and "the people's hearts." They sought to make manifest the twin virtues of loyalty and filial devotion, and stressed service to ruler and worship of ancestors. . . .[25] In short, the sages' teachings are virtually identical to Amaterasu's precepts. If only we had adopted Confucius' teachings to make Amaterasu's government and edification more illustrious still! If only we had upheld those teachings sedulously! But no, their limitless merits were lost to us. Wicked doctrines such as shaman cultism, Buddhism, the ideas of perverse Confucians, petty scholasticism, Christianity, and other teachings inimical to Imperial "transformation" (*kwa*) and injurious to morals arose one after another.

Amaterasu conducted Imperial Rituals properly, so that everyone in the realm joined Her in serving Heaven and revering forbears. The meaning in those rituals reached everyone without exception. But certain ancient territorial clans clung tenaciously to their hereditary shaman cults. Even today, in remote parts of the country, they revere vile gods and pray for personal fortune rather than serve Heaven and revere forbears. Devious thinkers provided such wicked folk cults with philosophical backing; they clung to old superstitions and delighted in the occult. They have spun out mystical, shamanistic nonsense about spirits being transferred to humans or men being possessed by demons. In later ages, shaman priests borrowed ideas from Buddhism and Confucianism in order to make their doctrines appear more reasonable and acceptable. They simply prayed for their own fortune in total disregard of "recompensing Amaterasu's original blessings" or "remaining true to ancestral will." Consequently, would-be loyal retainers and filial sons did not know where to direct their loyalty and filial devotion; the people's unity of spirit [achieved by Amaterasu] disintegrated.

When Buddhism first entered our Middle Kingdom, one group of ministers at Court argued that we should not tolerate this foreign idol because we already had Amaterasu's set of religious rituals. But the traitor, Soga no Umako, secretly revered it and erected temples to it in league with Shōtoku Taishi. The number of clerics attached to these temples steadily increased, and they engaged in sectarian disputes to gain followers. This further divided the people's hearts and minds. The *Taihō Code* [701], in that it placed the Office of Divinities above the Council of State and put clerics and nuns under the control of the Office of Barbarian Affairs, shows an understanding of the need to maintain popular spiritual unity which is essential to a nation (*kokutai*). But because folkways and morals had lost their former purity [due to Buddhism], the separation of government functions from religious rituals was unavoidable under this code. By the reigns of Emperor Shōmu and Empress Kō-ken, ministers at Court conducted all rituals and proceedings according to Buddha-worship. They built magnificent temples in each province which soon rivaled the provincial capitals in splendor. They disseminated Buddhism throughout the land and made government conform to Buddhist ritual. Since commoners below [always] submit eagerly to whatever rituals government officials choose to employ from above, absolute devotion to their foreign idol was evoked in the people's hearts throughout the realm.

Later, the *honji suijaku* doctrine arose.[26] This teaching gave our illustrious native gods Buddhist names. The clerics deceived Heaven and man; they convinced our people that the gods they worshipped were base manifestations of Indian Buddhas. The clerics sought to transform our Divine Land into another India,

to convert innocent subjects of our Middle Kingdom into followers of Indian barbarism. When transformed by barbarism
from within, how can "what is essential to a nation" (*kokutai*)
remain intact? Thus, Ex-emperor Go shirakawa[27] despaired of
bringing Buddhist clerics under control—and that despair be-
spoke a great watershed in our history.

[Soon] the fanatical True Pure Land sect arose. This sect did
not allow members to participate in the duly prescribed religious
rituals of our land or to worship at shrines dedicated to our
illustrious national gods. It suppressed its members' devotion
for Amaterasu and reverence for ancestors, and it forced them
to worship a barbarian idol. Due to their adoration of India, its
followers forsook our Middle Kingdom. Due to their devotion
to Buddhist clerics, they forsook ruler and parent. During their
treasonous uprisings, they labelled the nation's righteous and
loyal defenders "enemies of the Dharma."[28] Thus they turned
their courage and faithfulness against ruler and parent. Never
were loyalty and filial devotion more ignored, never were the
people's hearts more divided.

(Gloss: . . . If clerics can be made to obey the nation's laws,
there is no evil in their taking delight in Buddhist teachings
and living in the peace and solace of enlightenment. Only
when they violate the law do they menace the nation.)

The ancient sages taught rulers the Way—how to cultivate
themselves and rule over others—and nothing else. Scholars of
late cannot understand this. On the one hand, perverse Confucians expound pet theories and distort the true meaning of the
classics, trying to appear original or erudite. On the other, petty
men of letters vie for fame and fortune. But such riff raff are
the least of our problems. The true source of our malaise lies
in four other types of scholars. First there are those who designate the Ming and Ch'ing, rather than our Divine Realm, "Middle Kingdom Civilization."[29] They are ignorant of the virtue
of name and status, and disgrace our nation (*kokutai*). Second
are those who, misled by short-term trends in our history, distort names and abandon virtue by depicting the Emperor as a
defunct monarch in exile.[30] This impairs the Imperial Line's

transforming powers (*kwa*) and defames the bakufu's virtuous achievements. Third are picayune extollers of fiscal solvency and administrative efficiency who style themselves "political economists."[31] Finally are those who expound concepts from Sung Learning, such as "nature" or "Heaven's Will," in seemingly impressive tones and with an imposing mien, but who really are sham Confucians, indifferent to the tasks of the day. None of these four types of scholars represent loyalty, filial devotion, and the Way of Yao, Shun, and Confucius.

In short, Amaterasu's moral precepts have been disrupted by shaman cultists, transformed into something alien by Buddhist clerics, and debased by perverse Confucians and petty men of letters. Because such wicked doctrines were so diverse and contradictory, they destroyed the people's spiritual unity [achieved in antiquity by Amaterasu]. Loyalty of subject for ruler and affection between parent and child are now utterly ignored, leading us to wonder if the Way of Heaven and Man really exists.

In times past, even the worst spreaders of sedition were fellow-nationals working from within. But the Western barbarians are different. They all believe in the same religion, Christianity, which they use to annex territories. Wherever they go, they destroy native houses of worship, deceive the local peoples, and seize those lands. These barbarians will settle for nothing less than subjugating the rulers of all nations and conscripting all peoples into their ranks. And they are becoming aggressive. Having overthrown the native regimes on Luzon and Java, they turned their predatory eyes on our Divine Realm. They instigated insurrections in Kyūshū using the same methods as on Luzon and Java: Not only in Japan have nefarious commoners led people astray by spreading wicked doctrines. Fortunately, our enlightened lords and their astute advisors perceived the foreigners' pernicious designs and took steps to exterminate them. Due to our leaders' wise policies, Christianity was utterly eradicated. Not a single adherent remained alive to subvert our Middle Kingdom, and our people have been spared from the foreigners' wiles for two hundred years.

Even so, Amaterasu's Great Way is not fully elucidated, and the people have nothing to rely on spiritually. What is more, there are as many nefarious commoners in our midst as ever, and if they do not owe their allegiance to shamanism or Buddhism, then most surely they commit themselves to some perverse form of Confucianism or belletristic foolishness. Our present situation is like that of a patient recovering from a near-fatal disease: Though his life is no longer in danger, he is weak and in doubt about his best future course of action. He needs something spiritual to rely on within, and he is attracted to many harmful things from without.

One source of harm that has appeared of late is Dutch Studies. This discipline grew out of translation work—the reading and deciphering of Dutch books by specially trained interpreter-officials. There is no harm in Dutch Studies itself; the harm comes when some dupe with a smattering of second-hand knowledge of foreign affairs mistakenly lauds the far-fetched notions spun out by Western barbarians, or publishes books to that effect in an attempt to transform our Middle Kingdom to barbarian ways.[32] There are, moreover, many curiosities and concoctions from abroad that dazzle the eye and entice our people to glorify foreign ways. Should the wily barbarians someday be tempted to take advantage of this situation and entice our stupid commoners to adopt beliefs and customs that reek of barbarism, how could we stop them? [The *Book of Changes* tells us,] "The lining of frost on which we tread [in early winter soon] turns into a hard sheet of ice." We must adopt appropriate measures to thwart them now, before it is too late.

Now, when barbarians prowl about our coasts harboring pernicious designs on us, wicked doctrines of all sorts are rife within. Nurturing barbarism within our Middle Kingdom will trigger disturbances throughout the realm: Commoners will hatch evil conspiracies, and fawning men will collaborate. What would become of us? Would we still be Middle Kingdom Civilization? Or would we be transformed into another Ming or Ch'ing [China]? Or into an Indian [Buddha-Land]? Or into a Western [barbarian state]? Just what is essential for a land and people to be a nation (*kokutai*)? Without four limbs, a man is not a man. Similarly, a nation has some "requisite and defining entity" (*tai/t'i*) that makes it what it is. Some people stress the need to enrich

169

our country and strengthen our arms in order to defend our borders. But the foreign beasts now seek to exploit the fact that people in outlying areas crave a source of spiritual reliance: They furtively beguile our commoners into betraying us. Should the barbarians win our people's hearts and minds, they will have captured the realm without a skirmish. Then the "wealth and strength" that these people stress would no longer be ours to employ. In effect, we would provide arms for the brigand and provisions for the bandit. What a pity, if, after all our meticulous planning and painstaking effort, we merely ended up joining the enemy's ranks! No one who understands such matters can help being angry and vexed.

The bakufu has decreed resolutely that all contact between commoners in outlying areas and barbarians is strictly forbidden, that commoners may not aid and abet barbarians. This is to prevent the wily foreign curs from luring our people into their fold. Because of this decree, everyone in the realm, wise and foolish alike, is aware of the foreign beasts' loathsome nature and of their detestable designs on us. This is the indomitable spirit of our people.

Though present and past be far removed, His Imperial Majesty is a Descendant of the same Dynastic Line founded by Amaterasu. The masses below are descendants of those masses first blessed by Amaterasu's loving grace in antiquity. If we establish a set of doctrines for the people in keeping with their indomitable spirit, if we serve Heaven, if we revere forbears, if we recompense Amaterasu's original gifts to us, if we remain true to our ancestors in the spirit that She displayed in caring for Her subjects long ago, and if we rectify the loyalty of subject for lord and make warmer still the affection between parent and child, then it will not be difficult to edify the people and achieve spiritual unity. An opportunity like this will not come again in a thousand years—we must exploit it!

I have sought to outline the origin and development of the various ills now afflicting us, and I am deeply disturbed by those stemming from wicked doctrines. A Great Hero can, at a single stroke, alter history by infusing a touch of the Divine. He can accomplish anything at any time. The ancient sage kings maintained control over all within the Four Seas by means of the Great Way of Heaven. Though it assumes different forms [in different eras and places], the essence of the Great Way is immutable. Hence, the Way that Amaterasu used in antiquity to administer the realm, to achieve spiritual unity among the people, and to endear them inseparably to their rulers can be used today. The evils that stem from changing historical forces and from wicked doctrines are too numerous to relate. But by devising counter-measures [based on the Way] we can reform and revitalize the hearts of men. Need we do more?

New Theses: three

What is Essential to a Nation
[*Kokutai*] (II)

Long, long ago the Imperial Court established feudatories and brought its armed might to bear against the four quarters. Expert use of arms was evinced in the Age of the Gods, and the Sword is one of our Three Imperial Regalia. For good reason, then, our country derived its name, "The Land of Proficient Halberds Aplenty."[33] When Amaterasu bequeathed the Middle Kingdom to Ninigi, She dispatched Ame no Oshihi in command of the elite Kume regiment as an escort. This regiment also provided the spearhead of Emperor Jimmu's attack forces, with which he eventually pacified the Middle Kingdom. Emperor Jimmu established the Mononobe [of warriors] and combined this with the Kume regiment to form the Imperial Guard, which he ordered to defend the Palace and bring peace to the land.

Emperor Sujin dispatched generals to the Four Circuits and struck down the rebellious. One of those generals was Prince Toyoki, who suppressed insurrections in the east. Emperor Sujin ordered commoners to hunt during the agricultural off-season and to offer up their catch as a form of tax. These hunts also gave commoners military training and enabled Emperor Sujin to press them into service on His campaigns. Such discipline was upheld during succeeding reigns, and the nation's territory expanded further and further. We drove the Ezo off to the east, eliminated barbarism from Kyūshū, and subdued the Three Kingdoms of Korea. We set up an Imperial Magistrate[34] in Mimana, through which we governed the peninsula. At that time, our ruling prowess was manifest, and by Emperor Nintoku's time, the realm enjoyed such tranquillity that our armed might need no longer be exercised.

But beginning with the reigns of Emperors Richū [r. 400–05]

and Ankō [r. 453-56], our position gradually weakened and declined. After the next few reigns, we lost possession of Mimana, and the Three Kingdoms of Korea ceased bearing tribute.[35] Although Emperor Tenji restored the Dynasty's fortunes temporarily, he was vexed at the narrow sphere of our Dynasty's moral suasion and control (*kōkwa*). During our campaigns in Mimana, Emperor Tenji personally oversaw operations, but in the end, victory eluded us. Our campaigns in the east and north, however, met with triumph. We drove the Ezo even further eastward, and set up an Imperial Magistrate at Shiribeshi.[36]

(Gloss: There is a Mt. Shiribeshi in present-day western Ezo. This probably was the site of ancient Shiribeshi. I understand that in antiquity, there was a road running through this Shiribeshi mountain range and that the ancient Ezo constantly traversed it. But after a hundred years or so, they staged a rebellion, and after this was suppressed, they were forbidden to use the road, so it fell to ruin. In antiquity, Shiribeshi was an area of great strategic importance on our frontier. Because of its rugged, mountainous terrain, the Ezo barbarians could easily convert it into a staging ground for insurrection. That is probably why we forbade them access to the area and why we established an Imperial Magistrate there. We made full use of geographic advantages to check and control barbarians.)

We conquered the Jurchen on the mainland. These conquests actually took place during Empress Saimei's reign [655-61], but it was through [the future Emperor] Tenji's heroic efforts as Imperial Prince that our Dynasty's fortunes revived. Po-hai began to send tribute in recognition of our might and virtue; our ruling prowess was manifest once again.

Although the Way declined [due to Buddhism] for the next hundred years or more, during the reigns of Emperors Kammu [781-806] and Saga [809-23], we brought our northern and eastern regions under control and drove the Ezo across the seas [to Hokkaidō]. In short, our prowess was still intact. It was Amaterasu's manifest design that Her descendents repulse enemies and cultivate the frontiers of the earth, and this design

173

became an Imperial legacy. Ritual prayers addressed to Her, for example, contain the lines "may the realm ruled over by Amaterasu extend as high as Heaven and as broad as earth, may the unruly nations be reduced to subjugation, and may far-off lands be brought into our fold as if hauled in with numerous ropes."[37] During these rituals, His Majesty prays that the Imperial sphere of moral suasion (*kōkwa*) might encompass the four quarters. Herein lies the value that the Imperial Court attached to military prowess when it established its feudatories.

Yet normally in the universe, affairs change with time. Military organization, for example, has undergone many changes. In antiquity, a militia made up of commoners supplemented the Kume and Mononobe; and local feudatories, the *Kuni no miyatsuko* and *Agata nushi,* possessed military units to control their peoples and territories. In general, this was the system of military organization first set up by the state. [Subsequently that system underwent changes.] The first change was the establishment of a conscription system [under the Ritsu-Ryō state], and a second change was the emergence of specialized, family military units in the provinces called *bushi.* Under this latter form of military organization, agriculture and the military first became functionally distinct; military families became known as "houses of mounted bowmen." With the emergence of regionally-based warrior chieftains struggling for power in the Warring States era [1467-1590], feudalism again came into being, and this transition produced a third change in military organization.

In antiquity, people stored weapons in local shrines, and in times of war, prayed to the gods without fail. Not even the Emperor presumed to make decisions for war and peace by himself— he always obtained divine sanction. Through this divine medium, the people were spiritually unified; any dissipation of their energies in diverse directions was prevented. Sacred integration between gods and men characterized this form of military organization.

But after Buddhism entered our Middle Kingdom, spiritual unity dissolved. The people no longer worshipped our heavenly deities with wholehearted devotion, and the meaning behind divine sanction became obscured. Warfare lost its divine quality and became a purely human affair: This was the first Great Transformation in our history. Following the Minamoto regime, the Kamakura and Muromachi bakufus monopolized control over armed forces in the realm: This was the second Great Transformation in our past. In antiquity, all warriors lived on the soil, but by medieval times when warfare was endemic, warrior chieftains campaigned throughout the length and breadth of the realm. After the Warring States era ended, all fighting subsided and warriors settled permanently in castletowns, removed from the land that sustained them: This was the third Great Transformation in our history. Note that none of the three was a simple altering of institutions; instead, the three resulted from changing historical forces.

When warriors maintain roots in the land and the Emperor receives divine sanction, Heaven, Earth, and man form a triad. When men discipline themselves on the basis of this triad, when they train and study diligently, when they prepare for war in times of peace, thereby elucidating the awesome decrees of Heaven and promoting the work of the spirits, there is no limit to what they can achieve. But [after Buddhism came], the first Great Transformation occurred: Our people ceased revering Heaven, Heaven and man became disparate entities, and rulers had nothing to achieve spiritual unity with.

The Kamakura and Muromachi regimes [which ruled during the second Great Transformation] assumed control over the nation's armed forces. Thereafter, great baronial families divided the realm up among themselves, and during the Warring States era [1467-1568], fighting raged throughout the entire land. Because no single source of authority existed, warriors committed themselves to their own particular liege lords, and military power dissipated. Hence the realm was reduced to ruin. The only basis for optimism was that warriors remained on the land that sustained them, for warriors on the land are as plentiful as "water under the ground."[38] Even in the most out-of-the-way rural areas, warriors still defended their land. That is why armed strength remained the order of the day despite dynastic decline and chaos in the realm. Hence we drove off the Mongol enemy and [Hideyoshi] captured the Korean capital. Our immense military might still resonated to far-off shores.

But this tremendous military might greatly troubled Hideyoshi. He assembled the lords of the land in Ōsaka, set them to work on construction projects, or dispatched them to invade Korea. In either case, he prevented them from fortifying their own domains. Tokugawa Ieyasu continued this policy of strengthening central bakufu authority and weakening adversaries on the periphery. By forcing warriors to live permanently in castletowns, he sought to keep them from fortifying themselves in their domains, and to prevent peasants from learning the ways of war. He thus reduced the number of warriors in the land and made commoners ignorant of warfare: For the first time in our history, military weakness became the order of the day. The bold heroes of yesteryear docilely obeyed bakufu decrees. The astuteness of Ieyasu's strategem quickly revealed itself in the way he manipulated the realm.

Nothing in the realm that is of benefit can be without harm. In this case, military weakness led to stagnation. Yet an image of military strength persisted though military weakness was the real order of the day. Why was this? When Ieyasu founded his regime, his warriors were trained in the principles of honor; they willingly died in battle rather than live in shame. Even the strongest and most valiant of his enemies dared not oppose him. Although Ieyasu put an end to warfare in the realm, his officers and men continued to observe the principles of honor and to pride themselves on battlefield heroism. Warfare was still in living memory, and men of that generation continued to prepare for battle. Thus, although military weakness was the order of the day, it had yet to appear on the major thoroughfares and in the castletowns where warriors congregated.

Since the produce of the entire realm sustains warriors, it follows that wealth will accumulate wherever warriors reside. In turn, wherever wealth accumulates, merchants cluster. By nature, merchants follow every latest fashion and stock odd gadgets or novelties to make profits. Such a situation well suited [Ieyasu's] motive: to make valiant commanders and fearless warriors crave peace and loathe war. But after peace continued for a long time, evils appeared, such as the consumption of luxury items not permitted to one's status, or the failure to control one's passions according to the rules of propriety. To grow rich without moral teachings leads to insolent, licentious behavior that knows no bounds.

When wealth overflows, it gives rise to poverty, and poverty goes hand-in-hand with military weakness. To be poor yet indulge in extravagance creates a concern for one's livelihood. A concern for one's livelihood leads one to long for riches. A longing for riches drives one to seek profit without regard to virtue. Then high and low alike hanker for material benefits and are lost to all shame. When a nation falls to such depths, its vitality is sapped and military weakness appears in full view.

Skillful maneuvering of troops, appropriate countermoves in response to enemy tactics, adroit control over the battlefield situation achieved by exploiting topographical advantages—these are the demands of warfare. Yet present-day commanders do not set foot outside the city. They talk about women, banqueting, actors at the theater, flower arrangements, bird hunting, and fishing. Men who take up fencing and spearmanship do so only to fight duels. Those who practice archery or gunmanship do so only as sports to put on display. Those who train horses do so only for ritual events. Armor and weaponry are now antique curios, whose proper apparel and use are known to none. Actual battlefield conditions are beyond the imagination of all.

Warriors are of use only when physically fit. Strength, agility, endurance, indifference to the elements, simplicity and austerity in diet and dress—these constitute the warrior's way of life. That is why a wise commander picks men from tough, no-nonsense country boys reeking of paddy mud, and detests glib-tongued, quick-witted townsmen. When warrior youths live and grow up among merchants, they become frivolous and extravagant. They drink fine wines, relish sweet delicacies, and grow soft. Such a lifestyle inures them well enough to the rigors of late-night banqueting and merrymaking, but hardly prepares them for combat. A wise commander hates such qualities, for they make his men less than useless in wartime. The situation we face fits the adage, "Troops as now trained are worthless."

Military weakness is all too clear; our methods of cultivating strength are fundamentally wrong. [For example,] the rationale behind rice stipends is that each warrior receives a yearly allowance from his daimyo to maintain a personal retainer band.[39] But in reality, warriors cannot maintain these bands because they fritter away stipends in profligacy and presumptuous luxury. So they hire idle townsmen on a part-time basis instead. Should an emergency arise, even high-ranking warriors who receive generous stipends [and should be maintaining large retainer bands,] are essentially no different from commoners. This shows the dearth of warriors in our realm.

Commoners pay extremely heavy taxes to support the warriors [under our present system], so it is not possible to register and conscript them into armed service once again [as we did in antiquity]. Commoners today totally lack pluck and can hardly be expected to achieve great exploits in battle. Thus, there are no warriors to speak of except those in direct liege to bakufu or daimyo and who live in castletowns or traverse our nation's highways [on *sankin kōtai* duty]. Who is to defend the countryside? All warriors in the realm are concentrated in cities and castletowns where they practice fencing during the day. When we look only at the castletowns, we get the illusion of great numbers and military strength. But when we look at the realm as a whole, the virtual absence of warriors in the countryside attests to [the true situation]—paucity of numbers and military impotence. Land exists to support warriors, and warriors exist to defend the land. It is only natural that land without warriors is utterly depleted land, and warriors without land are feeble and few in number. Generations have passed since land and warrior were torn asunder and warriors were allowed to lead lives of ease and comfort. The population as a whole is far greater than in antiquity, but the number of fighting men is far, far fewer. The result of Ieyasu's policies was to debilitate the center as well as the periphery, the bakufu as well as the outer lords. This was not part of his motive for establishing peace and stability. The realm now presents a delusive aura of administrative strength that masks the reality of weakness and decay. I cannot help recalling the adage, "Secure your foundations before it is too late!"

All within the realm today rush headlong toward profligacy and dissipation. Daimyo take the lead in lavish spending beyond their allotted station in society. They are by no means wholeheartedly submissive to the bakufu, but their poverty and sloth prevent them from rebelling. Destitute commoners vent their wrath in peasant uprisings and urban rioting. Their treasonous behavior has not developed into armed insurrection only because of their natural timidity and their ringleaders' ignorance of military affairs. Nefarious commoners roam audaciously through the countryside, and adherents of seditious foreign doctrines infest the realm. Such deadly symptoms have not broken out in a nationwide plague only because of the bakufu's current policy of benevolence and the stop-gap, temporizing measures it adopts to deal with the grave problems before us.

[Tokugawa Ieyasu] sought to weaken the empire and make commoners ignorant, and he succeeded on both counts. Even if someone wanted to stir up trouble, it would be difficult. Our present lack of turmoil can be explained in one sentence: Everyone is afraid of war. When the phrase "fear of war" appears in books of history, even a child can tell that the nation under discussion is weak. How disgraceful! It has been many years since we lost possession of Mimana and since Po-hai ceased bearing tribute. The barbarians are now devouring the Ezo Islands, and here in our homeland (*naichi*), we are separated from their lair by only a strip of water. The lament "under Kings Wen and Wu the nation's territory expanded one hundred miles per day, but now it contracts one hundred miles per day," did not hold only for the Eastern Chou. We, who cower in abject timidity, and whose territory is daily contracting, must face the barbarians, veterans of a hundred campaigns, whose territory is daily expanding. This is enough to send shivers down one's spine.

People today look only at the lingering remnants of bakufu ruling power; they ignore the fact that weakness now prevails. They view the realm as though we were still living in the Bunroku and Keichō eras [1592–1614, when armed might was the order of the day]. How deluded can they be? Barbarian leaders possess the natures of dogs and goats, so it is pointless to compare strengths and weaknesses with them. But their customs are savage, and they constantly wage war; they could not establish and maintain their states through a policy of keeping their subjects ignorant and weak [as we do]. Hence they register and conscript their subjects into armed service, and they augment their ranks with other barbarian peoples [whom they convert] on their overseas campaigns. How can we despise them as few in number? Their nations constantly engage in battle, and they train their peoples in the use of arms. How can we despise them as weak? Because barbarian leaders seduce their peoples into spiritual unity through occult religions, they are more than fit to wage war; because their forte is the manufacture and use of large ships and cannon, they are well equipped to intimidate their foes. They present a mighty spectacle on the high seas and devour far-off lands and peoples at will. How can we despise them as stupid?

Such is the adversary we face. Can we rely on restrictive traditional policies, policies designed to weaken the realm and make commoners ignorant? Can we blithely ignore the need to adjust state policies to meet the demands of changing times? When our objective was to make the realm easy to control, it was wise indeed to make warriors weak and commoners stupid. But advantages always have drawbacks. The bakufu's decision for armed expulsion discloses a larger design: to transform our paucity of numbers into a great multitude and to turn our weakness into strength. This change in policy was dictated by changing historical forces.

To train troops in the principles of honor, and in accordance with Ieyasu's original *motive,* is the way to strengthen central bakufu authority. To allow daimyo to fortify themselves in their domains and to permit their vassals and sub-vassals to cultivate armed strength in the countryside, so that no land lacks warriors and no warrior lacks land, is the way to strengthen our periphery. When both center and periphery are strong and armed warriors exist in great multitudes, the people of our realm will be fearless and will know where to direct their allegiance. Then the spirit of virtue will abound within the four seas. We must raise a chastising army and utilize the might of the whole realm to remove every trace of the ugly barbarians from our shores and make sure they never return. That will more than uphold the nation's honor (*kokutai*).

Some may argue, "If we allow the daimyo to strengthen themselves, we run the risk of insurrection." I disagree. A Great Hero manipulates the realm by relaxing or tightening the institutional system according to his cognizance of contemporary needs. Restraints do not fetter him; he acts in an autonomous manner. With vastness of mind and clearness of vision, he accommodates himself to changed conditions in the realm. With discipline and rigor, he controls life and death within the realm. Therefore, disturbances will not occur. People in the realm understand the bakufu's astute decision [for *jōi*] and ardently await the chance to carry it out. Who would dare stage an uprising? Should the bakufu exploit the present chance to ally itself with the daimyo, to share their joys and sorrows, and to allow them to cultivate military strength, who would dare not comply? If some unruly daimyo did try to use his newly developed strength to defy the bakufu, it should mobilize loyal daimyo in the realm and liquidate that traitor summarily.

Moreover, though I advocate cultivating armed strength in the countryside, I do not mean that we should scrap the present military system totally, or that we should close down the castletowns and return all warriors to the soil. Earlier scholars have proposed doing that, and their arguments were wise on the whole. But they sought to implement military systems suited to a centralized empire though living in a feudal society, which made certain aspects of their proposals unworkable. I will present my own ideas on this subject in detail elsewhere.[40]

The Great Hero relaxes and tightens, adopts and discards [laws and institutions in autonomous fashion]. When he discards one thing, he does so better to adopt another, and when he relaxes one thing, he does so better to tighten up another. Now is the time for him to tighten up the realm. Yet if he is to concentrate tax grains and wealth in the cities, he must relax the system elsewhere. There must be a set criterion for determining what to tighten and what to relax, what to adopt and what to discard. Men and matter decay unless used constantly. The daimyo, their vassals, and sub-vassals should be given life, not left to decay. We must exploit the chance presented by *jōi* to allow the daimyo to strengthen themselves, and we must provide positions of responsibility for those who do. But this proposal is a temporary expedient; we should not make it permanent. Furthermore, we should provide incentives to make these lords perform deeds of merit on behalf of the whole state. The realm is a public trust; one does not cultivate wealth and strength to further private ends.

There is a proper method and a correct time for determining when to relax or tighten, when to adopt or discard. Particulars, such as the frequency and duration of visits to the Court in Edo[41] or the amount and types of taxes or military services imposed on the daimyo, must be dealt with on a case-by-case basis. If we are to adjust state policies to meet the requirements of changing conditions and stave off apathy among the masses, we must make the most of every chance that presents itself. Even if the bakufu insisted on controlling the realm through [obsolete] traditional measures, our coastal areas, for instance, are weakly defended. Should any daimyo's domain be attacked [by foreigners] and suffer defeat, the bakufu would have to send him back to his domain to strengthen his defenses anyway. It is far wiser to take the initiative and send him back to begin with, rather than wait until conditions deteriorate to the humiliating point where there is no other choice. Thus it is said, "seizing the initiative is the key to ruling over others; waiting until too late is to be ruled over by them." Whether the bakufu maintains or loses the realm hinges on its ability to make a decision now! As the ancients said, "When a man resolves and acts, even the spirits defer to him." How much greater are chances for success when his enterprise is one they look upon with favor.

Long ago, prior to his rise to power, Tokugawa Ieyasu esteemed martial prowess because he sought to establish a new regime and to end warfare and suffering in the land. Upon achieving power, he made the realm weak and the people ignorant in order to give them repose: By loosening what was

overly tight, he relieved pressures within. At present, the barbarians prepare for war. They annex territories and peoples
wherever they go; they conspire with one another and prowl
about our shores. The situation today is similar to that of Ieyasu
at Hamamatsu, surrounded as he was by Oda, Takeda, and Hōjō. That was no time for repose; it called for cultivating armed
strength by tightening up what was overly loose.

In sum, we must base ourselves on Ieyasu's *motive* for establishing his regime—not fetter ourselves by adhering to his specific
measures. An examination of our changed times can lead to no
other conclusion. It is said, "the caterpillar constricts itself in
order to lunge forward." We must loosen the realm so as better
to tighten it up, discard some things so as better to adopt others.
We should discard what we once adopted and adopt what was
once discarded, loosen what is now tight and tighten what was
once loose, disregard non-essentials and concentrate on urgent
problems, drop meaningless formalities and seek actual results.
Thus we can tighten up what was tight and adopt what was
used in antiquity. For this, we need a Man of Talent and Virtue.

When Ieyasu arose, the military prowess of Hamamatsu thun-
dered forth through the realm. By making the whole realm
Hamamatsu and thundering forth overseas, we will adhere to
Ieyasu's motive for training troops. We will establish government and elucidate [Amaterasu's] moral precepts, our armies
will obtain divine sanction, Heaven and man will be reunited,
and the spiritual unity [established by Amaterasu] will be re
established among the people. Then, [Amaterasu's] virtue will
shine forth in all its splendor, and [Her Heavenly tasks] will be
achieved. We will make the nation's prestige felt far across the
seas, repulse the barbarians, and cultivate the frontiers of the
universe. Truly, this was Amaterasu's manifest design and Her
legacy to the Imperial House.

New Theses: four

What is Essential to a Nation [*Kokutai*] (III)

Because Amaterasu attached great importance to Her people's livelihood, She provided them with the source of life—food and clothing.[42] The rice and silk that now abound in the realm all originate from Her august rice field and loom; we, Her subjects, continue to enjoy Her blessings even today. Our nation's bountifulness stems from Amaterasu's benevolence and the fertility of our soil, which is well-suited to growing cereals. Our Divine Realm lies to the east, in the direction of the sun. *The Book of Changes* says, "Emperors emerge from the east." The east corresponds to wood and is appropriate for cultivating grains. The east corresponds to spring; it gives life to, and sustains life in, all things. Our people do not eat flesh and drink blood as the barbarians do, so our country with good reason has been called "The Land of Ripening Rice Crests"[43] since ancient times.

In antiquity, the Emperor received cereal grains from the Heavenly Deities.

(Gloss: In "What is Essential to a Nation [Kokutai I]," I discussed how Amaterasu provided Ninigi with seeds from Her august rice field and how Ninigi offered these to the Heavenly Deities.)

All wealth came from a single source, the earth; it belonged to the people as a whole. In later ages, that wealth gradually dissipated; first passing into the hands of warriors, then ending up in the clutches of merchants. The ill effects of these two events are immeasurable, as I relate below in detail.

During Daijō Rituals in antiquity, the entire realm joined His Majesty in devoted worship of the Heavenly Deities. In the

184

autumn of each year when the grain ripened, His Majesty offered some of it to the gods as a symbolic act of thanksgiving, and afterward, consumed it with His people. At such moments, everyone in the realm was made to realize that the grain they consumed derived from Amaterasu's original rice seeds, and they stood in awesome veneration of Her will. They labored to bring forth the richest possible harvests that the soil would yield; their hearts were one with Heaven and Earth, and they gladly partook of the bounties that these provided. Heaven and Earth formed a union.

Even in antiquity, though, there was a time before Imperial rule fully developed, and there were eras of both decline and prosperity: Some people appropriated for themselves the wealth [intended for all]. Emperor Tenji rectified this evil [as part of the Taika Reform] by abolishing all private forms of wealth and equalizing its distribution throughout the realm—ideals instituted in the *Taihō Code* [701]. In the simple days of antiquity, the four classes worked dilligently.[44] Their only business dealings were simple exchanges of goods and services. The people engaged in production extensively, but in consumption, only slightly.

With the development of luxurious habits at Court, however, state revenues went to entertain Court ladies and handmaidens. [Buddhist] subversives appropriated state revenues to their hearts' content in order to build huge temples, and they squandered precious grain to feed a parasitic clergy. After the Fujiwara seized power, great families amassed huge fortunes, created private land holdings called *shōen,* and claimed ownership over the people living there. Since *shōen* lands paid few taxes, Court revenues dwindled. Later, [under the Kamakura regime,] the *shugo* and *jitō* surreptitiously amassed wealth and grain over many generations, until they finally became de facto rulers of the lands under their jurisdiction. At that point, the realm's wealth passed into the hands of warriors.

Since those warriors supported vassals and subvassals to uphold peace and tranquillity in the realm, the wealth they consumed was not wasted. Although the realm witnessed rebellion and disorder at times under early warrior rule, people did not suffer extreme poverty. Today, by contrast, we enjoy peace, but high and low alike are at their wit's end trying to escape destitution. This paradox stems from our failure to understand the Great Way as it applies to managing the realm's finances.

After the warriors left their land [for castletowns], they could no longer afford to maintain large retainer bands, so they hired idle townsmen as servants or workers when the need arose. Cities now teem with idlers and vagabonds who are less than useless in the event of war, and are a tremendous drain [on the realm's precious food supplies]. There are close to five hundred thousand Buddhist temples in the realm, and who knows how many million clerics, nuns, and servants belong to these.

(Gloss: The T'ang minister Fu I wrote a memorial stating, "If we provided husbands and wives for the monks and nuns, over ten thousand new households would come into being. . . ." From the year 845, Emperor Wu destroyed all temples in the land [except for two temples in both Ch'ang-an and Lo-yang and one in each of the other large cities]. He destroyed a total of 44,600 main and branch temples and converted some 260,500 clerics, nuns, and novices into useful, tax-paying subjects. In addition, the state reclaimed countless millions of acres of temple lands. As these figures show, despite the vastness of the T'ang Empire, it contained less than one-tenth the number of Buddhist temples now in our Divine Realm. Even so, the Chinese of that era were amazed at the numbers involved, which only underscores the size of the Buddhist establishment in our Divine Realm.)

The erection of palatial temples gave rise to, and now supports, hordes of merchants, artisans, and other townsmen [who should be working the land]. Tramps and beggars make their work a hereditary calling. Gamblers and thieves swagger through the countryside in countless numbers. Fortunetellers and shamans hoodwink and fleece the people of their wealth. Actors and entertainers of various types parasitically deplete the nation's grain supply, which is meager enough to begin with due to our production and consumption of luxury items such as *sake, mochi,* rice confections, and noodles.[45] We lose much rice on land and sea during shipment to Edo, Ōsaka, and other cities. The growing of cash crops such as tea, tobacco, dyer's saffron, sugar cane, and sweet-pears reduces farm production. Thus, our large-scale cultivation of commercial crops hinders farming, our methods of consumption are inefficient and wasteful, we have a tremendous number of idle mouths to feed, and our grain harvests are hardly enormous. Why is it that rice seems to abound and goes to waste throughout the realm while we suffer destitution? This is bewildering at first glance.

But the amount of rice we possess is not great at all—it is only made to appear so. If we store small amounts of some commodity in many separate places, its total volume might be quite large, despite appearances to the contrary. By the same token, even a relatively small amount of that same commodity naturally is made to appear large when stockpiled in one place. For example, one *koku* of rice stored in a farmer's house does not seem very much, but if ten thousand farmers each sold his one *koku* to a rice dealer, we could not help being impressed by how much flowed into the market.

Warriors live in cities and receive yearly rice-stipends, and have no trouble frittering these away on banqueting and women. That leaves them no surplus rice to repair or replace armor and weapons or to maintain a retainer band. They sell it [to meet living expenses] rather than store it at home. Farmers are extravagant and indolent despite being poor. They sell their crop to obtain a cash income, but the more rice they sell, the lower its market price falls, and the lower this falls, the more they must sell. No matter how much more they sell, their cash income is always lower than before, and this makes many of them abandon their village for the city. The fields they formerly cultivated go to waste for want of tillers, but the taxes owed by those who remain are as high as before. After paying taxes, selling the rest of their crop, and disposing of all valuables, these villagers still find themselves in debt.

Thus, the amount of rice sold on the market constantly increases, but the amount in the realm as a whole steadily decreases. The amount of rice in the realm as a whole steadily decreases, but the cities are full of rice. Looking at the cities full of rice shows just how depleted the rest of the realm is. But even so, the cities cannot store much more rice than the people consume there. They contain just a little more rice than is necessary to support their populations—and that is not really very much. The difference between a small surplus and a slight deficiency does not seem very great, but it can make all the difference in the world. Imagine a man who has just eaten his fill. If we offered him "just a little more" rice, he would think it far too much. But consider the poor man, who, even in the best of times, never receives quite enough to eat. If we made his rice ration "just a little less," he would think it a great deprivation. In this sense, the slight difference between "a little too much" and "not quite enough" is made to seem large indeed to those on the short end. Thus I say, the amount of rice stored in the cities is not very great, and the amount in the realm as a whole is even less.

Today we distress ourselves about the cheapness of rice and our lack of money. But these are not real problems: Rice is not cheap, nor is money in short supply. Our true problem is the high cost of goods and services. For example, let us say that 0.1 *koku* of rice sells for 5 *momme*. If a cotton garment also sold for 5 *momme*, we would be able to exchange 0.1 *koku* of rice for one garment. But in fact, it sells for as much as 0.6 or 0.7 *koku* of rice at current prices. In other words, rice is not cheap; cotton garments are too expensive. We eat rice to fill our stomachs; there is a limit to how much we can consume. This is not true with other commodities. We continually seek the fashionable or the novel, and there is no limit on our desire to possess, or our willingness to pay for, such articles. A single lady's hair ornament, for example, may cost as much as a middle-sized farm. Warriors exchange rice, a commodity that can be consumed only to a limited extent, for money. But with that money they purchase goods that they desire to possess, and are willing to pay for, to an unlimited degree. This is why rice alone is cheap, while other commodities are extremely costly.

Money [has no intrinsic value, it] simply measures the relative worth of commodities. When goods to be sold are abundant, their value is low, and that of money is high. As long as the value of money is high, it suffices to meet our needs even if there is little in circulation. For this simple reason there was never any destitution in earlier ages despite the extreme scarcity of money. Since the Keichō era [1596–1614], however, a great amount of gold has been mined and minted, so money now is of low value and goods and services are costly. To make ends meet, artisans and merchants must raise their prices. Living costs climb steeply, but the value of coinage plummets, and people mistakenly believe they need more money despite its plentiful supply.

(Gloss: According to one barbarian writer,[46] "Since the New World was discovered, the volume of trade between Europe and the Americas has been increasing steadily, and the quantity of gold and silver accruing to Europe from America is immense. Therefore, the value of gold and silver within Europe has declined steadily, and the cost of rice and other commodities has risen steadily. Many scholars are concerned about the disastrous effects of this excess coinage, but little can be done to help the situation because Europeans are so accustomed to garnering large profits from this arrangement that they are not likely to abandon their mercenary ways in the foreseeable future." Even the barbarians realize that too much coinage in circulation creates huge problems. Why is it that we in the Middle Kingdom remain ignorant of this fact?)

When some things are too expensive, others appear unduly cheap. Because the cost of goods and services in the realm is excessively high, coinage is made to seem worthless, and the price of rice falls. Warriors live in cities and must buy all necessities of life from merchants. They exchange rice, whose market value is steadily declining, for coinage, whose value is also steadily declining. With this depressed coinage, they purchase goods and services, whose prices are steadily rising. No wonder they cannot make ends meet.

Their hereditary retainers also are used to luxuries, so warriors cannot retain these sub-vassals with paltry sub-stipends. In time, they must discharge their hereditary retainers and hire followers on a contract (annual or biannual) basis. But later on, even these part-time followers (known as *nenkimono*) acquire expensive habits, and prove too large a burden. Warriors then must hire idle townsmen on a case-by-case basis. But because of their extravagant ways, these men also turn out to be a great financial strain. On top of that, household expenses, allowances to wives and mistresses, and entertainment fees, all keep rising. Because warriors cannot meet these expenses with stipends alone, they borrow money from rich merchants. This soon becomes an ingrained habit, and even the greatest daimyo today find themselves deep in debt. In short, cunning, tight-fisted profit-mongers manipulate the great lords of the land like so many puppets-on-a-string. Clearly, the realm's wealth has fallen into the merchants' clutches.

Rice is the object that the ancient sage-ruler [Amaterasu] greatly treasured. Not even the Emperor dares consume or distribute it without offering thanks to the gods. He obtains it from Heaven and nourishes His people with it. This is as it should be. [But today] lowly merchants enjoy the exclusive right to procure and market this treasured item while princes and great lords submit in mute deference: The people's very livelihood has been entrusted to contemptible merchants. We lack provisions for an army or to meet the needs of natural disasters; the entire realm is a depleted void, but no one finds this odd in the least. We look at one another complacently, our only concern being what to do with all the excess rice on our hands. How deluded can we be?

In antiquity, Amaterasu cared greatly about Her people's livelihood, and we enjoy Her blessings even today. The rice nurturing our bodies derives from the original seeds that She bestowed on our ancestors. But not only do we fail to cherish and conserve Her gift to us, we grumble about having too much of it, and fret over how to dispose of it. Some people even wish to barter it off to the foreign barbarians![47] They were born in "The Land of Ripening Rice Crests" yet despise rice. They would sell this precious gift of Amaterasu's to the dogs and goats of the world and gloat over having found a clever solution to our fiscal ills! Is this how a subject repays Amaterasu's blessings?

[Aside from that issue], it is easy to see why we should keep the rice we produce at home rather than dispose of it abroad. Our nation's farmers now grow about twenty-five million *koku* of rice. Since the average land-holding of one farm household is about ten *koku*'s worth[48] [or one *chōbu* of land], there must be approximately two and one-half million farm households in the nation. If each retained one *koku* above its actual needs, the amount stored in the nation's farm households would total two-and-a-half million *koku*. At present, the annual amount of rice bought and sold on the Ōsaka market comes to no more than two million *koku*.

(Gloss: According to records left by a certain Ōsaka merchant in the early Temmei era [1781–88], the total annual amount of rice transacted on the Ōsaka market from 1763 to 1780 was less than two million *koku*, and the amount stored in Ōsaka was anywhere from thirty or forty thousand *koku* to one million *koku* per year at the most. But since I know little about business, a merchant should be consulted on such matters.)

The general situation in other cities can be inferred from these figures. If each of our two and one-half million farm households stored one *koku* above its actual needs at home, two and one-half million *koku* would leave the market. And if the daimyo and warriors did likewise, the volume of rice in circulation would decrease even further. As the volume of rice sold on the market dwindled, we could look forward to its price going up. Then farmers could sell less and still make ends meet. If farmers sold less rice, city-dwellers would have less to waste and would have to find ways of conserving it. Of course, as the volume of rice flowing into the cities decreased, the amount remaining in the realm as a whole would have to increase. The people would not suffer from too much rice because they would store and consume it, rather than sell it at depressed prices.

If we really wanted to store rice in the realm, we could. Why do people advocate bartering it off to foreigners as a way to save the realm from destitution? There are any number of appropriate measures and incentives to make people store rice, but first we must admit the need to do so. Only when the

191

people have sufficient supplies of rice and have no anxieties about their livelihood, will they refrain from evildoing. And only when they refrain from evildoing can they be induced to stand in awesome veneration of Amaterasu's will, to labor to bring forth the richest possible harvests that the soil will yield, and to partake of Amaterasu's gifts, derived as these are from the bounties of Heaven and Earth.

New Theses: five

World Affairs

Change is the constant Way of Heaven and Earth. The world's nations have undergone innumerable changes. Two great land-masses [or hemispheres] exist amid the oceans; one contains our Middle Kingdom and the lands on the western side of the sea. The lands on the southern side of the sea may also be considered part of it.

(Gloss: This land-mass extends from a point twenty-five degrees east of Kyōto to a point seventy-five degrees west of it. Some think of it as comprising areas called "Asia," "Africa," and "Europe." But these names were coined by the barbarians, and are not generally used in the world. Furthermore, because the Imperial Court has not authorized their use, I shall not employ them here.)

The other great land-mass lies on the eastern side of the sea.

(Gloss: This extends from a point fifty degrees west of Kyōto to a point ninety-five degrees east of it. This land-mass is sometimes divided up into areas called "South America" and "North America," but these names too, were coined by the barbarians.)

There are many [independent] territories (*kuiki*) on these two great land-masses, and each defends itself against all others. Collectively, these territories are known as "the nations of the world."

In antiquity, prior to the dawn of civilization, barbarian tribes flocked and herded together like so many birds and beasts: They displayed no development worth outlining. On the other hand, we in the Middle Kingdom established feudatories in the form of *Kuni no miyatsuko* and *Agata nushi,* each of which defended its own territory. About midway through our history [the Nara period], we set up a centralized administrative system of provinces and districts. Later, regional lords divided up the land, and the feudal system again sprang up. [In China, by contrast,] the Yü, Hsia, Shang, and Chou ruled their realms through feudal princes, but after Ch'in and Han times, the system of provinces and districts remained with few modifications. The Yü, Hsia, Shang, and Chou periods witnessed unified rule, but during the Spring and Autumn period, there was a loose hegemony, and in the Warring States period, Seven Great Kingdoms fought among themselves. The many periods of unity and disunity thereafter are documented in works of history.

Barbarian peoples of times past scampered about like birds and beasts. Each, in turn, made a nuisance of itself, but on the whole, they were an intermittent menace at most. Only after Yü and Hsia times did the Hsien-yün appear, only after Shang and Chou times did the Hsiung-nu appear, only after Ch'in and Han times did the T'u-fan and Hui-ho appear, and only after Sung and T'ang times did the Khitan and Jurchen appear. Finally, only after Sung and Yüan times did the Western barbarians appear. They venture out to ravage and annex lands despite living ten thousand miles across the sea. As civilization steadily progressed, even the barbarians received its blessings; they learned [the technique] of creating religious injunctions and precepts to guide their peoples. Today their towering fortresses surrounded by deep moats are a far cry from their crude huts and tents of yesteryear; their huge warships and cannon are a great advance over their mounted bowmen of bygone days. Moreover, in past eras, their only means of securing obedience in their vast hordes was to lure followers with booty and intimidate them with force. As a result, those hordes lacked integration and permanence. But now Islam and Christianity have provided their leaders with these two elements and more. Today, each barbarian tribe, while maintaining its own territory, allies itself with all others to convert the entire world to their religion. Thus they are a far cry from the wandering nomads of centuries past.

In antiquity, periods of warring states signified fighting between small regional units within a single territory; today, entire territories go to war. Besides our Middle Kingdom and the Manchu Ch'ing Empire, five other states call themselves empires: Mogul, Persia, Turkey, Germany, and Russia. These constitute the world's Seven Great Empires. The small regional units that fought in previous periods of warring states are dwarfed by comparison.

(Gloss: According to scholars of Dutch Studies,[49] the barbarians call all the above nations "empires" (*teikoku*). In addition, other states such as Ethiopia, Morocco, Siam, and Sumatra in Java are often referred to as empires. Of these [lesser states,] Ethiopia considers itself a great power because of its size, and Morocco, because of its Islamic orthodoxy. But Ethiopia is populated by Negroes possessing foolish old customs, and Morocco is reeling from internal strife. Siam is rich but militarily impotent. Sumatra occupies a key position as the gathering place for the various barbarians, but is small and weak. None of these [lesser states] qualifies as a great power, so I omit them from this discussion. Scholars of Dutch Studies also label the kings of barbarian states "emperors." But they simply use the ideograph "*tei*" to convey a sense of nobility relative to baseness when translating the Dutch word "*keiser*," which originally designated the founder of ancient Rome. Because these barbarian kings bear no semblance to our Emperor, I do not refer to them with the ideograph "*tei*.")

The barbarians who menaced our periphery in ages past were the Kumaso, Hayato, Emishi, and Ezo. After subduing them, we induced the Three Kingdoms of Korea, the Su-shen, and the Po-hai to bear tribute to us. On the other hand, the Jurchen and Mongols tried to invade our shores from abroad.

(Gloss: After the Jurchen defeated the Khitan, they tried to invade the Sung, and in the Kannin era [1017–20], they attacked Kyūshū. We call this raid the "Attack of the Toi." Some two hundred years later the Mongols reigned supreme in the northeast and tried to annex the Sung. They too

195

attacked Kyūshū. Both cases represent southward thrusts made by northern peoples.) [50]

But blocked by rough seas, these would-be invaders could cause little damage. At that time, we took the ocean for granted as a natural barrier. Now, the barbarians traverse thousands of miles with whirlwind speed in their huge ships; they think of the ocean as a highway to distant lands. Because we are surrounded by water, we must be prepared on all sides. What was once a natural barrier is now a raiders' highway. Those seeking to defend our borders and pacify outlying areas cannot propose measures today based on assumptions belonging to eras past.

In today's era of warring states, the Mogul and Turkish Empires use Islam to strengthen their armies and enlarge their domains, Turkey being the more successful. But neither has attempted to invade our Middle Kingdom because they specialize in cavalry warfare to the detriment of naval operations. The Western barbarians, on the other hand, all believe in the Church of Rome. [51] The more outstanding of these are France, Spain, Sweden, and England. Their common mother-country is Germany, but it is no longer powerful. Its head of state simply maintains the title "Holy Roman Emperor" along with something of his former glory, and is therefore accorded a degree of respect by the other Western states.

Russia was once subject to Germany (as was France), but recently has acquired awesome strength and has reclaimed its ancient status as an empire. [52] Its territory includes states to the east and west, and borders our Divine Realm on the northwest. Russia contains vast expanses of frozen tundra, and longs to expand southward. But Turkey, Russia's long-standing nemesis, has been thwarting it. Russia has revived as an ally the Persian Empire (recently weakened by rebellion), and has defeated Turkey. [53] Should Russia and Persia again join forces, Turkey's left flank will be cut off. Russia, hegemon of the north, is now expanding southward to gain a stranglehold on the continent by dividing it in half, and is preventing Turkey from allying with the Mogul Empire. Ch'ing power has reached its limit, and can expand no further west. Russia has reduced neighboring domains to subservience and is a threat to all nearby states. It brandishes its power on the pretext that it is successor to the long-defunct Eastern Roman Empire. The lesser barbarians tremble in fear and brace themselves against Russia's mighty onslaughts. Russia will not desist until taking the entire world by storm.

In times past China (Kando) was plagued intermittently by barbarian tribes of various sorts [as previously mentioned]. One of them conquered China and became its emperor. Now Russia has annexed the homeland of these tribes, the Tungus area, and this will bring it into conflict with the Ch'ing Empire. But the Ch'ing, as strong as ever, is holding its own. So Russia has turned its predatory eyes on our Divine Realm. Russia plots to take over our Divine Realm first; then it will round up our people to ravage China's eastern seaboard and subvert the Ch'ing just as the so-called Japanese Raiders (*wakō*) subverted the Ming many years ago. Russia then will exploit this golden opportunity [while Ch'ing forces are held down in the east] to capture Hami, Manchuria, and other lands on the Ch'ing northern frontier. Then it will make a daring thrust on Peking itself, and the Ch'ing will have to capitulate. Having defeated China, Russia could easily topple the Mogul Empire. Then, with help from Persia, it would have no trouble conquering Turkey.

But if the Ch'ing prove more formidable than expected, and success seems unlikely in the east, Russia may strike to the west first. At the opportune moment, it will ally itself with Persia and seize Turkey. Having taken Turkey, it will assault the Mogul Empire and push on to Dzungar, to grapple with the Ch'ing. If successful against the Ch'ing, it will assemble a fleet and close in on our Divine Land.

In short, Russia either can sweep westward from the east, or eastward from the west. It will wait for the best time and consider all relevant factors before choosing. But whichever course Russia adopts, if successful, it will become ruler of the world. Naturally, it will opt for the easier of the two courses. That is why the Russians constantly prowl about our islands—they want to probe our defenses. Because navagation is Russia's forte, it is not timid about venturing on turbulent, stormy seas. Russia has already beaten Turkish land forces and seized various overseas islands (*kaigai shotō*). Russia is right on our doorstep, and is a far graver menace than the Jurchen or Mongols ever were. Those who seek to defend our borders and pacify outlying areas must realize that world conditions today are different from eras past; they must devise policies to deal with the present.

The world situation today, with its Seven Great Powers, presents striking similarities to that of the late-Chou period and its Seven Great Kingdoms. For example, Russia and Turkey are large, powerful states constantly at odds; in these respects, they resemble Ch'in and Ch'u. The wealth and power of the Ch'ing empire and its eastern location remind us of Ch'i. The Mogul and Persian empires resemble Han and Wei due to their central position. Germany, despite the respect accorded it by virtue of its title and former grandeur, is no longer an empire in reality; instead, Germany is on a par with France, Spain, or England. At most, Germany is a Han or a Wei; in lesser terms, a Sung or a Chung-shan.

(Gloss: Due to the respect accorded it by other barbarian nations, Germany appears analogous to the Eastern Chou. But viewed in today's world situation, there is a big difference that stops me from drawing that parallel.)

Our Divine Realm, due to its location east of the Ch'ing, would seem analogous to Yen, shielded from attack by Ch'i and Chao. But today the ocean is a raiders' highway; we alone cannot hope to escape the grim realities of war as Yen did in antiquity. Therefore, our position is more like that of Chou, bordered on by Han and Wei. France, Spain, and England all revere the same religion as Russia: Christianity.

(Gloss: Some say that Spain and England revere different religions, but these are simply variant sects, so there is little real difference. What is more important, both employ religion to annex territories whenever and wherever they please.)

It is only natural that these three countries conspire. They have already annexed Luzon and Java in the South Sea Islands, and have seized the Americas, located at the eastern end of the sea.

The Great Powers are dividing up the earth. Today we find ourselves alone in a hostile world; we defend a solitary castle under attack by enemies who erect fortresses along our borders.

The foremost adversary to stave off is Russia. If Turkey heeds conditions here in the east and coordinates troop movements accordingly, its power might keep Russia from striking in this direction. Or if the Mogul Empire allies itself with Turkey and they take over Persia [Russia's ally], this also would check Russia. The Manchu Ch'ing empire is the only nation besides ours unbefouled by either Islam or Christianity.

(Gloss: Countries such as Korea and Annam also maintain their independence (*tokuritsu*) by remaining unconverted to those occult religions. But these states are small and weak, so I omit them from this discussion.)

[Ch'ing China and our Divine Realm either stand or fall together:] "if the lips crumble, the teeth arc naked and exposed."[54]

This is the world situation facing us today. We must adjust to it and remain flexible enough to deal with constantly changing conditions. At home we must set up adequate defenses; in our foreign policy, we must "counteract the enemy's stratagems in advance and deprive him of would-be allies."[55] But to do all this, we first must select the right statesman-general.

New Theses: six

The Barbarians' Nature

For close to three hundred years now the Western barbarians have rampaged on the high seas. Why are they able to enlarge their territories and fulfill their every desire? Does their wisdom and courage exceed that of ordinary men? Is their government so benevolent that they win popular support? Are their rites, music, laws, and political institutions superb in all respects? Do they possess some superhuman, divine powers? Hardly. Christianity is the sole key to their success. It is a truly evil and base religion, barely worth discussing. But its main doctrines are simple to grasp and well-contrived; they can easily deceive stupid commoners with it. Using clever words and subtle phrases, they would have commoners believe that to deceive Heaven is to revere it, and that to destroy the Way is needed for ethical understanding.

They win a reputation for benevolence by performing small acts of kindness temporarily to peoples they seek to conquer. After they capture a people's hearts and minds, they propagate their doctrines. Their gross falsehoods and misrepresentations deceive many, particularly those who yearn for things foreign. Such dupes, with their smattering of secondhand Western knowledge, write books with an air of scholarly authority; so even daimyo or high-ranking officials at times cannot escape infection from barbarian ways. Once beguiled by Christianity, they cannot be brought back to their senses. Herein lies the secret of the barbarians' success.

Whenever they seek to take over a country, they employ the same method. By trading with that nation, they learn about its geography and defenses. If these be weak, they dispatch troops to invade the nation; if strong, they propagate Christianity to subvert it from within. Once our people's hearts and minds are captivated by Christianity, they will greet the barbarian host with open arms, and we would be powerless to stop them. Our people would consider it an honor and a privilege to die for this foreign god, and this willingness to die, this fearlessness, would make them fit for battle. Our people would gladly cast their riches into the sacrificial coffers of this foreign god, and those riches would finance barbarian campaigns. The barbarians believe it their god's will that they seduce other peoples into subverting their respective homelands; they borrow the slogan "universal love"[56] to achieve their desired ends. Barbarian armies seek only plunder, but do so in the name of their god. They employ this tactic in all lands they annex or conquer.

Only after developing their strength to the fullest did barbarian nations come to spy on us. The Portuguese were the first to enter our homeland (*naichi*). Their nation, Portugal, is under the control of Spain, but during the Tembun era [1532–54], it expanded greatly, annexing numerous islands in the South Sea and large parts of America. The Portuguese came to Kyūshū to propagate Christianity and incite our stupid masses to revolt, but they converted certain daimyo such as Ōtomo Sōrin and Konishi Yukinaga as well.[57] Oda Nobunaga himself erected a church to their god in Kyōto and invited barbarian clerics to preach there. As a result, Christianity gradually infected the realm. The barbarians quickly proceeded to comfort and care for the needy and distressed in an effort to capture our people's hearts and minds. When Oda Nobunaga perceived their ulterior motives, he vowed to destroy the church in Kyōto and eradicate all clerics from the land, but passed away before accomplishing this.

(Gloss: When Nobunaga first decided to build the church, his trusted retainer, Gyōbu Masanori, tried to dissuade him, but to no avail. Nobunaga probably planned to use Christianity to subvert his enemies as he once subverted Araki Murashige.[58] But he soon realized his mistake and lamented, "Gyōbu was right about those Christians. I have heard of believers in Buddha giving alms to clerics, but never have I heard of almsgiving from clerics to believers. Yet that is exactly what the barbarian clerics do. When they first came, they said they wanted to trade, but they do not seek profits. Quite the contrary, they engage in charitable works. They must be out to subvert out land.")

Toyotomi Hideyoshi banished overseas all stupid commoners whose minds had been polluted by this barbarian religion, and Tokugawa Ieyasu strictly prohibited propagation of it or belief in it. Thereafter, barbarians like the English or Spanish might come to our land, but never again could they bring their religion.

(Gloss: Tokugawa Ieyasu once sent a Nishi Munazane to the West, and he returned three years later.[59] Hideyoshi as well, sent a certain man named Ibi to the West, and he returned seven years later.[60] In both cases, the men were sent on reconnaissance missions, it is said, and they probably picked up a thorough knowledge of foreign languages. Without a doubt, their reports had much to do with the banning of Christianity. Iemitsu, in turn, sent an interpreter to India to inspect Buddhist temples there. His lordship undoubtedly had good reasons for doing so.)

At the beginning of the Kan'ei era [1624–44], the bakufu passed edicts forbidding the casting of barbarian images and forcing all stupid commoners who had been Christians to tread on the Cross as a test of loyalty. The barbarians probably surmised that they could not evade this bakufu decree; the mere thought of paying anchor at Nagasaki struck fear in their hearts. Ch'ing writers who advocated razing churches and eradicating Christianity in their own land lauded our policies.

(Gloss: The *Hsi-ho chih* and *T'ai-wan chih* are two good examples.)

When state power is on the upswing, Heaven lends a helping hand. So it was at Shimabara. Heaven brought all the realm's Christians together in one castle so that they could be exterminated. At that time, the barbarians were doing their best to propagate Christianity in our land. The King of Poland sent his niece, and the King of Navarre came in person, to win converts. But as soon as they arrived, they were cut down.[61] When other barbarians heard this news, they were so dejected that, according to one Ming writer,[62] they muttered to themselves, "[Japanese officials are so perceptive] they must have three eyes each." How gratifying to know that our nation's power looms this great in foreign eyes!

(Gloss: The Ming writer [Su Nai-yü] records that this occurred in "the year of elder-brother, earth-tiger," which corresponds to 1638. In a supplementary note to his text, he wrote, "This 'three eyes' lament stems from the fact that these two persons had returned to Japan and resumed their proselytizing only to be executed."

This note refers to the King of Navarre and the King of Poland's niece. But the King of Navarre was executed in 1636, two years before the year of elder-brother, earth-tiger, and the King of Poland's niece met her demise in 1639, one year after that year. Obviously, the Ming writer was mistaken. [I propose that our suppression of the Shimabara Rebellion was the true cause of the barbarians' dismay.] The Shimabara Christian insurgents were smitten in 1638, the year of elder-brother, earth-tiger. This event was more than enough to strike terror in the barbarians' hearts, but the Ming writer probably did not know this. That is probably why he attributed the Westerners' dismay to the executions of the two European nobles.)

After we enjoyed peace and tranquillity for many years, the barbarians appeared again, this time the English, who begged permission to trade.

(Gloss: The *Nagasaki yawa* has this to say about them.[63] "English ships frequently appeared in Nagasaki until the Genna era [1615–23], when they voluntarily closed their trading post and stopped coming; undoubtedly they realized that the times no longer favored them. But their mercenary spirit prompted them to return to Nagasaki in 1673, when they came begging permission to reopen trade. On that occasion, their request was denied." If we think carefully about the significance of this passage, it seems to be a realistic assessment.)

Next, Rome sent one of its clerics to propagate their faith surreptitiously among our people.[64] In this case, too, we foiled the barbarians' designs. But Russia has expanded tremendously of late. It utilized Christianity to seduce the Ezo tribes into submission and to capture island after island [to our north]. Now Russia has turned its predatory eyes on Japan proper (*naichi*). The English also appear at frequent intervals, furtively trying to beguile our commoners and peoples in outlying areas. Portugal was the first to use Christianity to spy on our Middle Kingdom, but was by no means the last.

The peoples of Europe happen to be at war with each other now. But they all revere the same god. When the opportunity for a quick kill presents itself, they combine forces, and [after attaining victory,] divide the spoils. On the other hand, when they encounter difficulties, each withdraws to its own territory. This explains why we enjoy peace here in the east whenever there is strife in the west, and why there is peace in Europe whenever they venture to the east seeking plunder and territory. Russia, after subduing the lesser barbarians to the west, has turned its attention to the east. It has captured Siberia, and wants to infiltrate the Amur River area. But the Ch'ing empire, as strong as ever, is frustrating Russian designs there. As a countermove, Russia now is invading our Ezo territories. This is the same stratagem Ssu-ma Ts'o [of the Ch'in] used to conquer Shu; [that is, to build up one's troop strength by annexing easily-conquerable states to begin with, and only then take on large, powerful enemies]. Moreover, after its crushing defeat at the hands of K'ung-ge erh,

(Gloss: I cannot identify this "K'ung-ge erh" for certain, but it probably refers to Germany. I have my own hypothesis about the etymology and Chinese transliteration of the name, but will not present it here.[65] Germany is no longer a great power, but the barbarian nations of the West still revere it as their mother country, and rushed to its defense against

Russia. From this, the Ch'ing historian who heard about Russia's defeat, erroneously inferred that Germany was a great power.)

Russia concluded a treaty of peace. Now Russia probably will try to expand in the east to recoup her losses and obtain reparation monies [to pay the West]. For these reasons, it has stepped up spying operations in our waters.

(Gloss: In the Gembun era [1736–40], a Russian ship appeared off the Mutsu and Awa coasts, but during the next few decades, Russian ships paid few visits to our land. The Russians concluded peace with K'ung-ge erh in 1770, and in the following year, a Russian named Benyowsky sailed by our eastern and southern coasts, measuring the ocean's depth and drawing a map of the Orient. He left a letter saying that Russia was about to launch an invasion of the Ezo Islands.[66] The next year, the Russians commenced hostilities against the Ezo to take over Uruppu, and after winning the natives over to their side with gifts, they captured it along with Shimoshiri. Next they infiltrated Nokkamapu, and lost no time disseminating their religion among the Ezo on Etorofu. Such events prompted the bakufu to draw up plans to develop the Ezo wilderness.)[67]

First, the Russians confined themselves to drawing sketches and maps of our terrain and coastline and to studying our moves and countermoves. Then they began to seduce our commoners into their fold and politely requested permission to trade.[68] But when we denied this request, they ravaged Ezo, seized our weapons, and set fire to our outposts there.[69] Then they requested permission to trade once more.[70] In other words, after slowly and methodically reconnoitering our position, they make their requests, sometimes under the cloak of politeness and correct protocol, sometimes accompanied by armed violence. They use every conceivable technique to achieve their ulterior motives, ulterior motives that are clear to any thinking man.

But our temporizing, gloss-it-over officials say, "They only come for provisions of rice; there is no cause for alarm." What simpletons! Unlike us, the barbarians eat flesh, not rice: A lack of rice should not bother them.

(Gloss: This is not entirely true. They do eat rice, but only in the form of *mochi* [glutinous rice cakes].)[71]

Even if they did want rice, there are many rice-growing areas in their home countries, in their colonies, and in their allies' lands.

(Gloss: India and the South Sea Islands all produce rice, as do other territories further to the south, no doubt. It is quite clear that their recent expansion has provided them with more than ample supplies of rice.)[72]

They use trade to probe for weaknesses and disseminate their occult religion [among their victims.] Russia seeks to enrich and populate her eastern provinces of Kamchatka and Okhotsk with profits garnered from trade. Then she could raise and supply large armies right here on the eastern front [instead of transferring men and provisions from the west.] Trade, then, is her single stone to kill two birds; this is why she has stepped up operations in the east. She is now fully committed on this front, and will not desist until attaining her goals here.

But the Russians have been strangely quiet of late, and in their place, the English have suddenly appeared. First they perpetrated violence in Nagasaki.[73] Then they forced their way into Edo Bay.[74] In short, the Russians, who have harbored designs on us for over one hundred years, suddenly disappear without a trace, and the English, who have rarely ventured to our coasts, just as suddenly zoom in to reconnoiter and probe. Can this be mere coincidence? Vicious birds of prey always pounce on their victims from dark shadows: The Russians are now hiding in wait for the kill. To facilitate their sly stratagem, they have English underlings do their reconnaisance work.

(Gloss: Once a castaway from Owari was saved by an English ship, and one from Satsuma, by a Russian ship. When the two ships met on the high seas, the Owari castaway was transferred to the Russian vessel, and both were sent to Russia.[75] On another occasion, when guardsmen at our outposts on Karafuto and Etorofu were captured by the Russians and interned in Kamchatka, an Englishman was among their interrogators.[76] This shows that the Russians and English are in league against us.

Furthermore, in 1807, the year that the Russians assaulted the Ezo Islands, a merchant ship from Boston [the *Eclipse*] "just happened" to call at Nagasaki seeking firewood and water. This town of Boston is the site of England's magistrate in her American colony of New England. In other words, Russians violate our northland and New Englanders reconnoiter our southern coast. Can this be mere coincidence?)[77]

When Chu-ko Liang sought to conquer Wei, he first enlarged his army by conquering small states to the south and enlisting captured troops. But the Wei remained oblivious to Chu-ko's moves and were taken aback when he attacked in force. The Russians are trying to pull this same trick on us now; how can we be so witless when they are so clever?

The bakufu once made it plain to Russia that Japanese law requires us to destroy on sight any barbarian ship approaching our coasts.[78] But now the English regularly appear and anchor off our shores, and we do not lift a finger to drive them away. [Quite the contrary, as in the recent Otsuhama affair,] when they have the gall to land, we go out of our way to provide for their needs and send them merrily along. Will the barbarians have any respect for our laws after they hear about this? The English come and go as they please, draw maps and sketch our terrain, disrupt our inter-island transport system, and win over our commoners with their occult religion and the lure of profit. If smuggling increases and we fail to stop commoners from aiding and abetting the barbarians, who knows what future conspiracies may hatch?

But our temporizing, gloss-it-over officials reply, "The foreigners are just fishermen and merchants doing nothing out of the ordinary; there is no cause for alarm." What simpletons! The barbarians live ten thousand miles across the sea; when they set off on foreign conquests, "they must procure supplies and provisions from the enemy."[79] That is why they trade and fish. Their men-of-war are self-sufficient away from home. If their only motive for harpooning whales was to obtain whale meat, they could do so in their own waters. Why should they risk long, difficult voyages just to harpoon whales in eastern seas?

(Gloss: The waters off Greenland, for example, teem with whales.[80] That is why barbarian whalers from all over the world go there. Moreover, Greenland is but a short voyage from England.)

Their ships can be outfitted for trading, or fishing, *or fighting*. Can anyone guarantee that their merchant vessels and fishing boats of today will not turn into warships tomorrow? The English barbarians come and anchor off our shores whenever they please; they learn all about convenient approaches to our islands, about the location of bays and inlets along our coastline, and about our climate and our people's spiritual make-up. Should we let them occupy the small islands off to our southeast,

(Gloss: Many of these lie quite near the Ogasawaras.)

and establish bases on Hachijōjima, Yaskushima, and Tanega-shima, they would be in a perfect strategic position to invade our Middle Kingdom. This would be another case of two birds with one stone. It is easy to see why the English conspire with the Russians and spy on our coastal fortifications: They are eager to combine forces and obtain spoils. Their constant fishing and trading in our waters is essentially the same tactic that Chao Ch'ung-kuo used to conquer the Ti and Ch'iang; [that is, to eliminate any need to maintain cumbersome supply lines from home].[81] How can we be so witless when the barbarians are so clever?

But Heaven has not forsaken our Divine Realm. The bakufu has discerned the barbarians' cunning designs. It has prohibited efforts by commoners to aid and abet the barbarians, thereby nipping in the bud any possible conspiracies. The bakufu will also revive the practice of "treading the Cross," no doubt. Furthermore, it has ordered daimyo to sink on sight all barbarian ships. This will remind Russia that bakufu decrees—even past bakufu decrees—are more than words on paper. Our armed might and our reputation as eagle-eyed extirpators of heresy will be revived and enhanced. Such a noble tactic, such heroic decisiveness! What better way to spark the samurai spirit and cow the barbarians into submission?

But those ignorant of the bakufu's astute reasoning and far-sightedness argue, "If we treat the barbarians with kindness, they will comply docilely; to intimidate them only invites reprisals." Such men cling to out-dated, erroneous views with unbelievable tenacity. They would have the bakufu issue injunctions when in fact the barbarians understand nothing but force.

For hundreds of years the barbarians have desired and resolved to subvert enemy nations through their occult religion and thus conquer the whole world. They will not be deterred by occasional acts of kindness or displays of force. When they wreak vengeance against us, they intimidate us into backing down; when they submit meekly before us, they lull us into a false sense of security. They employ these two tactics "to probe for strengths and weaknesses."[82] Those spied on can never fully fathom the thoughts and feelings of the spies: The barbarians "assume different guises and employ a variety of feints."[83] This forces us to commit ourselves one way or the other on each occasion and throws us off balance; so we often commit blunders in spite of ourselves. This should explain the acuity and astuteness behind the policy of armed expulsion.

But some dimwits argue, "The warriors of our Divine Realm have been peerless throughout the world since antiquity. The barbarians are puny runts; there is no cause for alarm." True, the fighting men of our Divine Realm are brave and skilled in warfare, and our customs reinforce this [native martial spirit]. But times change; there are eras of weakness as well as strength. During the Warring States period [1467–1568], our warriors were truly fit for combat; proper movements on the battlefield were simple reflex actions. Our warriors proved their valor through actual battlefield achievements, such as capturing enemy banners or beheading enemy generals. But two hundred years have passed since our warriors last tasted battle. How many of them today are trained well enough to cope with the sudden thrusts and feints or the other complexities of warfare? The weak-hearted would flee for their lives, disrupting the ranks; the courageous would die meaninglessly, their valor coming to naught. Our skill and valor do not guarantee victory. When the Mongols attacked [in 1274 and 1281], the military prowess of our Divine Realm was at its prime. But due to our ignorance of enemy formations and tactics, our valor counted for little. Our headlong charges led only to self-decimation. This is why I maintain that victory in war depends entirely on the statesman-general's stratagems and long-range planning. But the art of war as taught today consists of outmoded ideas and tactics employed by medieval generals like Takeda Shingen and Uesugi Kenshin. We do not observe foreign troops directly, nor do we gather information about them. Once war breaks out, they may engage us in a totally unexpected way, so it is a poor idea to rely solely on our reputation for valor.

Again the dimwits argue, "Because the barbarians live across vast oceans, they can dispatch but few troops. If they be so foolhardy as to attack us, let them. There is no cause for alarm." But a skilled barbarian general may assess the tide of battle and the drift of wartime conditions, and adroitly adjust his stratagems to turn our numbers against us. *Sun Tzu* says, "To take over the enemy's homeland intact is the best stratagem of all; to destroy it is only second best."[84] An inept Japanese commander might well turn our numerical superiority to the enemy's advantage, so strength of numbers alone does not ensure victory. To cite an example, once in the past, nefarious commoners from Kyūshū illegally put to sea and became pirates. Just then the Ming dynasty was plagued by decay and insurrection. Naturally, the Chinese rebels welcomed these Kyūshū pirates into their ranks, and called themselves "Japanese raiders" (*wakō*). They wreaked havoc along China's eastern seaboard almost every year. When they finally were apprehended and executed, it was discovered that only twenty-five Japanese nationals were among them. These twenty-five were extremely few in number, but by shrewdly exploiting given conditions, they did much to hasten the Ming dynasty's fall. The most important factor in warfare is to overawe the enemy; superiority or inferiority of numbers is secondary.

The skilled commander procures not only supplies from the enemy; he also conscripts manpower. The barbarians employ occult religions and other mysterious doctrines to seduce foreign peoples into their fold. Should they win our commoners over to their cause, their paucity of numbers would become a great multitude; they will have turned our numerical advantage against us.

(Gloss: One Ming scholar[85] writes, "The Western barbarians are adept in the ways of intrigue. Whenever they arrive in a country, it is doomed because they conquer it from within by recruiting the local inhabitants into their ranks. Over thirty nations have fallen in this way.")

Again the dimwits argue, "The barbarians' religion is a set of shallow, base doctrines. They may deceive stupid commoners with it, but they will never beguile our superior men (chün tzu). There is no cause for alarm." But the great majority of people in the realm are stupid commoners; superior men are very few in number. Once the hearts and minds of the stupid commoners have been captivated, we will lose control of the realm. The ancient sage kings enforced harsh penalties for seditious and subversive activities (in the Book of Rites); such was their hatred for those who incited stupid commoners to rebel. The barbarians' religion infiltrated Kyūshū once before, and spread like the plague among stupid commoners. Within less than a hundred years, two hundred eighty thousand converts were discovered and brought to justice. This indicates how fast the contagion can spread. Should we allow our stupid commoners to be deceived and converted once again, and in addition, should we permit nefarious lords such as Ōtomo Sōrin and Konishi Yukinaga to win over and employ these converts in furthering their wicked ends, the resulting insurrections will not be easy to suppress. It is of no avail for a few superior men to remain untouched by the pollution spreading around them. The immunity of superior men to Christianity does not permit complacence.

Again the dimwits argue, "Stupid commoners cannot be deceived and converted today because Christianity is strictly prohibited. Though the barbarians may display trifling shrewdness, there is no cause for alarm." The barbarians have been unable to work their wiles on us up to now only because the bakufu has strictly outlawed Christianity. And I might add, the people of the realm are very fortunate that it has. Nevertheless, the fact remains that mysterious evils are spreading throughout the land today, though under different names and in different forms. If the barbarians decide to work their wiles on us, they need not restrict themselves to old methods; they will adopt new ones.

The natural feelings of the people are such that they cannot but covet personal gain and hold the spirits in awe. Should someone capture their hearts by furtively appealing to such natural feelings, prohibition is impossible, no matter how harsh our penalties may be. For example, gambling and conspiratorial parties are strictly prohibited at present. But drifters, gamblers, and other nefarious elements swagger through the countryside, meeting clandestinely at night and dispersing at dawn. The reason we cannot bring them under control lies in the people's love of gain. Or again, prayers and incantations of various weird sorts designed to secure personal fortune and happiness are used by group leaders to call and bind together fellow-believers. The reason these bands are intermittently suppressed only to spring up again lies in the people's fear of spirits.

(Gloss: The *fuju fuse* sect of Nichiren Buddhism,[86] the Human Lotus Sacrificial Sect,[87] and other such groups have been uprooted. But recently, countless new forms of pseudo-Buddhistic miscreancy have arisen. The so-called Fuji Association,[88] for example, already has some seventy thousand adherents, it is believed. All such conspiratorial groups are made up of persons who hold spirits in awe.)

Should we again allow the barbarians to take advantage of the people's love of gain and fear of spirits, this time allowing them to lead our masses down evil paths other than Christianity itself, no law actually would be violated, but our people's hearts and minds would be captured just the same. What good do laws alone do? We must ponder this point carefully. Those who indulge in rumination without accurate knowledge or who are overly attentive to details without long-range, comprehensive policies are little more than blind men destined to fall prey to barbarian wiles. History has shown that such men, though adept enough at polemics or pedantry, are little more than desultory sophists. Confucius had them in mind when he said, "I detest clever talkers who bring the state to ruin."

The barbarians coming to spy on our Middle Kingdom during the past three hundred years arrived one after another from various nations. Though their homelands differ, they all revere the same god. This means that Christianity has had designs on our Middle Kingdom for the past three hundred years. In dealing with this [sustained threat], our Middle Kingdom has on each occasion adopted a different policy based on the then-prevalent opinion. The predators have a firm, fixed objective and steadfastly try to achieve it; the prey intermittently changes its defense posture, at times assuming the hard-line, at times, the soft-line, always vacillating between the two. Who can guarantee that the predators forever will meet frustration trying to discover our weaknesses? To turn our vacillation into constancy of purpose and eliminate the weaknesses we possess, we first must fully understand the barbarians' nature. We first must fully understand the barbarians' nature.

New Theses: seven

National Defense

To defend the nation and improve military preparedness, we first must determine our fundamental [foreign] policy—war or peace. Otherwise we will drift aimlessly, morale and discipline will slacken, high and low will indulge in the ways of ease and comfort, intelligent men will be unable to devise stratagems, and courageous men will be unable to work up their anger. Some people today fritter away precious time, assume an air of unruffled sedateness, and allow the barbarians slowly but steadily to attain final victory over us. In truth, this composure masks the cowardice in their hearts, a cowardice that precludes bold decisiveness.

By contrast, when the Mongols sullied our honor [in the thirteenth century], Hōjō Tokimune resolutely beheaded their envoy and ordered that an army be raised to smite them. His Imperial Majesty, Emperor Kameyama, prayed that disaster befall himself rather than the nation. In that hour of crisis, we willingly courted oblivion and the people ceased fearing death. Indeed, did anyone *not* aspire to die ardently in the realm's defense! Hence, we once again attained spiritual unity, and the purity and intensity of our sincerity unleashed a raging typhoon that destroyed the barbarian fleet. Ah, the ancients expressed it well when they said, "Place a man between the jaws of death, and he will emerge unscathed."[89] Or again, "If officials and commoners are led to believe that savage hordes are closing in, fortune will be with us."[90] Therefore I say that we must once and for all establish our basic foreign policy and place the realm between the jaws of death. Only then can we implement defense measures.

A discourse on war or peace seems out of place now because the barbarians seek only trade; hostilities have yet to break out.

But those ignorant of the evils stemming from trade are in truth too timid to assume a warlike stance, and inevitably they adopt policies of conciliation. Those who would strictly ban trade are immune to fear and unperturbed even if the consequences of their bold decision led to war. As a rule, if we make up our minds to do something, we usually achieve it. Now that the Expulsion Edict has been proclaimed and war has been decided on, the realm has a sense of purpose and direction. Only now will I present my proposals for national defense.

We must carry out four categories of reforms:

(1) Internal Administration. There are four specific items under this general heading: (a) reviving the samurai spirit, (b) prohibiting presumptuous luxury, (c) ensuring the people's livelihood, and (d) promoting men of ability.

First, reviving the samurai spirit. Licentiousness among warriors stems from their lack of shame. To foster a healthy sense of shame in them, we must institute a system of rewards and punishments. These rewards and punishments must be based on the affection between parent and child and be meted out according to the criteria of loyal devotion. When rewards are called for, not even enfeoffments or ministerial posts should be begrudged; when punishments are called for, not even royal personages or high-ranking officials should be exempted. "Favoritism and other heinous irregularities cannot be tolerated"[91] as long as righteousness and the Way exist. In times of peace, the ruler must do everything in his power to inspire his ministers, especially the complacent or hidebound among them. If he follows the practices established by Tokugawa Ieyasu and other wise leaders of that era to exhort and discipline his retainers, the samurai spirit will revive.

Second, prohibiting presumptuous luxury. Whenever presumptuous luxury appears, poverty develops and the morals of high and low alike inevitably decline. Then bribery and graft occur, and malice and discontent pervade the realm. To remedy this situation we must straighten out government finances, teach men the difference between good and evil, and make expenditures conform to income. Domain finances must be restored to a sound, normal footing, and the distinction of high and low must be upheld. Most of all, His Lordship should take the initiative and set an example for all by setting his household affairs in order, cleaning up administration, curtailing waste, eliminating inefficiency, rescinding complex or cruel regulations, and slashing expenditures for private construction projects or personal recreation. None of these proposals is new; all were introduced in antiquity. To eradicate presumptuous luxury, the ruler must make men forget about outward appearances and esteem sincerity above all else. To make men forget about outward appearances, he must get them to believe that they "are all aboard the same ship [of state], riding out the present storm together [or sinking together]."[92] To induce his people to feel concern for one another's livelihood, he must spell out the evils now plaguing the realm and inspire them to bear any burden, to withstand any suffering. If he carefully selects, trains, and outfits troops, and if he persuades the high and low alike to live each day prepared for war, the realm will be ready to meet any contingency. Thereafter he need only abide by regulations and practice diligence and austerity. Then the ways of presumptuous luxury will disappear.

(Gloss: After we beheaded the Mongol envoy at the beginning of the Kenji era [1275–77], we decided to give the enemy a sound drubbing. We slashed expenditures and practiced austerity at all levels of government, and [with the revenues thus saved,] cultivated armed strength. When a ruler issues laws to his people in this fashion, high and low alike are instilled with resolution and a desire to be prepared. Only then is government on a sound fiscal basis possible.)

Third, stabilizing the people's livelihoods. Agriculture is vital to the people's lives; it must take priority over the crafts and commerce, which are of secondary importance. We must regulate production, equalize the distribution of wealth in the realm, levy corvées only in the off-season so as not to obstruct agricultural production, institute the equal-field system to prevent the concentration of lands by the wealthy, root out nefarious elements from the countryside, chastise the indolent, carry out relief measures for the disabled and needy, reactivate the ten-man and five-man control systems, issue injunctions concerning mutual cooperation and surveillance, enrich the people, and increase domain population. Above all, we must induce the people to be filial and respectful, to care for the elderly, the orphaned, the widowed, and others in society who have no one to depend on. These measures are to ensure the people's well-being and have been proposed since antiquity. To implement them today, we must make high and low alike feel a genuine concern for one another, and this concern can be imbued in the people only through actual deeds, not through vain preaching.

Hence, by preparing the nation for war, we could stockpile food and supplies each and every year with the same sense of urgency as though last fall's crop had failed, and we could get the people to work at their jobs with the same diligence and intensity that they would display in beating off enemy marauders. The people's hearts would be united, their efforts would be coordinated, and not a single idler would remain among them. Thereafter, all we would need to do is issue injunctions and conduct benevolent rule. Then the people's livelihood would be ensured.

Fourth, promoting men of ability. The ancients compared men of ability to tigers roaming loose in the mountains: Neither may be left as is. By rewarding able men with government posts, political gravity is shifted from the periphery to the center; whereas if these men go unrecognized, political gravity remains on the periphery; and in the worst of all possible cases, if able men are allowed to remain in their domains, they are utterly beyond the reach of central [bakufu] control. Unless we make this central authority the focus of political gravity, we will not command respect in the realm. That is why the sages placed men of talent and ambition in ministerial posts where they could express their views on state policy. They monopolized the energies of ambitious men for state purposes and prompted the people to love and respect their government as children love their parents.

(Gloss: In antiquity, all men of ability, not just those belonging to certain houses or factions, were promoted to government

217

posts.[93] After the implementation of the *Taihō Code,* sons in provincial schools were enabled to enroll at the state university in the capital. On completing their studies, they took civil service examinations, and if successful in these, received office. [On the continent,] the Yü, Hsia, Shang, and Chou had systems of education, and the various feudal lords also maintained programs under which promising young nobles in their domains were sent to study in the capital. All this shows the importance attached to finding, training, and employing men of talent in antiquity. No man of ability went unrecognized.

State affairs are many and varied. If officials come from only one area, debate and policy formation will be monotoned and one-sided, since the men taking part all will have similar backgrounds and attitudes. Government would inevitably suffer from favoritism, narrowness of vision, and factionalism, rather than deal with matters in a manner equitable to the whole realm. That is why the sages paid so much attention to discovering and employing men of ability from all over the realm. The sage king, Yü, for example, said, "The ruler must employ men of talent. If not, he will fare well in nothing." Upon pondering the meaning of these words, we realize why Shun utilized the goods deeds of others to do good himself, and why he did nothing, yet kept the realm well ordered.)

Before we can promote men of talent, we must understand the correct method: Listen to what he says, look at what he does, and if he demonstrates his worthiness through actual deeds of merit, confer appropriate posts and titles on him. If we place the realm's talented men in a position to express their opinions fully and freely whatever these may be, we will relieve their pent-up frustrations. Then all of them will present their views enthusiastically in state councils. If we judge men by what they accomplish, they will have to turn their words into actual deeds. This would distinguish the wise from the foolish and the capable from the incompetent at a glance. We will bar from advancement those who are all talk and no action. This will promote the virtues of self-effacement and deference to superiors. If we confer posts and titles only on those who prove their worth through meritorious deeds, men of real ability will demonstrate it in concrete achievements. Then everyone in the realm will respect them and follow their example. Government will gain the services of all talented men, and they will propose and execute policies for the common good, with no tinge of bias. Who, then, would refuse to recognize and submit to central [bakufu] authority?

(2) The Military Command. There are three specific items under this general heading: (a) eliminating haughtiness from the ranks, (b) increasing troop strength, and (c) improving methods of training.

First, eliminating haughtiness from the ranks. Without a doubt, crack troops should command our respect. But insolent, overbearing troops both abuse the people and deprave morals at home, and flee before enemy spears and ruin military discipline at the front—which leads a nation to defeat. We must weed out such elements carefully at the start, so that we can train and discipline the remaining troops properly. Only then will we be able to ward off enemy attacks and take the offensive ourselves.

Second, increasing troop strength. Troop strength is difficult to increase because warriors are clustered together in castle-towns where they idly fritter away their rice stipends [and cannot maintain personal retainers]. To remedy this situation, we must study past and present military systems thoroughly, and increase troop strength by instituting an appropriate system of samurai-farmers that would allow us to meet any demand for more military manpower.[94] Moreover, attack from abroad normally occurs in conjunction with subversion at home. At present, swarms of nefarious commoners brandish swords and guns. They flock together like wild birds to drink, gamble, and pillage. After their evildoing has ended, they scatter like leaves before an autumn gale, only to flock together on another occasion. The countryside is a breeding ground for these subversives,[95] where they terrorize good, hardworking subjects, and present a sinister threat to the state. Should famine or plague occur [to aggravate the situation], who knows what crises would emerge, and should the barbarians take advantage of this situation to recruit our commoners into their ranks, the resulting horrors would be frightful indeed! We must act *now* to adjust our policies. If there are soldiers on the land to defend it, rebellion by subversives from within can be averted, attack from abroad can be deterred, and other unexpected crises can be nipped in the bud.

Third, improved methods of training. Drilling troops is neither a game, nor an exhibition. Military drill is to train warriors for real combat; all frills and stylistic elements must go. Drilling should center on signal flag and battle drum as actually employed in battle. We should drop useless, empty theories and make simplicity the rule, so that commands are easy to understand and execute. We should test the men's skills regularly on hunting expeditions or by making them pursue and apprehend fugitives. The men should be subjected to arduous duties of all sorts, inured to pain, hunger, and the elements, forced to march long distances wearing heavy armor, and accustomed to harsh training and discipline in order to cultivate toughness of mind and spirit. Only when tough in mind and spirit, will they be fearless and able to meet any contingency; only then will they be of use in wartime.

(3) Domain Finances. Most daimyo today are indolent and indulge in consumption not permitted to their status. Their tax systems lack regularity and their finances are in disorder. Their poverty is entirely of their own making. Throughout their lifetimes they live in the lap of luxury; they are mollycoddled by women in their inner chambers, duped by flatterers, and shielded from pain or difficulty.

At present, the great and small lords remain within domain borders because they are bound by fealty oaths to a common overlord, the bakufu (*kokka*). They uphold the [state] just as a centipede's legs support its body; so there is no fear that our political structure will collapse suddenly. Hence, the bakufu should make these daimyo shoulder some of the military burdens that it now bears alone, and force them to assume responsibility for defending their own local regions. It should order the daimyo to reform their domains with as much urgency as though they were locked in mortal combat. It should periodically check the state of each domain's preparedness, apportioning rewards and punishments not on the basis of traditional house-rankings, but as it deems proper case by case. Above all, the bakufu must make each daimyo realize the urgency of ministering to his subjects' needs. If the samurai spirit is revived, if extravagant ways are suppressed, if the people's livelihood is ensured, if men of ability are placed in positions of authority, if regulations are adhered to scrupulously, if finances are kept in the black, and if the people are spared maltreatment and abuse, domain wealth and strength is a matter of course.

All domains suffer financial distress because merchants monopolize the right to deal in rice.[96] Warriors cannot avoid dealing with merchants, since they must procure all necessities of life from the marketplace with money obtained by selling rice. For this reason, warriors suffer constant torment from rising costs. Moreover, the ceremonial offerings that the various domains make to the bakufu each year are all crafted and sold by artisans and merchants (except for a few food products famous in certain areas). Such items are mere ornaments of metal, bamboo, or lacquered wood, totally devoid of practical value. But they must be stamped "certified" by the appropriate licensed craftsman or merchant. Nowadays, daimyo hire townsmen [to replace the hereditary retainers they can no longer afford to maintain] as road clearers in front of their processions. Daimyo who hold banquets obtain the services of cooks and caterers from the city. In the furnishings of their mansions, in their attire, in the number of concubines and maidservants they support, in their pastimes and diversions; in short, in every aspect of their lives, a customary and extremely expensive "proper level of expenditure" has arisen, known as *"daimyō yaku."* The daimyo must adhere rigidly to this unwritten set of standards as though it were an ancestral law that not even the most powerful of them might dare alter.[97]

When daimyo desert their domains for Edo, bringing, as they do, the bulk of their tax revenues, their subjects eagerly follow suit. This leaves the countryside barren and destitute. To transform destitution into wealth, we must above all free ourselves from the fetters of custom. Of course, not all customs today deserve to be abolished, and not all past customs deserve to be revived. The Great Hero must weigh the relative merits and demerits of each case. He drops meaningless ritual to achieve actual results by discerning the right time and adopting the proper measure.

(4) The Deployment of Defense Forces. At present, the daimyo and their defense forces are concentrated in Edo. The original objective of this policy was to shift the nation's military center of gravity from the outlying provinces to the center [the bakufu]. But in Edo, warriors live in idleness and develop lavish, licentious habits—and this in truth weakens the realm. If but one strategic area in the nation is vulnerable to barbarian attack, our defenses contain a fatal weakness. Kyōto lies at the realm's forehead, Edo, at its heart. Ōsaka constitutes its midsection, and the Sagami [Kanagawa] and Bōsō [Chiba] peninsulas form Edo's jaws. The Ise and Atsuta Shrines house the Three Imperial Treasures and harbor the realm's "divine vital force" (*shen ch'i*). We must maintain strict security in all these strategic areas. But our defense forces are not well-organized or systematically deployed anywhere. Fortifications, for example, exist in some areas but not in others. How can we instill a sense of crisis in the people when such is the case? Appropriate security measures should be drawn up immediately.

Nagasaki Bay was originally fortified because that is where we make barbarian ships call. But today, the barbarians recognize no spot along our coastline to be off-limits and call wherever they please. In essence, the whole realm is [no different from] Nagasaki. Why isn't the whole realm fortified?[98] As for the Ezo territories and other overseas islands (*kaigai no shotō*), unless we dispatch officials and expeditionary forces to these areas, we can gain no accurate and detailed information, and will be unable to win the reverence and allegiance of inhabitants there.

(Gloss: Most people today believe that there is nothing to gain by taking over Ezo, and nothing to lose by leaving it as is. Is this really so? If we do not seize these islands, the barbarians surely will. What is more, if we allow them to establish a staging area there from which to attack Matsumae, the entire northern Honshū area will face the threat of insurrection, and if we allow their raiding parties to ravage our coasts, the whole realm will be threatened. True, even if we do not take over Ezo, the barbarians may choose to leave it alone, and in that case, there is nothing to worry about. But if, by our failure to act, we allow them to gain this territory, it will do them a world of good, and us, a world of harm. So we must do everything in our power to seize and defend it.)

We must formulate plans to develop and control this vital area, and must also make the daimyo in coastal domains shore up their defenses to eliminate any points of vulnerability. Then their warriors, now concentrated in Edo, can be deployed in their respective home domains. Then all habits of ease and luxury will be at an end: If the daimyo and their vassals resolutely man their lonely coastal garrisons, they cannot enjoy the city's pleasures. Their troops, inured to hardship and accustomed to garrison life, will be ready for any contingency. Only then will the realm's strategic areas be secure.

These, then, are the four general reforms we must undertake: internal administration, the military command, domain finances, and defense. I have presented my views on these topics in broad outline form: Once the main points are clear, the details can be worked out. The Great Hero must discern the right time and adopt the proper measures. There is no reason not to meet today's needs by implementing policies that did not exist in antiquity, for with proper study, this can be done.

Next, I discuss five specific programs to implement: (1) coastal garrisons, (2) communications networks, (3) a coast guard, (4) manufacturing firearms, and (5) stockpiling materiel and provisions.

(1) Coastal Garrisons. Presently, no spot along our coastline is immune to barbarian attack. Should the enemy land at some point, troops must be dispatched [from the nearest castletown, which might take days]. They would arrive exhausted, and would be too late to do any good. Therefore, we must implement a system of fortifications regularly manned by military units. Since Keichō and Genna times [1596–1623], building more than one

castle per province has been prohibited. This law was designed
to check the power of potentially rebellious daimyo, and it was
applied uniformly throughout the realm. Although we cannot
alter it now, we must take steps to deal with the barbarian
menace. Unless we build fortifications along the coast, where
local inhabitants may collect forces, we will have no rallying
point to instill spiritual solidarity in them. Unless we organize
the people into neighborhood [militia] units, we will be unable
to tap their energies.

The way of the soldier consists of regularized maneuvers and
skills. With proper training, even women and children can be
made to brave fire and water to beat off an attack; without it,
even grown men will scatter before an invading host. [Unless
appropriate steps are taken] all people in coastal regions will
flee for the hills under enemy assaults. The barbarian dogs and
goats would trample us underfoot, and nothing could save us.
For this reason, the ancients built fortifications in outlying
areas.

(Gloss: In the "Defense" section of the *Taihō Code,* it is
written, "The people living in frontier regions to the east,
north, and west will be deployed in fortifications except
when cultivating their fields, when they shall erect [and
live in] temporary dwellings. During the farming season, the
able-bodied are to leave the fortifications, labor in the fields,
and return after harvest time. All necessary repair work on
the fortifications will be done in the off-season." The *Ryō
no gige* reads, "An 'embankment' is a high earthen barrier
to ward off bandits.")

We cannot revive this ancient system completely, but certainly
some aspects of it warrant adaptation to meet today's needs.

Warriors originally were divorced from the soil to weaken
the realm and to prevent wars from breaking out in provincial
areas. But unless we garrison warriors in peripheral areas, we
will not be able to defend ourselves against barbarian enemies.
If we dispatch troops from a castletown to defend coastal areas,
they will exhaust their strength on long marches back and
forth, and the people along the way will rise up in vigorous

protest. On the other hand, if we enlist local commoners into militia service, their luxurious, slothful habits will make them demand high rates of pay. Moreover, they simply would be posted to warn of the enemy's approach; they would not actually fight. In advancing, they would seek to achieve no great feats of heroism, and in retreating, they would hold military discipline in contempt. Our only enlistees would be feeble old men or indolent delinquents, and neither would do us much good.

In addition, the lands to support troops [with rations] are already held in perpetuity by the peasants, and cannot be confiscated for this purpose. Generally speaking, agricultural lands in or near the realm's strategic areas are valuable, and the peasants living there are not destitute [enough to abandon these]. Agricultural lands not already under peasant control are few and far between, which means that there is very little land to distribute to the garrisons. But to supply them with rice [instead of rice fields] would be many times more expensive, since this rice first must be taxed from the peasantry, and then distributed to the men. Therefore we could not sustain a great number of troops.

(Gloss: We could support the troops by giving them tracts of land to cultivate, and allow each man a five to six *koku* tax exemption. At present, some daimyo employ such a system. On the other hand, if we allotted each man a rice stipend, much more rice would be needed to begin with, since taxes [on that five *koku*] computed at the usual rate of forty percent would amount to but two *koku*, which, of course, is insufficient for one household's annual needs. In other words, a two *koku* stipend could not support a soldier's family, but a five *koku* plot of land could.[99] This is the difference between rice fields and rice itself.)

Many people have pointed out these problems, but if we implemented a system that took the peasants' interests into account, we could reduce our expenses and still secure steady tax revenues. Generally speaking, lands that have gone to waste are found in oppressively-taxed, poor areas, and lands not yet under cultivation are infertile and of low value. In the realm's strategic areas, few wastelands or uncultivated lands exist, but in coastal areas, they can still be found. We must persuade troops to live on and cultivate such lands, exempting taxes if these be heavy, or supplying farm implements if the soil be unproductive. If some local peasants choose to enlist and enter the ranks, we should assess their holdings and exempt these from taxation. Thus, we would realize the original motive [of rulers in antiquity] for establishing garrisons.

The sea is an inexhaustible source of wealth we can exploit to cover the costs of building ships and maintaining maritime forces. It is both a training ground for our seamen and a source of food to sustain them wherever they may go. The Man of Talent and Virtue must devise the correct system to recruit brave, well-trained captains and crews.

The nation's defense must not be a burden for the garrisons to bear alone. The realm's pains and pleasures must be shared by all if our forces are to be of use. Garrison troops support themselves through farming and fishing, and they undergo rigorous training in their spare time. When the enemy approaches, it is they who first see action. Their lot is harsh indeed! But what of those warriors who live the year around amid the comforts of the city? Not one of them finds pleasure in defending the state. We must toughen them up on military drills and manuevers. We must inure them to hardship by making them go on hunts, apprehend fugitives, build roads and bridges, clear fields, and perform other unpleasant tasks. We must not permit the warriors in castletowns to indulge in license and debauchery. We must also make the peasant, artisan, and merchant classes realize that the realm is in dire peril, that only by hard work, frugality, and compliance with our laws, can they escape the horrors of war. We must convince the garrison troops that not only they, but everyone in the realm, is making sacrifices, that they should pluck up their courage to perform heroic feats. Only after we achieve all this, will our armed forces be of use.

A system of coastal fortifications, injunctions to create neighborhood [militia] units, the equal distribution of burdens in the realm—all are requisites of national defense. We must deliberate on these matters thoroughly while we still have time.

(2) Communications Networks. At present, observation towers do exist in coastal areas, but are few in number and isolated from each other. This makes sending and receiving messages between towers on hilltops all but impossible. Many observation posts lack the signal fires, flags, rockets, and other necessary equipment, or else the lookouts there are ignorant of the proper codes. These lookouts can only stare blankly at the open sea, and when the barbarians appear, they must report this fact to the authorities on foot. Since barbarian ships traverse miles in a matter of minutes, but our lookouts go on foot to report news of their approach, it is no surprise that their reports are too late to be of help.

By contrast, the law texts of antiquity state that observation towers existed in all frontier areas, everyone clearly understood the signal codes, and commanding officers supervised the lookout squads posted there.

(Gloss: In the "Defense" section of the Taihō Code, it says, "Signal posts may be set up at any convenient intervals, provided these posts are within sight of each other. Two officers shall be in command at each. At regular hours of the day and night, each post along the line will relay signals by smoke or fire. If the post immediately next to one's own fails to pass on the signal promptly, runners should be dispatched to find out why, and the entire mishap should be reported to the provincial governor. . . .")[100]

If we improve on these ancient systems, if we place observation towers within sight and earshot of each other, if we standardize signal systems and codes, if we keep lookouts under strict supervision and spur them on with rewards and punishments, we will never be caught off guard.

Since information is conveyed through our way-station system, its efficiency is imperative. If the distance between stations is too long, inhabitants along the way are spared toil and trouble, but horse and rider become exhausted. Yet if way-stations are too close together, more of them must be built, frequent demands on the local inhabitants must be made, and increased regulations and procedures along the line may actually cause delays.

At present, there are too many way-stations, and too many people jam the nation's road system on trivial personal business. This places great burdens on local inhabitants. An extreme example is that of lowly cooks and quartermasters who think nothing of traversing the nation's highways on non-official business. All of this interferes with the peasants' work at the busiest time of the year and hinders agricultural production by depriving it of precious labor. How can such abuses be excused in a time of peace and security? Furthermore, we do not distinguish urgent from routine business when using way-station facilities. The same plow-horse or man-carriage may serve in an emergency and on a leisurely excursion.

(Gloss: One Ch'ing writer boasts, "Our road and communications network is of the highest quality. Our western border, five thousand *li* away, can be reached in nine days; Hopei, Honan, and Sian can be reached in five. When Wu San-kuei launched his rebellion, he discovered that due to our good communications network, government forces were well prepared for him. He bemoaned his fate to Heaven, 'Alas, we cannot even begin to fight.' "

This writer goes on to state, "The Sung and Chin maintained a system of express runners and way-stations used exclusively in times of war or rebellion. But a distance of three hundred *li* per day was the best that either could attain. Never in history has a system achieved over five hundred *li* per day. This was due partly to the soft, lazy ways of the people and to the lack of proper training for runners. But the main responsibility lay with poor government planning. Our present-day system is far superior to anything that existed before. In emergencies, we can deliver messages at speeds of over six hundred *li* per day, and we maintain regularly scheduled communications with even the remotest rural districts." This shows that a nation's road and communications network depends on its leaders' skill at institutional planning.)

Since the Keichō and Genna eras [1596–1623], intercourse with overseas countries has been strictly prohibited, but in recent years, the barbarians have begun to seduce commoners in outlying areas again. It is extremely difficult to detect and ferret out stupid commoners who stealthily aid and abet the wily barbarians at sea.[101] Unless we institute an exhaustive system of informants and collective responsibility among commoners and assign able officers to investigate these illicit activities thoroughly, we will remain ignorant of the evildoings now perpetrated in our bays and inlets.

Thus, erecting coastal watchtowers, improving roads and relay systems, discovering methods to detect and ferret out nefarious commoners—all are of prime concern to leaders charged with developing communications networks. We must deliberate on these matters thoroughly while we still have time.

(3) A Coast Guard. In defending a castle, one [cannot remain within its walls, but] must engage the enemy outside. Likewise, in maritime defense [one must engage the enemy at sea].[102] The barbarians feel completely at home on the water and are superb at naval warfare. To repulse them, our warships must be of the finest quality, and our techniques of navigation must be highly refined. Establishing coast guard forces does not require us to assemble all men in one place and make them undergo military training for extended periods of time. But we must accustom the realm's warriors to deck life so that their normal functional skills are unimpaired on rough waters. Also, they must be able to handle large vessels as deftly as they now guide rowboats. The men must be put to work aboard transports or fishing boats so that they acquire sea legs and master skills such as how to steer, how to enter and leave harbors, how to adjust to shifting tides, how to sail in fair or foul weather, and how to use the compass and similar devices. All this will prepare them for service in a coast guard.

We should assign daimyo the tasks of building large, sea-going vessels. They would undertake this construction work as part of, and in accordance with, the prescribed duties of military service they now owe the bakufu.

(Gloss: In other words, shipbuilding should be thought of as similar to corvées that the bakufu now levies on daimyo.)

The vessels that each daimyo builds must be sturdy and well put-together, no less so than barbarian ships, for domain troops will be onboard and will see action in an attack.

(Gloss: In the "Construction and Public Works" section of the *Taihō Code,* it says, "An appropriate number of troops shall be dispatched from the capital to guard government ships wherever these be stationed.")

Accordingly, bakufu officials should supervise shipping operations. We must select these overseers with great care, since they will wield considerable authority. They must hold ranks high enough to command a large number of lesser officials, and must receive generous stipends to eliminate any need to accept graft. In peacetime we could use the ships to transport rice to Ōsaka or Edo. This also would let us transfer to the bakufu the right to deal in rice—a right now monopolized by merchants. This would free the daimyo from their dependence on profit-mongering merchants. Later on, we could conduct regular training sessions and military reviews to evaluate the performance of men and ships. If we upgrade our coast guard to the point where it can clear the enemy from our waters, we may go to war without fear. Then the barbarians' impudent behavior off our coasts will be at an end. "When we choose to fight, they will be unable to evade us; when we choose not to fight, they will be unable to harass us."[103] Only in this way can we gain the freedom of initiative to control them.

Some say, "We should mount cannon along our coast and repulse the barbarians from shore when they approach."[104] I do not belittle the importance of cannon. But they, along with other projectile weapons, must be fired at close range to be effective,[105] for their value lies in their shock effect, which temporarily throws the enemy into confusion. Our seamen must make a speedy attack utilizing small arms fire in boats of their own following the initial cannon barrage; cannon alone cannot demolish a strong enemy naval force. Boats on the water are extremely hard targets, and since barbarian ships are sturdily built, more than one or two direct hits is needed to sink them. At present, we do not conduct military training onboard ships; instead, we remain on shore and hope to demolish enemy fleets far out at sea. Can we be serious? Cannon are profitably employed in coastal defense only when mounted on high ground overlooking inlets or straits where barbarian ships are certain to anchor or pass. How can anyone maintain that mounting cannon along our shoreline is an effective way to defend our coasts?

(Gloss: When Arima clansmen burned and sank a Portuguese ship in the Keichō era [1596–1614], they employed small attack rafts and boats with flaming bales of straw piled on board. Kuroda clansmen used this same tactic to sink a barbarian ship in the Kyōhō era [1716–35].[106] In Ch'i Chi-kuang's "Attacking Fortresses Surrounded by Water,"[107] it says that "the standard range of firearms and flaming arrows is about fifty paces," but that "these weapons should not be used at such distances in an attack. Instead, small boats should press in on the enemy stronghold and pump these missiles in at close range." This is a prime example of Ming techniques for fighting on the water. Western barbarians, on the other hand, fire on each other's warships or attack in small boats lowered from the mother craft. When Coxinga demolished barbarian ships, he always plunged in through their cannon eyelets and set fire to the vessels from within their holds. All these examples clearly show that to sink and obtain victory over enemy fleets, we must attack them at close range in boats of our own.)

Some say, "We should not fight the barbarians on the water; it is unwise to try beating them at their own game. Instead, we should lure them ashore and only then engage them." Such reasoning is not fallacious. But the battle-wise barbarians will hardly discard their own forte and do battle as we would like. They will anchor off our coasts and disrupt our transport system [blocking the flow of food and supplies to Edo]. In the meantime they will probe carefully for weak spots in our defenses and wait for the right moment to attack. They zoom from place to place like lightning. How could we engage them on our own terms? How could we even keep track of their whereabouts?

The barbarians have full confidence in their own capabilities and hold nothing in fearful awe. They threaten in one spot and strike in another; they remain motionless, yet dominate peoples. We cannot launch a single raft[108] against them. We run around in circles on shore, and only wear ourselves out. The barbarians act as they very well please, and we can do nothing to stop them. Quite the contrary, flustered as we are, we simply play into their hands. Just how are we to "lure them ashore" in the first place?

Spirit (*ch'i*) is the key to victory in battle. When troops have full confidence in their own capabilities and hold nothing in fearful awe, their powers are heightened many times over by a feeling of inner spiritual strength. If we allow ourselves to fall behind the barbarians in military techniques, our inner spiritual strength will wither away before the battle begins. How could we attack and destroy them with confidence or composure?

Shipping originated [here in Japan] during the Age of the Gods.[109] Only later did it spread to foreign lands. Emperor Sujin revived sea transport to curtail the people's transportation costs and to gain additional state revenues.[110] Well over one hundred Imperial Majesties have been lain to rest since then, and never in all that time have foreign barbarians ravaged our transport system. [But what have we today?] We shrink from the water's edge in fear of the Western barbarians; even the great lords cannot put to sea. [In our own domain, for example,] certain officials seek to abolish seaborne transport altogether, and instead, dig a canal to ship goods to Edo. This proposal is all too attractive to those looking for easy answers. Such is the level to which our native courage has sunk. The ancients had a saying, "When we retreat one step, they advance one step." There are many island steppingstones between us and them: Iki, Tsushima, Tanegashima, Yakushima, and Hachijōjima, to name but a few. How can we sit back and watch the barbarians ravenously annex and convert these into military strongholds, while we diffidently mutter, "warfare on the water just isn't our long suit?"

Some say, "The key to ship handling lies in the captain's skill; nothing precludes a small ship from attaining naval victories." This reasoning is not fallacious. But it presumes that all our officers are masters of navigation. If not, our small flimsy ships will not always defeat their large sturdy ones. Moreover, skills vary from person to person; who can say for a fact that throughout the ages skilled navigators have never been found among captains of large ships? Indeed, history shows that most battles in which small boats defeated large ones took place in harbors or inlets. To stage such an encounter on the open sea would be like so many goldfish attacking a whale—one swish of its tail would end it all. . . . The outcome of sea battles is not a matter of courage and skill, but of ship size and construction, so we cannot ignore the advantages offered by large ships. Most of the battles that we lost [against the Mongols] in the Kōan era [1278–87] and [against the Koreans and Chinese] in the Bunroku era [1592–95] were lost not on land, but at sea. And we did not lose because we lacked courage: Our small boats proved no match for the enemy's large warships.

(Gloss: Tu Chung-lü of the Ming wrote, "Land warfare is Japan's strong point. Her weakness on the water stems from the inferior size of her ships and their lack of firepower." Yü Ta-yu[111] wrote that his countrymen's most urgent task was to repel us with their navy, that they should devote their utmost efforts to outfitting large ships. Ch'i Chi-kuang as well said, "Our huge sailing ships are like floating castles; Japanese ships are small and flimsy. With a strong wind in our sails, we smash them as the wheels of a cart crush insects on the road. Battles are fought between ships, not men. If Japanese ships were as large and powerful as ours, we would be in a fix." All these statements show that the key to victory at sea lies in ship size and construction.)

Therefore, attacking large warships in small boats is a stratagem we can resort to only when a particular captain's special skill and daring make victory probable. We cannot rely on it as a basic principle in maritime defense.

Small arms were first cast by the Western barbarians, but we in the Middle Kingdom imported and refined these weapons so much that the Ming Chinese named them "Japanese guns," not "barbarian guns." This shows their respect for our ingenuity. Let us repeat this *tour de force* in shipbuilding. There is no reason to be outdone by anyone.

(Gloss: The Russian khan, Peter,[112] once travelled to Holland disguised as a carpenter to learn the art of building large ships. This took place in the Genroku era [1688–1703], and there is little doubt that Russia began to possess huge warships and sophisticated navigating skills at that time. Even the barbarians heed this vital matter; how can we in the Middle Kingdom ignore it?)

Thus I say, "We must strengthen our arsenal with large ships to instill confidence in our own troops and fearful awe toward us in the barbarians. Only then will we put an end to their contemptuous and wayward behavior.

The creation of a coast guard is one of our top priorities. Training in navigation and the construction of large ships are the requisites of a maritime nation.[113] We must deliberate on these matters thoroughly while we still have time.

(4) Manufacturing Firearms. Firearms too are the barbarians' forte, and we cannot hope to control them with these weapons [alone]. But since cannon are effective in blowing apart solid structures, they are indispensable when attacking or defending castles. Furthermore, because sea battles today are encounters between floating castles, the cannon employed must be well-built. Though high-grade cannon are basically long-range weapons, capable of shooting vast distances and hitting even the smallest targets with precision, they also can be effective at close range—if we properly employ them. After all, how many men can one cannon shell actually kill? Rather, it is the thundering shock effect that takes a toll. If the enemy alone skillfully employs these weapons, our men will be gripped with terror before the battle even begins. How could we expect them to fight?

Ever since our Middle Kingdom first acquired guns, we have been casting and using mainly small arms. Warfare in our land ended soon after cannon were introduced, and the techniques of casting and firing these weapons became jealously guarded secrets of a few hereditary gunsmiths, who were loath to impart their skills to others. As a result, the number of qualified cannon-casters now falls far below the realm's needs. Unless all domains cast large cannon and all troops in the realm learn to employ these, our fighting spirit cannot be sparked, and these marvelous weapons cannot serve in the nation's defense. We must simplify methods of casting, mounting, and firing so that they are perfectly clear to everyone: We cannot put any trust in the family secrets and mystical nonsense now shrouding these procedures.

The barbarian ships closing in on us are floating fortresses; the protection of their hulls permits them to attack. To repel them, we must build and utilize a variety of firearms—offensive guns to demolish enemy ships far offshore, defensive guns to pin them down in our bays and inlets, and small arms for use on our patrol boats. In addition, we need flaming arrows, rockets, and other projectile weapons. Our rank-and-file must be fully trained to handle such auxilliary firearms in addition to their own handguns. Then the Man of Talent and Virtue would have to make the most of this army when he deemed proper.

There are many arguments about using shields in addition to body armor, bows and arrows to supplement firearms, and iron and stone to replace lead and copper in casting weapons. Although some fighting men in the Warring States period [1467–1568] mocked death by doing battle without shields, many warriors did avail themselves of shielding devices in that era.

(Gloss: In assaulting castles, large, tall bamboo shields were set up in front of the besieging troops to protect them against enemy missiles. On his campaigns in Korea, Katō Kiyomasa employed armored carts, much like those used in ancient China, called "tortoise shells." Any number of similar historical examples could be cited.

Of course, a cannon shell can pierce any shielding device. But even so, this shield absorbs most of the shell's force, so the body armor that each soldier wears will usually protect him from being wounded. And this sense of security allows the men to maintain their courage under a shower of enemy projectiles. For example, when Katō Kiyomasa attacked Konishi Yukinaga's stronghold at Udo in Higo Province, his officers and men were without shields and therefore had to improvise by using sliding doors removed from the houses of local residents. Yet even these makeshift devices allowed them to press their attack free from the fear of being struck by enemy projectiles. How much greater their composure would have been had they possessed genuine shields.

Moreover, the shells that the barbarians now use contain pellet-like shot and splatter on impact, so their total explosive power is slightly less than conventional shells. Therefore, the two-fold protection afforded by shield and body armor should be adequate, but we should conduct tests to make sure. In any case, the important thing about shielding devices is not whether they can withstand the impact of enemy shells. Instead, shields are valuable because they keep our men from looking at the enemy's muzzles. The wise commander understands this.)

Troops today are weak and used to soft living. Should they find themselves facing enemy fire without shielding, they would be panic-stricken. Hence, we must give them shields and armor to make them stouthearted and fearless. Serious studies as to types and methods is called for now, while we still have time.

The barbarians appropriate lead, copper, iron, sulfur, and other precious metals from their far-flung overseas possessions (*kaigai shokoku*), so they never suffer from a shortage of these metals. We, however, must rely solely on deposits of these metals found in our homeland, so we are at a clear [material] disadvantage when defending ourselves against foreigners.

(Gloss: At one time the Ming enlisted and garrisoned troops in frontier areas to ward off their enemies. Wang Ju-shun then wrote, "Our biggest headaches are our chronic shortage of gunpowder and trying to find armor and weapons for an ever-increasing number of troops." In other words, the Ming were plagued by shortages of gunpower, which is easily produced. How much greater are our problems with copper, iron, lead, and other metals, which can be produced only in limited quantities.)

Thus, we should not depend solely on firearms, but must supplement them with bows and arrows. In making firearms, we should not rely solely on copper and lead, but must use iron or wood to make the barrels, and iron or stone, or various other materials, to make shells. We must always be prepared to improvise with any odds and ends at our disposal. We should stockpile string, worn-out netting, wood-shavings, lumber scraps, sand, discarded pieces of metal, and the like. We must teach our men how to produce munitions from these odds and ends in peacetime so that we will not be found wanting in wartime. The volume of munitions we produce is small, but our habitual economizing will enable us to go all out when necessary. To attain victory at the precise moment requires grand stratagems from the mind of a master tactician. However, such matters should be discussed privately with those conversant in the art of war, not committed to writing in abstract, theoretical terms.

(Gloss: According to Ch'i Chi-kuang's "Methods of Warfare on the Water," bows, arrows, slings, and other projectile weapons should be employed along with firearms. Regarding "firearms," he says that "the amount of gunpowder placed onboard any one ship should be five hundred pounds, while the lead-encased cannon shells placed onboard should be no more than three hundred pounds." From this we can see that gunpowder was not used solely in firing cannon shells. Furthermore, since not only cannon shells, but flaming arrows and similar projectiles were also used, the term "firearms" did not refer only to cannon and cannon shells.)

The casting of cannon, the use of shielding devices, the techniques of bowmanship, the production of munitions from cast-off paraphernalia—all are methods of putting firearms to work in the nation's defense. We must deliberate on these matters thoroughly while we still have time.

(5) Stockpiling Materiel and Provisions. The munitions stored in castletown armories may be adequate for present purposes,

but fall short of massive wartime needs. Supplies and foodstuffs procured from city merchants may suffice for drilling and training in peacetime, but cannot meet sudden emergencies. Therefore, each domain should be ordered to increase the production of its local products such as nitrates, sulfur, tallow, glue, leather, hemp, and so on: Dependence on other domains cannot be allowed. Weapons and armor must be forged in volume and stockpiled now, while we still have time. Then, when war begins, we will have limitless supplies.

We must conserve the produce of our mines—gold, silver, lead, copper, iron, and precious stones—to the utmost. Squandering these irreplaceable resources is intolerable. The profligate use of gold and silver by Buddhist temples, the gilding of toys and ornaments, the use of precious metals by commoners, the making of women's jewelry and gold-laced kimonos—all squander valuable resources. We must act now to prohibit further melting down and recasting of gold and silver.

(Gloss: According to Chinese (*Saido*) works of history, dynastic rulers supplied gold and silver articles from their own households to be recast into armaments. They also prohibited the production of gilt and gold lace. We can surmise, then, that the ancients valued gold and silver mainly for military use, not for ornamentation. . . .

The Sung outlawed gold plating, the use of gold and silver on clothing, and the gilding of utensils. They also prohibited the use of gold on buildings, toys, and household furnishings. Women not belonging to the royal family could not wear gold hair ornaments. The emperor himself melted down his gold and silver personal effects for government use. Buddhist temples wishing to decorate statues or buildings with gold plate or gold foil could not do this themselves. Instead, they had to take unprocessed gold to one of the provincial government-run foundries which did the desired work for a fee. In addition, the government prohibited clerics from collecting donations of precious metals and gems for use in casting or decorating statues. At court, strict laws regulated the use of gold by non-members of the royal family. And of course, commoners were absolutely forbidden to use gold.

These and other carefully detailed injunctions appear repeatedly throughout history. From them we see how important it is to conserve the riches that Heaven provides for us.)

Frequent recoinages cause the lamentable destruction of precious metals through melting down and reminting. Foreign trade is largely a frittering away of our precious metals for useless commodities and must be banned. In town and village, people nowadays squander untold amounts of wealth on luxury items. We must stop all this!

(Gloss: High and low alike adore luxury items, and townsmen continually seek out new conveniences. People once were content with houses or tools made of wood and bamboo; now they demand iron and bronze. Grindstones and flints are indispensable to a military state. Our finely wrought, delicate tools—gimlets, chisels, knives, handsaws—wear away in no time. Our supply of pure iron-ore and high quality grindstones is just about depleted. People are so used to luxury that they reject simple lacquerware for fine china. We waste precious flints in great quantities to fire blast furnaces used in producing the useless items of glass that abound everywhere. Our list of squandered resources is endless. We must find ways to conserve these natural riches and eliminate waste before our irreplaceable treasures are completely gone.)

If we stopped producing and consuming things devoid of practical value, our mines and quarries would not be drained of their deposits so readily; our resources of divine spirit, also, would not be exhausted.

Not only do our people's lives depend on rice, it is vital as a source of rations for our troops. The surplus rice now amassed in urban areas may fatten decadent city dwellers, but these valuable rations cannot be distributed to fighting units. If we really want to store rations for our men, we must return to our original calling [agriculture], cultivate rice diligently, and treasure

it. Both the people and domain governments must store this
precious grain throughout the countryside.

(Gloss: See "What is Essential to a Nation.")

Then decadent city dwellers gradually will have to return
to the villages they once deserted. Then the processing of
food products wasteful of rice—such as *sake, mochi,* rice confections, and noodles—will be reduced. Also, the cultivation
of cash crops that lower agricultural production—such as
tea, tobacco, and dyer's saffron—will come under some control.

With proper study and adaptation, many ancient institutions—
the ever-normal granary system and the Leveler's Office [of
Nara times] to name but two—could be revived to meet today's needs. If we restored agriculture to its proper place
of primacy in society, if we kept the price of rice fixed all
year round every year, if we prevented avaricious merchant
princes from garnering exhorbitant profits and trampling
underfoot small proprietors, and if we taught high and low
alike to curb their acquisitiveness, then everyone from the
daimyo on down would store rice voluntarily in their homes
and could make ends meet. When warriors and peasants are on
sound financial footing, benefits will accrue to merchants as well.

An orderly system to regulate rice transactions would be a
boon to high and low alike, and would help curb acquisitiveness
throughout the realm. Rice should be the primary medium of
trade between domains and should serve as legal tender for
transactions between firms or individuals; coinage or silk products would supplement it only when necessary. Then rice would
circulate freely among the people all over the realm instead of
piling up in city storehouses. If a system of relief granaries,
whether government- or privately-run, were set up in the countryside, even the most destitute would be free from hunger in
lean years. Granary rice dispensed in times of need would be re-
plenished, and old rice [remaining at summer's end] would be
replaced by newly harvested grain [each fall]. Ancient institutions such as these all possess certain merits that we should
select and utilize in our famine-relief or defense programs. Then
the good bounties of earth and nature would circulate freely

and abundantly throughout the realm, and our vital life force (*yuan ch'i*) would not weaken.

(Gloss: Techniques for managing finances or a relief granary system are far from simple: When we implement them, we must realize that for every benefit we obtain, a disadvantage arises. Hence we must implement measures as each situation dictates, rather than adhere strictly to some set program. For this reason, I confine myself here to one aspect [of a much vaster problem]. On another occasion, I will state my views in more detail.)

We must end wastefulness in consuming rice, using the produce of our mines, and fashioning products from earth and sea. We must eliminate harmful practices and establish beneficial programs. We must ponder deeply, plan with broad vision, and tighten or relax our institutions after carefully discerning the needs of the day. None of these things can be accomplished until the Man of Talent and Virtue has been found. All my proposals are ways to stockpile materiel and provisions. We must deliberate on them thoroughly while we still have time.

I have thus outlined five specific programs to implement: coastal garrisons, communications networks, a coast guard, manufacturing firearms, and stockpiling materiel and provisions. I have written in general terms because I believe that after we outline guidelines and programs, we can work out details accordingly. We must reestablish institutions that existed in antiquity but are gone today, and revive the discipline that was upheld strictly in antiquity but is lax today. We must implement and rigorously enforce laws that should be but have not yet been drafted.

In this section, I have presented a basic outline of my views on national defense. But whenever knowledgeable men ponder the consequences of their proposals, they must bear in mind that harmful and beneficial results always come together; they must recognize the sources of both harm and benefit. Therefore, I conclude this section with a few words on the evils [encountered in political reform].

Anything of benefit to the realm must also be of harm. The *Book of Changes* [as interpreted by Chu Hsi] states, "Profit must accord with virtue." Unless we deem virtue itself to be profit, any benefits obtained will be specious. If we revive the samurai spirit without differentiating virtue from profit, we will be unable to tell the sincere from the wicked, we will have no just criteria to base rewards and punishments on; the realm will plunge into turmoil, and we will be unable to elevate the people's manners and morals. Efforts to eliminate luxurious habits and consumption denied to one's status will lead to indolence and furtive, large-scale graft; meanwhile, diligence and frugality will be impossible to instill. Measures designed to stabilize the people's livelihood will lead to distrust and estrangement between high and low: Commoners might feign compliance and industriousness, but their hearts would not be in it. Promoting men of ability will lead to favoritism and partisanship in government. Eliminating insolent, overbearing troops from the ranks will earn us the enmity of officers and men. Increased troop strength will tempt us into foolhardy belligerence. Improved methods of military training and the conduct of field maneuvers would amount to nothing more than cadenced flamboyance. Enriching the domains will tempt them to be insolent. Deploying defense troops throughout the land will precipitate warlord insurrections. Establishing garrisons will turn marauders loose in the countryside to pillage and to deprave folkways and morals. Setting up an intricate system of observation posts and way-stations will heap immense, unbearable burdens on the people. Building large ships and transporting goods in them will make smuggling all the more easy for nefarious commoners. Casting weapons and training troops in bowmanship and gunnery will open up avenues of advancement to phony tacticians and show-offs. Exploiting and stockpiling nature's treasures will breed embezzlers and swindlers. Retrenchment and austerity will cause the loss of many people's livelihood. Restoring agriculture to its proper place of primacy in society and stabilizing rice prices will usher in illegal marketing practices. In other words, none of our reforms would achieve hoped-for results.

Confucius once said, "Superior men (*chün tzu*) keenly perceive virtue; petty men (*hsiao jen*), profit." If we permit petty men—who cannot tell virtue from profit—to wield princely authority, programs designed to benefit the realm may well end up harming it. For that very reason, I argue that reviving the samurai spirit is the key to national defense and that we must lead the realm through virtue. To lead the realm through virtue, we must base ourselves on its interests as a public trust (*kōgi*). The bakufu has proclaimed a policy of armed expulsion throughout the land, thus appealing to our sense of shame; it has elucidated great virtue, and provided a focal point toward which all should direct their loyalty and energy. We must plunge into our work day and night with dedication; the intelligent must formulate stratagems, and the courageous must prepare for death. We must fire up our spirits, annihilate the impudent barbarians, and thereby demonstrate the greatness of our virtue to the entire world.

But alas, our slothful, indolent ways are as deeply ingrained as ever. How many of us are truly prepared to risk death? By nature, man does not willingly forsake pleasure for pain: We all long to remain in our soft, familiar ways. Even though the Expulsion Edict has been promulgated, none of us has actually executed it; momentous, long-needed reforms for national defense remain unimplemented. No wonder the masses long for peace and remain skeptical about armed expulsion. We have yet to fix our hearts on a policy of war. No wonder warriors remain unresolved to die.

Sun Tzu says, "In the face of death, men know not the meaning of fear."[114] Hōjō Tokimune [realized this when he] beheaded the Mongol envoy: Like it nor not, our warriors found themselves staring death in the face. If we expelled the barbarians but once, even the realm's laggards would bestir themselves to confront the nation's peril. We would "make them climb to great heights," and "take away the ladder from behind [to make them forget their fear]."[115] As *Sun Tzu* says, "Place men with their backs to the wall and they will die before fleeing to the rear."[116] Can there be a better way to dispel fear from men's hearts?

Whenever sovereigns in antiquity set out to accomplish a goal, they vigorously seized the initiative and boldly plunged into action. They disposed of routine business at Court in the

early hours of dawn. During the remainder of the day they debated vital matters of state, reviewed and exhorted their troops,
or held audiences with ministers to relate opinions to them. The
rulers of old made plain everything in their hearts: They clearly
revealed their aims and aspirations to their people and shared
joys and sorrows with them. Intelligent and courageous men
throughout the realm then responded resolutely by offering
their talents to the state in a spirit of sincere and loyal devotion;
they vowed never to co-exist with the barbarians. Sovereigns in
antiquity, then, succeeded in attracting intelligent and courageous men to government service. When such is the case, the
central government needs but issue a decree and it is executed
all over the land. Only when the spirit of righteousness per-
meates the realm can our spirits thus be sparked.

New Theses: eight

A Long-Range Policy

Before the Great Hero undertakes any important enterprise in the realm, he makes a panoramic survey of contemporary conditions, considers the broad vista thus obtained against the vast sweep of historical change, and establishes an immutable, long-range policy. Once this policy is implemented within, it will accommodate infinite changes from without. For this reason, the Great Hero is unperturbed by changes of fortune and unabashed when plans go awry. He may meet with innumerable setbacks, but is certain to achieve ultimate success because his objective is fixed. Although he pursues it through diverse methods, his efforts are constant and sustained.

It was this [timeless, immutable policy,] the Way, that enabled Amaterasu and Sage Emperors [in antiquity] to expel barbarians and extend our frontiers. Thus, our Middle Kingdom has always possessed a definite stratagem to bring barbarian tribes under control. Our rulers achieved great enterprises through indomitability of spirit by which they extended the Imperial sphere of moral influence (*kōkwa*). In ages past, barbarian tribes [surrounding our Middle Kingdom] were at times strong, and at times weak, at times rebellious, and at times submissive; but in the end, all were encompassed within it. The barbarians could not oppose our long-range policy because they could not achieve enterprises or pursue far-sighted goals through sustained planning.

The successful ruler possesses a boundless spirit and always begins an enterprise by surveying conditions in the realm. He meticulously ascertains topographic and climatic conditions in his land and the spiritual make-up of his people with a view to devising effective military and political stratagems. Only then does he implement his measures, slowly and methodically, so that he controls all affairs of the realm in the palm of his hand. For example, when Emperor Jimmu pacified our Middle Kingdom, he thoroughly surveyed lands to the east to determine their worthiness of Imperial rule before setting off to conquer them. He first formulated clear plans for conquest, and then executed them. As a result, his forces were victorious everywhere.

Emperor Sujin aspired to enhance the nation's power and prestige and to make these felt abroad.

(Gloss: During his dream, a divine messenger appeared and said, "Nations across the sea should also submit to our sphere of moral suasion (*kikwa*)." This dream was no chance occurrence.)

Even before the capital region was fully pacified, His Majesty drew up plans to administer the realm. He divided the land into four administrative circuits and [placed warrior-gods] in charge of these, a measure he no doubt decided on after carefully assessing prevailing conditions. His future administrative system was thus mapped out [before he went on to pacify the land]. No sooner did Sujin subdue barbarian tribes close at hand than those far away submitted to him. Thus dynastic fortunes revived magnificently.

The Emperors succeeding Sujin followed his example, eradicating the customs of savagery and enlarging the nation's territory so that foreign peoples [on the Korean peninsula] submitted in good order. During Empress Genshō's reign [715-24], we dispatched an expedition to the continent to survey the terrain and climate. This shows that we still aspired to conquer foreign territories.

(Gloss: During the Yōrō era [717-23], we dispatched Morogimi no Kurao, the provincial governor of Watarishima and Tsugaru.)

Amaterasu and Sage Emperors [in antiquity] keenly perceived the situation confronting them and administered the realm through policies so profound and sublime that their divine resplendence endures to this day. When we look back on these

Sage Emperors [in antiquity], we see how broad and vast their spirit was.

(Gloss: When the Sage King Yao of the T'ang [in high antiquity] set up his regime, he dispatched Hsi and Ho to live at the remotest ends of the realm. He ordered them to observe the movements of the Heavens and to teach the people when to sow and reap based on the knowledge they thus gained. After first exhaustively studying the warp and woof of the universe in all its vastness, Yao, Shun, and their retainers slowly and methodically went on to achieve great tasks. They would have failed utterly had they not first discerned the nature of the situation confronting them.

At the beginning of the "The Heavenly Officers" section of the *Rites of Chou,* it says, "They establish order over the state, over political organs, and over people by means of the *Six Classics.*" This means that the Heavenly Officers exercised comprehensive control over all government processes. At the beginning of "The Earthly Officers," it says, "They manage geographic and demographic affairs," which means that they performed the basic functions necessary to political administration. When the Duke of Chou established his capital at Lo-i, he made sacrifices to Heaven before doing anything else, because to honor Heaven—which presides over the people—is the most important requirement of government. When Liu Pang, who became the first Han emperor, occupied Ch'in, he first seized all maps and domicile registers. With the aid of these, he became thoroughly familiar with the terrain and where the people lived, and as a result, he greatly offset the power of his rival, Hsiang Chi. Thus, one must be quick to size up the situation and determine one's course of action.)

For many and varied reasons, however, foreign peoples in later ages ceased bearing tribute to our Middle Kingdom. The Court lacked men of vision and planning, our territory contracted day after day, and Emperors lost the will to govern. The Western barbarians have grown tremendously powerful in recent times, and what is more, they too have learned how to discern prevailing situations confronting them and to ply stratagems of their own. Thus, they have been annexing territories at will for over three hundred years, slowly and steadily making their way toward our Divine Realm. They have appropriated the very stratagem that Amaterasu and our Sage Emperors [in antiquity] once used to subjugate barbarians; now they seek to turn it against our Middle Kingdom. Yet we in the Middle Kingdom have yet to establish a coherent policy to deal with them. Councils are divided both in and out of government. We waver indecisively, or at best, adopt gloss-it-over, stop-gap measures. We even allow these foreign beasts to come ashore and run amok! Ours is the Land of the Illustrious Gods—have we no sense of shame?

The ruler of men is both prince and edifier to the multitudes. He who rules over others has a broad spirit that encompasses the four seas; he tends to affairs in the realm in a poised, self-assured manner, and accomplishes every task. By contrast, he who is ruled over by others is capable of perceiving only short-run advantages; he acts without thinking and lacks the capacity to manage affairs in the realm.

Since we have yet to observe conditions in foreign lands, it comes as no surprise that the wily barbarians take advantage of us and deride us for our shortsightedness. To determine our basic [foreign] policy, we first must assess conditions in the realm and then compare strengths and weaknesses. I have already presented a brief account of conditions at home and abroad. Thus informed of the situation confronting us, we now must make our islands into a castle and think of the ocean as a moat. We must adopt defense measures dictated by conditions in the realm as a whole. Yet before comparing specific strengths and weaknesses with the barbarians, we must determine just whose forces enjoy preponderance [in this theater]. Then we must devise ways to gain the freedom of initiative to control them.

Our forces should enjoy overall preponderance, since we await them in our homeland, and they must travel thousands of miles to spy on us. But in truth, they have turned the tables on us. They have a superb stratagem at their disposal and rule their territories in a poised, self-assured manner. Through fishing and trade, they procure food and supplies without having to maintain supply lines far from home: They are truly masters at the art of "securing provisions in the enemy's homeland."[117] They "transport men and materiel effortlessly and without loss or damage"[118] in their huge ships. They remain motionless at sea, but we scurry from place to place on shore, exhausting ourselves in an attempt to cover all possible weak spots: They are truly adept at "subduing the enemy without resorting to battle."[119] They lure our commoners over to their side through their barbarous religion, for they have learned well the lesson, "to take over the enemy's homeland and people intact is the best strategy of all."[120]

Sun Tzu says, "Only when enjoying a ten to one advantage in men does one lay siege to fortresses."[121] The enemy must cross vast oceans to reach us, and even if they assembled all their forces to make a sudden assault, they lack sufficient numbers to surround us [and lay siege]. But in effect, they do enjoy a ten to one edge over us because we must "spread our forces thin" to defend ourselves on all four sides, and theirs are "concentrated"[122] in a single fighting force. Moreover, [because they control the seas,] "they are free to maneuver and choose the best time and place to do battle."[123] They need only dispatch one or two ships to incite an uprising by commoners on shore, so it takes little insight to see just who is strong and who is weak.

To turn our weakness into strength, we must outwit the enemy and throw him off balance. To do this, we must put him on the defensive; there is no defense apart from offense. As the ancients put it, "To attack is the key to defense." If we take the offensive, the enemy will have to assume a defensive posture, and freedom of initiative will revert to us. We must shore up our defenses and seize the opportune moment to cut off barbarian forces on the open sea. Though they seek to incite rebellion in outlying areas, they possess only a few ships and men. Therefore they would lose effective strength by dividing up the small squadrons they dispatch. If we prevented them from inciting our commoners here, there, and everywhere along our coastline, the troops we deploy, though few in number, would suffice.

Furthermore, as long as their ships remain huddled together for defensive purposes, the barbarians cannot secure needed provisions through fishing and trade as they normally do. As a result, they will have to leave our coastal waters as soon as their supplies run out. They will not be able to employ their stratagems against us, and their insolence will be a thing of the past. Moreover, since we await the enemy in our homeland (*naichi*), we are in [what *Sun Tzu* terms] "defection-prone territory," whereas the enemy, who has yet to penetrate our territory deeply, is in "falter-prone territory."[124] As *Sun Tzu* says, "When in defection-prone territory, one must unify the [the people's] wills."[125] If we determine our basic [foreign] policy now, lead the people along the proper path, and thus unify them spiritually, defeating the barbarians should not be difficult, since they are still in falter-prone territory. What keeps us from devising stratagems to slaughter them?

By taking the offensive, I do not necessarily mean killing enemy troops, vanquishing enemy armies, and capturing enemy strongholds. Rather, what we must do is "fortify ourselves so that we are invincible and devise measures to defeat the enemy."[126] We first must rejuvenate ourselves spiritually and study conditions [at home and abroad]. Externally, we must "counteract the enemy's stratagems in advance."[127] Then we must "disrupt his alliances,"[128] and devise tactics to stop him cold. Internally, we must shore up our defenses and increase troop strength to bring the enemy under control. Our government and edification must be so perfect that we can transform barbarian ways to those of civilization. Then, if they attempt to spy in our coastal waters, we could exterminate them; and if they choose to submit, we could spread the blessings of Imperial Virtue far and wide, to the remotest regions of the world.

We should annex the Ezo Islands and absorb the barbarian tribes on the continent; we should roll back the tide of barbarism and extend our frontiers ever forward. This is what I mean by "measures to defeat the enemy." In this way we could attack and capture the hearts and minds of the foe before the battle begins. Then we need but assault their strongholds, strike their weak points, and take advantage of every opportunity to wreak

Heavenly Devastation on them. This is the way to ensure victory. In short, we then will have put the barbarians on the defensive, and our forces will have reclaimed the overall preponderance that theirs now enjoy. This is what I meant earlier by "outwitting the enemy, throwing him off balance, and making him take the defensive." We will have turned their strength into weakness and our weakness into strength. Thus we will have revived the stratagem so adroitly employed [in antiquity] by Amaterasu and Sage Emperors to control the barbarians, and which they have recently turned against us. Can there be a better method of counteracting the stratagem that they now use to subvert us? Thus we will have recovered the freedom of initiative to control them.

Now that the bakufu has proclaimed armed expulsion, high and low alike are spiritually united, and all our efforts are directed toward one objective. This indeed was the Way for controlling barbarism that Amaterasu and Sage Emperors employed: a resolute strategy decided on within, and impenetrable safeguards against encroachment from abroad. Then no matter how often the barbarians might come spying, they could not wreak havoc on shore.

(Gloss: Tokugawa Ieyasu once sent an interpreter named Shimano Kenryō to India. Shimano set off in a Dutch vessel, and after visiting many lands, finally arrived in a huge country three thousand miles to the east. Firmly believing that this territory should belong to our Divine Realm, he erected a small sign saying, "Part of Japan (*Nihonkoku*)." This shows the breadth of vision men had in those days. This land "three thousand miles to the east," I believe, was the territory that the Western barbarians now call "America.")

Simply bringing the barbarians under control with a definite stratagem should be enough to achieve spiritual unity among the masses. But there are two methods to strengthen further the bonds binding our people together: performing short-term feats of greatness through inspired effort, and implementing gradualistic programs whose successful culmination must be left to future generations. The former method is impossible without timing, resourcefulness, and the presence of an able statesman-general. The latter method is impossible without long-range vision and unless we resolutely achieve the enterprise [delegated to us by Amaterasu] by extending the sphere of Imperial moral suasion (*kōkwa*). The former method calls for rewards and punishments periodically applied to inspire the people; the latter, for prescribed rituals and edification eternally upheld to discipline them. [*Mencius* says,] "The people fear good government and love good teachings." This means that they occasionally hold authority in fearful awe, but always yearn for timeless moral precepts. Thus, [*Mencius* says,] "good teachings capture the people's hearts."

In maintaining the realm for all eternity, [a sage] first takes into account any and all problems that might arise and prescribes broad guiding precepts to deal with them. He clarifies the decrees of Heaven, the nature of men's hearts, the laws inherent in things, and the ethical principles by which men live. Then he lays down teachings and injunctions to disseminate in good order: Immutable precepts originate from [the sage's] mind. In antiquity Amaterasu "established teachings in accordance with the 'spirit-like processes of nature'" (*shen tao*), thus elucidating loyalty and filial devotion and prescribing the rules of conduct by which men live. It is through these teachings that the realm can be maintained for eternity.[129] That the present dynasty was founded in antiquity, that it has been maintained for countless generations, and that therefore its sphere of moral suasion (*kōkwa*) should extend far and wide—all this accords with the august motive that inspired Amaterasu to "establish her precepts" for posterity.

Whenever Emperor Jimmu, the founder of our Imperial Line, waged war, he looked to divine powers for help in performing great heroic feats.

(Gloss: While pacifying the Middle Kingdom, Emperor Jimmu prayed to the deities, obtained divine assistance, and marched with the Sun [Goddess] at his back. Guided by the Yata Crow and armed with the Futsunomitama Sword, He displayed obedience to the instructions of Amaterasu and Takemikazuchi.

By worshipping the Heavenly and Earthly Deities at the upper reaches of the Nyū River and by ordering His sub-lieutenant, Michinoomi, to worship the god Takamimusubi, His Majesty displayed reliance on divine assistance.)

After pacifying the Middle Kingdom, He established a site to worship godly spirits at Tomi, where He paid reverence to Amaterasu and to His Heavenly Ancestors. Thus, he was a living exemplar of filial devotion.

(Gloss: Emperor Jimmu attained victory over Nagasunehiko only after the auspicious appearance of the Golden Kite (*tobi*). For this reason, he named this area "Tobinomura," or [after a euphonic change,] "Tomi." This is probably why His Majesty worshipped the godly spirits there.)

When Emperor Sujin acceded to the Throne, local chieftains rebelled. In those days, the Court still followed the ancient custom of worshipping [the Sacred Mirror, the embodiment of] Amaterasu, [privately] within the Imperial Palace. Emperor Sujin, however, was awe-struck and ill at ease.[130] Therefore he transferred this Imperial Treasure to Kasanui, where he worshipped it publicly, and turned it into an object that everyone in the realm might revere with him. His Majesty intended to make reverence for Amaterasu a feeling shared by Court and people alike. [He sought] to show the people that their worship of Amaterasu constituted reverence for the Imperial Court.

(Gloss: It is true that by worshipping Amaterasu [privately] within Court enclosures, [earlier Emperors] had offered the full measure of their sincere devotion to Her. But the meaning in Their Majesties' ritual acts was lost on the realm's people. By worshipping Amaterasu [publicly,] outside Court enclosures, Emperor Sujin displayed sincere devotion together with the whole realm. Thus, the realm's people grasped the significance of His Majesty's act [directly and sensually,] not through explanations or exhortations. Since His Majesty's sincere devotion alone touches the gods' hearts, how much greater is the effect when the entire realm joins in!)

The ancients [Mencius] said, "Filial devotion by the realm *en masse* is the ultimate in filial devotion." When the Duke of Chou was praised in antiquity for having attained "the ultimate in filial devotion," it was because everyone in the realm [joined him] in worshipping his ancestors, each person in accordance with his proper status. The Duke of Chou did not worship his parents within ritual-hall confines, but in public, together with his people. No doubt he had the same idea as Emperor Sujin.)

[Emperor Sujin] also worshipped the local deities Ōmononushi and Yamato no Kunitama. Because the inhabitants of the capital region revered these two gods, His Majesty gave their rituals Imperial recognition and official standing. Thus, he captured the minds and allegiances of the people in the capital area, and they revered the Court thereafter.

(Gloss: Local commoners worshipped Ōmononushi, a god who performed heroic deeds in pacifying the realm. Therefore, [Emperor Sujin] allowed their descendants to conduct religious rituals dedicated to Ōmononushi. These people were deeply moved that Emperor Sujin joined them in worshipping their clan god, and thereafter looked to the Imperial Court for fulfillment of their hopes and prayers.

The meaning behind Emperor Sujin's worship of Ōmononushi is no doubt similar to that of the 'Great *Shê*' religious ritual in Chou times. According to the *Book of Rites,* "the *shê* instituted by the king for the people's benefit are 'Great *Shê*.'" "*Shê*" are rituals in which people worship local deities and heroes who have performed meritorious services. Thus, for example, in *Tso Chuan* it says, "Kung Kung-shih had a son named Chü Lung who became the god Hou T'u. This Hou T'u is worshipped during the *shê.*"

Likewise, the god Yamato no Kunitama is probably "the deity who pacified Yamato Province." Since the nation's capital then was located in Yamato, this god probably was worshipped by many inhabitants there. This form of worship is very similar to that displayed by the Chinese people during their "Kingly *Shê*" in Chou times. The *Book of Rites* says, "'Kingly *Shê*' are those established by the emperor himself." The land is the basis of the people's livelihood, and the local deities of the land are the objects of their worship. If the Emperor takes the lead in worshipping these local deities, He will gain the allegiance of and create spiritual unity among His people.)

[Emperor Sujin] proceeded to worship provincial clan deities in area after area, establishing Heavenly and Earthly shrines to Heavenly and Earthly Deities throughout the realm. He captured the hearts of the people, and thereafter they revered the Court.

(Gloss: In antiquity, the term "Heavenly Deities" designated Amaterasu and Her august offspring as well as the gods and heroes who served and aided the Emperors in Their Majesties' Imperial government. The term, "Earthly Deities," referred to old clans of long-standing who subdued outlying districts. These deities are worshipped at "Heavenly Shrines" and "Earthly Shrines" respectively. In the *Ryō no gige* it says, "Ise, Kamo [in Yamashiro], Sumiyoshi, and the deities worshiped by the Izumo Kuni no Miyatsuko are examples of "Heavenly Deities;" Ōmiwa, Ōyamato, Kamo [in Katsuragi], and Ōnamuchi [of Izumo] are examples of "Earthly Deities." The shrines at which these gods are worshipped are "Heavenly Shrines" and "Earthly Shrines," respectively.)

In addition, Emperor Sujin set up special rice fields for the deities and appointed villagers to tend these and secure stable supplies of rice for offerings at ritual time. Thus, the people were made aware of the homage paid by the Imperial Court to their local deities. The weapons of war were also employed during rituals to the gods. Through these rituals, the people were made aware of the divine sanctions attached to military commands, the realm's strategic areas were always well guarded, commoners were impressed with the inviolability of the Imperial Court, and they were induced to hold it in ever greater religious awe.

(Gloss: According to the "Suinin Chronicle" in *Nihon shoki,* "Bows, arrows, and swords were stored in shrines. The use of weapons in worshipping the gods during religious festivals began at this time." But actually even before this, during the reign of Emperor Sujin, halberds and shields were used to worship deities in festivals at Sumisaka and Ōsaka. I believe that because these two regions were of strategic importance to the realm, religious festivals also served as a means of storing weapons and tacitly conveying the need to shore up defenses to people in those key spots. This [use of religious rituals] continued as late as Emperor Suinin's reign [29 B.C. to 70 A.D.].)

The people revered the Court, the rebellious were subdued as a matter of course, and the likes of Takehani Yasuhiko and Izumo Furune promptly received their just deserts.[131] The "spirit-like processes of nature" (*shen tao*) were elucidated, the Imperial Line was maintained, and an official list of recognized rituals and deities [as part of the *Engi shiki*] was distributed throughout the realm. Bona fide deities who had been overlooked were added to the list and granted official standing.

(Gloss: According to the *Engi shiki,* the total number of shrines in the Court, capital region, and the seven administrative circuits are over 3,100. There are 492 Great Shrines, of which 304 received Imperial Cloth Offerings from the Office of Divinities and conducted the *anjō kampei* ceremony during the Toshigoi, Tsukinami, and Niiname Rituals. Of these 304, 71 participated in the Ainame Ritual. The remaining 188 Great Shrines received Imperial Cloth Offerings from the Office of Divinities. There were 2,640 Lesser Shrines, of which 433 received Imperial Cloth Offerings during the Toshigoi Ritual. The above-mentioned rituals—the Toshigoi, Tsukinami, Niiname, and Ainame—were accorded the highest official rankings, and these rankings applied to all shrines in the realm.)

Gods who had performed feats of heroism on Imperial campaigns were appointed tutelary deities in the regions they had helped to conquer.

(Gloss: Those gods and heroes who conquered and pacified particular regions during Imperial campaigns in antiquity were worshipped. Their descendants were placed in charge of religious rituals, and in this capacity, they continued to pacify the peoples in those areas. For example, Takemikazuchi, the god enshrined at Kashima Shrine, performed great heroic feats in pacifying the east. . . . Because of these gods' and heroes' great deeds of merit in antiquity, the inhabitants of these areas continued to worship them for countless generations. Likewise, Ōnamuchi pacified Izumo, and Prince Toyoki pacified Kōzuke and Shimotsuke. The descendants of these deities continue to watch over and conduct religious rituals at the various shrines dedicated to them in these regions. Numerous examples of this sort in all areas of the nation can be cited. By winning the devotion of the local inhabitants, we keep the provinces in peace, and instill an attitude of respectfulness in the people.

When the Chou established their capital at Lo-i, they gave official standing to as yet unrecognized deities, and they deified any local inhabitants whose ancestors had performed meritorious deeds in antiquity. Thus, the actions of the Chou were prompted by motives similar to those of [Sujin and other] early Emperors in our history.)

In these regions, they unified the people's hearts, drove off barbarian tribes, and transformed barbarous customs to civilized ways. Thus, our sphere of moral influence became more extensive with each passing day and the common people enjoyed harmony. The innumerable deities and myriad shrines near the capital and in the provinces watched over and protected their respective lands and peoples. The descendants of those peoples continue to revere and worship those deities even today, since the virtues of recompensing the blessings bestowed by Amaterasu and remaining true to ancestral will [outlined in "What is Essential to a Nation"] has been tacitly conveyed.

Amaterasu and Sage Emperors [in antiquity] established broad guiding teachings and thus maintained the realm forever; Their Majesties prescribed rituals which were made manifest and dutifully followed. When viewing the vestiges of these teachings and rituals today, we can judge for ourselves just how broad and vast Imperial solicitude once was. But various heresies sprang up in later ages and the Way became obscured. The Court lacked men of planning and vision, Dynastic decay set in, [the Imperial House] gradually lost its hold on the people's hearts, and Impe-government breached Amaterasu's manifest will that Sage Emperors should rule the realm for ages eternal.

In recent years, the wily barbarians have established ethical precepts of their own that sound very much like the genuine ones prescribed [by the sages] in antiquity; armed with their "Way of Wickedness," they eat into the peoples' hearts and minds. The barbarians' teachings are not "good teachings,"[132] but they pass these off as "teachings" just the same, and manage "to capture the people's hearts." In every country they go to, they raze the dwelling-places of native deities, trying to introduce their own god and win over the inhabitants' allegiance.

The barbarians are triumphant everywhere and have begun to disseminate their poisonous doctrines in our Divine Realm. They have their hearts set on transforming us to barbarism by turning against us the very stratagem that Sage Emperors [in antiquity] employed to encompass them within our Middle Kingdom. Yet we in the Middle Kingdom remain without an unswerving moral basis of action; our people lack unity and spiritual cohesion, our leaders can dream up nothing better than stop-gap, gloss-it-over measures to tide them over each day's new crises. Our Land of Illustrious Gods has fallen to such depths that we now sit by idly and allow these foreign beasts to lure the common people away from us. Have we lost all sense of shame?

Nothing is more awe-inspiring than Heaven. That is why the Sages venerably serve and fear it. They do not think of Heaven as inanimate matter [informed by Principle and discernible to human reason; but instead, view it as a living entity]. By venerably serving it, they evoke a sense of reverent awe and respectful submissiveness in commoners. Nothing is more possessed of spirituality than man. His soul is of an imperishable nature, unlike that of the grasses and trees, or the birds and beasts. He is conscious of his own life and death, particularly when faced with the prospect of dying. That is why the Sages elucidated the proper religious rituals. With the aid of these, they soothed man's doubts and fears and assured him of a place to rest his soul after death, so that his uncertainties about the hereafter would not lead him down evil paths. When commoners stand in reverent awe of Heaven and respectfully submit to its decrees, wicked doctrines will not beguile them on the threshold of death, and [fictive tales of] paradise in the afterworld will not mislead them.

The responsibility for performing these rituals, that is, for recompensing Heaven, worshipping ancestors, praying for fortune, and eliminating calamities and evils, rests with rulers. Commoners need only do as their ruler tells them; by respecting their ruler as they would serve Heaven, they worship their ancestors. In addition, by binding their families together with warmth and affection, they cherish their ancestors as they do their parents. When the masses below are spiritually unified, outlandish doctrines hold no attraction for them. But when religious rituals fall into neglect, people are cut off from Heaven, and they become disdainful toward it. In death, they are reduced to insignificant floating spirits in a cosmic sea, futilely seeking some place of repose. In life, their hearts are unsettled, and they are fearful of the hereafter.

This makes them susceptible to notions of paradise and hell. They crave happiness in the world to come and reject virtue in this life; they shirk their ruler's commands as they would avoid the incursions of enemy raiders; they embrace the foreigners' [religious] teachings as they long for a mother's compassion. They are attracted to pernicious doctrines from without because they need a basis of spiritual reliance within. It is only natural that the barbarians take advantage of this spiritual void and this fear of the hereafter. They beguile commoners into embracing barbarian notions of paradise or hell, fabulous places that no one has ever seen or visited.

(Gloss: It is written, "Whenever pure vital force conglomerates, matter is formed; when it disperses, floating spirits are released and transformed." Unless the proper religious rituals are duly performed to soothe the spirits of the dead on their way to Heaven, there can be no repose for the living or the dead, for the common people by nature cannot help feeling a vague sorrow [at the thought of dying]. Unless they possess an inner source of composure that puts their minds at ease when faced with death, they cannot help being deceived by tales of paradise and hell. It is to relieve their fears that we perform religious rituals to ancestors.

Ancestors and offspring belong to the same original *ch'i:* The progenitor is the fountainhead and the offspring are temporal extensions. [This *ch'i* cannot be severed] so how can the spirit of a deceased ancestor, even though it be floating about the cosmos, be separated from his offspring? Through religious rituals the ancestral spirit in Heaven is soothed and comforted. [As explained in the *Chung-yung,*] "Heaven is a mass of luminous *ch'i.*" Man exists between Heaven and Earth and is permeated by the vital force (*ch'i*) flowing therein, which imparts life to him. In other words, Heaven, Earth, and man are composed of the same *ch'i.* Man's primordial vital force (*yuan ch'i*), which sustains all life and order, is common to Heaven and Earth as well. When man conducts the proper religious rituals to Heaven and Earth, he can make contact with them, and [through this ritual medium,] they reveal their secrets. Therefore, when the sages served Heaven and revered ancestors, the people's sorrow [at the thought] of dying disappeared, and the realm readily submitted.

In subsequent ages rulers lacked vision and planning, and they belittled the need to serve Heaven and revere ancestors. As a result, the people lost their object of reverent awe in life and their place of repose in death. Doubts and fears arose among them, and they began to yearn for a source of spiritual reliance. Then the Western barbarians struck further anxiety in the commoners' hearts by spreading doctrines of paradise and hell. This is [what Mencius meant when he said,] "Only when one demeans himself do others scorn him.")

To achieve resolutely the great enterprises [delegated by Amaterasu], we first must prescribe broad guiding precepts and make perfectly clear the difference between justice and evil, Middle Kingdom Civilization and barbarism. I have already outlined the great essence of our nation as prescribed by the gods in antiquity. Since our broad guiding principles are established, we must extend these to all within the Four Seas, as if they formed one large family, and we must uphold these precepts for all eternity while making necessary modifications as changing times dictate. To clarify the difference between justice and evil, and between our Middle Kingdom Civilization and barbarism, we must elucidate the great Way of Heaven and make it the standard for our actions.

Our Divine Realm stands at the vertext of the world, where the *"ch'i* of justice" and the "clear *ch'i* of dawn" prevail.

(Gloss: Our Divine Realm is the land that the gods first created. The Chinese (*Kanhito*) call [our land] off to their east "The Area of the Sun." The Western barbarian also call our Divine Realm, the Ch'ing Empire, India, and Tungusland, "Asia" or *"Morgenland."* These names are based on [the earth's] natural configurations.)

The *"ch'i* of justice" and *"ch'i* of dawn" are *yang.* Therefore, the Way of our Divine Realm is just and bright. By clarifying the Five Human Relationships, we serve Heaven; by honoring the gods, we exert our human powers to the limit; and by sustaining the myriad things, we embody "the life-nurturing virtue of Heaven and Earth" [as elucidated in the *Book of Changes*]. By contrast, the barbarians inhabit those parts of the world [that correspond to the] legs and feet [of the human anatomy], where the *"ch'i* of wickedness" and "the murky *ch'i* of dusk" prevail. The *"ch'i* of wickedness" and "the murky *ch'i* of dusk" are *yin.* Therefore, the barbarians seek out the dismal and practice the occult. They destroy the Way of man and preach doctrines of the hereafter. They desecrate Heaven and curry favor with the spirits. They amuse themselves by fabricating absurd [Biblical] fables. They spell death and devastation for all creation, and they adhere to the Way of darkness and ill-omen.

If we truly are to roll back this tide of devastation, we must supplant barbarian destruction with the power of Life. We must transform (*kwa*) their darkness into our light; we must refute their fanciful tales of life and death with the great, resplendent Way that encompasses the Will of Heaven and the hearts of men. If we illuminate the entire world with the sun's radiant splendor, how can the flickering flame of barbarism maintain its hold over men? Then we will have counteracted the prime stratagem that they use to annex peoples and nations. In short, we must transform them by appropriating the very Way that they now seek to use to transform us; this is the most pressing need behind setting up broad, guiding precepts.

Barbarians are, after all, barbarians. It is only natural that they adhere to a barbarous Way, and normally we could let things go at that. But today they have their hearts set on transforming our Middle Kingdom Civilization to barbarism. They will not rest until they desecrate the gods and destroy the Way of Virtue, until they lure all peoples into their ranks and take over all lands in the world. Our Way of Virtue and their deceitful techniques are as incompatible as fire and ice. The universe is not vast enough to contain us both: "Unless their barbarous way is blotted out, the Way of Amaterasu and our Sage Emperors remains unelucidated."[133] Until the Way of Amaterasu and our Sage Emperors is elucidated, their barbarous way remains to be blotted out. Either we transform them or they will transform us—we are on a collision course. How can a leader of planning and vision shirk his duty of counteracting [their] deceit with our justice? Only thus can he spare future generations from pestilence!

Benevolence and universal love extend as far as the sun shines; men are men no matter what part of the earth they inhabit. But how can a benevolent ruler sit back and watch the barbarians propagate their occult religion, destroy the Way of Heaven, trample underfoot accepted rules of human conduct, and deceive and reduce commoners to the level of beasts and demons? Indeed, the benevolent ruler aspires to transform barbarism to our Middle Kingdom Civilization. Thus he would rescue the whole world from the ravages of savage cunning—just as Heaven radiates to all corners of the earth. The benevolent ruler must promote learning and military prowess at home and make these felt abroad if he is to display great virtue and resolutely achieve the tasks [delegated by Amaterasu].

(Gloss: Yü's great personal achievement in antiquity was to edify the entire realm. Yi Yin's claim to greatness was his deep sense of personal responsibility. If but one commoner in the realm was denied the blessings of sagely rule, Yi Yin felt as though he himself had pushed that poor man into a ditch. Similarly, though the flood was certainly none of Yao's doing, he interpreted it as Heaven's admonition to himself— such was the extent of his benevolence. When Emperor Wu of the Han took it on himself to avenge his great-great-grand-father's disastrous defeat by the Hsiung-nu, he did so not be-cause he specifically had been charged with this task. Instead, he felt constrained by his great sense of duty. Such examples indicate the keen sense of personal accountability felt by rulers of old.)

To realize this aspiration, we first must strive to clarify "our national essence" (*kokutai*). We must make the present conform to the past by adhering to the great methods [laid down by Amaterasu]. With broad mind and vision, we must reign supreme over Middle Kingdom Civilization and barbarian lands alike. By boosting troop strength we will be true to our name The Land of Proficient Halberds Aplenty, and by raising agricultural out-put we will be true to our name The Land of Ripening Rice Crests. To make the people trust us, we must elucidate loyalty and filial devotion and thereby elevate the realm morally. To amass supplies of food, to cultivate adequate troop strength, and to make the people trust us; to elucidate loyalty and filial devotion, and to reestablish the union of Heaven and man; to eliminate the doubts and fears that the masses now hold regard-ing death and the hereafter; to convert [barbarian] deceit into justice; and to transform barbarism to our Middle Kingdom Civilization—these are the enterprises delegated by Amaterasu for Her Descendants to achieve resolutely. To accomplish these tasks, we must induce the people simply to submit [to Her Way without asking why]. How can this be done? I say, "Through [the mystical, suggestive power of] ritual, and through ritual alone." There are five categories of rituals, but religious rituals are the best means of teaching commoners respectfulness.

(Gloss: In the *Offices of Chou* it is written, "When the people are taught respectfulness by means of religious rituals, they become deferential.")

There are different categories of religious rituals, every ritual has a meaning of its own. We must clarify meanings before speaking of categories. By worshipping the deities of Heaven and Earth, the Emperor recompenses Heaven; by reverently worshipping Amaterasu, he honors his ancestors; by worshipping the deities of the Yamato Plain, he pacifies the earth; and by worshipping the god Ukemochi, he shows his concern for the people's livelihood. . . .[134] There are detailed rituals for worshipping the gods of the wind, rain, grasses, trees, and all creation,

(Gloss: These deities are Yamatsumi, Mizuwa, Watatsumi, Shinato, Haniyama, Kayano, Kukunochi, and so on. The reason so many famous mountains are places of worship to Izanagi, Ōnamuchi, and Ōyamatsumi is that these gods pacify the land. The sea god, Sumiyoshi, is worshipped in coastal areas in hopes of calm seas. The other gods whose names are listed [in the *Engi shiki*] all are worshipped by the people to obtain bountiful harvests and protection from natural disasters. . . .)

There are rituals for worshipping Imperial Princes, Imperial Offspring, illustrious retainers, and others who rendered service to the Court.

(Gloss: For example, Prince Yamato Takeru, Prince Toyoki, Takemikazuchi, Futsunuchi, Ame no Koyane, and Sugawara no Michizane are worshipped at the Ōtori, Futawara, Kashima,

Katori, Kasuga, and Kitano Shrines, respectively. The Chinese [*Kando*] customarily worship deities who performed services on the people's behalf. . . .)

The ritual procedures are prescribed in our classics in detail. No worthy deity or person, no spirit of Heaven and Earth is overlooked during these rituals, and as a result, every corner of the land is pacified. The religious rituals performed by various lesser functionaries at Court serve to protect His Majesty and to assist Him in ordering the realm.

(Gloss: These are the Mikan no Ko, who conduct rituals to the gods of antiquity; the Ikasuri, who conduct rituals to the spirits of the Imperial Palace Grounds and the deity of the Palace Well; and the Ikushima, who conduct rituals to the spirits of the various provinces and islands. In addition to the above Court functionaries, in the Department of the Imperial Household, rituals are performed at the Sono and Kara Shrines. In the Court kitchens, rituals are performed to the deities of foods and fire. In the Distiller's Agency, rituals are performed to the spirits of *sake*. And in the Waterworks Agency, rituals are performed to the god of thunder. Protection is afforded to the Imperial Line through all these rituals. In China [*Kando*], the Five Rituals serve this same purpose.)

[The five categories of rituals can also be divided into three groups according to the length of purification involved great, intermediate, and lesser.] There is but one great ritual, the Daijō, which is after the Emperor's Coronation. By acceding to the Throne, His Majesty recompenses Amaterasu's blessings and carries on Her Manifest Will [that Her Descendants reign over the land for ages eternal]. Therefore, this ritual deserves our highest veneration.

There are [five] intermediate rituals; the Toshigoi, during which prayers are offered so that the year's religious rituals might be conducted in good order at all shrines throughout the land; the Tsukinami, during which the Court makes offerings to the Heavenly and Earthly shrines throughout the realm (much as commoners make offerings to the protective deities watching over their homes);

(Gloss: However, the Emperor thinks of all within the Four Seas as his household. Because His Majesty distributes offerings to the gods of the whole realm and to those of the islands within our seas, and because He prays that His blessings might extend far and wide, it is quite clear that His Majesty's prayers and rituals are not performed to benefit his own household alone.)

the Niiname, the significance of which is similar to that of the Daijō; the Kammizo, during which offerings of Heavenly Garments are made in summer and autumn at the Ise Shrines; and the Kanname, which is performed on the same day as the autumn Kammizo ritual.

Through the first three of these [five] intermediate rituals, the Emperor nourishes the people and brings security to the state; and by means of the last, the Kanname, His Majesty pays thanks to Amaterasu for Her original gifts of rice and silk to the people. In addition, there are numerous lesser rituals such as the Ōimi, Kaze no kami, Hanashizume, and Hishizume, to placate the gods of nature or to prevent crop failures, fires, natural disasters, and plagues. By performing these rituals, His Majesty prays for good fortune and eliminates calamities and suffering in the land.

(Gloss: The Chou also performed a sort of Toshigoi ritual along with their Five Rituals . . . for much the same reasons as our Emperor performs the above rituals.)

Each religious ritual possesses its own particular meaning; the Court performs each, and its ritual effects pervade the Four Quarters. The meaning of recompensing Amaterasu's original blessings and remaining true to ancestral will, as well as an awareness of His Majesty's concern for the realm and for the people's happiness and well-being, are imbued in all the realm's people. The responsibility for conducting these lies with rulers; the common people should do as they are told. If they but pay homage to the Imperial Court, they can do no evil. This is how to achieve spiritual unity.

Before performances of the Daijō Ritual in antiquity, sacrificial rice fields and ritual sites were selected through divination, and reapers were dispatched to the areas selected. After obtaining the cooperation of the provincial governors there, the reapers enlisted commoners to cultivate, reap, and prepare rice for sacrificial offerings. All provinces equally possessed the opportunity of being chosen to serve the gods in this manner; and the common people aspired to toil mightily to offer rice for use in this ritual. His Majesty's desires to serve Heaven, revere ancestors, be filial, and ensure His people's livelihood were manifested throughout the Four Quarters. The provincial governors led their people in transporting the sacrificial rice, and all people along the nation's highways assisted; so the meaning behind the Emperor's ritual acts was conveyed along the highways [of the entire nation.]

Moreover, each province paid a ten-thousand bale levy to defray expenses [for the Daijō Ritual], so all people in the realm understood its symbolic meaning. Ritual purifiers were dispatched throughout the realm, so everyone recognized the need to purify himself and serve the gods. The Court distributed Imperial Cloth Offerings to all shrines in the realm, so people everywhere realized that their local deities were united under Amaterasu's aegis. These Cloth Offerings conveyed the meaning behind the Emperor's ritual acts to everyone in the realm—His service to Heaven, reverence for ancestors, and love of the people. A ritual existed for every meaning to be conveyed, and through these rituals the Emperor made his will understood to the people day-in and day-out, without recourse to explanations or exhortations. Each person was loyal to his ruler, and all of them in turn revered the Imperial Court. Thus, the hearts and minds of the people were one.

In later ages, rulers conducted rituals and politics in an abbreviated, simplified manner. The sacrificial rice fields and ritual sites employed in the Daijō Ritual, [which formerly had been located in different provinces yearly,] were permanently established [in Tamba and Bitchū]. The Ritual itself [which had been conducted in all regions of the realm] was now limited to the area near the capital. The Emperor's intentions and the meaning behind his religious rituals went unknown to the people in the realm. The transporting of sacrificial rice took place over but a few tens of miles, [so people] along the nation's highways lost sight of what it stood for. Special rice levies were no longer collected from the provinces [involved], so the people living there became ignorant of the rituals' meaning. The practice of dispatching ritual purifiers died out, and with it, the meaning of purity before the gods. The Court ceased distributing Imperial Cloth Offerings to shrines throughout the realm, so everyone forgot that local deities were once united under Amaterasu's aegis. [Thus in later ages,] rulers might explain to every household and exhort every domicile in the land, but no one could be made to understand. These same rituals, though extant today, are devoid of their [suggestive, transforming] function. How lamentable indeed!

In antiquity the great shrines in the capital and outlying provinces were all consecrated to gods who had assisted or performed deeds of merit on Amaterasu's behalf. The myriad gods of mountain and stream pacified man and matter, aroused wind and rain, and assisted the works of the Heavenly Deities. The local people could not help recompensing these deities' virtue, and the Imperial Court as well, felt bound to repay them. This it did through Imperial Cloth Offerings presented to provincial shrines before every Tsukinami and Niiname Ritual.

(Gloss: In an earlier gloss I listed those shrines to which Imperial Cloth Offerings were distributed.)

The performance of all religious rituals was under Court control and the myriad deities of the land were integrated within a [centralized] system.

(Gloss: At present, the god Uka no Mitama is worshipped in the eleventh month. This is a carry-over from the ancient practice of worshipping local deities when the Imperial Cloth Offering was made at Niiname Ritual time. On this day, commoners prepare *sake* and festival foods in their homes, and they feast the entire day, much as the Chinese did during the *Cha* festival of Chou times. This *Cha* festival was conducted to give pleasure to elderly persons, and in it, one finds many ancient practices such as "playing the *pin sung* and beating the earthen drum," [as outlined in the *Rites of Chou.*] On this day, the elderly were tenderly cared for, and commoners were taught filial devotion through strict respect for age order. [In the *Book of Rites,* it says,] "Whether the year's crop is plentiful or poor is shown in the *Pa-cha* ritual." This means that when the realm (*tenka*) suffers a lean year, the *Pa-cha* ritual is dispensed with in order to conserve the people's tax revenues. During the *Cha* ritual the elderly were tenderly cared for, and people all across the land became drunk and delirious with wine and joy. Confucius said, "The one-day *Cha* festival following one hundred days of labor is a means of alternating work with play; it has something in common with the Way of Kings Wen and Wu." This is how the ancients provided the people with pleasure and harmony. It is yet another meaning that religious rituals tacitly convey.)

Shrine storehouses contain treasured objects, weapons, supplies, provisions, documents, and other items for use at ritual time and for regulating the people's daily affairs through awe-inspiring divine powers. Stockpiling provisions in shrines enables rulers to carry out the sages' original intent: "to make daily life easier for, and to ensure the livelihood of, the common people."[135] Moreover, it also tacitly conveys the idea that shrines can serve as defense posts when our military state faces emergencies.

(Gloss: I have already noted that in antiquity, government and edification were [conducted in and] conveyed through religious rituals and that the weapons of war were stockpiled in shrines. But in addition, the *Kuni no miyatsuko* and *Agata nushi* worshipped their respective domain gods, and in each domain, there were lesser officials known as "rice-stockpilers" who stored rice seedlings and plants in the villages. If we established a system modeled after this, we would always have adequate provisions against famine, and our armies would have extra supplies of rations. The awe-inspiring power of divinities would benefit the people's daily activities. But I will present my views on this subject in detail on another occasion.

The Chou rulers also utilized religious rituals to call people together and communicate decrees to them, to admonish them for misconduct, to place them in proper order by age, or to present awards to men of ability. . . . "Religious rituals" heads the list of The Twelve Teachings, and "service to the gods" appears at the beginning of The Eight Precepts; these served to make commoners deferential. There are countless similar examples of making them take part in religious rituals.

In later eras, ever-normal granaries were built to benefit the people. If we incorporate the good features of such institutions found in antiquity and utilize the awe-inspiring power of divinities to carry out projects to benefit the people, they undoubtedly will submit to us, since we will have provided them with precisely what they desire. The people will submit to us just as water flows downward. At present, when Buddhist festivals are employed to call commoners together and set them to work on tasks, they respond like an echo. If the people respond this quickly when the spiritual powers of Buddhas are invoked, how much swifter would their response be when prompted by the awe-inspiring powers of our [native] gods!)

In antiquity, then, religious ritual corresponded to government, administration was identical with edification, and the people looked to their leaders for the fulfillment of their desires. The Emperor's sincere will [to serve Heaven, embody filial devotion, and love his people] touched all deities in the realm. There was a religious ritual for every meaning His Majesty sought to convey, and through it, the people became aware of their ruler's will. They rejoiced in and respected it; their loyalty and filial devotion were unified and had a clear object to be directed to. In later ages, however, rulers conducted rituals in perfunctory fashion, ignoring their meaning to be conveyed; the myriad deities and countless rituals lacked systematic organization and coherence; the people's devotion was not directed toward a single object; and the religious rituals lost their [suggestive, transforming] function. How lamentable indeed!

Imperial Mausolea have always been objects of solemn worship. But after an Emperor's relatives all passed away, it was only natural that his mausoleum became lost through neglect. The great virtue and exploits of Emperors Jimmu (who pacified the realm), Sujin (who conquered vast new areas), and Tenji (who reestablished order in the realm), however, were not forgotten; their meritorious deeds remain known even today. Our array of official shrines and rituals remain incomplete until we properly identify their mausoleum sites and thus can conduct rituals in their honor.

(Gloss: It is generally thought that the Kamo Shrine is dedicated to Emperor Jimmu, but some scholars are skeptical of this due to a lack of documentation in ancient records. It is time for us to recompile our list of shrines and rituals so that no deserving deity or hero is overlooked.)

With the spread of Buddhism, funerals were conducted according to Buddhist rituals, and many Imperial Rituals and Mausolea were lost through neglect even before relatives passed away. This created a serious defect in our array of official shrines and rituals. Likewise, the exploits of many Imperial offspring and illustrious ministers in antiquity come down to us [in legend] but remain unrecognized in our official set of rituals. As a result, their descendants find themselves in pathetic circumstances, being unable to pay proper worship to their ancestors. This too stems from our incomplete set of official shrines and rituals. To remedy this, we must consider antiquity in the light of present-day needs, revive rituals that have fallen into disuse, reinstate rituals now missing from our classics, and tacitly convey their didactic value to people. By thus inducing all people in the realm to be loyal and filial, to be sincere in their reverence for forbears, to feel gratitude and indebtedness to rulers for blessings bestowed, to hold the spirits in awe, and to respect the deities, we will make them submit [to the Way, without asking why].

Then the people will prostrate themselves *en masse* echoing, "Amaterasu inaugurated the Heavenly enterprises from on high, and Her legions of godly retainers aspired to assist Her in

271

pacifying the realm. By conducting rituals to our local gods, we requite them for their services performed on our behalf, and we recompense Amaterasu for Her original gifts to us." In short, we will have unified the myriad gods and countless rituals. The people will continue, "Amaterasu [the sun itself,] beams down on us from on high, Her Divine Descendant carries on Her Manifest Will by lovingly nurturing us, the Shogun upholds the Imperial House by maintaining peace throughout the realm, and the daimyo rule their domains—all of this allows us to enjoy stability of livelihood and security of possession. By following our lord's decrees and obeying bakufu laws, we look up to the Imperial Court and recompense Amaterasu's original gifts to us." In short, we will have unified bakufu and domain rule. When each family in the realm gathers together to conduct rituals in reverence of its ancestors, its members will say, "to revere our main house is to revere our progenitor; to live in peaceful harmony by submitting to our lord's decrees, obeying bakufu laws, looking up to the Imperial Court, and recompensing Amaterasu's original gifts to us, is to carry on the will of our ancestors." In short, we will have given unity to the people's loyalty and filial devotion.

The benevolence of Amaterasu and Her Divine Descendants will reach the whole realm, the virtue of bakufu and domain lords will fill all under Heaven, parental love and filial reciprocity will endure forever, reverence for ancestors and gratitude to Amaterasu for Her original gifts will be elucidated to all, and the teachings of loyalty and filial devotion will be firmly established. The people will live by this Way day in and day out, and will be blind to all heresies.

(Gloss: In the Chou period, high officials were in charge of state religion [*hōkyō*] and carried out the Twelve Teachings, the first of which reads, "When respectfulness is taught through religious rituals, the people become deferential." This shows how important rituals are to state religion [*hōkyō*].)

Rituals can be established only when there is loyalty between ruler and subject and affection between parent and child. We must discriminate prudently the different roles for men and women, uphold the hierarchic relationship between old and young, and be of good faith in dealings with friends. If we make commoners cooperate and assist one another at all times, prevent crimes together, care for the sick and needy, feel affection for their rulers and leaders even to the point of dying for them, then their minds can never be led astray though faced with a thousand heresies. The barbarians' grand stratagem—to raze the dwelling places of our native deities in an attempt to introduce their own god and to incite our stupid commoners to rebel and subvert our country from within—will be counteracted. [As Sun Tzu said,] "the ultimate in warfare is to counteract the enemy's stratagems before hand." This is truly our best long-range policy.

Those scoundrels who ruined our powers of moral suasion (*kwa*) and depraved our folkways in days past—shamans, Buddhist clerics, perverse Confucians, and petty scholastics—were nevertheless little children of our Middle Kingdom. If we make them live in the solace of their homes, bask in our great sphere of moral suasion, accept Imperial Benevolence, and obey bakufu and domain laws, they may pursue personal gratification as they wish throughout their lives. But should anyone swallow whole the Western barbarians' absurd tales or laud the barbarians publicly in a blind and excessive manner, thereby aiding and abetting foreigners in their attempts to subvert us, he must be prosecuted most severely. Should anyone violate these bans, he should be punished in accordance with the "Sedition and Insurgency Statutes" in the *Rites of Chou*. All Western goods, medicines, woolens, and the like, must be burned on sight—the sale or use of imported articles must be absolutely forbidden. Commoners must be made to despise foreigners as they would despise dogs and goats, to hate the barbarians as they would hate wild boars and wolves.

(Gloss: An Imperial Edict issued in the Tempyō era [729–49] reads, "Should persons study heretical doctrines, practice the occult, or cast harmful spells on others, their leader shall be beheaded, and his followers, exiled. Any persons who live in mountainous woodlands and teach false, heretical doctrines under the guise of Buddhism, or who concoct poisons by mixing medicinal herbs, or who engage in other mysterious practices that violate this Imperial Edict, are subject to the same punishments as stated above." This is how rulers prohibited evil heretical doctrines in antiquity, and how we must prohibit these now if we are to teach commoners the Way.

After we build up our military strength, put an end to the barbarians' encroachments, and extend our virtuous teachings to them so that they become our vassals and bear tribute to us, it is perfectly all right to accept and use the tribute articles they bear.)

Anyone informing us about nefarious traitors who secretly aid and abet foreigners at sea will be rewarded the same as if he had beheaded an enemy general; anyone withholding such information will be punished the same as if he had harbored a renegade criminal. Any domain that destroys a barbarian ship will be decorated the same as if it had captured an enemy fortress; any that fails to fire on the barbarians will be punished for cowardice in the face of the enemy. Such measures [for armed expulsion] are temporary expedients, but should inspire both warriors and commoners to respect and obey bakufu injunctions. By thus strengthening our defenses, by prevailing on the realm to reform itself in the name of a [national] emergency, and by sincerely sharing the people's joys and sorrows, we should be able to rouse the realm to action.

If we implement decrees, laws, and punishments together with rituals of edification, if we base ourselves on the *ch'i* of justice and carry out the Way of Righteousness, and if we firmly establish grand procedures to administer the realm, commoners will possess a basis of spiritual reliance within. [The *Book of Documents*] says, "Heaven obeys what the people desire." If the people obey us, and Heaven obeys them, the barbarians will be unable to turn against us the long-range policy that Amaterasu and Sage Emperors used to transform their barbarous folkways and subdue them in antiquity. Quite the contrary, we will turn against them the very stratagem that they have been trying to employ against us. Then we will regain the freedom of initiative

to exercise powers of edification over them. The bakufu's decision [for armed expulsion] has been made, and the hearts of
high and low alike are united.

Diverse though our modes of action may be, all are based on
the Way. Today we are prompted to extend our Imperial sphere
of moral suasion (*kōkwa*) by the same inspiration that prompted
Amaterasu and Sage Emperors to extend it [in antiquity]. If we
resolutely achieve the tasks bequeathed by Amaterasu at home,
and establish impenetrable safeguards against subversion from
without, the foreign beasts will never be able to beguile our
people no matter how hard they try.

Naturally, achieving [Amaterasu's] tasks within the realm and
implementing an eternal, long-range policy [to deal with heresies
from without] cannot be done overnight. The enterprises delegated by Amaterasu were begun by Emperor Jimmu, enlarged
on by Emperor Sujin, and continued with unswerving dedication by later Emperors. Therefore our Imperial sphere of moral
suasion (*kōkwa*) extended over all within the seas. [Today,] we
first must determine our fundamental [long-range] policy and
establish an unswerving moral basis for action. Only then will
we encompass the barbarians within Middle Kingdom Civilization, only then will we base ourselves on antiquity and clarify
[the Sage Emperors'] meaning, only then will we bequeath
political stratagems to our descendents in keeping with Amaterasu's precepts and carry on Ieyasu's grand traditions forever,
only then will we rescue all nations in the world from suffering,
only then will we eliminate every vestige of the Western barbarians' occult religions from the face of the earth, and only
then will we spare the children of our Middle Kingdom from
barbarian cunning. If we first establish this [immutable long-
range] policy within, we will be able to deal with the infinite
changes occuring from without.

By spreading benevolence throughout the four quarters and
treating the barbarians as children [of our Middle Kingdom], we
will induce them to regard the Imperial Court as their loving
parent. Antiquity is our guide. Making the present approximate
the past prevents the future from diverging from the present:
We will achieve timelessness and immutability. The barbarians

will bear tribute to us for all eternity. Patriots of humanity and high resolve will aspire to offer their lives to advance our cause. No matter how bewilderingly the situation before us may change, we will never lose sight of our objective; we will remain with fixed resolve forever and a day. Nourished by the rations of our Heavenly Deities, brandishing the weapons of our Heavenly Deities, and inspired by the benevolence of our Heavenly Deities, we shall wage war against the enemies of our sovereign. Our might will reverberate all over the earth. "[Our] small nation will expand, and the unruly nations will be subdued."[136] Our invincible might stemming from gentleness and humanity will extend beyond the farthest reaches of the earth, and will induce foreign barbarians to approach us seeking virtue. Never again will we need to worry about commoners in outlying areas being lured into their fold.

The ancients said, "The state's greatest concerns are rituals and war." Through war, we draw up a definite stratagem; through rituals, we indomitably achieve Amaterasu's enterprises. Indeed, these are the state's greatest concerns. That is why the Hero makes a panoramic survey of contemporary conditions in the realm, considers the broad vista thus obtained against the vast sweep of historical change, and establishes a timeless, immutable long-range policy. Elucidating "what is essential to a nation" (*kokutai*), being informed on world affairs, understanding fully the barbarians' nature, strengthening national defense, and establishing a long-range policy—these represent the best form of loyalty and filial devotion, the best method of recompensing Imperial Ancestors and Heavenly Deities, and the best way for bakufu and daimyo to rescue their peoples and dispense benevolent rule for eternity. The theses I respectfully submit are not a set of private theories: The spirits of Heaven and Earth themselves seek to share them.

I have long kept these five theses (in seven parts) to myself, but not because I was loath to share my opinions. It is said, "The universe is a living entity." Man as well is a living entity. When one living thing operates amidst another, transformations occur which we cannot fully fathom. With the passing of ages, innumerable transformations take place, and the moment at which each transpires is instantaneous. Most people are so caught up with specifics that they neglect overall processes. To present my theses on overall processes, I believed, would expose me to the censure of those preoccupied with specifics. [On the other hand, I feared,] discussing how to solve difficult problems as these and how to deal with changed situations now would commit me to proposals lacking future applicability. Once ideas are verbalized they become vacuous, once committed to paper they become so many dead letters. That is why I refrained from addressing Your Lordship.

But deep in my heart, I believe that all men, whether noble or base, have maintained the same natural *ch'i* that connects parent and offspring from the beginning of time to the present. Though of low status, I have received the blessings of Amaterasu and generations of Sage Emperors; I observe bakufu laws, enjoy Your Lordship's benevolence, and lack nothing to sustain my family and observe rituals to my ancestors. How can I remain silent any longer in this time of the realm's peril? Thus, I have drafted the present memorial, which outlines our present crisis in broad, long-range terms.

The *Book of Changes* says, "The Way does not implement itself; that requires the Man of Talent and Virtue." To solve difficult problems as these arise and to devise methods of dealing with changed situations—these tasks await the appearance of the Great Hero.

Aizawa Yasushi   Spring, 1825

Appendix
Notes
Bibliography
Glossary
Index

appendix

Sources Cited by Aizawa in
Chishima ibun (1804)

1. *Taisei yochizusetsu* 泰西輿地図説
   translated by Kuchiki Masatsuna (1788)
2. *Hsi-yü wen-chien lu* 西域聞見録
   by Ch'i-shih i ch'un yüan 七十一椿園 (1777)
3. *Chih-fang wai-chi* 職方外記
   by Julio Aleni
4. *Li-shih chi-shih* 歴世記事
5. *Lung-sha chi-lüeh* 龍沙記略
6. *Ti chih* 狄誌
7. *Ch'uan-hsin chi-shih* 伝信記事
8. *K'un yü wai-chi* 坤輿外記
9. *Ming-t'ien-chu* 明天竺
10. *San-ch'ao shih-i* 三朝事異
11. *San-ch'ao shih-lu* 三朝実録
12. *Tsūran hoi* 通覧補遺
    by Hayashi Shihei (三国通覧図説) ? (1786)
13. *Shih chuan* 世伝
14. *Kunsatsukaki* 東砂葛記
    translated by Maeno Ryōtaku
15. *Fūsetsukō* 風説考
    by Kudō Heisuke, *Kansatsuka fūsetsukō* or *Akaezo fūsetsukō*
    (1783) カンサツカ風説考   赤蝦夷風説考
16. *Riisukoku zukō* リイス国図考
17. *Oranda zensekai chizusho* 阿蘭全世界地図書
    translated by Motoki Ryōei
18. *Suiko hikki* 酔古筆記
    by Kimura Ken (Mito clansman)
19. *Bunkai zukō* 分界図考
    by Kondō Jūzō, *Henyō bunkai zukō* 辺要分界図考

20. *Akitsu shingo* 秋蟬新語
21. *Ch'ao-chi wen-chi* 朝隮文集
22. *Sōshi* 草紙
    by Mogami Tokunai, *Ezo sōshi* 蝦夷草紙
23. *Heidan* 兵談
    by Hayashi Shihei, *Kaikoku heidan* 海國兵談
24. *Shūi* 拾遺
    by either Satō Genrokurō or Honda Toshiaki, *Ezo shūi*
    蝦夷拾遺
25. *Kansei jin-shi no sho* 寛政壬子の書
    by Honda Toshiaki, *Ezo kaihatsu ni kansuru jōsho* (1792)
    蝦夷開発に関する上書
26. *Takahashi shūki* 高橋集記
27. *Matsumae zokusho* 松前属書
28. *Zōsetsu* 増説

Notes

FOREWORD AND ACKNOWLEDGMENTS

1. A readily-accessible Japanese language edition (*kakikudashibun*) which I consulted is in Mukyūkai bunko at Machida-shi, Tokyo.
2. Hōjō Shigenao, *Mitogaku to ishin no fūun*, pp. 110–111.
3. Hashikawa Bunzō, *Jidai to yoken*, pp. 339–340.
4. The biographical information on Aizawa presented here is sparse—perhaps overly so—because little reliable information exists, and also because my analysis neither turns on, nor gains from, a recounting of events in his life. Two standard biographies of Aizawa are Nishimura Fuminori, *Aizawa Hakumin* and Seya Yoshihiko, *Aizawa Seishisai*. Both are based largely on the 1863 panegyric by Aizawa's disciple, Terakado Kin. A printed version of this work is appended to Aizawa's *Kagaku jigen*.
5. In Hashikawa Bunzō, ed., *Nihon no meicho*, 29: *Fujita Tōko*.
6. To list a few examples, "*shen tao*" rather than "*shintō*," "*yuan ch'i*" rather than "*gen ki*," "*ch'üan*" rather than "*ken*."
7. Herbert Butterfield, *The Whig Interpretation of History*, p. 96.

ONE: PROLOGUE: LOOKING BACKWARD

1. Modern historians divide "Mito Learning" (Mitogaku, itself a neologism dating from the 1830s) into "Early" and "Later" Schools. Throughout this work I refer solely to the Later Mito School when I employ the term "Mito Learning." The Early Mito School centered on the Mito-sponsored compilation of *The History of Great Japan* (Dainihonshi), particularly the "Main Annals" and "Lives" portions, which took place between 1657 and 1720. The Later Mito School refers to the Mito-style politicization of Confucianism expressed in ideals such as "Honor the Emperor, Expel the barbarian," "practice both military and literary arts," "the identity of loyalty and filial submissiveness," and "the unity of government and religious rituals." This Later Mito School is represented by scholar-activists such as Fujita Yūkoku (1774–1826), his son Tōko (1806–1855), and his grandson Koshirō (1842–1865); Aizawa Seishisai (1781–1863); and Toyota Tenkō (1805–1864). Key writings include Fujita Yūkoku's "On Rectifying Names" ("Seimeiron") of 1791, Aizawa's *New Theses* (*Shinron*) of 1825, and Tōko's *Commentary on the "Inscription to the Mito Domain School"* (*Kōdōkanki jutsugi*) of 1847. See Kikuchi Kenjirō,

Mitogaku ronsū, pp. 1–4; Bitō Masahide, "Mitogaku no tokushitsu"; and Hashikawa Bunzō, "Mitogaku no genryū to seiritsu."

2. For a recent revisionist work on the subject of *"sakoku"* to which I am greatly indebted, see Ronald P. Toby, *State and Diplomacy in Early Modern Japan,* especially pp. 240–246.

3. This is the standard interpretation of Mito Learning formulated by Tōyama Shigeki, see his *Meiji ishin.*

4. The following insights derive mainly from W. G. Beasley, *Select Documents in Japanese Foreign Policy, 1853–1868.*

5. Conrad Totman, "From *Sakoku* to *Kaikoku.*"

6. This view is that of Maruyama Masao, "Kindai Nihon shisōshi ni okeru kokka risei no mondai"; also Uete Michiari, "Bakumatsu ni okeru taigaikan no kaiten," in his *Nihon kindai shisō no keisei.*

7. Matsumoto Sannosuke, "Sonjō undō ni okeru kindaiteki seiji ishikishi no keisei" pp. 119–168; H. D. Harootunian, *Toward Restoration,* pp. 47–128.

8. Takahashi Shin'ichi, *Yōgaku shisōron;* Donald Keene, *The Japanese Discovery of Europe;* Haga Tōru, "Jūkyūseiki Nihon no chiteki senshi-tachi"; Calvin French, *Shiba Kōkan.*

9. G. B. Sansom, *The Western World and Japan,* p. 247.

10. W. G. Beasley, p. 5.

11. I borrow the term from Benjamin Schwartz, *In Search of Wealth and Power,* p. 15.

12. See Joseph Levenson, *Confucian China and Its Modern Fate,* pp. 95–116; Yen-p'ing Hao and Erh-min Wang, "Chapter 3, Changing Chinese Views of Western Relations, 1840–95," in John K. Fairbank and Kwang-ching Liu, ed., *The Cambridge History of China Volume 11, Late Ch'ing 1800–1911, Part 2;* Paul A. Cohen, *Between Tradition and Modernity.*

13. See Takano Chōei's "Tale of a Winter Night's Dream in 1838" (*Bojutsu yume monogatari*) and Watanabe Kazan's "On Grim Forebodings" (*Shinkiron*) in *Watanabe Kazan, Takano Chōei, Sakuma Shōzan, Yokoi Shōnan, Hashimoto Sanai.*

14. However, as we shall see in Chapter 3, Takahashi's proposal differed in certain important respects from the edict that actually was promulgated.

15. For a critical discussion of the various interpretations current in Japanese and Western secondary scholarship on Western Learning and its impact on Tokugawa politics and society, see Bob Tadashi Wakabayashi, "Aizawa Seishisai's *Shinron* and Western Learning."

16. For a revisionist view to which I am greatly indebted, see Bitō, "Mitogaku no tokushitsu."

17. Because of its blatantly anti-bakufu contents, Yamagata Daini's 1759 tract, *New Theses* (*Ryūshi shinron*), was ruthlessly suppressed after his execution in 1767. Thus, Daini's *New Theses* was not widely disseminated

or known in the Tokugawa period, but the "newness" of his views as well certainly was associated with deviance.

18. Yoshida Shōin, *Yoshida Shōin zenshū* 3:564–565.

19. Ibid., pp. 606–607.

20. Ibid., p. 607.

21. Kawashima Suminosuke, *Meiji yonen Kurume-han nanki*, p. 87.

22. However, this is not to ignore the obvious fact that Aizawa was first and foremost a scholar of the Chinese classics. He wrote *New Theses* in classical Chinese and derived much of his thought from classical Chinese sources. See Imai Usaburō, "Mitogaku ni okeru jukyō no juyō," pp. 525–555; also Imai Usaburō, "Aizawa Seishisai ni okeru jukyō keiden no kenkyū," pp. 501–542.

23. Aizawa, *Shinron*, p. 94.

TWO: THE CIVILIZED AND THE BARBARIAN

1. See Fairbank, ed., *The Chinese World Order*, pp. 1–32; and Uete Michiari, *Nihon kindai shisō no keisei*, p. 21 and pp. 235–245. I also profited from Harry D. Harootunian's insights into the metaphorical nature of the terms "Chūka" and "Chūgoku" which expressed the idea of "civilization" for Tokugawa thinkers and could be detached from China and transferred to Japan. See his "The Functions of China in Tokugawa Thought," pp. 9–36. In addition to Fairbank and Uete, see Tsuda Sōkichi, "Ōdō seiji shisō," pp. 133–172; Hihara Toshikuni, *Shunjū kuyōden no kenkyū*, pp. 235–266; and Ogura Yoshihiko, *Chūgoku kodai seiji shisō no kenkyū*, pp. 320–335.

2. *Shisho shitchū* 1:160–161, 428. Quoted in Bitō Masahide, "Sonnō jōi shisō," pp. 47. Note however that Bitō rejects this Chu Hsi gloss as a source for *sonnō jōi* thought in Tokugawa Japan, arguing that political concepts of "nation" or "state" were more important. On the other hand, I hold that cultural considerations of "customs" and "ritual" should be given priority over military or political factors in analyzing the formation of *jōi* ideas in the early Edo period. Moreover, Bitō's main emphasis is on "*sonnō*" thought; he does not treat "*jōi*" extensively.

3. The original terms are "Chūgoku," "Chūka," "Chūdo," and "Ka."

4. Mencius wrote: "Good rule is not as good as good teachings. The people hold good rule in awe and have love for good teachings. Good rule wins the people's revenues; *good teachings win the people's hearts*" (emphasis added). See *Mōshi*, p. 443. To avoid confusion between *ka* meaning "Middle Kingdom Civilization" (華 or 夏) and *kwa* (化) meaning "moral transformation" or the "extent of a dynasty's moral suasion," I have employed historical *kana* usage in transliterating the latter term alone throughout this essay and the translation of *New Theses*.

5. *Taionki, Oritaku shiba no ki, Rantō Kotohajime,* p. 411.

6. Thus Chinese "literati-officials" (*shih*) supported the alien Manchu ruling house in suppressing the Taiping Rebellion led by the Chinese national, Hung Hsiu-ch'üan.

7. *Shisho shitchū* 1:160–161, 428.

8. This is a modified version of D. C. Lau, tr., *Confucius: The Analects,* pp. 126–127.

9. Tsukamoto Manabu, "Edo jidai ni okeru 'i' kannen ni tsuite," pp. 1–18. I gratefully acknowledge my heavy debts in this chapter to Tsukamoto and Uete for elucidating the concepts of *ka* and *i.* Tsukamoto's article was extremely enlightening, particularly about early Tokugawa perceptions of Japan as barbarian.

10. See Satō Shōsuke, *Yogakushi kenkyū josetsu,* pp. 15–23, where he argues that Japanese animus against Western learning developed only after Dutch Studies achieved academic respectibility, that such an attitude did not exist to a significant degree during the early Edo period.

11. See Uete, pp. 22–23.

12. Kate Wildman Nakai, "The Naturalization of Confucianism in Tokugawa Japan: The problem of Sinocentrism," pp. 157–199.

13. See *Rongo,* I, 59–60; Hihara, pp. 242–243.

14. Of course the term "chu Hsia" (here translated "Middle Kingdom") can also be taken as plural, and this is probably a more valid interpretation considering the historical conditions of Confucius' day. But I am concerned with how Tokugawa Confucians construed this passage, and they often neglected this factor of historical context in making their interpretations.

15. *Shisho shitchū* 1:66–67, 400. The two different interpretations are reflected in the translations by Waley, *The Analects,* pp. 94–95, and Lau, *Confucius,* p. 67.

16. This gloss is from Itō Jinsai's *Rongo kogi* (compiled in 1683), p. 32.

17. Ibid., pp. 137–138. The English translation is adapted from Lau, p. 98, to fit Jinsai's interpretation.

18. Itō, *Rongo kogi,* pp. 137–138.

19. Ibid., pp. 137–138.

20. Ibid., pp. 137–138.

21. Ibid., p. 4.

22. Ibid., p. 212.

23. It was on these grounds that Nishikawa Joken (1648–1724) and Terashima Ryōan (dates unknown) designated Westerners *i.* See Tsukamoto, p. 9.

24. The following remarks are all taken from essays of Sokō's that were compiled between 1663 and 1665. See Yamaga, *Yamaga Sokō zenshū* 5:22.

25. Ibid., p. 22.

26. Ibid., p. 17.

27. Ibid., p. 31.

28. Ibid., p. 22.

29. Ibid., p. 366.

30. Ibid., p. 23.

31. Ibid., p. 23.

32. Ibid., p. 49.

33. Ibid., p. 47.

34. As Nakai notes (pp. 197-199), their arguments, fraught with logical inconsistencies as these were, probably left the thinkers themselves unconvinced.

35. See Harootunian, "Functions of China," p. 12. However, I again wish to emphasize that this "centrality" should not be viewed solely on the horizontal geographical plane, but also on the perpendicular socio-political hierarchy: The "noble" and the "high" were considered superior to the "base" and "low."

36. *Henji zokusan no sakai* or *Zokusan henji no sakai.* For two early examples of such perceptions of Japan's geographical position and size, see *Heike monogatari* 1:144 and 172; *Heiji monogatari*, p. 342.

37. This work was first composed in 1688-89, but was revised and published in 1701. See pp. 416-420. Also see Maruyama Masao's essay, "Ansaigaku to Ansaigakuha" in the same volume.

38. "Chūgoku ben," p. 417.

39. Ibid., p. 417.

40. Nakayama Shigeru, *A History of Japanese Astronomy*, p. 94, p. 105. Moreover, Francis Xavier had introduced the theory in 1552. See Ayuzawa Nobutarō, "Kinsei Nihon ni okeru chikyūsetsu chidōsetsu no tenkai," p. 33.

41. "Chūgoku ben," p. 416.

42. *Ichibun no tenka.* The *"ichibun"* here should not be interpreted as "a part of" or "a unit of," but rather as "pride" or "honor," as in the phrase *"otoko no ichibun."* Thus the phrase comes to mean, "full-fledged."

43. *"Sore nari no tenka."* "Chūgoku ben," p. 416.

44. Ibid., p. 416.

45. Ibid., p. 417.

46. Ibid., p. 417.

47. Ibid., p. 417.

48. Ibid., p. 417.

49. Ibid., p. 419.

50. Ibid., p. 419.

51. Ibid., p. 416.

52. In *Gakusoku* [1717], Sorai wrote: "[Countries such as Japan in] the Eastern Sea have produced no sages; [countries in] the Western Sea have produced no sages. Hence, ritual and music as expounded in [Chinese classics such as] the *Book of Odes* or *Book of Documents* are all that they [may rely on] as teachings." Sorai, *Gakusoku*, p. 188.

53. Quoted in Maruyama, "Ansaigaku to Ansaigakuha," pp. 624–625.

54. Motoori Norinaga, *Kuzubana*, p. 168.

55. Ibid., p. 168.

56. *Kojiki den*, p. 60.

57. *Genji monogatari tama no ogushi*, pp. 237–238.

58. *Kojiki den*, p. 52.

59. *"Gūgen," "hyōji," "kasetsu."*

60. *Kojiki den*, pp. 51–52.

61. When Norinaga was accused of employing Taoist arguments of "nature" (*shizen* or "things as they are") to justify criticism of "cleverness" (*sakashira*) and artificiality, he retorted that the Chinese Taoists made a conscious attempt to set up nature (*shizen*) as an alternative norm in opposition to cleverness, which they disliked. Therefore, he argued, the Taoists' "nature was not 'true' nature." "If they really considered 'leaving things to nature' to be good, they should have gone along with 'cleverness' when the world became clever, for such cleverness would constitute true 'nature' (*shizen*, or 'things as they are')." In contrast to the Taoist's normative nature, Norinaga held that Japan's Way of the Gods was truly natural because it was "as the gods would have it" (*kannagara*), and if the gods would have it "clever," Japanese should submit to it as such. *Kuzubana*, p. 163.

62. Ibid., p. 137.

63. Ibid., p. 137.

64. Ibid., p. 159.

65. Ibid., p. 133.

66. *Kakaiga*, p. 406.

67. *"Chikyū no zu."* Note the acknowledged sphericity of the world in the term *"chikyū,"* or "globe."

68. *Kakaiga*, p. 402.

69. Ibid., p. 405.

70. Ibid., pp. 405–406.

71. Motoori, *Tamakatsuma*, p. 213.

72. Ibid., p. 213.

73. Yoshikawa Kōjirō and Kate Nakai have pointed out that Sorai possessed more ethnic pride than is usually recognized. But the fact remains that in the late Edo period, that element of his thought was not usually recognized: The image he cast was that of worshipping Chinese moral culture to the detriment of Japan. For Mitogaku thinkers' views, see Aizawa, *Taishoku kanwa*, p. 243, p. 287.

74. Ōtomo Kisaku, ed., *Hokumon sōsho, 4:Kankai ibun*, p. 415.

75. See Sugita, *Kyōi no gen*, pp. 237–238. Helpful modern Japanese translations of Sugita's major works are to be found in Haga, ed., pp. 87–374.

76. *"Shina"* did not assume pejorative connotations until the Meiji period. Scholars of Dutch Studies began using "Shina" as a value-free designation for China because "Chūka" or "Chūgoku" connoted Chinese moral and cultural superiority. In this respect, they were motivated by the same sentiments that induced Keisai to call China "Kara," and foreign countries, *"ikoku."*

77. Sugita, *Kyōi no gen*, pp. 227-228.

78. Ibid., pp. 227-228.

79. Satō, *Yōgakushi kenkyū josetsu*, pp. 15-23.

80. Sugita, *Kyōi no gen*, p. 237.

81. Ibid., p. 237.

82. Ibid., p. 237.

83. Ibid., pp. 228-229.

84. Ibid., p. 229.

85. Ibid., p. 229.

86. Ibid., pp. 227-228.

87. Ibid., p. 229.

88. Ibid., p. 229.

89. Ibid., p. 228.

90. Ibid., p. 257.

91. Sugita, *Kaitai shinsho*, p. 215.

92. Sugita's "empiricism" owed much to the method of inductive criticism applied by Jinsai and Norinaga to literary texts and to *shinshi jikken,* the "close personal observation, actual experience in curing" procedure employed by Yamawaki Tōyō (1705-1762), Yoshimasu Tōdō (1702-1773), and others of the School of Ancient Method.

93. Sugita, *Yasō dokugo*, pp. 291-292.

94. Satō plays down Sugita's examples of the Han Confucian idea of "interaction between Heaven and man" as being mere "rhetorical flourishes," but is unconvincing. See *Yōgakushi no kenkyū*, p. 144.

95. In precisely this era, the Kokugakusha and students of Western Learning such as Honda Toshiaki and Shiba Kōkan were arguing to end the practice of writing in Chinese and instead use Japanese *kana* or the Western alphabet. See Motoori, *Tamakatsuma*, p. 479; and Keene, *Japanese Discovery*, pp. 69-73.

96. Sugita, *Rangaku kotohajime*, p. 498.

97. Numata, *Shisō taikei* 64, pp. 581-583.

98. Ibid., p. 586.

99. Maeno translated this term as "the study of things 'in their original state'" (*honzengaku*).

100. On similarities in the thought of Yamagata Bantō, see Albert Craig, "Science and Confucianism in Tokugawa Japan," pp. 145-149.

101. Maeno, *Kanrei higen*, p. 129. The following paragraphs discussing

Maeno's views of the West owe much to Satō Shōsuke, *Yōgakushi no ken-kyū*. My debts to Satō are gratefully acknowledged.

102. Maeno, *Kanrei higen*, p. 129.

103. Ibid., p. 162.

104. Ibid., p. 162.

105. Ibid., pp. 162–163.

106. Ibid., p. 147.

107. Ibid., p. 147.

108. Ibid., pp. 145–146.

109. Maeno considered the earth a sphere whose "center" was not on its surface, but rather, was at its "core." Ibid., pp. 142–143.

110. Ibid., pp. 142–143.

111. Ibid., p. 148.

112. Western cartographers conjectured that "Magellanica" was a large continent in the southern hemisphere. See ibid., p. 144.

113. Ibid., pp. 147–148.

114. Ibid., p. 147.

115. Ibid., pp. 147–148.

116. But note that Maeno mistakenly believed Islam (*fuifui no oshie*) to be a sect of Christianity (*tenshukyō*). See ibid., p. 147 and the note on p. 148.

117. Ibid., p. 147.

118. Ibid., p. 128.

119. In *Rangaku kaitei* (p. 337), Ōtsuki Gentaku lists many of Ryōtaku's works including *Kanrei higen* and presumably had access to them.

120. Aizawa cited at least one of Maeno's works, a translation entitled *Kansatsuka-ki* (An account of Kamchatka) in *Chishima ibun*.

121. Fujita Yūkoku, "Seimeiron," p. 227.

122. For a good example, see Aizawa's *Tekiihen* (esp. pp. 274–276), wherein he justifies Confucian hierarchical relations in society on the basis of analogies to nature.

123. "Nagakuko Sekisui ate shokan," pp. 703–704. This passage is quoted in Tōyama Shigeki, "Mitogaku no seikaku," p. 188 and *Meiji ishin*, p. 80.

124. *Shōsho*, pp. 621–623.

125. Yūkoku's analysis was anachronistic, since commoners did not normally join in military campaigns during Shang and Chou times.

126. *Yūkoku zenshū*, p. 123.

127. Aizawa, *Taishoku kanwa*, pp. 246–247.

128. However, we should make a clear distinction between Confucians such as Aizawa who merely acknowledged the value of assimilating advanced technology from abroad and Confucian-Rangakusha like Sugita, Sakuma Shōzan, and Hashimoto Sanai, who invested enormous amounts of time and energy to study Dutch and thereby actually assimilate such knowledge.

129. Aizawa, *Shinron*, p. 124.

130. Ibid., pp. 124–125.

131. *Kagaku jigen*, p. 25.

132. Ibid., p. 70. For similar sentiments, see Aizawa's *Taishoku kanwa*, p. 244.

THREE: KNOWLEDGE AND HATRED OF THE WEST

1. *Bojutsu yume monogatari*, pp. 165–166.

2. Ibid., p. 167.

3. Yokoi Shōnan believed that Toyotomi Hideyoshi had instituted *sakoku*. See *Yokoi Shōnan ikō*, p. 692.

4. Ronald P. Toby has broken new ground on this subject with his excellent study, *State and Diplomacy in Early Modern Japan*.

5. Inobe Shigeo, *Shintei ishin zenshi no kenkyū*, p. 147.

6. Ibid., pp. 120–147.

7. Tokutomi Iichirō, *Kinsei Nihon kokuminshi, 25: Bakufu bunkai sekkin jidai*, pp. 314–315.

8. *Tokugawa kinreikō*, pp. 609–610.

9. See Toby, *State and Diplomacy*, and Tashiro Kazui, *Kinsei Nitchō tsūkō boekishi no kenkyū*.

10. Iwao Seiichi, *Nihon no rekishi, 14: Sakoku*, p. 344.

11. Ibid., p. 426.

12. Inobe, p. 10; *Ofuregaki Kampō shūsei*, pp. 628–629.

13. Inobe, p. 11.

14. Ibid., p. 10; *Tsūkō ichiran* 5:27.

15. Inobe, pp. 12–15; *Nagasaki-shi shi: Tsūkō boeki hen Seiyōshokoku bu*, pp. 485–502.

16. Inobe, p. 14.

17. Ibid., pp. 18–19.

18. Ibid., pp. 16–17.

19. Ibid., pp. 19–21.

20. Iwao, pp. 434–437.

21. Ibid., pp. 433–434.

22. Numata Jirō, *Nihon zenshi, 7: Kinsei, 2*, p. 288.

23. Inobe, pp. 37–38.

24. For accounts of Benyowsky, see Tabohashi Kiyoshi, *Zōtei kindai Nihon*, pp. 90–122; and Donald Keene, *The Japanese Discovery of Europe*, pp. 31–35.

25. Inobe, *Shintei ishin*, pp. 40–41.

26. For the account that follows, see Inobe, pp. 120–147.

27. The key term is "*hyōryū*," which was not limited in meaning to "shipwrecked." In Japanese documents of the period, this term at times

refered to ships landing in areas other than Nagasaki whether by design or due to bad weather.

28. On the problem of diplomatic protocol, see Toby, pp. 178–179.

29. Ōhara, *Chihoku gūdan*, p. 115.

30. Aizawa, "Tsuzuki Hakuei ni kotauru no sho," *Seishisai bunko 1*.

31. Ibid.

32. Ibid.

33. "Arai Chikushū Rōmajin o satosu sho ni gisu," contained in *Seishisai bunko 4*.

34. Their terms were "*kokkyō*" and "*hōkyō.*" See Maeno, *Kanrei Higen*, p. 148; Aizawa, *Shinron*, p. 154.

35. Ōhara, *Chihoku gūdan*, p. 112.

36. Aizawa, *Shinron*, p. 137.

37. Both are brush-copied manuscripts in cursive script held by Mukyū-kai bunko, Tokyo, Japan.

38. Tsushima and Satsuma were authorized to trade with Korea and the Ryukyus, respectively. In addition, Tsushima conducted diplomacy on the Bakufu's behalf with Korea. But these exceptions are not directly relevant to this discussion. See Tashiro Kazui, *Kinsei Nitchō*, pp. 37–201; and Toby, pp. 53–167.

39. *Sankoku tsūran zusetsu*, p. 260.

40. Ibid., p. 260.

41. Ibid., p. 260.

42. Indeed, a glance at the maps Hayashi attempted to publish shows that such expansion would roughly double Japan's total land area. See maps appended to *Hayashi Shihei zenshū*, vol. 2.

43. Inobe, pp. 158–161. Also Uete, pp. 243–244.

44. Inobe, pp. 158–161.

45. Ibid., pp. 158–161.

46. Ibid., pp. 158–161.

47. Ibid., pp. 158–161.

48. Donald Keene treats this problem in *Japanese Discovery*, pp. 115–122 and pp. 134–137.

49. *Sankoku tsūran zusetsu*, p. 261.

50. Ōhara, *Chihoku gūdan*, pp. 115–116.

51. Honjō Eijirō, ed., "Honda Toshiaki shū kaidai," pp. 9–10.

52. See Ōtomo Kisaku, ed., "Kaisetsu," pp. 38–40; Inobe Shigeo, pp. 153–155.

53. Ibid., pp. 153–155.

54. Aizawa quotes Honda directly in *Chishima ibun* and expresses opinions similar to Ōhara's.

55. See *Mito han shiryō: bekki, 1*, pp. 255–257 concerning the passing-on of Kimura's information to Aizawa by Yūkoku.

56. Aizawa is incorrect about the year. Laxman's visits to Ezo took place

in 1792 and 1793, not 1794. This passage is found in Aizawa's *Kyūmon ihan* (p. 790), which was composed in 1850.

57. See the list in the appendix.

58. Aizawa, *Chishima ibun.*

59. Ibid.

60. Ibid.

61. Ibid. The same observation is made by Ōtsuki Gentaku in *Hoppen tanji*, p. 426.

62. *Chishima.*

63. Ibid.

64. See *Mito-han shiryō: bekki, 1*, pp. 249-309.

65. Irokawa Daikichi, *Nihon no rekishi, 21: Kindai kokka no shuppatsu*, pp. 245-250.

66. *Chishima.*

67. Ibid.

68. Ibid.

69. Ibid.

70. Ibid.

71. Ibid.

72. Englebert Kaempfer was a German physician serving in the Dutch trading post on Dejima from 1690 to 1691. A partial Japanese translation of his work, entitled *History of Japan* (in English), was prepared by Shizuki Tadao in 1801, the same year that Aizawa wrote *Chishima ibun.*

73. *Chishima.*

74. Compiled in 1777 by Ch'i-shih-i.

75. *Chishima.* See also the supplementary note in *Shisō taikei, 53*, p. 457.

76. *Chishima.*

77. Ibid.

78. Ibid.

79. Ibid. For more detailed accounts of the Benyowsky affair than that presented earlier in this chapter, see Tabohashi Kiyoshi, pp. 90-122; Donald Keene, pp. 31-40.

80. *Chishima.*

81. Ibid. Aizawa quotes verbatim from Honda's *Ezo shūi.* See *Honda Toshiaki shū*, p. 310.

82. *Chishima.*

83. Ibid. Aizawa paraphrases loosely from Mogami Tokunai's *Ezo sōshi*, see p. 380.

84. *Chishima.* This quote is from Kondō's *Henyō bunkai zukō* (p. 55), which Aizawa relied on heavily for his Western Learning.

85. *Chishima;* Kondo, *Henyō bunkai zukō*, p. 67. This account by Kondō Jūzō is also quoted by Honda Toshiaki. See Keene, p. 117.

86. *Chishima.* On *sake* and *mochi* as barter items, see Satō Genrokurō's

expedition report to the Bakufu, *Ezo shūi,* p. 307; Ōtomo's "Kaisetsu," pp. 129–132; and Mogami's *Ezo sōshi,* p. 392, where he identifies the *mochi* as *"manjū."*

87. Ōtomo Kisaku, ed., *Hokusa ibun, Hoppen tanji,* p. 348.

88. *Chishima.*

89. Ibid. Ōtsuki Gentaku also notes this fact. See *Hoppen tanji,* p. 425.

90. *Chishima.*

91. Ibid.

92. Ibid.

93. *Chihoku gūdan,* p. 191.

94. For details, see George Alexander Lensen, *The Russian Push Toward Japan: Russo-Japanese Relations, 1697–1875,* pp. 196–262.

95. Tokutomi Iichirō, *Kinsei Nihon kokuminshi, 25: Bakufu bunkai sekkin jidai,* pp. 314–315.

96. Ibid., p. 315.

97. Aizawa and Yūkoku specifically cite Hakuseki's name in reference to the Sidotti incident. In addition to mentioning Hakuseki's interrogation of Sidotti, Aizawa quoted the following passage (in single quotation marks) regarding "Marabariko Island" from *Seiyō kibun* in *An'i mondō.*

[Hakuseki:] ". . . Mata Roson [Luzon] no chi ni hakugin ōku idenuru koto, mata 'waga kuni tōnan no kaitō yori kingin ōku idenuru wo Isupaniyajin no toriuru' koto nado iite. . . "

[Aizawa:] "Marabariko wa Ogasawaratō yori nampō e tsuranaritaru shotō no sōmei nari. Anzuru ni, Shōtoku-chū mo rōmajin no Arai-shi ni kotaeshi nimo, 'Shinshū tōnan no kaitō yori kingin ōku toriidasuru wo Isupaniyajin toriuru' to iishi mo sunawachi kono shima no koto narubeshi."

Assuming that the copied manuscript of Aizawa's held by Mukyūkai bunko in Tokyo is authentic, Aizawa's citation of Hakuseki by name plus the above evidence leave little room to doubt that Aizawa did in fact read Hakuseki's *Seiyō kibun.*

98. For an account of this incident, see *Mitoshi-shi,* pp. 460–467.

99. See also the partial English translation of a variant text of *An'i mondō* included in Ernest W. Clement, "Mito Samurai and British Sailors in 1824."

100. *An'i.*

101. "Kōshin teisho," p. 723.

102. *An'i.*

103. Ibid.

104. Ibid.

105. Ibid.

106. Ibid.

107. Ibid.

108. Ibid.

109. Ibid.

110. Ibid.

111. Ibid.

112. Shinobu Seizaburō, *Shōzan to Shōin: Kaikoku to jōi no ronri*, pp. 47–52.

113. *An'i.*

114. See Ōtsuki's *Hoei mondō*, pp. 401–441, especially pp. 405–409 and pp. 419–421.

115. Tabohashi, *Zōtei kindai Nihon*, pp. 301–306.

116. Ibid., pp. 255–269.

117. A report in 1799, for example, declared that French royalist forces had squashed the revolution there. See Satō Shōsuke, *Yōgakushi no kenkyū*, p. 146. The following account of Ōtsuki's *Hoei mondō* is presented by Satō in ibid., pp. 145–154.

118. Ibid., pp. 148–149.

119. Ōtsuki, *Hoei mondō*, p. 149 and p. 148.

120. Ōtsuki, *Kankai ibun*, pp. 431–432.

121. Ōtsuki, *Hoei mondō*, p. 423.

122. Ibid., pp. 422–424. Gentaku specifically mentions "the Cape of Good Hope, Ceylon, Bengal, and various places in India."

123. Ibid., pp. 423–427.

124. Ibid., pp. 423–427.

125. Ibid., p. 426.

126. Ibid., pp. 435–441.

127. As further evidence that Aizawa read Hakuseki's *Seiyō kibun*, note the following passage from *An'i mondō*, in which Aizawa asserted that Gibson refused to reveal his true identity as a Christian, and added, "Gibson's surname is 'John,' the name of one of Christ's disciples, which he has assumed for himself—a custom described in Arai's writings. Moreover, the fact that many believers in Christianity are named 'John' is another piece of evidence [to show he is a Christian]."

128. Aizawa, *Shinron*, p. 243.

129. See his undated essay, "Arai Chikushū Rōmajin o satosu sho ni gisu."

130. For example, Takahashi Shin'ichi, *Yōgaku shisōshi ron*, pp. 44–47.

131. *Seiyō kibun*, p. 82.

132. Ibid., p. 82.

133. Ibid., pp. 65–66.

134. Ibid., p. 66.

135. Ibid., p. 66.

136. Ibid., pp. 66–67.

137. Ibid., pp. 66–67.

138. See *Mōshi*, p. 206; Lau, *Mencius*, pp. 113–114. According to Mencius, this situation resulted from the teachings of Yang Chu and Mo Tzu, individualism and universal love, respectively.

139. *Seiyō kibun*, pp. 57–58.

140. Ibid., pp. 57–58.

141. Ibid., pp. 62–63.

142. Ibid., pp. 62–63.

143. Ibid., pp. 64–65.

144. Ibid., pp. 64–65.

145. *"Kōsei, riyō, seitoku no michi."* See Bitō Masahide, "Mitogaku no tokushitsu," pp. 575–576; also *Mitoshi-shi* 2:2, pp. 484–486.

146. Ibid. Bitō stresses the reversal in emphasis from *seitoku*, which is traditionally placed ahead of *riyō* and *kōsei*, and argues that Yūkoku and Aizawa viewed the latter two as being primary.

147. *Seiyō kibun*, p. 64.

148. Of course China's relationship to surrounding barbarians changed according to historical conditions—the relative strengths of Chinese and barbarian forces. Under the first Ming emperor, for example, China adopted a militant, expansionist policy. Under weaker dynasties such as the Sung, more emphasis was placed on "virtue" and non-military means of "transforming" barbarians. And under barbarian conquest dynasties such as the Yuan, Confucians were at a loss to explain why the reversal of "civilization" and "barbarism" had taken place. See Lien-sheng Yang, "Historical Notes of the Chinese World Order," and Wang Gungwu, "Early Ming Relations with Southeast Asia: A Background Essay," pp. 20–62. For a revisionist critique of Fairbank, see the essays in Morris Rossabi, ed., *China Among Equals*.

149. Lau, tr., *Mencius*, p. 69, pp. 194–195.

FOUR: AIZAWA AND HIS NEW THESES

1. For Tokugawa Nariaki's view, see *Mito-han shiryō: bekki 2*, p. 679. For Watanabe Kazan, see *Shinkiron*, p. 47. For Yokoi Shōnan, see *Yokoi Shōnan ikō*, pp. 242–243.

2. Wang Fu-chih, a late Ming Confucian widely regarded as "protonationalistic," held the same view of "cultural *jōi.*" The *shih*, or literati-official class, had to maintain the distinctions of civilization and barbarism, and of superior men (*chün-tzu*) and small men (*hsiao-jen*). To maintain these distinctions, Wang said, the *shih* must "build barriers" between Chinese commoners and alien barbarians. See Gotō Motoi and Yamanoi Yū, ed., *Mimmatsu-shinsho seiji hyōron shū*, pp. 212–213.

3. *Tokugawa kinreikō* 6:608–609.

4. Ibid., p. 610.

5. Four years later Takahashi was sentenced to be executed in the Siebold Incident by the very bakufu that he strove so diligently to serve. He died during imprisonment, but his corpse was preserved in salt to await sentencing. See Keene, p. 152.

6. I used the text in Uehara, *Takahashi Kageyasu no kenkyū*, pp. 289–

294, checking it against the one in Tokutomi Iichirō, *Kinsei Nihon koku-minshi, 27: Bunsei-Tempō jidai*, pp. 371–384.

7. Uehara, *Takahashi kenkyū*, pp. 289–293.

8. Ibid., pp. 289–293.

9. Ibid., pp. 289–293.

10. On this point, see Ichiko Chūzō, *Sekai no rekishi, 21: Chūgoku no kakumei*, p. 16.

11. Uehara, *Takahashi kenkyū*, pp. 289–293.

12. Ibid., pp. 289–293.

13. Ibid., pp. 289–293.

14. Ibid., pp. 289–293.

15. Ibid. Inobe (p. 323) suggests that this may be interpreted as the beginning of the idea of "territorial waters" among Japanese officials. However, we should note that Takahashi would not allow Japanese vessels to venture beyond this ten *ri* limit. Thus, his ideas should be thought of as a logical extension of *"sakoku"* to the seas surrounding Japan.

16. Uehara, *Takahashi kenkyū*, pp. 289–293.

17. Ibid., pp. 289–293.

18. Aizawa, *Shinron*, p. 51.

19. Tokutomi, *Kokuminshi: 27*, p. 386.

20. For Chōei, see *Bojutsu yume monogatari*, pp. 168–169.

21. Shinobu, *Shōzan to Shōin*, p. 23.

22. Fujita Yūkoku, *Yūkoku zenshū*, p. 723. Also quoted in Shinobu, *Shōzan to Shōin*, p. 19.

23. Uehara, *Takahashi kenkyū*, p. 290.

24. A good example is Ueda Jō, "Shinron keiseihen ni mirareru sekai chiri chishiki," pp. 223–236. Interestingly, Ueda believes that Aizawa employed the map, *Shintei bankoku zenzu*, compiled by Takahashi Kageyasu in 1810, because both thinkers established zero-latitude as running through Kyoto. This view is also held by Nagakubo Mitsuaki, "Shinron no chiri-gakuteki kōsatsu," pp. 46–51.

25. *Kuwaji Toshiakira monjo* 5: 360. Cited in Satō Seizaburō, "Seiyō no shōgeki e no taiō," p. 40, note.

26. Aizawa, *Shinron*, p. 93.

27. Ibid., pp. 137–138.

28. Ibid., p. 92.

29. Ibid., pp. 100–101.

30. Ibid., p. 137.

31. Ibid., p. 89.

32. Although Aizawa did hold a view of history as a recurring cycle of "orderly rule and anarchy," (ibid., p. 63) this linear aspect of his thought—the progression from "simplicity" (*shitsu*) to "refinement" (*bun*)—should not be overlooked.

33. Aizawa, *Shinron*, pp. 89–90.

34. The Chinese thinker, Wang Tao, would not make this analogy until 1873–1874. But note that Wang did *not* extend the analogy to include China among those "warring states." See Paul Cohen, *Between Tradition and Modernity*, pp. 93–94.

35. Aizawa, *Shinron*, p. 93.

36. Ibid., pp. 127–128.

37. Ibid., pp. 92–94.

38. Ibid., p. 92.

39. Ibid., p. 94.

40. Ibid., p. 93.

41. Ibid., p. 77.

42. Ibid., p. 75.

43. Ibid., p. 75.

44. Ibid., p. 95.

45. Ibid., pp. 73–74.

46. Ibid., pp. 73–74.

47. Ibid., pp. 73–74.

48. Ibid., pp. 77–80.

49. Ibid., p. 77.

50. Ibid., p. 79.

51. Ibid., pp. 120–124.

52. Ibid., pp. 115–117.

53. Ibid., p. 116.

54. Ibid., p. 116.

55. I agree with Yasumaru Yoshio, who sees Mito thinkers as understanding the need to tap popular energies, to create a "Japanese nation" (*kokumin*) that would work actively toward fulfilling national goals rather than "serfs" (*nōdo*) who merely acquiesced in passive fashion. See Yasumaru, *Nihon nashonarizumu no zenya*, pp. i–ii, and pp. 155–157. However, such a change would have placed burdens on the feudal *mibun* order that it could not have borne.

56. Bitō Masahide, "Mitogaku no tokushitsu," pp. 556–582; Bitō, "Kaisetsu"; Bitō, "Mitogaku no hatten to sonnō jōi ron;" Hashikawa Bunzō, "Mitogaku no genryū to seikaku," pp. 55–60. This last volume contains useful modern Japanese translations of basic *Mitogaku* texts, including Aizawa's *Shinron*. My understanding of both Sorai and *Mitogaku*, as will be apparent in the following paragraphs, owes much to the excellent works of Professors Bitō and Hashikawa, which is gratefully acknowledged.

57. Bitō Masahide, "Kokkashugi no sokei toshite no Sorai," pp. 7–61; Bitō, "Ogyū Sorai no shisō."

58. *Ogyū Sorai*, p. 70.

59. *Rei-gaku no myōyō*. See Aizawa, *Kikōben*.

60. *Ogyū Sorai*, p. 25.

61. Ibid., p. 13.

62. Aizawa, *Kikōben*.

63. This is Mencius' well-known usage in the "Li-lou" chapter. See D. C. Lau, tr., *Mencius*, pp. 124–125; also see Lau's discussion of the term, "*ch'üan*" in "Appendix 5," of the same volume.

64. Professor Ōba Osamu of Kansai University has called my attention to this aspect of "*ch'üan*." He contends that "*ch'üan*" should be interpreted according to the Japanese usage of "*gon*," as in "*gon-dainagon*" or other "*gon-kan*," of the Nara and Heian periods. The *gon-dainagon* was a permanent extra-legal post with real administrative functions, but at other times, particularly in cases of envoys to the Sui or T'ang court, a "*gon*" rank or office would be granted as a temporary expedient. It would be in effect only during the envoy's term in China, was purely nominal in nature, and was instituted to obtain favorable treatment relative to envoys from other nations who possessed lower official ranks in their home countries.

65. Yamazaki Anzai quotes Chu Hsi to this effect in *Hekki*, p. 245. Even when a sage employed it, *ch'üan* might become the object of criticism by Japanese Confucians when associated with the idea of the Heavenly Mandate as a justification for overthrowing an existing dynasty. See for example, Asami Keisai's usage in *Kōyū sōshi setsu*, pp. 233–234, where he approvingly quotes Confucius' words of censure, "King Wen's was the ultimate in virtue; [the overthrower] Wu did not fully perform goodness."

66. *Kikoben*.

67. *Shinron*, p. 104.

68. *Sōen wagon*, p. 14.

69. *Shinron*, p. 144.

70. Ibid., p. 144, p. 149.

71. *Kikōben*.

72. *Shinron*, p. 142.

73. The author and date of composition are unknown. It is traditionally attributed to Honda Sado no Kami Masanobu (1538–1616); hence the title, "Accounts (*rohu*) by *Honda Sado* no Kami." However, some scholars attribute it to Fujiwara Seika, and the text that I consulted is included in a volume of writings by Seika and Hayashi Razan. See note 74 below.

74. *Honsaroku*, p. 293.

75. *Kikōbun*.

76. *Shinron*, p. 144.

77. *Kikōbun*.

78. Ibid.

79. *Shinron*, p. 143.

80. Ibid., p. 66.

81. Aizawa's term "*kokutai*" is extremely difficult to translate. Basically, it has two meanings—"the nation's honor or prestige" (*kuni no taimen*) and "what is essential" to a land and people in forming a "nation." In this latter sense, "*tai*" assumes roughly the same meaning of *t'i* in the Ch'ing

Confucians' "t'i-yung" thinking. That is, "tai" is some defining quality or group of characteristics that may not be allowed to undergo "transformation." In the Ch'ing context, however, t'i was what was of essence to the shih, or literati-official class; it did not become connected to a "nation."

81. Ibid., p. 69.

82. Ibid., p. 52.

83. "Mitogaku no tokushitsu," "Kaisetsu."

84. Shinron, p. 70.

85. "Kōsei, riyō, seitoku no michi." Ibid., p. 27 and pp. 151–152; Kagaku jigen, p. 58.

86. Shinron, pp. 53–54.

87. Ibid., pp. 86–87.

88. Ibid., pp. 53–54.

89. Ibid., p. 81.

90. Ibid., p. 53.

91. Ibid., pp. 81–82.

92. Kagaku jigen, p. 58.

93. Hashikawa Bunzō, "Mitogaku no genryū to seiritsu," p. 55.

94. Shinron, p. 140.

95. Ibid., p. 64.

96. Ekikyō "kuan" hexagram, 1:341.

97. Shinron, p. 53.

98. Ibid., p. 152.

99. Ibid., pp. 81–82.

100. Ibid., pp. 81–82.

101. Ibid., pp. 150–151.

102. Ibid., p. 54, pp. 150–151.

103. Ibid., p. 54, pp. 150–151.

104. Ibid., p. 54, pp. 150–151.

105. Ibid., p. 140.

106. Ibid., p. 140.

107. Ibid., p. 141.

108. I have profited from J. Victor Koschmann, "Discourse in Action: Representational Politics in Mito in the Late Tokugawa Period," pp. 92–93. Koschmann describes Aizawa's use of ritual to induce popular obedience and allegiance as "a principle of 'magical' government" according to the definition of "magic" given by Herbert Fingarette. However, Fingarette explains, "The user of magic does not work by strategies and devices as a means toward an end . . ." See Confucius: The Secular as Sacred, p. 3. Yet in my opinion, this is precisely what Sorai and Aizawa argue that the former sage kings, Amaterasu, and barbarian leaders had done. Ritual and music were deemed a "technique" (jutsu) by Sorai, and a "device" (gu) by Aizawa: The sages and Amaterasu had invented and utilized religious ritual

for the purpose of securing order in the realm, and the Westerners had invented a false imitation for similar purposes.

109. *Shinron*, pp. 150–151.

110. Ibid., p. 151, note.

111. Ibid., p. 151.

112. The Early Mito compilers of *Dainihonshi* did not refrain from criticizing emperors for immoral conduct. In addition to Bitō's "Mitogaku no tokushitsu," see his "Rekishi shisō," pp. 188–203; also see his *Nihon no rekishi, 19: Genroku jidai*, pp. 186–213. Also illuminating on this topic is Matsumoto Sannosuke, "Kinsei ni okeru rekishi jojutsu to sono shisō," pp. 578–615.

113. *Shinron*, pp. 60–63. See also, the term *"jōri"* on p. 60.

114. Ibid., p. 145.

115. Ibid., p. 144.

116. Ibid., p. 136, p. 143.

117. Ibid., p. 146.

118. In 1741, the bakufu revived the Niiname ritual, which had been discontinued in the reign of Emperor Gohanazono (r. 1428–64). The Daijō ritual, which had been discontinued in 1466, was revived in 1687, was again discontinued for a span of fifty-one years until revived by the bakufu once more in 1738. See Ono Shinji, "Bakufu to Tennō," p. 353.

119. *Shinron*, p. 137.

120. Ibid., pp. 70–74.

121. See Yasumaru Yoshio, *Kamigami no meiji ishin*, pp. 13–44.

FIVE: EPILOGUE: LOOKING AHEAD

1. Cited in a letter by Yokoi Shōnan dated 1855/11/3, *Yokoi Shōnan ikō*, p. 229.

2. Letter dated 1853/6/5 in *Mito-han shiryō: jō hen kon*, p. 4.

3. Dated 1853/6/6, included in *Mito-han shiryō, jō hen kon*, p. 5.

4. *Kaiten shishi*, p. 39.

5. But not the rhetoric of reverence for the Emperor *in general*. By the late 1850s, just before his death, Yoshida Shōin was advocating the idea of "one ruler over all the people" *(ikkun bammin)*. This idea entailed eliminating the existing class-bound form of loyalty within the hierarchic status order. Under that system—ideologically reinforced by Mito Learning—daimyo and samurai owed loyalty to the bakufu which in turn owed loyalty to the emperor. Commoners owed no loyalty, only submission. After Shōin, however, samurai and commoners both were seen as owing loyalty directly to the emperor, overriding the daimyo and bakufu who were deemed superfluous.

6. Dated 1860/2/4, *Mito-han shiryō, jō hen kon*, p. 690.

7. *Jimusaku*, pp. 352–367.

8. Imai et al. ed., *Nihon shisō taikei, 53: Mitogaku*, pp. 230–231, p. 242, and p. 278.

9. Tokugawa Nariaki understood the need to assimilate advanced Western knowledge in military technology, medicine, and foreign affairs. In 1842, he urged Senior Councillor Mizuno Tadakuni to continue supporting the "inexperienced and clumsy" Takashima Shūhan, then studying Western artillery techniques. See *Mito-han shiryō: bekki, 1*, pp. 124–127. Nariaki learned that innoculation was successful against smallpox in the West, and in 1849, introduced it to Mito domain, vaccinating his own children first of all to eliminate popular fears. He innoculated 13,400 persons in Mito during the early 1850s. See *Mito-han shiryō: bekki, 2*, pp. 320–323. In 1857, he encouraged Toyoda Tenkō, a Mito ideologue and Rangaku student, to drink "cow's milk" in order to increase resistance to disease. See *Mito-han shiryō: jō hen ken*, pp. 928–929. Such little-known facts suggest that Nariaki recognized the superiority of Western science—at least to some extent—and strove to assimilate it, often in the face of stubborn opposition from less-enlightened segments of Japan's ruling class. But his motive for sponsoring Western studies was to reinforce and preserve bakufu and daimyo rule by assimilating advanced Western technical knowledge about armaments, shipbuilding, and medicine, which was unobtainable through traditional forms of Chinese or Japanese learning.

10. *Mito-han shiryō: bekki, 2*, p. 226, 231.

11. Saitō, *Ahen shimatsu*, p. 209. See also Masuda Wataru, *Seigaku tōzen to Chūgoku jijō*, pp. 69–72.

12. *Ahen Shimatsu*, pp. 69–72.

13. Aizawa's term is *"kuiki,"* *Shinron*, p. 89.

14. Ibid., p. 127.

15. He used the term on ibid., p. 77, p. 97, and p. 138.

16. *"Kaigai shokoku,"* or *"kaigai no shotō."* Ibid., p. 127, and p. 114. Aizawa also uses the term *"kaigai shokoku"* to denote "countries overseas" that Russia had seized. See ibid., pp. 92–93 and 99.

17. Though as we have seen, his idea of "Ezo" was quite vague; it included the Kuriles, Sakhalin, and Siberia.

18. Aizawa's attacks on Westerners and Christianity were qualitatively different from what Paul Cohen has called "the foul and obscene calumnies" that nineteenth-century Ch'ing literati gave vent to in anti-Christian tracts such as *Pi-hsieh chi-shih*, which focused on the alledged salacious and perverted practices of Western missionaries in China. See Paul A. Cohen, *China and Christianity*, pp. 45–60.

19. *Shinron*, p. 103.

20. See Watanabe Hiroshi, "'Michi' to 'miyabi' (IV)," pp. 7–18.

21. *Yokoi Shōnan ikō*, pp. 242–243.

22. For a different appraisal of how Japanese intellectuals understood Christianity in the mid-nineteenth century, see George Elison, *Deus*

Destroyed, pp. 245-246. Elison labels Aizawa's attacks on Christianity "antique fulminations" that "have neither rhyme nor reason."

23. Quoted in Shimizu Shin, *"Teikokukempō seitei kaigi,* pp. 88-89; also quoted in David Anson Titus, *Palace and Politics in Prewar Japan,* p. 36; and in Maruyama Masao, *Nihon no shisō,* pp. 28-30. I have rendered the passage into English somewhat differently from Titus. He translates Itō's metaphor, *"kijiku,"* literally, as "axis." Itō's figurative use of the term, however, was to characterize something deemed vital to hold the state together. In this figurative sense, "linchpin" seems more appropriate.

24. *"Okuchō kokoro o itsu ni shite...."* This point is also made by Iwai Tadakuma, *Meiji kokkashugi shisōshi kenkyū,* pp. 166-167.

25. See his use of *"kokka"* in *New Theses:* "At present, the great and small lords remain within domain borders because they are bound by fealty oaths to a common overlord, the bakufu *(kokka).* They uphold [the state] just as a centipede's legs support its body....)" *Shinron,* p. 112.

NOTES TO THE TRANSLATION

1. Two early Chinese uages of the term *shinshū (shen-chou)* are noteworthy. First, the Warring States period thinker, Tsou Yen, considered China to constitute but one-eightieth of the world's surface area, and not to be the major, central portion of it. Second, in 356, Huan Wen of the Eastern Chin attempted to recover the north from barbarian conquest, and is reported to have exclaimed, "That this Wondrous Realm *(shen-chou)* [or China] should have sunk away to become but an empty waste for these hundred years is something for which Wang Yen and those others cannot escape the responsibility." Both of these Chinese usages are quoted from Kung-chuan Hsiao, *A History of Chinese Political Thought,* p. 63, and p. 646. Thus, in China as well as in Japan, the claim of divinity *(shen)* for one's homeland was induced or accompanied by a consciousness of geographical insignificance or military weakness toward alien powers deemed barbarian.

2. On translating the philosophical term *"ch'i"* see Wing-tsit Chan, tr., *Reflections on Things at Hand,* p. 360. Also Fukui Fumimasa, "Seiyō bunken ni okeru 'ki' no yakugo," pp. 557-567. On *yuan ch'i* as a Later Han concept, see *Ki no shisō,* pp. 3-11 and pp. 181-208.

3. Aizawa did not really believe that the world was shaped like the human anatomy. He had access to and utilized Chinese translations of Western atlases and gazetteers and to maps drawn by Japanese geographers and explorers. Moreover, in 1824 when he was ordered by Mito *han* to interrogate the English seamen who came ashore at Ōtsuhama (Mito territory), he brought a global map of the world *(chikyūzu)* with him for use in the interrogation. See *An'i mondō.*

4. The *locus classicus* is *Shih chi,* "Wu Tzu-hsü." See *Shiki,* p. 83; also Watson, tr., *Records of the Historian,* p. 22.

5. *Son shi,* p. 89; Samuel B. Griffith, tr., *Sun Tzu: The Art of War,* p. 114.

6. See *Shiki,* p. 83; Watson, *Records of the Historian,* p. 22. In the original context, Aizawa's two quotes are found as a single sentence rather than being divided into two.

7. This phrase, "all the people of the realm be of one heart and mind" (*okuchō kokoko o itsu ni shite*), appears in, and can be considered the guiding principle behind, *The Imperial Rescript on Education.*

8. Two excellent studies of the Daijō ritual exist in English. See D. C. Holtom, *The Japanese Enthronement Ceremonies;* also Robert S. Ellwood, *The Feast of Kingship.*

9. *Kuni no miyatsuko* were provincial officers established by the Yamato Court before the Taika Reform, in the sixth century at the latest. Most appointments were given to local magnates. The office itself was abolished during the Taika Reform, but most of the Kuni no miyatsuko continued to function as District Governors (*gunshi*) under the Ritsu-Ryō System.

10. Aizawa here quotes extensively from the *Book of Changes, Book of Rites, Doctrine of the Mean, Classic of Filial Piety, Book of Documents,* and *Analects* to support his assertions. He ends this long gloss by stating that because geographical and climatic factors (outlined in the *Book of Changes*) in Japan are similar to those in China and the spiritual make-up (*ninjō*) of the Japanese people is similar to that of the Chinese, the numerous quotations he has just made hold for both nations and peoples.

11. *Tomo no miyatsuko* were provincial officers established by the Yamato Court before the Taika Reform. They were similar to the *Kuni no miyatsuko* except that they held jurisdiction over people—the various *be* owned by the Imperial Court, rather than territorial districts. *Nihonshi jiten,* p. 696. The point here is that the Imperial Court in antiquity established the "*hōken*" system—which I translate as "feudal." Aizawa later argues that Tokugawa Ieyasu revived this system; therefore the existing bakuhan state structure accords with the polity Japan possessed in high antiquity.

12. Of course Aizawa considered Japanese history to have begun in 660 B.C., with the accession of Jimmu.

13. Examples include Ex-emperors Gotoba, Tsuchimikado, and Juntoku in 1221, after the Jōkyū Uprising; and Emperor Godaigo in 1332, after the Genkō Uprising.

14. Quotations from *Mencius, Spring and Autumn Annals,* and *Rites of Chou* here support Aizawa's arguments.

15. By Soga no Emishi and his son, Iruko, in 645.

16. To obtain lucrative trade rights with Ming China, Ashikaga Yoshimitsu accepted the degrading terms imposed by the Ming tribute system.

He willingly acknowledged himself "king" of the tributary state of Japan bearing tribute to the Ming court in return for gifts bestowed by the Chinese Son of Heaven. Under such an arrangement, the Emperor in Kyoto occupied the position of the Ming emperor's sub-tributory, or so it seemed in Aizawa's eyes.

17. This practice was the source of much political corruption, intrigue, and unrest in daimyo houses. In many cases, the adoption of a son as family heir was accompanied by large sums of money or political favors, so that the heirship went to the highest bidder. In other cases, high-ranking retainers plotted the assassination of a legitimate heir in order to adopt a bribe-bearing candidate from the outside. In 1830, the Fujita reform faction, to which Aizawa belonged, used the argument that an heir must be a direct male descendent of the Mito daimyo house to confirm the selection of Tokugawa Nariaki (brother of the deceased daimyo Narinobu). This was in opposition to the conservative faction then entrenched in power, which sought to adopt an heir from a Tokugawa collateral house.

18. Here Aizawa quotes passages from Kumazawa Banzan and Arai Hakuseki, who also lamented and opposed the practice.

19. This passage is taken from *Mencius* 3A/3. This view of history as a cycle of anarchy and orderly rule did not preclude progressive, linear development. Aizawa believed that history basically represented the progressive movement from "simplicity" (*shitsu*) to "cultured refinement" (*bun*); and moreover, he held that this progressive view of historical development was true also for Western "barbarians."

20. This is the Ōtsuhama Incident of 1824 in which the captain and crew of a British whaler came ashore at Mito, were captured, and were interrogated by Aizawa.

21. Aizawa's reference, of course, is to the bakufu's 1825 Expulsion Edict, originally proposed by the Rangakusha, Takahashi Kageyasu.

22. This interpolation is based on Aizawa's statements in *Kagaku jigen*, p. 62.

23. Here Aizawa uses the term "*Shinsei*," which he also employs on p. 214. But in the same quotation from the *Book of Changes* made on p. 332, he employs the term, "*Tenso*." This indicates that he used these terms interchangeably to designate Amaterasu. See *Shinron*, p. 64, p. 65, and p. 140.

24. The distinction between *shen tao*, the Chinese "spirit-like processes of nature" and the Japanese *shintō* is of the utmost importance. In attacking an assertion made by Motoori Norinaga that Japan's "*kami*" and "*shintō*" were essentially different from the "*shen*" and "*shen tao*" of China, Aizawa merely quoted from the *Book of Changes* and insisted that these were the same; he could not logically refute Norinaga, but made a counter-assertion. For Aizawa's criticism of Norinaga, see *Toku naobi no mitama*. For Norinaga's views, *Motoori Norinaga zenshū* 1:534-535.

25. A gloss containing a passage quoted from *The Doctrine of the Mean* along with Aizawa's commentary are deleted.

26. Traditionally attributed to Kūkai (774–835), but in fact dating from the tenth century. The doctrine held that native deities were earthly manifestations of buddhas.

27. An erroneous reference on Aizawa's part. The Cloistered Emperor Shirakawa, not ex-Emperor Go shirakawa, is reported to have made remarks to this effect in *Heike monogatari*.

28. This refers to the Shimotsuma clan, which participated in *Ikkō* Uprisings. See *Kagaku jigen*, p. 7.

29. Ogyū Sorai is the target of Aizawa's criticism. See Aizawa's *Taishoku kanwa*, p. 243.

30. Arai Hakuseki. See ibid., p. 243.

31. *"Keizai no gaku."* The followers of Sorai such as Dazai Shundai and Hoashi Banri.

32. Aizawa is not criticizing professional Rangaku scholar-officials, but rather, "Rangaku enthusiasts" such as Shiba Kōkan or Hayashi Shihei, who possessed secondhand knowledge of conditions in the West, and used it to criticize political, social, or military conditions in Japan publicly.

33. The original reads, *"kuwashihoko chitaru no kuni."* It is instructive to compare this Mito interpretation of this ancient name with Motoori Norinaga's. Norinaga held that *"kuwashihoko"* was merely a pillow word for *"chi,"* and maintained that the appellation meant "wealthy nation." This contrasts sharply with the martial overtones that Aizawa and Fujita Tōko wished to stress. See *Motoori Norinaga zenshū* 3:457.

34. In another work Aizawa wrote, "After Jingū Kōgō conquered and incorporated the Three Kingdoms of Korea, an Imperial Magistrate (*fu*) was established to pacify the new territory. This 'Mimana Magistrate' was much like the 'Nagasaki Magistrate' (*bugyō*) of today." See *Sōen wagon*, p. 17. Aizawa, then, definitely considered the Three Kingdoms to have been part of Japan in ancient times, and clearly lamented their subsequent loss.

35. According to Confucian political theory, by "ceasing to bear tribute," the Three Kingdoms and other tributory states signified that they no longer recognized the virtue of Japan's Emperor and his claim to be dispensing virtuous government. In short, they bolted from Japan's "sphere of moral suasion" (*kwa*).

36. This is in present-day Hokkaidō. This "Imperial Magistrate" in Shiribeshi was similar to that established in Mimana, mentioned earlier. In Aizawa's mind, all of Ezo, which was then uncharted territory, was under Japanese rule in antiquity.

37. These prayers are recited during the Toshigoi and Tsukinami Rituals.

38. This quote is taken from the *Book of Changes*.

39. This military system, characteristic of warrior rule, was known as

"gun'yaku," and dated from the Kamakura period. Under it, each retainer was responsible for maintaining a certain number of followers to be placed at his overlord's disposal on command. This duty was in return for stipends or grants of land. Bakufu edicts on *gun'yaku* date from 1616 and 1630, and stipulate five men per two-hundred *koku*. See Takayanagi, *Nihonshi jiten,* p. 307.

40. Presented most coherently in *Kagaku jigen,* pp. 79–82.

41. *"Chōhei."* This refers to the *sankin kōtai* system. That Aizawa uses the term "Court" (*chō*), a term usually reserved to designate a ruling dynasty, is of considerable significance.

42. By providing the people with the "Way of convenience and livelihood," (*riyō kōsei no michi*) in antiquity, Amaterasu, in Aizawa's mind, was equivalent to China's ancient sage kings. Aizawa insisted that Amaterasu bestowed rice and silk on the Japanese people, but in his ignorance of the true conditions of the daily lives of peasants, he unwittingly ascribed rice and silk, everyday consumption and use items for the samurai class, to peasants as well. In fact, peasants (except for *gōnō*) rarely if ever wore silk and only occasionally ate boiled white rice. As scholars of Japanese folklore have pointed out, boiled white rice unmixed with other cereals was an item consumed on special occasions (*hare*), such as festival days, not in everyday life (*ke*). It is therefore unlikely that Aizawa had much success in his campaign to instill reverent gratitude toward Amaterasu and Her Imperial Line among the mass of the peasantry through such arguments.

43. *"Mizuho no kuni."*

44. An instructive anachronism on Aizawa's part. He read the four-tiered Confucian *mibun* system back into his idealized picture of ancient Japanese society.

45. *Sake, mochi,* rice confections called *dango,* and noodles are all (*hare*) food items, and as such, played an important part in the people's spiritual lives. Decrees banning the distillation of *sake* were periodically issued (particularly during famines) to conserve rice. *Mochi* and *dango* are made from a special type of glutinous rice (*mochigome*), which yields less per acre than regular rice. Hence the obstruction to agricultural production.

46. The Italian Jesuit, Giuglio Aleni, who served as a missionary to China during late Ming times. Aizawa's quote is from Aleni's *Chih fang wai chi* which (along with Arai Hakuseki's *Sairan igen*), were regarded essential reading for Japanese students of the West during the latter half of the Tokugawa period. See Miyazaki Michio, *Arai Hakuseki no yōgaku to kaigai chishiki,* p. 182.

47. Two such advocates were Shiba Kōkan and Baba Masamichi. See Keene, pp. 109–110; Inobe, pp. 177–178.

48. That is, the amount of land required to produce ten *koku*.

49. Ōtsuki Gentaku was one such Dutch Studies scholar: He listed as

"empires" Russia, China, Japan, Germany, Turkey, India, and the Mogul. Gentaku then went on to state:

Japan is a small land compared with others, but it is an empire whose ruling Imperial Line has remained intact throughout the myriad ages. This is why Japan is superior to other countries, and why they stand in awe of her. . . .

Kankai ibun, p. 415.

50. This idea was fairly common at the time and served to heighten Japanese anxieties about Russian encroachment during the latter half of the eighteenth century. Hayashi Shihei, for example, quoted Arend Willem Feith (Dutch Commander of the Nagasaki Trading Post from 1771–1781) as follows:

A Dutchman named Heito (Japanese transliteration) told me, "It is easier for armies from northern lands to take over territories to the south, but it is difficult for armies from southern lands to take over territories to the north. . . . Hence Holland took over Java, Tartary took over China, and Muscovy took over Tartary. All these cases represent northern states taking over lands to their south."

Sankoku tsūran zusetsu, p. 263. In his *Ezo sōshi* (pp. 382–383), Mogami Tokunai cites this same "Captain Arento Ueruremu Heito" (Japanese transliteration) indirectly through Nagasaki Magistrate Natsume Masanobu to the same effect.

51. Here Aizawa lumps all Christian peoples under the heading, "Church of Rome," but in a later section he does distinguish certain European peoples as belonging to different sects of Christianity.

52. Aizawa here refers to the fact that Russian heads of state began to employ the title "Czar" from the fifteenth and sixteenth centuries onward and that Russia claimed to be the successor to the Byzantine Empire.

53. The Russo-Turkish War, 1768–1774.

54. The connotation of this classical metaphor is "interdependence," but in this context, the interdependence is clearly not between equals: Japan needs China more than China needs Japan.

55. A quotation taken from *Son shi,* pp. 36–37; Griffith, tr., *Art of War,* pp. 77–78. This idea of counteracting the enemy's strategy in advance through expulsion edicts and persecutions of Christians was a key element in Aizawa's *jōi* thought.

56. Aizawa used Mo Tzu's term *chien ai* to represent the Christian idea of universal love.

57. Ōtomo Sōrin (1530–1587) at the height of his power controlled six of the nine Kyūshū provinces. He engaged in trade with Korea and Portugal, became baptized in 1578, and established seminaries and novitiates in his territories. In 1582, together with Arima Harunobu and Ōmura Sumitada, he sent a mission to visit the Pope in Rome, which was Japan's first mission to Europe. Konishi Yukinaga (d. 1600), another Christian daimyo,

was the son of a wealthy Sakai merchant serving the Ukita clan. Yukinaga, however, became a military commander under Hideyoshi, and in 1588 became lord of Udo in control of half of Higo Province. After Hideyoshi's death, he along with Ishida Mitsunari, plotted to depose Tokugawa Ieyasu but suffered defeat at Sekigahara and execution.

58. Nobunaga cleverly used the Jesuit missionary Gnecchi-Soldi Organtino to induce Araki (whom Nobunaga suspected of treachery) to stage an unsuccessful uprising.

59. Nishi was originally a samurai from Ōmura domain but later became a "red-seal ship" merchant licensed by the bakufu. Aizawa is incorrect in his assertion that Nishi was sent to the West. In fact, Nishi was baptized and travelled to Manila, where he learned Spanish. Upon his return to Japan, he became a trusted advisor to Ieyasu, supplying the bakufu with information on foreign affairs.

60. Ibi Masakichi spent seven years in Kyūshū (saigoku), not the West, where he gathered information on Christianity and its adherents.

61. These two incidents were recorded by Arai Hakuseki. See *Arai Hakuseki zenshū* 4:821 and 824.

62. The reference is to a late Ming work, Su Nai-yü's *Hsieh tu shih chü*.

63. The correct title is *Nagasaki yawa sō*, a work completed in 1720 by Nishikawa Joken (1648–1724), a Nagasaki astronomer. Nishikawa also related the Sidotti incident in this work.

64. This reference is to Giovanni Battista Sidotti.

65. It is related in Aizawa's *Chishima ibun*.

66. For an account of the Benyowsky affair in English, see Donald Keene, pp. 31–35.

67. Tanuma Okitsugu made this decision based on a suggestion in Kudō Heisuke's memorial, later rewritten to form the first half of *Aka ezo fūsetsu kō* (also called *Kamuchatsuka fūsetsu kō*), a work which Aizawa consulted.

68. This refers to the Laxman and Rezanov missions in 1792–93 and 1804–05, respectively.

69. The attacks were made on the order of Rezanov's subordinates there in 1806–07.

70. This is clearly untrue. The Golovnin-Takadaya affair dragged on for three years, but was amicably settled in 1813. The Russians made no requests for trade. Quite the contrary, they apologized for their acts of violence in the above-mentioned incidents, saying that the attacks on Karafuto and Etorofu did not have the Czar's sanction, and the Russian government would take steps to punish the offenders.

71. Aizawa received this piece of information from explorers such as Kondō Jūzō and Mogami Tokunai, *Ezo sōshi*, p. 393. Satō Genrokurō, of the bakufu expedition to Ezo from 1785–86 correctly identified these items distributed by the Russians to the Ainu as bread (*pan*), not *mochi*. *Ezo shūi*, p. 307.

72. This gloss is not found in the 1931 Iwanami bunko edition of *Shinron, Tekiihen* edited by Tsukamoto Katsuyoshi.

73. This is the *Phaeton* Incident of 1808 in which an English warship forced its way into Nagasaki harbor in search of Dutch ships to destroy, since the two nations were then at war. The Nagasaki magistrate, Matsudaira Yasuhide, committed suicide to atone for indignities suffered.

74. In 1818, the *Brothers* called at Uraga and requested permission to trade. This request was refused; and the crew is reported to have left two copies of Bibles translated into classical Chinese before leaving. Then in 1822, an English whaler, the *Saracens,* landed at Uraga and received firewood and provisions.

75. This incident took place in 1816.

76. This incident took place in 1806.

77. These last two sentences are not as ridiculous as they appear. Although the bakufu learned about America's independence in 1809, this fact did not become publicly known until much later. The Rangakusha Ōtsuki Gentaku shared precisely the same suspicion as Aizawa. See *Hoei mondō,* pp. 419-420 and pp. 424-427.

78. This reference probably is to Matsudaira Sadanobu's reply to Laxman's request for trade and diplomatic relations in 1793. Sadanobu boldly asserted that national exclusion and the expulsion of Western ships other than the Dutch were sacred national laws in effect since ancient times despite the lack of historical evidence supporting his claims. On this point, see Inobe, pp. 142-147. Aizawa may also have been referring to the bakufu's statement to the Russian negotiators following the Golovnin-Takadaya Incident in 1813.

79. *Son shi,* pp. 29-30; Griffith, *Art of War,* p. 74.

80. Aizawa owes this piece of information to Arai Hakuseki. See *Arai Hakuseki zenshū* 4:826.

81. This reference is to the fact that Chao (137-52 B.C.) was the first to institute the garrison system in China. His troops farmed and lived off the frontier land where they were stationed. The Ti and Ch'ing were barbarian tribes that he and his troops conquered.

82. *Son shi,* pp. 68-69; Griffith, p. 100.

83. *Son shi,* p. 65; Griffith, p. 98.

84. *Son shi,* pp. 36-37; Griffith, p. 77.

85. Su Chi-yü.

86. The bakufu prohibited and persecuted this sect throughout the Tokugawa period. As an article of faith, the *Fuju fuse* sect accepted offerings from, and performed religious services for, its own members alone. In addition, it strictly forbade its members to worship at Shinto shrines or at the temples of other Buddhist sects. The sect was not anti-bakufu, but rather, sought to maintain its independence as a religious body distinct from political and secular authority.

87. A believer sat on a lotus-leaf platform, and priests chanted the *Lotus Sutra*. When the lotus petals wilted away, he was stabbed to death. It was believed that death in this manner guaranteed rebirth in paradise.

88. A religious organization founded in the Sengoku period whose members adopted Mt. Fuji as their object of worship. Members were primarily from the merchant, artisan, and peasant classes. After 1724, edicts banning the organization were periodically issued.

89. *Son shi*, pp. 133-134; Griffith, p. 139.

90. This is attributed to Ch'en Liang (1143-1194).

91. *Son shi*, pp. 133-135; Griffith, p. 139.

92. *Son shi*, pp. 126-127; Griffith, pp. 135-136.

93. This is a subtle hint to the effect that talented but low-ranking members of the Fujita reform faction (to which Aizawa belonged) in Mito domain should be granted posts in the domain government at the expense of the conservative faction then entrenched in positions of authority by virtue of their hereditary house rankings.

94. Aizawa criticized the *dochaku* theses advocated by Kumazawa Banzan and Ogyū Sorai on the basis that the systems they sought to implement were suited to "centralized empires" (*gunken no sei*), not "feudalism" (*hōken no sei*), and that therefore, these two thinkers failed to take "historical conditions" (*jisei*) into account. Aizawa presented his own theory in *Kagaku jigen*, pp. 79-82.

95. Chinese historians employed this term, "subversives," or "*ryūzoku*," to designate the peasant armies of Li Tzu-ch'eng and Ch'ang Hsien-chung, whose rebellions toppled the Ming dynasty prior to the Manchu conquest.

96. One of Aizawa's primary aims behind putting the nation on a wartime footing was to impose state controls over the merchant class and to allow bakufu and daimyo to appropriate the merchants' right to deal in and transport rice within Japan. Honda Toshiaki and Satō Shin'en also advocated such ideas.

97. This point was also made by Ogyū Sorai in *Seidan*, although he used the term "*kaku*." These *kaku*, Sorai said, had not been prescribed in the rituals of ancient times, nor had they been established by the bakufu, but had sprung up spontaneously, and were not informed by coherent or logical principles. See *Ogyū Sorai zenshū* 6:126.

98. This point was also made by Hayashi Shihei. See *Hayashi Shihei zenshū* 1:126.

99. Put differently, a 12.5 *koku* tax yield would be required to obtain the 5 *koku* stipend.

100. Two quotations from Ming sources have been omitted.

101. Aizawa is referring to the exchange of money or other valuables and food, water, and firewood taking place between Japanese commoners in coastal areas and Western sailors. Aizawa conceived of such activities solely as smuggling, or illicit trade, since all trade conducted by Japan

with foreign countries according to bakufu law had to be conducted under bakufu control or with bakufu permission.

102. We should note that the role Aizawa envisioned for these warships is purely a defensive one. For this reason, I call his naval forces a "coast guard" throughout this translation.

103. *Son shi*, pp. 63–64; Griffith, p. 97.

104. The reference is to Hayashi Shihei and Takahashi Kageyasu. See Hayashi, *Kaikoku keidan*, p. 126. Moreover, Hayashi argued that large cannon should be fired from shore, not mounted aboard ships because the recoil when fired might break open and sink the small, frail Japanese ships. For Takahashi, see *Takahashi Kageyasu no kenkyū*, pp. 289–294.

105. Aizawa owes this idea to Chi Chi-kuang (1528–1585).

106. Aizawa refers to the ship in question as "barbarian" (*ryohaku*), but it was in fact Chinese (*karabune*). See *Tsūkō ichiran* 5:294.

107. A chapter in his *Chi hsiao hsin shu*.

108. This was taken from Hayashi Shihei's *Kaikoku heidan* (pp. 127–128). Aizawa's original term, *"sumpan,"* might be translated "board." Hayashi wrote, "The Westerners call their ships 'castles on the water' while the Chinese call theirs 'boards' (*han*); and the difference between the two is as great as night and day."

109. This statement probably refers to the *"ama no iwakusubune"* and *"tori no iwakusubune"* that were used to set adrift the Leech Child born by Izanami mentioned in *Nihon shoki*. See *Nihon shoki*, p. 87 and p. 89.

110. Ibid., p. 249.

111. Yü Ta-yu (d. 1580) and C'hi Chi-kuang were Ming commanders who did much to suppress piracy and eliminate the *wakō* menace along China's eastern seaboard.

112. Aizawa's esteem for Peter the Great is evidenced in *Chishima ibun*, which Aizawa compiled in 1801. Aizawa's reference to Peter as a "khan," is instructive because it reveals his early image of Russians as horseriding nomadic hordes. Here he expresses admiration for their attainment of naval power.

113. *"Kaikoku."* Aizawa clearly surpassed Hayashi's *Kaikoku heidan*, both in tactical thinking and assessing the international situation. For example, Hayashi believed that cannon and small ships were sufficient to ward off attackers, and he conceived of the Ch'ing Chinese, not Westerners, as probable enemies.

114. *Son shi*, pp. 123–126; Griffith, p. 134.

115. *Son shi*, pp. 128–130.

116. *Son shi*, pp. 123–126; Griffith, p. 134.

117. *Son shi*, pp. 29–30; Griffith, p. 74.

118. *Son shi*, pp. 29–30; Griffith, p. 74.

119. *Son shi*, pp. 34–35; Griffith, p. 77.

120. *Son shi*, pp. 34–35; Griffith, p. 74.

121. *Son shi*, pp. 38-39; Griffith, p. 79.

122. *Son shi*, pp. 65-68; Griffith, p. 98.

123. *Son shi*, pp. 65-68; Griffith, p. 98.

124. *Son shi*, pp. 118-121. Griffith translates these terms "dispersive ground" and "frontier ground," respectively. See *Art of War*, p. 131.

125. *Son shi*, pp. 131-133. This is to prevent them from defecting.

126. Ibid., pp. 43-45.

127. Ibid., pp. 36-37; Griffith, p. 77.

128. *Son shi*, pp. 36-37; Griffith, p. 78.

129. The term *"shen tao"* should not be interpreted according to the Japanese reading *"shintō."* Aizawa adapted his portion of his text from a passage in the *Book of Changes* ("kuan" hexagram) that reads, "When they [the sages] gaze on the spirit-like processes of nature *(shen tao)*, the seasons unfold in proper order. The sages establish teachings in accordance with these spirit-like processes of nature, and the realm submits [in proper order]." Aizawa obviously substituted "Amaterasu" for "the sages," and inserted "loyalty and filial devotion" as the specific teachings that were "in accordance with *shen tao.*" By means of these precepts, Aizawa believed, the realm could be induced to submit voluntarily and forever.

130. Aizawa's probable source for this assertion, *Nihon shoki* (p. 238), reads simply, ". . . so fearful was Emperor Sujin of Her divine power that he did not feel at ease in the same abode." This mentions nothing about publicly worshipping Amaterasu to achieve spiritual unity: Aizawa clearly misused the source for political purposes.

131. According to the *Nihon shoki* (pp. 244-246, 250-252), Takehani Yasuhiko led an uprising in 88 B.C., and Izumo Furune killed his brother for having surrendered the Divine Jewels of Izumo upon the demands of the Imperial Court in 38 B.C.

132. That is, the sages' "true" good teachings that according to Mencius "capture the peoples' hearts."

133. Aizawa consciously adapted this sentence from a statement in *Mencius*, "Unless the way of Yang Chu and Mo Tzu are blotted out, the Way of Confucius remains unelucidated." Itō Jinsai also quoted this passage along with another, "Some call me disputatious [but when battling heresies how can I be otherwise?]" in his *Dōjimon*, p. 140. Aizawa used this same phrase, "Some call me disputatious," as the title of an essay written in 1828 wherein he inveighed against Christianity. In short, Aizawa conceived of himself as carrying on this tradition of heresy-extirpation begun by Mencius and continued by Jinsai. Christianity was the most recent in a long list of dangerous heresies that intermittently sprang up during the course of history.

134. A long gloss comparing similarities between religious rituals in China and Japan is deleted here. In this and numerous other glosses Aizawa

asserts that the function of religious ritual observances and the nature of the deities worshipped by the Chinese and Japanese people were virtually identical. This shows Aizawa's intellectual debts to the Kimon School of "coincidental correspondences."

135. This concept is found in the *Book of Documents*, "Ta Yü mo." According to Aizawa, both the ancient sage kings in China and Amaterasu in Japan achieved these ends for their peoples. See *Kagaku jigen*, pp. 51–59.

136. This is part of a Shinto prayer delivered during the Toshigoi Ritual. Aizawa, like twentieth-century nationalists, here interprets it in an expansionist fashion.

Selected Bibliography

PRIMARY SOURCES

Aizawa Seishisai 会沢正志斎 . *An'i mondō* 諳夷問答 . Manuscript in Tokyo, Mukyūkai bunko 無窮会文庫

———. "Arai Chikushū Rōmajin o satosu sho ni gisu" 擬新井筑州
諭邏瑪人書 . Manuscript in Tokyo, Mukyūkai bunko.

———. *Chishima ibun* 千島異聞 . Manuscript in Tokyo, Mukyūkai
bunko.

———. *Jimusaku* 時務策 , in Imai Usaburō 今井宇三郎 , et al.,
ed., *Nihon shisō taikei, 53: Mitogaku.* 日本思想大系 53 水戸学
Tokyo, Iwanami shoten, 1973.

———. *Kagaku jigen* 下学通言 . Mito, n.p., 1892.

———. *Kansei manroku* 閑聖漫録 . Manuscript in Mito, Ibaraki-ken
rekishikan.

———. *Kikōben* 豈好弁 , in Seki Giichirō 関儀一郎 , ed., *Nihon
jurin sōsho* 日本儒林叢書 , vol. 4. Tokyo, Ōtori shuppan 鳳
出版, 1971.

———. *Shinron* 新論 , in Imai Usaburō, et al., ed., *Nihon shisō taikei,
53: Mitogaku.*

———. *Sōen wagon* 草偃和言 . Ibaraki-ken shinshokukai 茨城県
神職会 ed., Mito, n.p., 1931.

———. *Taishoku kanwa* 退食間話 , in Imai Usaburō, et al., ed.,
Nihon shisō taikei, 53: Mitogaku.

———. *Tekiihen* 迪彝編 , in Tsukamoto Katsuyoshi 塚本勝義 ,
ed., *Shinron, Tekiihen* 新論迪彝編 . Tokyo, Iwanami bunko,
1974.

———. *Toku Naobi no mitama* 読直毘霊 , in Seki Giichirō, ed., *Nihon jurin sōsho*, vol. 4.

———. "Tsuzuki Hakuei ni kotauru no sho" 答都築伯盈書 , Manuscript in Tokyo, Mukyūkai bunko.

Arai Hakuseki 新井白石 . *Seiyō kibun* 西洋記聞 , in Matsumura
Akira 松村明 et al., ed., *Nihon shisō taikei, 35: Arai Hakuseki.*
Tokyo, Iwanami shoten, 1975.

Asami Keisai 浅見絅斎 . "Chūgoku ben" 中国弁 , in Nishi Junzō
西順蔵 et al., ed., *Nihon shisō taikei, 31: Yamazaki Ansai gakuha*
山崎闇斎学派 . Tokyo, Iwanami shoten, 1980.

———. *Kōyū sōshi setsu* 拘幽操師説 , in Nishi Junzō, et al., ed.,
Nihon shisō taikei, 31: Yamazaki Ansai gakuha.

Ekikyō 易経 . Suzuki Yoshijirō 鈴木由次郎 ed., *Zenshaku kam-bun taikei, 9-10: Ekikyō* 全釈漢文大系 9-10 易経 , 2 vols. Tokyo, Shūeisha 集英社 , 1974.

Fujita Tōko 藤田東湖 . *Kaiten shishi* 回天詩史 , in Kikuchi Kenjirō 菊池謙二郎 ed., *Shintei Tōko zenshū* 新訂東湖全集 . Tokyo, Hakubunkan 博文館 , 1940.

———. *Kōdōkanki jutsugi* 弘道館記述義 , in Imai Usaburō, et al., ed., *Nihon shisō taikei, 53: Mitogaku*. Tokyo, Iwanami shoten, 1973.

Fujita Yūkoku 藤田幽谷 . "Kōshin teisho" 甲申呈書 (Dated 6/6/1824), in Kikuchi Kenjirō 菊池謙二郎 ed., *Yūkoku zenshū* 幽谷全集 . Tokyo, n.p., 1935.

———. "Nagakubo Sekisui ate shokan" 長久保赤水宛書簡 , in *Yūkoku zenshū*.

———. "Seimeiron" 正名論 , in Imai Usaburō, et al., *Nihon shisō taikei, 53: Mitogaku*.

Hayashi Shihei. *Kaikoku heidan* 海国兵談 , in Yamamoto Yutaka 山本豊 , ed., *Hayashi Shihei zenshū* 林子平全集 , vol. 1. Tokyo, Seikatsusha 生活社 , 1933.

———. *Sankoku tsūran zusetsu* 三国通覧図説 , in Yamamoto Yutaka, *Hayashi Shihei zenshū*, vol. 2.

Heiji monogatari 平治物語 . Nagazumi Yasuaki 永積安明 and Shimada Isao 島田勇雄 , eds., *Nihon kotenbungaku taikei, 31: Hōgen monogatari, Heiji monogatari* 日本古典文学大系 31 保元物語 平治物語 . Tokyo, Iwanami shoten, 1977.

Heike monogatari 平家物語 . Takagi Ichinosuke 高木市之助 , et al., ed., *Nihon kotenbungaku taikei, 32: Heike monogatari, 1* 平家物語 1. Tokyo, Iwanami shoten, 1959.

Honda Toshiaki 本多利明 . *Ezo shūi* 蝦夷拾遺 , in Honjō Eijirō 本左栄治郎 ed., *Kinsei shakai-keizaigakusetsu taikei: Honda Toshiaki shū* 近世社会経済学説大系 本多利明集 Tokyo, Seibundō shinkōsha 誠文堂新光社 , 1935.

Honsaroku 本佐録 . In Ishida Ichirō 石田一良 and Kanaya Osamu 金谷治 , eds., *Nihon shisō taikei, 28: Hayashi Razan, Fujiwara Seika* 林羅山 藤原惺窩 . Tokyo, Iwanami shoten, 1975.

Itō Jinsai 伊藤仁斎 . *Dōjimon* 童児問 , in Ienaga Saburō 家永三郎 , ed., *Nihon kotenbungaku taikei, 97: Kinsei shisōka bunshū* 近世思想家文集 . Tokyo, Iwanami shoten, 1966.

———. *Rongo kogi* 論語古義 , in Seki Giichirō 関儀一郎 ed., *Nihon meika shisho chūshaku zensho: Rongo bu, 1* 日本名家四書注釈全書論語部 上 . Tokyo, Tōyō tosho kankōkai 東洋図書刊行会 , 1922.

Kawaji Toshiakira 川路聖謨 . Diary entry dated 8/29/1849 in Nihon shiseki kyōkai 日本史籍協会 , ed., *Kawaji Toshiakira monjo* 川路聖謨文書 , vol. 5. Tokyo, Nihon shiseki kyōkai, 1934.

Kawashima Suminosuke 川島澄之助 . *Meiji yonen Kurume-han*

nanki 明治四年久留米藩難記 . Kurume, Kimbundō 金文堂 , 1911.

Kondō Jūzō 近藤重蔵 . *Hen'yō bunkai zukō* 辺要分界図考 , in Toyokawa Ryōhei 豊川良平 , ed., *Kondō Seisai zenshū* 近藤 正斎全集 , vol. 1. Tokyo, Kokushokankōkai 国書刊行会 , 1905.

Maeno Ryōtaku 前野良沢 . *Kanrei higen* 管蠡秘言 , in Numata Jirō 沼田次郎 , et al., ed., *Nihon shisō taikei, 64: Yōgaku, 1* 洋学 上 . Tokyo, Iwanami shoten, 1976.

Mito-han shiryō 水戸藩史料 , 5 vols. Tokyo, Yoshikawa kōbunkan, 1970.

Mogami Tokunai 最上徳内 . *Ezo sōshi* 蝦夷草紙, in Ōtomo Ki-saku 大友喜作 , ed., *Hokumon sōsho, 1: Akaezo fūsetsukō, Ezo shūi, Ezo sōshi* 北門叢書 1 赤蝦夷風説考 蝦夷拾遺 蝦夷草紙 . Tokyo, Kokushokankōkai reprint paperback edition, 1972.

Mōshi 孟子 . Kanaya Osamu 金谷治 , ed., *Shintei Chūgoku kotensen, 5: Mōshi* 新訂中国古典選 5 孟子 . Tokyo, Asahi shimbunsha, 1973.

Motoori Norinaga 本居宣長 . *Genji monogatari tama no ogushi* 源氏 物語玉の小櫛 , in *Motoori Norinaga zenshū* 本居宣長全 集 , vol. 4. Tokyo, Chikuma shobō 筑摩書房 , 1969.

———, and Ueda Akinari 上田秋成 . *Kakaiga* 呵刈葭 , in *Motoori Norinaga zenshū*, vol. 8. Tokyo, Chikuma shobō, 1972.

———. *Kuzubana* くず花 , in *Motoori Norinaga zenshū*, vol. 8.

———. "Naobi no mitama" 直毘霊 , *Kojiki den* 古事記伝 , in *Motoori Norinaga zenshū*, vol. 9.

———. *Tamakatsuma* 玉勝間 , in Yoshikawa Kōjirō, et al., ed., *Nihon shisō taikei, 40: Motoori Norinaga*. Tokyo, Iwanami shoten, 1978.

Nagasaki-shi shi 長崎市史 . Nagasaki shiyakusho 長崎市役所 , ed., *Nagasaki-shi shi: Tsūkō bōeki hen, Seiyō shokoku bu* 長崎市史 通交貿易篇 西洋諸国部 . Nagasaki, Nagasaki shiyakusho, 1935.

Nihon shoki 日本書紀 . In Sakamoto Tarō 坂本太郎 , et al., ed., *Nihon kotenbungaku taikei, 67: Nihon shoki, 1* 日本書紀 上 . To-kyo, Iwanami shoten, 1967.

Nishikawa Joken 西川如見 . *Nagasaki yawasō* 長崎夜話草 , in Iijima Tadao 飯島忠夫 and Nishikawa Tadayuki 西川忠幸 eds., *Chōnin bukuro, Hyakushō bukuro, Nagasaki yawasō* 町人囊 百姓囊長崎夜話草 . Tokyo, Iwanami bunko, 1942.

Ofuregaki Kampō shūsei 御触書寛保集成 , in Takayanagi Shinzō 高柳真三 and Ishii Ryōsuke 石井良助 , eds., *Ofuregaki Kam-pō shūsei*. Tokyo, Iwanami shoten, 1973.

Ogyū Sorai 荻生徂徠 . *Bendō* 弁道 , in Yoshikawa Kōjirō, et al., ed., *Nihon shisō taikei, 36: Ogyū Sorai*. Tokyo, Iwanami shoten, 1973.

———. *Gakusoku* 学則 , in Yoshikawa Kōjirō, et al., ed., *Nihon shisō taikei, 36: Ogyū Sorai*.

317

Ōhara Sakingo 大原左金吾 . *Chihoku gūdan* 地北寫談 , in Ōtomo Kisaku, ed., *Hokumon sōsho, 3: Chihoku gūdan, Hokuchi kigen, Ezo sōshi kōhen* 北門叢書 3 地北寫談 北地危言 蝦夷草紙後編 . Tokyo, Kokushokankōkai, 1972.

Ōtsuki Gentaku 大槻玄沢 . *Hoei mondō* 捕影問答 in Numata Jirō, et al., *Nihon shisō taikei, 64: Yōgaku, 1.* Tokyo, Iwanami shoten, 1976.

———. *Hoppen tanji* 北辺探事 , in Ōtomo Kisaku, ed., *Hokumon sōsho, 6: Hokusa ibun, Hoppen tanji* 北門叢書 6 北槎異聞 北辺探事 . Tokyo, Kokushokankōkai, 1972.

———. *Kankai ibun* 環海異聞 , in Ōtomo Kisaku, ed., *Hokumon sōsho, 4: Kankai ibun* 北門叢書 4 環海異聞 . Tokyo, Kokushokankōkai 1972.

———. *Rangaku kaitei* 蘭学階梯 , in Numata Jirō, et al., ed., *Nihon shisō taikei, 64: Yōgaku, 1.*

Rongo 論語 . Yoshikawa Kōjirō, ed. *Shintei Chūgoku kotensen, 2, Rongo,* 2 vols. Tokyo: Asahi Shimbunsha, 1969.

Saitō Chikudō 斎藤竹堂 . *Ahen shimatsu* 鴉片始末 , in Sumida Seiichi 住田正一 , ed., *Nihon kaibō shiryōsōsho* 日本海防史料叢書 , vol. 3. Tokyo, Ganshōdō 巌松堂 , 1932.

Satō Genrokurō 佐藤玄六郎 . *Ezo shūi* 蝦夷拾遺 , in Ōtomo Kisaku, *Hokumon sōsho, 1: Akaezo fusetsukō, Ezo shūi, Ezo sōshi.* Tokyo, Kokushokankōkai 1972.

Satō Shin'en 佐藤信渕 . *Bōkaisaku* 防海策 , in Takimoto Seiichi 滝本誠一 , ed., *Satō Shin'en kagaku zenshū* 佐藤信渕家学全集 , vol. 3. Tokyo, Iwanami shoten, 1927.

Shiba Kōkan 司馬江漢 . *Shumparō hikki* 春波楼筆記 , in Takimoto Seiichi, ed., *Nihon keizai taiten* 日本経済大典 , vol. 20. Tokyo, Keimeisha 啓明社 , 1929.

Shiki 史記 . Noguchi Sadao 野口定男 , ed. *Chūgoku kotenbungaku taikei, 11: Shiki.* Tokyo, Heibonsha, 1976.

Shisho shitchū 四書集注 . Suzuki Yoshijirō 鈴木由次郎 ed., *Shushigaku taikei, 7: Shisho shitchū* 朱子学大系 7 四書集注 Tokyo, Meitoku shuppan 明徳出版 , 1974.

Shōsho 尚書 . Ikeda Suetoshi 池田末利 ed. *Zenshaku kambun taikei, 11: Shōsho.* Tokyo, Shūeisha, 1976.

Son shi 孫子 . Kanaya Osamu, ed., *Son shi* 孫子 . Tokyo, Iwanami bunko, 1963.

Sugita Gempaku 杉田玄白 . *Kaitai shinsho* 解体新書 in Hirose Hideo 広瀬秀雄 , et al., ed., *Nihon shisō taikei, 65: Yōgaku, 2* 洋学下 . Tokyo, Iwanami shoten, 1972.

———. *Keiei yawa* 形影夜話 , in Numata Jirō, et al., ed., *Nihon shisō taikei, 64: Yōgaku, 1.*

———. *Kyōi no gen* 狂医の言 , in Numata Jirō, et al., ed., *Nihon shisō taikei, 64: Yōgaku, 1.*

————. *Nochimigusa* 後見草 , in Ichijima Kenkichi 市島謙吉 , ed., *Enseki jisshu* 燕石十種 . Tokyo, n.p., 1907.

————. *Rangaku kotohajime* 蘭東事始 , in Odaka Toshio 小高敏郎 and Matsumura Akira 松村明 , eds., *Nihon kotenbungaku taikei, 95: Taionki, Oritaku shibanoki, Rantō kotohajime* 戴恩記 折たく柴の記 蘭学事始 . Tokyo, Iwanami shoten, 1964.

————. *Yasō dokugo* 野叟独語 , in Numata Jirō, et al., ed., *Nihon shisō taikei, 64: Yōgaku, 1.*

Takahashi Kageyasu 高橋景保 . "Kempakusho" 建白書 , in Uehara Hisashi 上原久 , *Takahashi Kageyasu no kenkyū* 高橋景保 の研究 . Tokyo, Kōdansha, 1977.

Takano Chōei 高野長英 . *Bojutsu yume monogatari* 戊戌夢物語 , in Satō Shōsuke 佐藤昌介 , et al., ed., *Nihon shisō taikei, 55: Watanabe Kazan, Takano Chōei, Sakuma Shōzan, Yokoi Shōnan, Hashimoto Sanai* 渡辺崋山 高野長英 佐久間象山 横井小楠 橋本左内 . Tokyo, Iwanami shoten, 1971.

Tokugawa kinreikō 徳川禁令考 . Kikuchi Shunsuke 菊池駿助 , ed., *Tokugawa kinreikō* 徳川禁令考 . Tokyo, Yoshikawa kōbunkan, 1932.

Tsūkō ichiran 通交一覧 . Hayakawa Junzaburō 早川純三郎 , ed., *Tsūkō ichiran* 通交一覧 , 8 vols. Tokyo, Kokushokankōkai, 1913.

Watanabe Kazan 渡辺崋山 . *Shinkiron* 慎機論 , in Satō Shōsuke, et al., ed., *Nihon shisō taikei, 55: Watanabe Kazan, Takano Chōei, Sakuma Shōzan, Yokoi Shōnan, Hashimoto Sanai.* Tokyo, Iwanami shoten, 1971.

Yamaga Sokō 山鹿素行 . *Yamaga gorui* 山鹿語類 , in Hirose Yutaka 広瀬豊 ed., *Yamaga Sokō zenshū* 山鹿素行全集 , vol. 5. Tokyo, Iwanami shoten, 1941.

Yamazaki Ansai 山崎闇斎 . *Hekii* 闢異 , in Nishida Ta'ichirō 西田太一郎 , ed., *Nihon no shisō, 17* 日本の思想 . 17. Tokyo, Chikuma shobō, 1970.

Yokoi Shōnan 横井小楠 . "Tachibana Iki e" 立花壹岐 (dated 11/3/1855), in Yamazaki Masatada 山崎正董 , ed., *Yokoi Shōnan ikō* 横井小楠遺稿 . Tokyo, Nisshin shoin 日新書院 , 1943.

Yoshida Shōin 吉田松陰 . Yamaguchi-ken kyōikukai 山口県教育会 ed., *Yoshida Shōin zenshū* 吉田松陰全集 , 12 vols. Tokyo, Iwanami shoten, 1939.

SECONDARY SOURCES

Ayusawa Shintarō 鮎沢信太郎 . "Kinsei Nihon ni okeru chikyūsetsu chidōsetsu no tenkai" 近世日本における地球説地動説の 展開 , in *Nihon rekishi* 日本歴史 71 (1954).

Beasley, W. G. *Select Documents in Japanese Foreign Policy, 1853–1868.* London, Oxford University Press, 1955.

Bitō Masahide 尾藤正英 . "Kokkashugi no sokei toshite no Sorai" 国家主義の祖型としての徂徠 , in Bitō, ed., *Nihon no meicho, 16: Ogyū Sorai* 日本の名著 16 荻生徂徠 . Tokyo, Chūōkōronsha, 1974.

———. "Mitogaku no hatten to sonnō jōi ron" 水戸学の発展と 尊王攘夷論 , in Itō Tasaburō 伊東多三郎 ed., *Mito-shi shi* 水戸市史 . Mito, Mito-shi yakusho 水戸市役所 , 1976.

———. "Mitogaku no tokushitsu" 水戸学の特質 , in Imai Usaburō, et al., ed., *Nihon shishō taikei, 53: Mitogaku.* Tokyo, Iwanami shoten, 1973.

———. "Ogyū Sorai no shisō" 荻生徂徠の思想 , in *Tōhōgaku* 東方学 58 (1979):154–168.

———. "Rekishi shisō" 歴史思想 , in Bitō, ed., *Chūgoku bunka sōsho, 10: Nihon bunka to Chūgoku* 中国文化叢書 10 日本文化と中国 . Tokyo, Taishūkan, 1968.

———. "Sonnō jōi shisō" 尊王攘夷思想 , in *Iwanami kōza Nihon rekishi, 13: Kinsei, 5* 岩波講座日本歴史 13 近世 5. Tokyo, Iwanami shoten, 1977.

———. "Sonnō jōi shisō no genkei: Motoori Norinaga no baai" 尊王攘夷思想の原型 本居宣長の場合 , in *Nihon shisōshi* 13 (1980):100–114.

Butterfield, Herbert. *The Whig Interpretation of History.* New York, Norton, 1965.

Cohen, Paul A. *Between Tradition and Modernity: Wang Tao and Reform in Late Ch'ing China.* Cambridge, Harvard University Press, 1974.

———. *China and Christianity: The Missionary Movement and the Growth of Chinese Antiforeignism, 1860–1870.* Cambridge, Harvard University Press, 1963.

Craig, Albert M. "Science and Confucianism in Tokugawa Japan," in Marius B. Jansen, ed., *Changing Attitudes Toward Modernization.* Princeton, Princeton University Press, 1972.

Ebisawa Arimichi 海老沢有道 . *Nambangakutō no kenkyū* 南蛮学統の研究 . Tokyo, Sōbunsha 創文社 , 1958.

Elison, George. *Deus Destroyed: The Image of Christianity in Early Modern Japan.* Cambridge, Harvard University Press, 1973.

Ellwood, Robert S. *The Feast of Kingship.* Tokyo, Sophia University Press, 1973.

Fairbank, John, K., ed., *The Cambridge History of China, Volume 10: Late Ch'ing 1800–1911, Part 1.* Cambridge, England, Cambridge University Press, 1978.

———, and Liu Kwang-ching, eds., *The Cambridge History of China,*

Volume 13: Late Ch'ing 1800–1911, Part 2. Cambridge, England, Cambridge University Press, 1980.

————. *The Chinese World Order.* Cambridge, Harvard University Press paperback edition, 1974.

Fingarette, Herbert. *Confucius—The Secular as Sacred.* New York, Harper and Row Torchbook edition, 1972.

French, Calvin. *Shiba Kōkan: Artist, Innovator, and Pioneer in the Westernization of Japan.* New York, Weatherhill, 1974.

Fukui Fumimasa　福井文正　. "Seiyō bunken ni okeru 'ki' no yakugo" 西洋文献における気の訳語　, in Onozawa Seiichi 小野沢 誠一, et al., ed., *Ki no shisō: Chūgoku ni okeru shizenkan to ningenkan no tenkai*　気の思想中国における自然観と人間 観の展開　. Tokyo, Tokyo University Press, 1978.

Gotō Motomi and Yamanoi Yū 後藤基巳・山井湧　, ed. *Chūgoku kotenbungaku taikei, 57: Mimmatsu-Shinsho seiji hyōron shū* 中国 古典文学大系　57：　明末清初政治評論集　　 Tokyo, Heibonsha 平凡社 , 1971.

Griffith, Samuel B., tr. *Sun Tzu: The Art of War.* London, Oxford University Press, 1963.

Haga Tōru 芳賀徹　. "Jūkyūseiki Nihon no chiteki senshitachi" 十九世紀日本の知的戦士達　, in Haga, ed., *Nihon no meicho, 22: Sugita Gempaku, Hiraga Gennai, Shiba Kōkan* 日本の名著　22： 杉田玄白平賀源内司馬江漢　　 Tokyo, Chūōkoronsha, 1971.

Hani Gorō 羽仁五郎　. *Meiji ishinshi kenkyū* 明治維新史研 究.Tokyo, Iwanami shoten, 1956.

Harootunian, Harry D. "The Functions of China in Tokugawa Thought," in Iriye, Akira, ed., *The Chinese and the Japanese.* Princeton, Princeton University Press, 1980.

————. *Toward Restoration.* Berkeley, University of California Press, 1970.

Hashikawa Bunzō 橋川文二　. *Jidai to yoken* 時代と予見　. Tokyo, Dentō to gendai sha 伝統と現代社 , 1975.

————. "Mitogaku no genryū to seikaku" 水戸学の源流と性格 in Hashikawa, ed., *Nihon no meicho, 29: Fujita Tōko* 日本の名 著 29 藤田東湖　. Tokyo, Chūōkoronsha, 1974.

Iihara Toshikuni 日原利国　. *Shunju kuyōden no kenkyū* 春秋公羊 伝の研究　. Tokyo, Sōbunsha, 1972.

Hōjō Shigenao 北条重直　. *Mitogaku to ishin no fūun* 水戸学と 維新の風運 . Tokyo and Osaka, Shūbunkan 修文館 , 1932.

Holtom, D. C. *The Japanese Enthronement Ceremonies.* Tokyo, Sophia University Press, 1972.

Honjō Eijirō 本庄栄次郎　, ed. "Honda Toshiaki shū kaidai" 本多 利明集解題　, in *Kinsei shakai keizai gakusetsu taikei: Honda Toshiaki shū* 近世社会経済学説大系本多利明集 Tokyo, Seibundō shinkōsha 誠文堂新光社 ,1939.

Bibliography

Ichiko Chūzō　市古宙三　. *Sekai no rekishi, 21: Chūgoku no kakumei*
世界の歴史　21　中国の革命　. Tokyo, Kōdansha, 1978.

Imai Usaburō　今井宇三郎　. "Aizawa Seishisai ni okeru jukyō keiden
no kenkyū"　会沢正志斎における儒教経伝の研究　　,
in Yamagishi Tokubei　山岸德平　ed., *Nihon kambungakushi ronkō*
日本漢文学史論考　. Tokyo, Iwanami shoten, 1974.

———. "Mitogaku ni okeru jukyō no juyō"　水戸学における儒教
の受容　, in Imai, et al., ed., *Nihon shisō taikei, 53: Mitogaku*. Tokyo, Iwanami shoten, 1973.

Inobe Shigeo 井野辺茂雄　. *Shintei ishin zenshi no kenkyū* 新訂
維新前史の研究. Tokyo, Chūbunkan shoten　中文館書店
1937.

Irokawa Daikichi　色川大吉　. *Nihon no rekishi, 21: Kindai kokka no
shuppatsu* 近代国家の出発　　. Tokyo, Chūōkoronsha, 1966.

Itō Tasaburō　伊東多三郎　. *Kinseishi no kenkyū, 2: Kokugaku to
Yōgaku*　近世の研究 2　国学と洋学. Tokyo, Yoshikawa kōbunkan, 1982.

———, ed. *Mito-shi shi*　水戸市史　. Mito, Mito shiyakusho, 1969.

Iwai Tadakuma　岩井忠熊　. *Meiji kokkashugi shisōshi kenkyū*
明治国家主義思想史研究. Tokyo, Aoki shoten 青木書
店, 1972.

Iwao Seiichi　岩生成一　. *Nihon no rekishi, 14: Sakoku* 日本の歴史
14 鎖国. Tokyo, Chūōkoronsha, 1966.

Kanazashi Shōzō　金指正三　. *Kinsei kainan kyūjo seido no kenkyū*
近世海難救助制度の研究　. Tokyo, Yoshikawa kō-
bunkan, 1968.

Keene, Donald. *The Japanese Discovery of Europe, 1720–1830*. Palo Alto,
Stanford University Press paperback edition, 1969.

Kikuchi Kenjirō　菊池謙二郎　. *Mitogaku ronsū* 水戸学論藪
Tokyo, Seibundo shinkōsha　誠文堂新光社, 1934.

Koschmann, J. Victor. "Discourse in Action: Representational Politics in
Mito in the Late Tokugawa Period." Ph.D. dissertation, University of
Chicago, 1980.

Lau, D. C., tr. *Confucius: The Analects*. Middlesex, England, Penguin,
1979.

———, tr. *Mencius*. Middlesex, England, Penguin, 1970.

Lensen, George Alexander. *The Russian Push Toward Japan: Russo-Japanese Relations, 1697–1875*. Princeton, Princeton University Press, 1959.

Levenson, Joseph. *Confucian China and Its Modern Fate*. Berkeley, University of California Press, 1969.

Maruyama Masao. "Ansaigaku to Ansaigakuha" 闇斎学と闇斎学
派　, in Nishi Junzo, et al., ed., *Nihon shisō taikei, 31: Yamazaki Ansai gakuha* 山崎闇斎学派　. Tokyo, Iwanami shoten, 1980.

———. "Kindai Nihon shisōshi ni okeru kokka risei no mondai" 近代

日本思想史における国家理性の問題 , in *Tembō* 展望 , 1949, pp. 4-15.

———. *Nihon no shisō* 日本の思想 . Tokyo, Iwanami shoten, 1961.

———. *Studies in the Intellectual History of Tokugawa Japan*, Mikiso Hane, trans. Tokyo, University of Tokyo Press, 1974.

Masuda Wataru 増田渉 . *Seigaku tōzen to Chūgoku jijō* 西学東漸 と中国事情 . Tokyo, Iwanami shoten, 1979.

Matsumoto Sannosuke 松本三之助 . "Kinsei ni okeru rekishi jojutsu to sono shisō" 近世における歴史叙述とその思想 , in Matsumoto and Ogura Yoshihiko 小倉芳彦 , eds., *Nihon shisō taikei, 48: Kinsei shironshū* 近世史論集 . Tokyo, Iwanami shoten, 1974.

———. "Sonjō undō ni okeru kindaiteki seiji ishiki no keisei" 尊攘 運動における近代的政治意識の形成 , in Sakata Yoshio 坂田吉雄 , ed., *Meiji ishinshi no mondaiten* 明治維新史 の問題点 . Tokyo, Miraisha 未来社 , 1962.

———. *Tennōseikokka to seiji shisō* 天皇制国家と政治思想 . Tokyo, Miraisha, 1969.

Miyazaki Michio 宮崎道生 . *Arai Hakuseki no yōgaku to kaigai chishiki* 新井白石の洋学と海外知識 . Tokyo, Yoshikawa kōbunkan, 1973.

Muraoka Tsunetsugu 村岡典嗣 . *Nihon shisōshi kenkyū* 日本思想. 史研究 . Tokyo, Iwanami shoten, 1930.

Nagakubo Mitsuaki 長久保光明 . "Shinron no chirigakuteki kōsatsu" 「新論」の地理学的考察 , *Mito shigaku* 水戸史学 6 (March 1977):46-51.

Nakai, Kate Wildman. "The Naturalization of Confucianism in Tokugawa Japan: The Problem of Sinocentrism," *Harvard Journal of Asiatic Studies* 40 (June 1980):157-199.

Nakayama Shigeru. *A History of Japanese Astronomy.* Cambridge, Harvard University Press, 1969.

Nishimura Fuminori 西村文則 . *Aizawa Hakumin* 会沢伯民 . Tokyo, Shōkasha 章葦社 , 1936.

Numata Jirō 沼田次郎 . *Bakumatsu yōgakushi* 幕末洋学史 Tokyo, Tōkō shoin 刀江書院 , 1951.

———. *Nihon rekishi bunko, 13: Kaihoku zengo* 日本歴史文庫 13 開国前後 . Tokyo, Kōdansha, 1975.

———. *Nihon zenshi, 7: Kinsei, 2* 日本全史 7 近世 2. Tokyo, University of Tokyo Press, 1959.

———. "Sakokuka no Nihon to Seiyō" 鎖国下の日本と西洋 in Numata, ed., *Tōzai bummeishi no kōryū, 6: Nihon to Seiyō* 東西 文明史の交流 6 日本と西洋 . Tokyo, Heibonsha, 1971.

———. "Shiba Kōkan to Rangaku" 司馬江漢と蘭学 , in Numata, et al., ed., *Nihon shisō taikei, 64: Yōgaku, 1.* Tokyo, Iwanami shoten, 1976.

———. *Yōgaku denrai no rekishi* 洋学伝来の歴史 . Tokyo, Sōbunsha, 1960.

Ōba Osamu 大庭脩 . *Edo jidai ni okeru tōsen mochiwatarisho no kenkyū* 江戸時代における唐船持渡書の研究 . Osaka-fu, Kansai 関西 University Press, 1967.

Ogura Yoshihiko 小倉芳彦 . *Chūgoku kodai seiji shisō no kenkyū* 中国古代政治思想の研究 . Tokyo, Aoki shoten, 1979.

Ono Shinji 小野信二 . "Bakufu to Tennō" 幕府と天皇 in *Iwanami kōza Nihon rekishi, 10: Kinsei, 2* 岩波講座日本歴史 10 近世 2. Tokyo, Iwanami shoten, 1962.

Ōtomo Kisaku 大友喜作 . "Kaisetsu" 解説 in Ōtomo, ed., *Hokumon sōsho, 1: Akaezo fūsetsukō, Ezo shūi, Ezo sōshi.* Tokyo, Kokushokankōkai, 1972.

———. "Kaisetsu," in Ōtomo, ed., *Hokumon sōsho, 3: Chihoku gūdan, Hokuchi Kigen, Ezo sōshi kōhen.* Tokyo, Kokushokankōkai, 1972.

Rossabi, Morris. *China Among Equals.* Berkeley, University of California Press, 1983.

Sansom, G. B. *The Western World and Japan.* Tokyo, Tuttle, 1977.

Sato Seizaburō 佐藤誠三郎 . "Seiyō no shōgeki e no taiō" 西洋の衝撃への対応 , in Shinohara Hajime 篠原一 and Mitani Ta'ichirō 三谷太一郎 , ed., *Kindai Nihon no seiji shidō* 近代日本の政治指導 . Tokyo, University of Tokyo Press, 1965.

Satō Shōsuke 佐藤昌介 . *Yōgakushi kenkyū josetsu* 洋学史研究序説 . Tokyo, Iwanami shoten, 1964.

———. *Yōgakushi no kenkyū* 洋学史の研究 . Tokyo, Chūōkōronsha, 1980.

Schwartz, Benjamin. *In Search of Wealth and Power: Yen Fu and the West.* New York, Harper and Row Torchbook edition, 1977.

Seya Yoshihiko 瀬谷義彦 . *Aizawa Seishisai* 会沢正志斎 . Tokyo, Bunkyō shoin 文教書院 , 1942.

Shibusawa Eiichi 渋沢栄一 . *Tokugawa Yoshinobu-kō den* 徳川慶喜公伝 , 4 vols. Tokyo, Heibonsha Tōyō bunko edition, 1967–68.

Shimizu Shin 清水伸 . *Teikoku kempō seitei kaigi* 帝国憲法制定会議. Tokyo, Iwanami shoten, 1940.

Shinobu Seizaburō 信夫清三郎 . *Shōzan to Shōin: Kaikoku to jōi no ronri* 象山と松陰開国と攘夷の論理 . Tokyo, Kawade shobō shinsha 河出書房新社 , 1975.

Tabohashi Kiyoshi 田保橋潔 . *Zōtei kindai Nihon gaikoku kankeishi* 増訂近代日本外国関係史 . Tokyo, Tōkō shoin 刀江書院 , 1938.

Takahashi Shin'ichi 高橋碩一 . *Yōgaku shisōshi ron* 洋学思想史論 . Tokyo, Iwanami shoten, 1972.

Tasaki Tetsurō 田崎哲郎 . "Yōgakuron saikōsei shiron 洋学論再構成試論, *Shisō* 思想 , 665 (November, 1979):48–72.

Tashiro Kazui 田代和生 . *Kinsei Nitchō tsūkō bōekishi no kenkyū* 近世日朝通交貿易史の研究 . Tokyo, Sōbunsha, 1981.

Teng, Ssu-yu and Fairbank, John K. *China's Response to the West: A Documentary Survey, 1839–1923*. New York, Antheneum, 1963.

Titus, David Anson. *Palace and Politics in Prewar Japan*. New York, Columbia University Press, 1974.

Toby, Ronald. *State and Diplomacy in Early Modern Japan*. Princeton, Princeton University Press, 1984.

Tokutomi Iichirō 德富猪一郎 . *Kinsei Nihon kokuminshi, 25: Bakufu bunkai sekkin jidai* 近世日本国民史 25 幕府分解接近時代 . Tokyo, Meiji shoin, 1936.

———. *Kinsei Nihon kokuminshi, 27: Bunsei-Tempō jidai* 近世日本国民史 27 文政天保時代 . Tokyo, Meiji shoin, 1935.

Totman, Conrad. "From 'Sakoku' to 'kaikoku'," in *Monumenta Nipponica* 35.1 (Spring 1980):1–19.

Tōyama Shigeki 遠山茂樹 . *Meiji ishin* 明治維新 . Tokyo, Iwanami shoten, 1975.

———. *Meiji ishin to gendai* 明治維新と現代 . Tokyo, Iwanami shoten shinsho edition, 1968.

———. "Mitogaku no seikaku" 水戸学の性格 in Nakamura Kōya 中村孝也 , ed., *Seikatsu to shisō* 生活と思想. Tokyo, Shōgakkan 小学館 , 1944.

Tsuda Sōkichi 津田左右吉 . *Bungaku ni arawaretaru waga kokumin shisō no kenkyū* 文学に現はれたる我国民思想の研究, 8 vols. Tokyo, Iwanami bunko edition, 1977–78.

———. "Ōdō seiji shisō" 王道政治思想 , in *Tsuda Sōkichi zenshū* 津田左右吉全集 , vol. 18. Tokyo, Iwanami shoten, 1965.

Tsukamoto Manabu 塚本学 . "Edo jidai ni okeru 'i' kannen ni tsuite" 江戸時代における「夷」観念について , *Nihon rekishi* 371 (April 1979):1–18.

Ueda Jō 上田穰 . "Shinron 'Keisei-hen' ni mirareru sekai chiri chishiki" 『新論』形勢篇にみられる世界地理知識 , in Arisaka Takamichi 有阪隆道 , ed., *Nihon yōgakushi no kenkyū* 日本洋学史の研究 . Osaka, Sōgensha 創元社 , 1974.

Uehara Hisashi 上原久 . *Takahashi kageyasu no kenkyū* 高橋景保の研究 . Tokyo, Kōdansha, 1977.

Uete Michiari 植手通有 . *Nihon kindai shisō no keisei* 日本近代思想の形成 . Tokyo, Iwanami shoten, 1974.

Wakabayashi, Bob Tadashi, "Aizawa Seishisai's *Shinron* and Western Learning." Ph.D. dissertation, Princeton University, 1982.

Waley, Arthur, tr. *The Analects of Confucius*. New York, Vintage paperback edition, no date.

Wang Gungwu. "Early Ming Relations with Southeast Asia: A Background

Essay," in John K. Fairbank, ed., *The Chinese World Order*. Cambridge, Harvard University Press, 1974.

Watanabe Hiroshi 渡辺浩 . "'Michi' to 'Miyabi'" 「道」と「雅び」, parts 4, 5; in *Kokka gakkai zasshi* 国家学会雑誌 , 88.5-6 (May 1975):1-72.

Watson, Burton, tr. *Records of the Historian: Chapters from the* Shih chi *of Ssu-ma Ch'ien*. New York, Columbia University Press, 1969.

Yang, Lien-sheng. "Historical Notes on the Chinese World Order," in John K. Fairbank, ed., *The Chinese World Order*. Cambridge, Harvard University Press, 1974.

Yasumaru Yoshio 安丸良夫 . *Kamigami no Meiji ishin* 神々の明治維新. Tokyo, Iwanami shoten shinsho edition, 1979.

———. *Nihon nashonarizumu no zenya* 日本ナショナリズムの前夜 . Tokyo, Asahi shimbunsha, 1977.

Yoshida Toshizumi 吉田俊純 . "Kōki Mitogaku to kiheitai shotai" 後期水戸学と奇兵隊諸隊 , in *Ibaraki-ken rekishikampō* 茨城県歴史館報 2 (February 1975):89-102.

Glossary of Japanese and Chinese Terms

Abe Masahiro 阿部正弘
Agata nushi 県主
Ahen shimatsu 鴉片始末
Aizawa Kyōkei 会沢恭敬
Aizawa Seishisai 会沢正志斎
Aizawa Sōbei 会沢総兵衛
Ama no iwakusubune
　天磐樟船
Amaterasu 天照
An'i mondō 諳夷問答
Asami Keisai 浅見絅斎
Arai Hakuseki 新井白石
Ashikaga Yoshimitsu
　足利義満

Bankoku kōkai hyōkizu
　万国航海慓旗図
Bemmō 弁妄
bumbutsu 文物
bun 分
bunka 文華

Chao 趙
Chi Chi-kuang 戚継光
Chi hsiao hsin shu 紀効新書
Ch'i 斉
ch'i 気
chien ai 兼愛
Chihoku gūdan 地北寓談
chikyū no zu 地球の図
Ch'in 秦

Ch'ing 清
Chishima ibun 千島異聞
chōbu 町歩
Chou 周
Chu Hsi 朱熹
chu Hsia 諸夏
Ch'u 楚
ch'üan 権
ch'üan tao 権道
Chūgoku 中国
Chūka 中華
chūkō 中興
chün tzu 君子
Chung-shan 中山

Daijō 大嘗
Dazai Shundai 太宰春台
Dejima 出島
daimyō yaku 大名役
dochaku 土着

Engi shiki 延喜式
Etorofu 月多頼 (択捉島)
Ezo 蝦夷
Ezo sōshi 蝦夷草紙

Fuifui no oshie 回々の教
Fujita Tōko 藤田東湖
Fujita Yūkoku 藤田幽谷
Fuju fuse 不受不施

gaichi 外地
gaikan 外患
Genji monogatari 源氏物語
gokuraku 極楽
goseidō 御政道
gūgen 寓言
gumin 愚民

Habuto Seiyō 羽太正養
Han 漢
Han 韓
Hayashi Shihei 林子平
heihaku 幣帛
heinō bunri 兵農分離
hō 法
Hoei mondō 捕影問答
hōken 封建
hōkoku no kokoro 報国の心
hōkyō 邦教
Honda Toshiaki 本多利明
honji suijaku 本地垂迹
Honsaroku 本佐録
honzengaku 本然学
Hsia 夏
hsiao jen 小人
hyōji 表彰
hyōryū 漂流

ichibun no tenka 一分の天下
Igirisu 嘆咭唎
Ikkō 一向
ikkun bammin 一君万民
ikoku 異国
Itō Jinsai 伊藤仁斎

jasetsu 邪説
jigoku 地獄

jimbun 人文
Jimmu Tennō 神武天皇
jinsei 仁政
jinwa 人和
jisei no hen 時勢の変
jitō 地頭
jōi 攘夷
jōsei 常勢
jutsu 術

ka-i 華夷
kaibō 海防
kaigai shokoku 海外諸国
kaigai shotō 海外諸島
kaikoku 開国
Kaitai shinsho 解体新書
kaku 格
Kamoi dono 神殿
kami 神
kampaku 関白
Kando 漢土
Kan'ei 寛永
Kanrei higen 管蠡秘言
kansai 漢才
Karafuto 唐太（樺太）
Karahito 唐人
Karakuni 漢国
kasetsu 仮説
Katsuragawa Hoshū 桂川甫周
Kawaji Toshiakira 川路聖謨
Kawashima Suminosuke
　川島澄之助
Keiei yawa 形影夜話
kijiku 機軸
Kikōben 豈好弁
kikwa 帰化
Kimon 崎門

Kimura Ken 木村謙

kinchū narabi ni kuge sho-
　hatto 禁中並公家諸法度

kōgi 公議

Kojiki 古事記

Kōken Tennō 孝謙天皇

kokka 国家

kokkyō 国敎

koku 石

Kokugaku 国学

Kokugakusha 国学者

kokumin 国民

kokutai 国体

Kondō Jūzō 近藤重蔵

Konishi Yukinaga 小西行長

kōsei riyō seitoku 厚生利用正德

Koyama Zenkichi 古山善吉

Kuan Chung 管仲

kuiki 区域

Kumazeki (Kumaishi) 熊石

Kumaso 熊襲

K'ung-ge erh 控噶爾

kuni 国

Kuni no miyatsuko 国造

kuni no taimen 国の体面

Kudō Heisuke 工藤平助

kūshin 空心

kwa 化

kyōkwa 敎化

kyōhō 敎法

Kyōi no gen 狂医の言

kyūri 窮理

Li Ching 李靖

Li Ma-tou 利瑪竇

Maeno Ryōtaku 前野良沢

Mamiya Rinzō 間宮林蔵

Man'yōshū 万葉集

Matsudaira Sadanobu
　松平定信

mikuni 御国

Minhito 明人

Mito 水戸

Mitogaku 水戸学

miyosashi (go-inin) 御奉仕

Mogami Tokunai 最上德内

Morokoshi 唐

Motoori Norinaga 本居宣長

myōkei 妙契

naichi 内地

naiyū 内憂

Nakai Chikuzan 中井竹山

Nakai Riken 中井履軒

Nakajima Hirotari 中島広足

Nihonkoku 日本国

Nihon shoki 日本書紀

Niiname 新嘗

Ninigi 瓊々杵

Nintoku Tennō 仁德天皇

Nokkamapu 訥加桝

Ōhara Sakingo 大原左金吾

Ōjin Tennō 応神天皇

osadame 御定

Ōtomo Sōrin 大友宗麟

Ōtsuki Gentaku 大槻玄沢

pa 霸

Pi-hsieh chi-shih 辟邪紀実（實）

Rangaku 蘭学

Rangaku kotohajime 蘭学事始

Rangakusha 蘭学者
reigaku no myōyō 礼楽の妙用
ri 理
ryojō 虜情
Ryō no gige 令義解
Ryūshi shinron 柳子新論
ryūzoku 流賊

Saitō Chikudō 斎藤竹堂
sakoku 鎖国
sankin kōtai 参勤交代
sei 勢
Seiken igen 靖献遺言
Seiyō kibun 西洋記聞
sekkan 摂関
sennō 先王
sesshō 摂政
Shang 商
shen ch'i 神気
shen tao 神道
Shiba Kōkan 司馬江漢
Shimoshiri 失毋失利
shimpai 信牌
Shina 支那
Shinkokinshū 新古今集
Shinron 新論
shinsei 神聖
shinshi jikken 親試実験
Shinshū 神州
Shintan 震旦
shishi 志士
shitsu 質
shōen 荘園
Shōkōkan 彰考館
Shōmu Tennō 聖武天皇
Shu 蜀
shugo 守護

Shun 舜
Soga no Umako 蘇我馬子
sonnō 尊王
Sugita Gempaku 杉田玄白
Suiko hikki 酔古筆記
Sujin Tennō 崇神天皇
sumpan 寸板
Sun Tzu 孫子
Sung 宋
Sung Kao 嵩高

Tachihara Suiken 立原翠軒
tai/t'i 体
Takahashi Kageyasu 高橋景保
Takano Chōei 高野長英
Tamakatsuma 玉勝間
Tanuma Okitsugu 田沼意次
teikoku 帝国
teiō 帝王
Tempō 天保
tenchi 天地
Tenjiku 天竺
Tenji Tennō 天智天皇
tenka 天下
tenka no aku wa hitotsu nari
　天下の悪は一つ也
tenso 天祖
Tenshukyō 天主教
t'i-yung 体用
Toba Yoshiaki 鳥羽義著
tochi 土地
Toda Tadaakira 戸田忠敞
Toi 刀伊
Tokugawa Nariaki 徳川斉昭
Tokugawa Narinobu 徳川斉脩
tokuritsu 特立
Tomo no miyatsuko 伴造

Tori no iwakusubune
鳥磐橡樟船
Tōyō 東洋

uchiharai 打払
Ueda Akinari 上田秋成
uji 氏
Uruppu 獵虎

waga kuni 我国
Wakō 倭寇
Wakon 和魂
Watanabe Kazan 渡辺崋山
Wei 魏・衛

Yamagata Bantō 山片蟠桃

Yamagata Daini 山県大弐
Yamagata Taika 山県太華
Yamaga Sokō 山鹿素行
Yao 堯
Yasō dokugo 野叟独言
Yen 燕
yin-yang 陰陽
Yokoi Shōnan 横井小楠
Yoshio Chūjirō 吉雄忠次郎
yōsai 洋才
Yuan 元
yuan ch'i 元気

Zokusan henji no sakai
粟散辺地の境

Index

Abe Masahiro, x, 135
Abe no Hirafu, 77
Ability: need to recognize, 217-218, 244
Agriculture: regulation of, 216-217, 240; need to increase, 263. *See also* Rice
Aizawa Kyōkei (father of Seishisai), xi
Aizawa Seishisai, ix, xi, 3; and *jōi,* 3, 54-55, 86 (*see also Jōi*); on Western threat, 6, 15-16, 89-90, 131-132, 133, 141-142, 149-150, 168, 169-170, 180, 198-199; on Japanese superiority, 8-9, 98, 140-141; xenophobia of, 10-11, 51, 61, 70, 77, 98; Westerners denigrated by, xiii-xiv, 10, 21, 109, 141; and state religion, 13-15, 71-72, 133, 142; Western Learning of, 14, 72-73, 77, 85-86, 97, 98, 113, 114, 115, 116, 132, 133, 140; as understanding West, 14, 72, 107, 141-142; and *sakoku,* 16, 59 (*see also* National isolation or seclusion); and *kokutai,* 16, 69, 124-125, 145 (*see also Kokutai*); and Sinocentric world view, 42, 52, 56, 138, 140, 290 n.122; and Maeno Ryōtaku, 49, 51; on civilized/barbarian, 55-56; and Christianity, 56, 69-72, 93, 112, 117, 140-141, 141-142, 200, and Peter the Great, 56, 71, 83-85, 234, 312n.112; on assimilation of Western techniques, 56-57, 138; original anti-Western inspiration of, 70; on Russia, 70, 78-85, 111-112; and Fujita Yūkoku, 76; on common people, 76, 113, 115, 120-121, 178; on Ezo, 77-78; English crewmen interrogated by, 87-89, 295n.127; on sagehood, 96; on Takahashi Kageyasu's viewpoint, 105; "counter transformation" proposed by, 109, 262; dilemma of, 115; on *ch'üan,* 119-123; and politics behind ritual, 129, 132; on emperors, 129-131, 132, 133, 134, 136, 145 (*see also* Emperor(s), Japanese); and *sonnō,* 136; in retreat from *New Theses* views, 137; and "Japan proper," 141. *See also New Theses*

Aizawa Sōbei, xi
Amaterasu (Sun Goddess), 152-158, 255, 307n.42; and Japanese superiority, 39, 139; decline in influence of, 98, 99, 130, 162, 168; and long-range policy, 109, 275; and *ch'üan,* 124; and Sacred Mirror, 125, 128, 152-153, 253; teachings of, 125-126, 150, 153, 159-160, 171, 257-258, 272; and *shen tao,* 126-127, 164, 252; Sujin's worship of, 128-129; revival of, 132; emperors as descended from, 149, 152, 153, 170; and Ninigi, 153, 154, 172, 184; blessings from, 155, 170, 184, 190, 277; Jimmu's worship of, 165; versus Buddhism, 166; and military prowess, 173-174, 183; rice from, 184, 185, 190, 192; versus barbarians, 245, 251, 274, 275; policy wisdom of, 246; Westerners using stratagems of, 248; military instruction from, 252; tasks delegated by, 261, 263-264; Western threat against, 262; and rituals, 265, 266, 267, 268, 271-272, 276
America, 79, 92, 149, 189, 193, 207, 251
An'i mondō (Aizawa), 73, 87, 90
Ansai. *See* Yamazaki Ansai
Anti-foreignism. *See Jōi;* Western threat; Xenophobia
Arai Hakuseki, 19, 71, 86, 87, 89, 93-96, 105, 134, 295n.127
Araki Murashige, 201
Armed expulsion. *See Jōi*
Armed forces. *See* Military organization; National defense
Asami Keisai, 30-35, 36, 41, 42, 44, 50, 126, 127, 138
Ashikaga Yoshimitsu, 162

Bakufu: and *New Theses,* x, 137; and expulsion of Westerners, 4, 15, 136-137; and role for Emperor, 14, 134, 137, 145; and trade, 61, 230, 311n.96; and need for military reorganization, 182; and daimyo responsibilities, 220-221

Index

Bakuhan system, 8; repudiation of, 5; and Japan as Middle Kingdom, 9, 140; and *New Theses,* 14-15, 16; and hatred of West, 51; as natural, 52; and Christianity, 93, 94; and *hōken* system, 125; and spiritual authority of Emperor, 133-134, 137; Aizawa's reforms incompatible with, 145

Bakumatsu ("End of Shogunate") era, 4, 5, 7-8

Barbarians: commoners and aliens as, 18-19, 20, 28, 29; Japanese as, 22, 23, 24, 26, 27, 34; in Confucian interpretations, 22-26, 27-28; Dutch as, 42, 44; Chinese culture overcome by, 43-44; Christianity as transforming, 51-52; in Aizawa's viewpoint, 55-56; in Ezo, 73; and sage-rulers, 98; "transformation" of, 131-132; long-range policy against, 245. *See also* Civilization

"Barbarians," Westerners as. *See* Western nations; Western threat

Beginnings of Dutch Studies (Rangaku kotohajime), 46-47

Benyowsky, Baron Moritz Aladar von, 65, 67, 81, 205

Bering, Captain Vitus, 79

Bitō Masahide, xii, 124

Book of Changes, 35, 126, 169, 184, 241-242. 261, 277

Book of Documents, 53, 273

Book of Rites, 31, 211, 254-255, 269

Brothers Incident (1818), 90, 103

Buddhism: geographical views from, 30; in Maeno Ryōtaku's critique, 50; expedient method from, 121-122; and *kokutai,* 123; as divisive, 129, 142-143, 174; and demise of ritual, 131, 132; and wicked doctrines, 165-166, 167, 168; revenues appropriated by, 185, 186; Tokugawa Iemitsu's inquiries on, 202; uprooting of, 212; gold and silver use by, 238; funerals under, 271; Imperial Edict against, 273-274

Butterfield, Herbert, xiii

Cannon: deployment of, 103, 104, 230-231, 234, 312n.104; as Westerners' forte, 180; and end of warfare in Japan, 234-235; need for, 235; versus shields, 235-236. *See also* Firearms

Changing historical forces, 130-131, 160-164, 167-168, 175, 180

Chao Ch'ung-kuo, 109, 208

Chinese civilization. *See* Sinocentric world view

Ch'ing Empire: as untouched by Christianity and Islam, 13, 199; trade with, 64; Russian designs on, 78, 80, 109, 111, 197, 204; Japanese dictate relations with, 106; Aizawa's view of, 111-112; Japan contrasted with, 139; among world's empires, 195; limits of, 196; and prohibition of Christianity, 202

Chirikov (Russian soldier), 79

Chishima ibun (Aizawa), 73, 76, 77, 83-84, 85, 98

Chōei. *See* Takano Chōei

Chou, Duke of, 37, 126, 129, 165, 247, 254

Christianity: extent of, 13, 50, 51-52, 97, 199; as unifying, 13-14, 69, 106, 112, 133, 142, 143, 194; Japanese persecution of, 21, 201, 202-203; in Maeno Ryōtaku's analysis, 49-50; moral transformation by, 50, 51, 83, 84, 98, 109, 140-141; European spreading of, 51-52, 52-53, 95; Fujita Yūkoku's fear of, 53, 69, 70, 71; Aizawa's views on, 56, 69-72, 93, 112, 117, 140-141, 141-142, 200; Expulsion Edict against, 60; national seclusion policy against, 61, 64; as Confucian ritual and music, 71, 143; Japanese banning of, 86, 168, 201-203, 208, 212; Hakuseki on, 93-95, 96-97; British seamen's spreading of, 103; in *Kikōben,* 117; and *ch'üan,* 121, 122, 143; as divisive in Japan, 129; and cessation of ritual, 131. *See also* Church-state relationship; Religion

Christianity in Western threat, 13, 68-69, 70, 72, 100-101, 200-201; and Japanese commoners, 53, 55, 90, 113, 142, 211-212; Russian use of, 82-83; and Arai Hakuseki, 93-94; and missionary tactics, 95; and Western rulers' faith, 96-97; and Western Learning, 98; Takahashi Kageyasu on, 106; strategy of, 109, 110-111; and *kokutai,* 132, 142; in sixteenth as opposed to nineteenth century, 143; as wicked doctrine, 165; and aggressive policies, 168; sect differences in, 198; in Japan of previous centuries, 201-202, 211-212; and Japanese policy, 213; stories of hereafter in, 259, 260

Index

Index

No Two Thoughts Expulsion Edict. *See* Expulsion Edict of 1825
Nochimigusa (Sugita), 46
Norinaga. *See* Motoori Norinaga
Numata Jirō, 104

Observation towers, 227
Oda Nobunaga, 201
Ogyū Sorai, 34, 39–40, 117–119, 120, 126, 127, 134, 137
Ōhara Sakingo, 52, 68, 69, 71–72, 73, 75, 76, 86, 97, 131
"Opening the country." *See Kaikoku*
Opium War, and Ch'ing dynasty, 139–140
"Origins and Outcome of the Opium War" (Ahen shimatsu), 139
Ōtsuhama Incident, 87–90, 207
Ōtsuki Gentaku, 40, 73, 83, 90, 92–93
Ottoman Empire. *See* Turkey

Patriots of high resolve (*shishi*), x, xiii, 137
Perry, Matthew C., 4, 14, 115, 135, 136
Peter the Great, 56, 71, 83–85, 234, 312 n.112
Phaeton Incident (1808), 60, 90, 91, 92–93, 310n.73
Political economists, 168
Popular unity and integration. *See Jinwa*
Portugal: Japanese expulsion of, 61–62, 63, 64; entry into Japan by, 201
Poverty: and military weakness, 177; rebellion prevented by, 179; in early versus present times, 186; from presumptuous luxury, 215

Rangaku. *See* Dutch Studies
Raw materials: Japanese versus Western access to, 111, 141, 236; domestic production of, 238
Realpolitik: *jōi* succeeded by, 6, 136
"Regulations for Court and Nobility," 133–134
Religion: *kokutai* through, 13–14, 133–134, 142–144 (*see also Kokutai*); in Maeno Ryōtaku's analysis, 49–50; Western use of, 100, 132, 142, 211 (*see also* Christianity in Western threat); as unifying, 143–144, 158–159; wicked doctrines in, 165–166; and human spirituality, 258–260. *See also* Christianity; Chruch-state relationship; Islam; Rituals

Return (English ship), 64
"Revere the Emperor, expel the barbarian" movement, and *New Theses,* ix, 137
"Revering the emperor" (*sonnō*), 136
Rezanov, Nicolai Petrovich, 60, 92
Ricci, Matteo (Li Ma-Tou), 47–48, 95
Rice: and Japanese superiority, 39; and *kokutai,* 125, 127; as Amaterasu's gift, 125, 127, 154–155, 184, 185, 190, 266, 307n.42; for rituals, 154–155, 184–185, 255, 267, 268, 269; scarcity and price of, 186–189, 191; trade in, 190, 191–192; need for storing of, 191–192; and Westerners' motives, 206; monopoly in, 221; as troop rations, 225, 239–240, 269; and bakufu and daimyo, 230, 311n.96; regulation of trade in, 240–241
Rituals: in concept of civilization, 18, 19, 21, 24, 25, 27–28, 44–45; transforming power of, 20, 117–118; Sugita Gempaku on, 44; Christian/Confucian, 71, 132, 143; as *ch'üan,* 117–121, 122, 143; Daijō Ritual, 125–126, 130, 154–158, 184–185, 265, 267; and *kokutai,* 127–130, 132, 134, 256–258, 264–273; Emperors in, 128–129, 131, 132, 133–134, 155, 184–185, 253–258, 259, 265–268; of filial devotion, 125–126, 154, 155, 157–158, 165, 270; from Amaterasu, 153, 154, 165, 166, 257–258; as government, 154, 158, 269, 270, 300–301n.108; prayers to Amaterasu in, 174; when meaningless, 222; by Sujin, 255–256; from Sage Emperors, 257–258; as spiritual comfort, 259–260; categories of, 264–266; as state concern, 276
Road system, 228
Russia: threat from, 52–53, 69–70, 71, 73, 74, 76–77, 78–84, 89, 93, 197–198, 199, 204, 205–207; Fujita Yūkoku on, 52–53, 76; and Peter the Great, 56, 83–85, 234, 312n.112; and *sakoku* development, 59, 60, 61, 62, 65–66; religious unity in, 68–69; Aizawa's views on, 70, 78–85, 111–112; and Ezo, 73, 74–75, 75–76, 77, 80, 81–83, 98, 111–112, 204, 205, 207; expansion of, 78–79, 81, 84, 196–197, 204–205; *jōi* against, 86, 208–209; among world's empires, 195

340

Index

Talent, need to recognize, 217-218, 244
Tanuma Okitsugu, 76
Tempō Learning: Mito ideas as, 12
Tenji, 126, 161, 173, 185, 271
Three Imperial Treasures, 125, 152-153, 156, 159, 172, 222
Toba Gi (Yoshiaki), 35
Tobita Shiken, 87
Toda Tadaakira, 135
Tokugawa Hidetada, 55
Tokugawa Iemitsu, 55
Tokugawa Ieyasu, x, 113, 163, 176, 179, 182-183; son of (Yorifusa), xi; and *jōi*, 55; and daimyo, 115-116; and *hōken* system, 125, 164; and bakufu rule, 131; versus Christianity, 202; and samurai spirit, 215; interpreter sent by, 251; and long-range plan, 275
Tokugawa Nariaki, ix, xii, 71, 79, 135-136, 137, 138, 302n.9
Tokugawa Narinobu, ix
Tokugawa state: and Mito Learning, 3; as bakufu-led federation of daimyo domains, 8, 55, 57, 144; and emperor's role, 14, 145; and social system as natural, 52; as feudal system, 113, 125, 164, 181; Aizawa's dilemma over, 115; and *kokutai*, 145. *See also* Bakufu
Tokugawa Yorifusa, xi
Toyotomi Hideyoshi, 77-78, 163, 175-176, 202
"Tract to Enlighten the Roman (As Might Have Been Written by Arai Hakuseki)" (Aizawa), 71
Trade: under Western powers' rules, 5, 106; illicit, 102-103, 207, 229, 311-312n.101; Takahashi Kageyasu's view of, 106; Japan opened to, 136-137; between Europe and America, 189; in rice, 190, 191-192; English request for 203; and Russians, 205, 206; evils from, 214-215; as loss of resources, 239; Westerners' supplies from, 249
True Kings. *See* Sage rulers and Emperors
True Pure Land sect, 167
Tsudayū, 92
Tsukamoto Manabu, 21
Tsunoda, Ryūsaku, xii
Turkey (Ottoman Empire): Aizawa's view of, 111-112; among world's empires, 195; versus Russia, 196, 197, 199
Tzu-ssu, 118

Ueda Akinari, 38

Uete Michiari, 18
United States. *See* America.
Unity: through *kokutai*, 13, 133, 144-145, 158, 263 (*see also Kokutai*); from Christianity, 13-14, 69, 112, 133, 142, 143, 194; national defense through, 54, 133, 250, 251, 273

Vespucci, Amerigo: Maeno Ryōtaku on, 49
Wang An-shih, 11
Wang Mang, 11
Warfare, cessation of in Japan, 234-235. *See also* Military organization; National defense
Warring States era (in China, 403-221 B.C.), 28, 140, 194
Warring States era (in Japan, 1467-1568), 174, 175, 209, 235
Warriors. *See* Military organization; Samurai
Watanabe Kazan, 10, 59
Western Learning, 6-7; and *jōi*, 6-7, 10, 15, 101; and *New Theses*, 6-7, 86, 107; and xenophobia, 10-11, 61, 98; and Aizawa, 14, 72-73, 115, 116; and Japan as Middle Kingdom, 22; and Japanese superiority, 39, 40; and Confucian world view, 40, 97-98; versus Sinocentrism, 51-52, 138, 140; Aizawa on dangers of, 56-57; national isolation prompted by, 61; and Aizawa's view of Russia, 77, 85-86; and Aizawa's linguistic ability, 88; and Aizawa's Sinocentrism, 97-98, 140; and church-state separation, 100; and domestic policy, 101; and Aizawa's domestic proposals, 113, 114; and Aizawa on *kokutai*, 132, 133, 145. *See also* Dutch Studies
Western nations: and rules of international order, 5, 106; church-state relations in, 71-72, 100, 132, 133, 142, 143; national unity of, 106, 107, 112-113; overseas raw materials of, 111, 141, 236; *chüan* of, 116; and Seven Great Powers, 140, 198; geography of, 193; development of, 194; empires among, 195; and Church of Rome, 196; war and unity among, 204; *ch'i* of wickedness in, 261
Western origins: of *kokutai*, xi, 13, 69, 133; and Aizawa's ideas, 14
Western technology: equality through, 4-5; in meeting Western threat, 5, 8,